Timothy Sprigge

CRIME *and* PUNISHMENT *in* BRITAIN

An Analysis of the Penal System
in Theory, Law, and Practice

★

CRIME

and

PUNISHMENT

in

BRITAIN

★

NIGEL WALKER

Reader in Criminology
University of
Oxford

[*Revised edition*]

★

at the University Press
EDINBURGH

© N. D. Walker 1965, 1968
Edinburgh University Press
22 George Square, Edinburgh
ISBN 0 85224 038 4
North America
Aldine · Atherton, Inc.
529 South Wabash Avenue, Chicago
Library of Congress Catalog
Card Number 77-363543
First published, 1965
Second, Revised Edition, 1968
Reprinted, with minor revisions, 1970
Reprinted 1971
Printed in Great Britain
by T. & A. Constable Ltd, Edinburgh
Printers to the University

TO MY FATHER AND MOTHER

PREFACE

This book is an attempt to describe our penal system in a particular way. It is not about the criminal law except to the extent that this defines and sets limits to the types of conduct which we call 'offences', and curtails the flexibility and severity of the penalties which we apply to offenders. It is not about the philosophy of punishment, although it tries to describe objectively the aims, assumptions, and the techniques of current penal measures. It does not offer a unified explanation of crime, although it tries to sort out some of the tangles between contemporary theories. What it attempts to be is a study of our present ways of defining, accounting for, and disposing of offenders, regarded simply as a system in operation. To the extent that the book succeeds in adhering to this ascetic principle it is a work of criminology.

Criminology is not, and does not include, moral or political philosophy. It does not argue about the right of states or societies to limit the freedom of individuals to rob, rape, murder, or commit suicide; or about the sense in which a stupid or deluded man can be said to be responsible for a crime. At the same time, the criminologist is interested in differences between, and changes in, the views held by legislators, lawyers, philosophers, and the man in the street, on such topics, and the extent to which they reflect the facts established and the theories propounded by psychologists, anthropologists, and sociologists.

Nor does criminology overlap with jurisprudence. To the criminologist the arguments of Beccaria and Bentham, Hart and Wootton, are flags that show where the wind of change is blowing, not battle standards round which to rally and skirmish.

Perhaps the hardest impression to eradicate is that the criminologist is a penal reformer. It is true that he is concerned to establish the truth or falsehood of some of the assertions upon which campaigns for penal reform are based – for example, the assertion that the death penalty is not a deterrent. But since the driving force of such campaigns is not a purely logical or purely scientific appreciation of fact, but a humanitarian motive, it is to that extent non-criminological. The criminologist may confirm (or refute) the facts or methods of inference which are used to support the arguments of penal reformers; he may note with scientific interest the changing objectives of the Howard League, or the establishment of a society known as the Anti-Violence League with the aim of restoring corporal punishment; but it is no more his function to attack or defend the death penalty than it is the function of a political scientist to take part in an election campaign. The confusion, however, between criminologists and penal reformers has been encouraged by criminologists themselves, many of whom have also been penal reformers. Strictly speaking, penal reform is a spare-time occupation for criminologists, just as canvassing for votes would be for political scientists. The difference is that the criminologist's spare-time occupation is more likely to take this form, and when it does so it is more likely to interfere with what should be purely criminological thoughts.

The result of this process of reasoning may be to allot criminology to the discipline of sociology – if discipline is not too strong a term. If so, this still leaves the criminologist considerable room for manoeuvre, since the boundaries of sociology are wide. Nor need this disqualify him from appraising, for example, sociological attempts to explain delinquency just as critically as he must approach psychological or economic theories.

To some readers much of this book may sound inhuman. If so, I shall have achieved an important objective. Admittedly the machinery of justice, which is only metaphorically mechanical, involves the interaction of human beings in their roles of victim, offender, policeman, judge, supervisor or custodian, and there must be a place for human sympathy in the understanding, and still more in the treatment, of individual offenders. Humanity also sets a limit nowadays to the unpleasantness of penal measures, whether these are regarded as retributive, deterrent, prophylactic, or remedial. Ideological notions and moral judgements, too, may be relevant when the aims of the penal system are under discussion. But when we are concerned, as I am, with the efficiency of the system as a means to these ends, emotions such as sympathy or horror, praise or blame, pity or vindictiveness, are irrelevant, or even confusing. One of the main reasons why penal institutions develop more slowly than other social services is that they are a constant battlefield between emotional prejudices; and battlefields are unproductive places.

One function of a preface is to create the illusion that the book was written on a preconceived and logical plan; and certainly the sequence of subjects in this book requires an explanation. Since one cannot have a penal system without deciding what conduct to penalise, the first chapter discusses the scope of the prohibitions imposed by the criminal law, and the principles on which attempts to justify them are based. In the second half of the chapter the accuracy of the system in identifying those who break the law is discussed. This is followed by a chapter on the current trends and patterns of serious and minor crimes. The second part of the book analyses the essential features of fashionable explanatory theories, the relationship between them, and the reasoning which has caused them to be overshadowed by the predictive approach in recent years. The third part is an outline of what I call 'the system of disposal'. A description of the underlying aims and assumptions of our penal measures is followed by a chapter on the law of disposal as it applies to the mentally normal adult male. The disposal of the young offender is the subject of the next chapter. Part Four describes the sentencing process and attempts to assess the efficacy of sentences. To reduce complexity, the main part of the book mostly ignores three minor but important groups of offenders – recidivists, women and girls, and the mentally abnormal; these are dealt with in Part Five.

The bibliography has one unusual feature. Since the value of many of the investigations reported in the literature depends to a great extent on the methods by which their samples of delinquents and non-delinquents were obtained, the references to reports of major investigations are supplemented by short specifications of the samples on which these were based. This saves digressions in the text of the book. In the footnote references, the date of publication is followed by the chapter, section, or page number, when appropriate, thus:

K. Friedlander, 1947, chapter IV, and E. Glover, 1960.23 &.175.

To save elaborate cross-references, the letters q.v. are used after a name or phrase to indicate that a fuller explanation of it will be found by consulting the index and looking up the page reference followed by the letter 'E'. Abbreviations of statutes and the special meanings of some phrases used in Parts Three and Four are explained at the beginning of Chapter Nine. Unless otherwise ascribed, all statistics in the text, in tables, and in figures are based on the published or supplementary Criminal Statistics for England and Wales for the year 1961, which was the year of the decennial census.

Here and there in the book I have drawn attention to features of the Scottish penal system where these seem to differ markedly from their English counterparts. These references are not prompted by mere nostalgia or desire for comprehensiveness; they are addressed to the reader who finds it difficult to imagine alternatives to the English practice which would be countenanced within this island. Not long ago a professor of law discussed the idea that a majority verdict might be accepted from juries, and said 'a verdict of guilty by a bare majority could not be tolerated'[1]; yet, had he known it, such verdicts are not only tolerated but even defended north of the Tweed. This is not to suggest that Scottish differences (of which Scots themselves are proud to the point of narcissism) are necessarily for the better; but merely to emphasize the fact that the boundaries of practical possibility are wider than supporters of the *status quo* believe.

Nigel Walker, *Oxford, January 1964*

[1] Listener, 10 May 1962. Majority verdicts are now acceptable even in England.

PREFACE TO THE SECOND EDITION

The first edition was reprinted in 1967 with a few amendments and corrections. For this second edition, however, the book has been much more thoroughly revised, and takes account not only of the important innovations of the Criminal Justice Act, 1967, but also of recently published research. A new final chapter deals briefly with the important sources of influence on the penal system.

I have also profited by criticisms and suggestions from reviewers, friends and complete strangers. One reviewer's criticism, however, drew my attention to a misunderstanding which I should like to put right. He complained that I had omitted to mention some important research outside Britain. I must therefore emphasise that this is not intended to be a general textbook about criminals and penal systems the world over. Such books have been written, but we are beginning to realise their limitations. One thing that sociology has taught us is that generalisations about, say, delinquent sub-cultures in Chicago cannot safely be applied to English cities, any more than descriptions of French prisons can be taken for descriptions of their American counterparts. Of course there are fields of research in which the findings can more safely be generalised (on the assumption that the research was properly done): an example is Christiansen's follow-up of Danish twins, which seems relevant to the explanation of criminal behaviour wherever it occurs. But when dealing with the behaviour of British offenders, or the measures which we take to deal with them, I have naturally relied on British studies, although even so I have been deliberately selective. Where no British study has yet been reported, I have relied on others: for example, on Kalven and Zeisel's admirable investigation of the decisions of American juries. But as soon as an equally sound British study on this subject is available, I am logically bound to turn to it. This is not insularity, but science.

Nigel Walker, *Oxford, January 1968*

ACKNOWLEDGEMENTS

One of the most thankless labours which can be demanded of anyone is the criticizing of someone else's chapters in draft. I have succeeded in imposing parts of my typescript on more than twenty men and women. It would be unfair to associate individuals with specified sections of the book, since this might implicate them in my errors and distortions, and so embarrass those whom I mean to thank. I therefore simply record that this book owes more than a little to corrections, additions and deletions suggested by those listed below. I also thank Miss J. Bond for a particularly accurate final typescript, Miss N. Wright for her help with the bibliography and index, and Mrs C. Frey for help in revising them. N.D.W.

Dr C. E. Blank
Detective-Inspector A. S. Bowley
Professor K. O. Christiansen
Professor A. R. N. Cross
Miss A. Dunlop
Mrs J. Floud
Mrs E. Gibson
Miss W. M. Goode
Mr L. I. Gordon
Mr W. H. Hammond
Professor H. L. A. Hart
Miss P. Hooper
Mr J. J. Hulme

Mrs S. F. McCabe
Mr R. H. Maudsley
Mr C. T. Morris
Mr D. A. C. Morrison
Miss J. Packman
Mr A. W. Peterson and other officers of the Prison Department of the Home Office
Dr H. R. Rollin
Mr R. D. Shuffrey
Dr Ann Smith
Mr T. R. Tudor
Mr R. J. Whittick
Mr H. D. Willcock

CONTENTS

PART ONE

★

INTRODUCTION

THE SCOPE

AND ACCURACY

OF THE

PENAL SYSTEM

Those who attempt to describe the essentials of any system for dealing with offenders must make up their minds at the outset what questions they are trying to answer. Some are of a kind which can be answered only by making moral judgements: for example, 'Is the system of trial a fair one?' or 'Are inhumane punishments awarded?' The answers to these are bound to be to some extent emotional, and to beg other questions, if not whole philosophies, of morals and politics. There are, however, questions which are less ambitious, and to which the answers can be more factual. The most import-ant of these seem to be:

1. 'What forms of conduct are dealt with by penal measures?': in more popular language, 'What is criminal?'
2. 'How accurate is the system in identifying those who indulge in prohibited conduct?': in popular language, 'How many of the guilty escape conviction, and how many of the innocent are wrongly punished?'

In this chapter I shall try to give answers to these questions in relation to the British penal system; or at least to show the lines on which they could be answered.

WHAT IS CRIMINAL?

Penal measures are not of course the only way – merely the most formal and drastic – of dealing with types of behaviour which people find objectionable. An enormous sector of our actions is regulated simply by what we believe to be the expectations of our fellow citizens and by our occasional experience of their disapproval when we fail to fulfil these expectations.

Codified Rules. When it is necessary that these expectations should be observed with precision, they become rules, which are sooner or later systematised and promulgated; the 'unwritten convention' becomes the published code. For example, when sport becomes competitive it requires precise rules, although when it is non-competitive conventions seem to be sufficient. Thus in rock-climbing there is simply a convention that one may cut footholds in ice but not in rock, whereas in golf there is a published code of some complexity, which even limits the designs of clubs, and in chess the permissible moves are similarly defined.

Rules with sanctions. Most uncodified conventions are enforced simply by the ordinary man's dislike of being regarded as abnormal by his neighbours or acquaintances, or, worse still, of being treated as abnormal. He fears ridicule, criticism and in the last resort ostracism. Many written codes are enforced by similarly informal sanctions. Just as one does not go rock-climbing with someone who cuts holds in rock, so one does not play golf against someone who lifts his ball out of bunkers.

Independent sanctions. But violations of some written codes are discouraged by more formal sanctions, that is, sanctions which are themselves imposed according to rule. This is common in groups of people which have a formal organisation. Associations of doctors and other professional workers, trade unions and similar organisations expel, suspend and otherwise punish members for infringement of their rules.

Civil Law. In all societies, however, some forms of behaviour are so frequent and at the same time so objectionable that they are prohibited under a code which both provides for certain sanctions and is universal in its application to members of the society. In its elementary forms this code allows a person aggrieved by certain actions of another to retaliate. What distinguishes this system from mere spontaneous vengeance is that it is approved by the other members of the community; and indeed in some primitive societies there does not seem to be any other authority to which the aggrieved person can apply. Perhaps this might be called the stage of 'approved retaliation'. Something of the sort was observed by Rasmussen among Eskimo communities. Probably because this leads to vendettas, it is replaced by an approved system of compensation with approved retaliation to fall back on if the compensation is not paid. At some later stage of development it becomes possible to raise the matter before a formal meeting of the older men, and eventually some sort of 'court' is evolved. The result is control of behaviour by civil law, of which the essential features seem to be an impartial authority, administering and interpreting a code[1] accepted as binding upon all members of the society, acting only at the application of the aggrieved party, and pronouncing decisions designed to compensate the aggrieved or put an end to whatever harm is being done.

In some societies this is the only form of law.[2] In others – and in all sophisticated societies – a distinct system has grown out of the civil law. The courts by which it is administered may or may not be distinct from civil courts – in Britain the same man often sits as judge in civil and criminal cases in the same week; but there are more important differences:

---

[1] It is true that it is often alleged that there is no 'code' of civil or criminal law in England. But this is so only to the extent that in comparison with some other codes it is more fragmentary, less difficult to modify by interpretation, and less easy to study in writing; it is still a 'code' in the sense that it is a body of rules which is intended to be consistent.

[2] See, for example, Hoebel, 1955.

1. The procedure is initiated by some kind of public prosecutor and not by the private person who has been aggrieved.[1] The private individual may report a breach of the criminal law, but he no longer initiates the legal process, nor can he halt it by withdrawal. This system has the advantages that a public prosecutor is more competent, less open to bribery or intimidation, and more economical in manpower.

2. Practically none of the measures which the criminal court can order are designed to compensate the private person who has suffered from the prohibited behaviour. The aims of modern penal measures will be discussed in Chapter 8, and we shall see that while there are exceptions to this statement they are insignificant. It is most exceptional for a penal measure to confer any material benefit upon anyone: even fines – unless they are very large – do no more than reduce the cost to the state of dealing with the offender.

3. Although many of the types of conduct which can be the subject of a criminal prosecution can also be the subject of civil actions (a fact which illustrates the development of criminal law out of civil law), in practice few types of crime lead to civil actions; the only important exception is careless driving which leads to personal injuries or damage to property. Civil suits for compensation for loss of stolen property or for personal injury caused by criminal violence are rare, though not unheard of. Moreover, not only is criminal prosecution regarded as the natural recourse against virtually all the common offences, but there are some which cannot be the subject of civil proceedings – attempts at crimes, and offences of drunkenness or indecency which do not result in loss or damage to another party. It is very difficult, if not impossible, to state any general principle which will distinguish satisfactorily between actions which are dealt with as crimes and those which are not; as Kenny found, such principles turn out to be either circular or subjective. It may well be that there is no rational principle, merely an historical explanation in terms of the concern caused by the nature or frequency of the behaviour and the ability of the aggrieved parties to afford the cost or trouble of civil proceedings.

Borderline Offences. It is noticeable, however, that the boundary between the criminal and the civil law, and the boundary between the criminal law and mere discouragement by social disapproval, are drawn at slightly different points in different penal systems. All civilised and most primitive codes prohibit homicide, unjustifiable personal violence, rape, theft, and the intentional destruction of another's property. Civilised societies also use criminal procedure to enforce taxation and discourage behaviour which obstructs roads, or endangers life or health. But there are some types of behaviour which in some countries are criminal, and in others merely civil wrongs or simply matters of private morals.

Most of these involve, directly or indirectly, sexual conduct:

---

[1] Private prosecutions are more or less obsolete, though not impossible, in Britain.

1. Extra-marital intercourse. In some American states the crimes created by the Puritans of fornication between unmarried persons, or adultery between a married person and someone other than his or her spouse, are still on the statute book, although seldom prosecuted. Adultery by a wife is a crime which is still prosecuted in France and Italy, and in France a husband who imports his mistress into the marital home can be convicted of concubinage. In Britain adultery by either spouse is not criminal, although it is a ground for a matrimonial suit, and a husband may sometimes seek damages at civil law from a co-respondent.

2. Homosexual acts. In a diminishing number of countries, including Western Germany and most states of the U.S.A., a homosexual act between males but not between females is an offence. This was the position in Britain until recently. The Wolfenden Committee recommended in 1957 that homosexual acts in private between consenting males over the age of 21 should no longer be criminal. Although the recommendation was too controversial for the Government of the day, prosecutions were gradually restricted, and eventually a Private Member's Bill which implemented the recommendation was passed in 1967.[1]

3. Abortion. In some countries abortion is criminal only if performed by unauthorised persons. But in most Western countries, including Britain, it is criminal unless there is a special justification for it. In this country the special justifications are that the continuance of pregnancy would involve risk to the woman's life, or injury to her physical or mental health or that of her existing children; or that there is substantial risk that if the child were born it would suffer from such physical or mental abnormalities as to be seriously handicapped.[2]

4. Prostitution. In some states of the U.S.A. this is a crime, although seldom prosecuted unless the authorities have special reasons for wishing to do so. In most other countries, including Britain, it is not of itself a crime, but certain methods of practising it are: for example, soliciting in the street, brothel-keeping, or living on the earnings of prostitution. Proposals that it should be made possible to prosecute the clients of prostitutes have been made but not seriously considered by the legislature.

There are a few 'borderline crimes', however, which are not sexual:

5. Attempted suicide. For over a century attempted suicide was prosecuted as a crime in England but not in Scotland, although even in that country a person who unsuccessfully but publicly attempted to kill himself has been prosecuted for a breach of the

---

[1] But such acts are still criminal if one of the parties is under 21, or if more than two persons are present, or if committed in a public lavatory, or on a U.K. merchant ship by members of the crew; and male prostitution, like its female counterpart, can give rise to offences (such as living on a prostitute's earnings) although it is not itself criminal. See the Sexual Offences Act, 1967.

[2] See the Abortion Act, 1967.

peace. As a result of the Suicide Act, 1961, this form of behaviour is no longer a crime in England.

6. Negligent injury. In some countries, for example Canada, a person whose negligence causes injury to another person can be convicted of a crime. In Britain, if the injury is fatal and the negligence gross, the person may be charged with manslaughter. If the injury is caused by a moving vehicle the driver may be charged with careless or dangerous driving; but these charges could be brought even if no injury resulted. Yet a person who negligently cripples someone for life by driving into him at golf, demolishing a building or cutting down a branch of a tree, can be sued at civil law but not charged with a crime.

There are other offences which, though they appear in almost all civilised criminal codes, have recently been criticised in England as unnecessary:

7. Incest. Until 1908 this was not a criminal offence, although until 1857 it had been punishable under ecclesiastical law and – more important – was strongly discouraged by social pressure. A growing acquaintance with ways of life other than those of the middle and upper classes brought it home to the Church of England that social and religious sanctions were not completely effective, and they persuaded a private member of Parliament to introduce a Bill to make incest criminal. After several sessions of resistance the Government eventually complied. It has been argued that while children certainly need protection against incestuous adults, this protection is already provided by other statutes; and that incest between consenting adults in private, like homosexual acts in similar circumstances, is not a proper subject for the criminal law.

8. Euthanasia. The general abhorrence of the deliberate taking of human life is so strong that civilised criminal codes permit very few exceptions. They include in this prohibition even the killing of sane adults who have good reasons – such as a painful, fatal and incurable disease – for wanting to die. It has been argued[1] that with suitable safeguards such cases should be excluded from the definition of murder.

9. Bigamy. The felony of bigamy, created in 1603, is no longer punishable by death, but has nevertheless been criticised even by nineteenth-century judges. A married man who leaves his wife to live with another woman commits only a matrimonial offence, even if they pretend to be married; but if they go through a ceremony of marriage he commits a crime punishable with seven years' imprisonment. This is so even if he wrongly believes himself to be divorced,[2] or even if his new 'wife' knows him to be married. Glanville Williams has argued[3] that in many cases the only

[1] For example, by Glanville Williams, 1958.
[2] Though not if he wrongly believes himself a widower!
[3] 1945.76 ('Language and the Law' in *Law Quarterly Review* for 1945).

anti-social consequences of bigamy are the waste of the time of the
minister (or registrar) and the falsification of official records. He
points out that similar consequences would result if a man
contracted several 'marriages' with his adult nieces, one after
another. None of them would be valid, and none would be criminal;
but there would be a similar waste of time and falsification of records.
Other prohibitions are criticised as too wide in their scope. For example:

10. The use of narcotic and other addictive drugs without medical prescription is prohibited in most civilised countries (with the notable
exception of alcohol and nicotine), and is the subject of increasing
efforts by police and other social services. It is often argued, however,
that some drugs – especially marihuana – should not be subject to
this strict control, on the grounds that they are neither addictive
nor harmful. A more extreme section of opinion argues that even
heroin and other 'hard' drugs would be less of a menace if their use
were controlled in non-penal ways.[1]

There have also been unsuccessful agitations for the creation of new
crimes. A recent example, again concerned with sexual behaviour, is

11. Artificial insemination. In 1958, after the Scots judge, Lord
Wheatley, had ruled in a divorce case that artificial insemination
was not adultery, some members of the House of Lords, led by the
Archbishop of Canterbury, urged that it should be made a crime.[2]
Instead the Government appointed the Feversham Committee,
which preferred the *status quo*.[3]

The arguments which are usually advanced for removing offences from
the criminal code are of two kinds. On the one hand, reformers point to the
positive harm that seems to result from treating some of these types of
behaviour as criminal. Male homosexuals are subjected to blackmail, or (it
is argued) turned into enemies of society. Women who wish to rid themselves of their pregnancies resort to unskilled and unhygienic 'back-street
abortionists', at great risk to their life and health. Sufferers from agonising
disorders with no hope of recovery are kept alive by doctors who dare not
administer the *coup de grâce*.

Quite distinct from these arguments is the case which is founded on the
general principle that there should be a limit to the intrusion of the criminal
law into private conduct. The Wolfenden Committee, for example, which
was concerned with homosexual acts and prostitution, contended that

... the function of the criminal law ... is to preserve public order and
decency, to protect the citizen from what is offensive or injurious,
and to provide sufficient safeguards against the exploitation and
corruption of others, particularly those who are specially vulnerable
because they are young, weak in body or mind, inexperienced, or in
a state of special physical, official or economic dependence.

It is not ... the function of the law to intervene in the private
lives of citizens, or to seek to enforce any particular pattern of

[1] See Schur, 1962.
[2] Hansard (Lords), 2nd February 1958, col. 1000.
[3] 1960.79 (Cmnd. 1105).

behaviour, further than is necessary to carry out the purpose we have outlined. . . .[1]

They concluded that neither prostitution as such nor homosexual behaviour between consenting adults in private should be criminal, and a similar principle was adopted by the Feversham Committee on Artificial Insemination[2] when the Government was pressed to legislate on this subject. It seems possible to apply this reasoning also to incest between consenting adults in private, and perhaps to abortion, euthanasia and bigamy in certain circumstances.

This liberal attempt to preserve an area of human conduct from the intervention of the criminal law has been attacked, notably by Sir Patrick Devlin[3]:

> . . . it is not possible to set theoretical limits to the power of the State to legislate against immorality. . . . Society is entitled by means of its laws to protect itself from dangers, whether from within or without. . . . An established morality is as necessary as good government to the welfare of society. Societies disintegrate . . . when no common morality is observed, and history shows that the loosening of moral bonds is often the first stage of disintegration, so that society is justified in taking the same steps to preserve its moral code as it does to preserve its government and other essential institutions.

He argued that there was a danger signal which infallibly told us when the point had been reached at which interference with private conduct in order to enforce a common morality was justified: this was when the man in the street felt not mere disapproval of the private conduct, but 'intolerance, indignation and disgust'. His argument has been criticised in its turn by Hart and others,[4] and the controversy continues.

In practice, the definitions of most crimes yield marginal examples in which moral principles, compassion, public sentiment, the difficulty of obtaining evidence, or other considerations, discourage strict and literal enforcement of the law; and this borderland is especially wide in the area of controversial crimes. In England bigamists are seldom prosecuted unless they seem to have deceived their partner with a view to gain or seduction. Women are not prosecuted for procuring their own abortion or resorting to 'abortionists', sometimes because they have suffered enough illness as a result, sometimes because their evidence is needed. Teenage males are seldom prosecuted for homosexual behaviour which is genuinely private, consenting and unmotivated by gain. Sexual intercourse with girls under the age of 16, even when reported to the police, is often unprosecuted, especially if the girl is just under the official age of consent, and the boy of much the same age.

Attempts to formulate a simple rule by which to decide whether a certain

---

[1] 1957. The Committee must either have forgotten or disapproved of the use of the criminal law to enforce the collection of revenue, or to protect the citizen against what is neither injurious nor offensive, but merely inconvenient – for example, obstruction of the road by car-parking. [2] loc. cit.

[3] 'The Enforcement of Morals': the Maccabaean Lecture in Jurisprudence (1959).

[4] Hart, 1959 and 1963; Wollheim, 1959; Walker, 1969.

type of conduct is a proper subject for the criminal law are unlikely to be realistic. The more intellectually satisfying the formula the less likely it is to fit the actual state of the law in any civilised country. The assembly of prohibitions which constitutes the substantive part of the English criminal law is the result of additions made over a long period of development and in response to demands from very different bodies of opinion, of which the churches, the police, and government departments are only the most obvious examples. Some of these additions undoubtedly reflected a wide-spread feeling; for example, those dealing with cruelty to children. Others were inserted in the statute book by well organised or tactically skilful minorities or even individuals.

The consequence is that if we attempt to summarise the functions which are served by our present list of prohibitions, it is impossible to reduce them to less than thirteen:

1. the protection of persons – and to some extent animals – against intentional violence or cruelty (for example, against assault);
2. the protection of the person against some forms of unintended harm (for example, as a result of a traffic accident, or through poisoning by impure foods);
3. the protection of easily persuadable people – that is, the very young or the very feeble-minded – against the exploitation of their persons or property (for example, against sexual intercourse);
4. the prevention of acts which, even if the participants are adult and willing, are regarded as 'unnatural' (for example, bestiality, homosexual acts between men, or incest);
5. the prevention of acts which, though not included in any of those other groups, are performed so publicly as to shock people who are not directly involved in them (such as nakedness, obscene language, blasphemy, heterosexual copulation between consenting adults in public);
6. the discouragement of behaviour which might provoke disorder (for example, using insulting words at a public meeting);
7. the protection of property (for example, the offences of theft, arson, or forgery);
8. the prevention of inconvenience (such as the obstruction of roads by parked vehicles or the falsification of records);
9. the collection of revenue (for example, keeping a motor car, dog or radio without a licence);
10. the defence of the realm (for example, espionage, or the obstruction of manœuvres);
11. the enforcement of justice (for example, perjury or resisting arrest);
12. the protection of other social institutions, such as marriage or religious worship (for example, against bigamy or blasphemy);
13. the enforcement of what might be called 'compulsory benevolence' (for example, by ensuring children's attendance at school).

In some cases – for example, when personal violence is involved – the strongest argument for using the criminal law is that if we were content with other methods such as private action, the result would be retaliation, vendetta, and disorder. Innocent people would be lynched and the guilty would protect themselves by superior force. Recourse to private litigation, although it is a feature of those primitive systems which do not have a distinct criminal law, tends to break down for similar reasons. A strong aggressor may intimidate claimants. An indignant victim or his relatives may not accept money in payment for intentional harm. The injury may be assessed so dearly that the aggressor cannot pay, and so runs away or is enslaved, either of which may lead to more violence.

In other cases it is difficult to find more than an economic justification. Why does not the state use the civil law to recover some forms of unpaid revenue, for example, the fee for a dog-licence, although it does so in the case of income-tax? Whatever the historical reason, the present justification can only be that this would be more wasteful of time, manpower and money, for the civil law is a more complex and cumbersome machine. Again, the protection of the ordinary householder against burglary could be achieved – as it sometimes was in past centuries – by private guards; but it is obviously more economical to employ a handful of public police. Nevertheless, when the property at stake is very valuable and its owner a large organisation, private guards again become an economic proposition, and are in fact employed by banks, dock authorities and other public undertakings.

A purely economic justification of this kind would lead us to question the logic of treating as criminal – or at least of prosecuting – petty thefts, such as shoplifting, where the value of the goods stolen is probably less than the cost of turning the mills of justice. It was probably considerations of this kind which led the Chief Constable of Southend to announce that he would not 'waste public money' on prosecutions for shoplifting where the value of the stolen goods was small and the offender unlikely to repeat his theft.[1]

It is easiest to accept economic considerations of this sort when the measures that would result from the penal process are mild; for example, when they consist of probation, a recognisance, or a fine. If, on the other hand, the reaction of people to the disapproved conduct is so strong that they tend to apply drastic measures, it may actually be desirable to invoke the criminal law in the interests of the offender. Not only does this sometimes protect the innocent from retaliation; the penal measures permitted by law may be more humane – or even possibly more effective – in preventing a repetition of the offence than the measures which would be taken by a temporarily outraged community. Nor does this argument apply only to communities where lynching is a genuine possibility. Even in this country a man can suffer severely from expulsion from his trade union or professional association, and it is arguable that the decisions of such bodies in disciplinary cases – and especially the penalties awarded – should be subject to appeal to a court of law.[2]

[1] *Daily Telegraph* for 26th February 1963.
[2] Some disciplinary bodies – such as the Disciplinary Committee of the General Medical Council – model their procedure as closely as possible upon that of criminal courts: see C. P. Harvey, 'The Disciplinary Committee and the Courts', in *British Medical Journal* for 22nd November 1958. For a fuller discussion of economic and administrative aspects of this subject see Walker, 1969.

DETECTION AND TRIAL

The second question which should be asked about a penal system is 'How accurate are its methods of identifying those who indulge in the conduct which it prohibits?' This is in the nature of things a very difficult question to answer, and it is hardly possible to do much more than indicate the important sources of inaccuracy.

Unreported Offences. For example, a large number of offences are never reported to the police. This may happen for a number of reasons:

1. all those involved may fail to realise that an offence has been committed. Children at play commit assaults and indecencies without being aware of their criminality;

2. all those involved may be willing participants. This is especially frequent in the case of abortions, homosexual offences, incest, and carnal knowledge of girls under 16;

3. even an unwilling victim may not wish to involve the offender in the consequences of prosecution. This happens not only with sexual offences such as indecent assault, but also in minor cases of pilfering, embezzlement, or fraud;[1]

4. the victim may himself be antagonistic to the police. Many assaults in certain districts of large cities are not reported because this would be regarded as handing the aggressor over to a common enemy;

5. the victim may regard the offence as too trivial to be worth the trouble of reporting. Many minor thefts are not reported for this reason;[1]

6. the victim may be so pessimistic about the chances of bringing the offender to book that he does not bother to report the offence. This is more likely with minor offences;

7. the victim may be too embarrassed to report the offence. Women – especially the very young – are often inhibited in this way from reporting indecent exposure. Men may keep silent about homosexual importuning in case they are suspected of attracting such advances. Parents of child victims of sexual offences may wish to spare the child the experience of interrogation and appearance in court;

8. the offence may be observed only by someone who disapproves of the law. Poaching is often unreported for this reason;

9. the victim or observer may be intimidated by the offender's threats of violence or by blackmail. Prostitutes' thefts from clients are seldom brought to the notice of the police;

10. the offence may be unknown to anyone but the offender, as must often happen in the case of speeding motorists.

The Untraced Offender. Secondly, many reported offences are not traced to the offender. Less than 50 per cent of reported thefts are cleared up by the police. The importance of this factor, however, is often exaggerated. Few reported murders are not cleared up. Serious assault is cleared up in

---

[1] See for example, J. P. Martin, 1962, who investigated the extent to which employers refrain from reporting employees to the police.

more than four cases in five, largely because the victim knows the identity of the offender. Even where the percentage of cases not cleared up is high, as it is in the case of theft, this does not mean that there is an enormous number of undetected thieves. Let us suppose that offenders in general have three chances in four of committing a single offence without detection (this is the level of 'general immunity' suggested by McClintock et al., 1968). If so, on average, an offender who commits two offences reduces his chances to slightly more than half ($0.56 = 0.75^2$); and if he commits seven his chances fall to about one in eight ($0.13 = 0.75^7$). Of course there are intelligent and experienced criminals who are probably responsible for the more lucrative crimes of dishonesty, and whose 'immunity' declines less steeply. But the number of unsolved crimes, especially against property, can give rise to wildly inflated estimates of the numbers of uncaught property offenders.

The Unprosecuted Offender. Many offenders are traced but not prosecuted, at least for the offence in question. This may happen for several reasons: the evidence may be insufficient to make a prosecution worth while; the offender may turn out to be a child under the age of criminal responsibility,[1] or a person under treatment for mental disorder[2]; or the police may consider that a mere warning is sufficient to deter the offender from repetitions. More will be said about police 'warnings' in Chapters 9 and 10. Even in a case where the reason for not prosecuting an offender is simply lack of evidence it should not be assumed that the penal system is ineffective, since the effect of police enquiries alone may deter an unseasoned offender from repetitions.[3]

The Courts. If prosecuted, the accused is tried by one of three kinds of court. For the gravest offences he can be tried only by Assizes,[4] where a professional judge presides and decides upon the sentence, but the issue of guilt is decided by a jury. For other serious offences he may be tried by Quarter Sessions, where a jury decides the issue of guilt, but the sentence is chosen by a 'recorder' (who is a lawyer) or – in County Quarter Sessions – by a bench of magistrates which usually has a legally qualified Chairman or Deputy Chairman. For lesser offences he is tried by a Magistrates' Court, where both the issue of guilt and his sentence are determined by a bench of at least two lay magistrates. Assizes and Quarter Sessions (and courts with juries in Scotland) are known as 'higher courts', those without juries as 'lower' or 'summary' courts. In England, an offender cannot be tried at a higher court unless he has been committed for trial by a court of 'examining justices' which has heard the evidence against him.

The decision as to the type of court in which the accused is to be tried is an important one for him, since the sentences imposable by higher courts are more severe, while at the same time his chances of acquittal – as we shall see – are greater if he pleads not guilty before a jury. In England the decision rests sometimes upon the nature of the offence. At one extreme are

---

[1] See Chapter 10.   [2] See Chapter 13.

[3] I am not of course concerned here with the possibility that innocent persons may suffer from enquiries, since I am discussing only the efficiency and not the humanity of the system.   [4] Or the equivalent, i.e., by the Central Criminal Court in London.

PART ONE * INTRODUCTION

'summary', often called 'non-indictable offences',[1] which can be tried only by a summary court: for example, being drunk and disorderly in a public place. Among indictable offences, however, there are several subdivisions. Some offences can be tried only on indictment: murder and other serious offences against the person can be tried only by assizes; while housebreaking, for instance, can be tried at quarter sessions. There are, however, two intermediate kinds of indictable offence. One is known as the 'hybrid offence', for which the statute fixes two maximum fines and terms of imprisonment, one to apply if it is tried summarily, the other if it is tried on indictment, which in the case of hybrid offences almost always means at quarter sessions. An example of a hybrid offence is embezzlement, for which quarter sessions can impose a sentence of fourteen years' imprisonment, while a magistrates' court is limited to six months', or a fine of £100, or both. Such offences can be tried summarily if the prosecutor requests the magistrates to do so and they agree; or if, after they have begun to enquire into the case in their capacity as examining justices, they are persuaded by the prosecution, the accused, or the nature of the case, to do so.[2]

Similar to, but distinguishable from, hybrid offences, are indictable offences which are simply triable summarily at the discretion of the magistrates. In such cases they begin by acting as examining justices but can at any stage, after hearing the views of the prosecutor and the accused, decide instead to try the case summarily themselves.[3] Finally, whether the offence is non-indictable, hybrid, or indictable but triable summarily, there is a rule that if conviction would render the accused liable to more than three months' imprisonment he can claim to be tried on indictment.[4]

Since the magistrates' court is not allowed to see reports about the history and background of the accused until he has been convicted, it sometimes finds that it has dealt summarily with an offender who seems to require the sort of sentence that only a higher court can impose. If the offence is an indictable one the court is allowed to commit him to quarter sessions for sentence.[5]

Scottish Courts. In Scotland there is a similar distinction between summary trial and trial on indictment before a jury. Corresponding roughly to the Central Criminal Court, Crown Courts and Assizes is the High Court of Justiciary which sits usually in Edinburgh but also in other cities as occasion requires. It consists of one of the professional judges and a jury of fifteen. Its powers of imprisonment and fining are limited only where a

[1] The old distinction between 'felonies' and 'misdemeanours' was replaced in 1967 by the distinction between 'arrestable' and 'non-arrestable' offences. In the case of arrestable offences, constables and ordinary persons have certain powers of arrest and search without warrant. In the case of other offences (unless a statute expressly declares otherwise) a warrant is required for arrest. Any offence for which the sentence is fixed by law (e.g. murder) or for which a statute allows the offender to be imprisoned for five years or more, is arrestable. (See the Criminal Law Act, 1967.)
[2] Magistrates' Court Act, 1952, s. 18.
[3] *ibid*, s. 19.
[4] *ibid*, s. 25.
[5] *ibid*, s. 29.

statute provides an express limit.[1] It is the only court competent to try murder, treason, rape, incest, the deforcement of messengers, and breach of duty by magistrates. But it can also try any other crime which the prosecutor thinks fit to bring before it. In practice he chooses this form of trial only for serious crimes against the person, or serious property offences by offenders with long criminal records.

Corresponding roughly to quarter sessions are the local Sheriffs Substitute sitting in solemn jurisdiction – that is, with a jury. They are legally qualified holders of full-time appointments, and have the power to imprison for up to two years, although they can remit a convicted offender to the High Court for sentence if they feel their powers to be inadequate. All indictments not tried by the High Court are dealt with by these courts. The Sheriff Substitute, however, also sits as a summary court, with powers to impose not more than three (or in some cases six) months' imprisonment or a fine of not more than £150 (unless a different limit is fixed by statute). A stipendiary magistrate – of which Glasgow has at present the only example – has similar powers. These courts may try any offence which can be tried summarily – that is, any offence for which summary trial is not excluded by the terms of the statute. A lower form of summary court is the burgh court (sometimes called the 'police court') and its county equivalent, the justice of the peace court. These are the only Scottish criminal courts presided over by lay magistrates (who sit singly in the burgh court), and where the prosecution is brought not by an officer of the Crown but by a locally appointed public prosecutor. Their powers of sentence are limited to 60 days' imprisonment or a fine of £50, and they are statutorily debarred from trying a number of serious offences; in practice they try very minor offences of the kind that in England would be non-indictable, and occasional thefts, frauds and embezzlements where the value of the goods or money is under £25,[2] or where the accused has no criminal record.

Within these very broad limits it is the police and the prosecutor in Scotland who decide which type of court is the most appropriate, although a burgh or justice of the peace court which is trying a case can decide that it is more suitable for a higher court and discontinue its proceedings, leaving the Sheriff Court's prosecutor to proceed.[3] The accused himself has no say in the matter.

In England the verdict of the court must be either 'guilty' or 'not guilty'.[4] In Scotland, it can take a third, intermediate form, 'not proven'; the legal effect of this verdict is the same as that of an acquittal, while it leaves the accused under the same public suspicion as a conviction. Its merits are hard to explain to anyone who is not Scots.[5] An English jury (of twelve men or women) is expected to reach unanimous agreement on its verdict, although if it fails to do so the court can eventually accept a verdict on which at

[1] In Scotland many serious crimes are still defined only by common law, so that the High Court can in theory impose life imprisonment for them.

[2] For the jurisdiction of summary courts, see the Summary Jurisdiction (Scotland) Act, 1954, as amended.   [3] *ibid*, s. 5.

[4] Except in certain special cases of mental abnormality: see Chapter 13.

[5] But see Lord Clyde's defence of the practice in *McNicol* v. *H.M. Advocate* [1964] *Scots Law Times*, 151.

least ten members agree[1]. Scots juries of fifteen members are allowed to return verdicts by majorities of eight. In both countries the foreman must state publicly whether the verdict is unanimous or not.

Trial. The trial of guilt in these courts, its procedures and principles, is the subject of a huge corpus of legal literature. As a stage in the selection of offenders for penal treatment, however, the trial is a negligible source of inaccuracy. It is negligible not because of its perfection, which lies largely in the moral field; that is, in the safeguards with which the law protects the accused from 'unfairness'. Indeed, it has been argued (for example, by Glanville Williams[2]) that these safeguards are now excessive; and certainly the innocent persons who are mistakenly convicted must be numerically insignificant in comparison with genuine offenders who are acquitted. In fact, it is only in a small minority of cases that the safeguards come into operation at all. In practice the accused usually pleads guilty, and the court is left with the problem of disposal. Evelyn Gibson (1960) found that in higher courts 75 per cent. of accused persons plead guilty, and in lower courts the percentage must be higher still, although the increasing availability of legal aid has probably reduced these percentages recently. It is only where the charge is murder that the court usually refuses to accept a plea of guilty and insists on trying the issue.

If, on the other hand, he does plead 'not guilty', the accused's chances of acquittal vary with the type of court. English juries seem to acquit about two in every five persons who plead 'Not Guilty'.[3] In summary courts their chances are less than one in twenty-five. The reason may be partly that the sentences imposable by magistrates are less drastic, and so give rise to less hesitation; but an important factor must also be that juries, whose members are usually attending their first criminal trial, are more impressed than the seasoned magistrate is by the stories of an experienced and ingenious offender. Since magistrates' courts must try over 100,000 pleas of 'not guilty' every year, and must be rejecting well over 90,000 of them, it can be assumed that if the percentage of wrongly convicted persons were substantial, the volume of protest would be formidable. It is much more likely that juries, in acquitting two fifths of accused persons, are operating with a larger factor of error.

In summarising the accuracy of the penal system in identifying and dealing with people who infringe its prohibitions it can be said that the process of trial is a minor source of inaccuracy simply because so many of the accused plead guilty; in so far as it is inaccurate, most of its mistakes operate in favour of the individual, and not against him. But a much more important source of error is failure at one of the earlier stages in the process – for example in the reporting of an offence, or in the tracing of the offender. From the criminologist's point of view the function of a scrupulous system of trial is not to increase the efficiency of the system but to satisfy the public demand for fairness, so that the man in the street will not wreck the system.

---

[1] See the Criminal Justice Act, 1967, s.13, and the Lord Chief Justice's Practice Direction of 31st July 1967 (e.g. in *The Times* for 1st August).   [2] 1963 (3rd edition).
[3] See the figures for 1965 collected by the Chief Constables' Association and published in the *New Law Journal* for 9th June, 1966.

TRENDS

AND PATTERNS

IN CRIME

The forms of behaviour which we try to discourage by means of this system are infinitely heterogeneous. They range from elaborate frauds, involving protracted planning and execution, to an impulsive blow that is over in a second; or from failure to renew a car licence to the deliberate sabotage of an airliner. In theory it would be possible to prosecute any behaviour simply on the ground that it is contrary to one of the objectives which I listed in Chapter 1 (or any other objective to which society attached enough importance). In practice, however, this would leave too much scope for the arbitrary judgement of police and courts as to what was or was not contrary to these aims, and it has been found necessary to attempt definitions[1] of the types of behaviour which are to be officially discouraged. These definitions have been kept down to a reasonable number by deliberately lumping together what is recognisably different, and by giving the courts sufficient freedom to enable them to allow for such differences when deciding how to deal with the individual offender. The crime of bigamy consists of marrying a person while still married in the eyes of the law to another person. It can be committed, however, in very different circumstances: for example, by a man who mistakenly believes himself divorced, by a man who deliberately conceals his former marriage from his second 'wife', or by a man who frankly explains to her that he is married but cannot obtain a divorce.

This can have unfortunate results if the system prescribes a fixed penalty for a group of acts which are only nominally the same, as the British system did, and to some extent still does, for murder. The consequence may be that some, offences are punished in ways that are either inappropriate from a retributive point of view or inefficient from a prophylactic point of view. Sophisticated systems try to avoid this danger by allowing courts great freedom in the choice of penal measure[2]; even so they cannot always prevent sentencers from being consciously or unconsciously influenced by the name of the crime.[3]

---

[1] For definitions of many (but by no means all) offences in English law, see Archbold, 1967. For Scottish definitions, see Gordon, 1967.

[2] See Chapter 7, and especially the section on 'individualisation'.   [3] See page 216.

B

Another consequence is that anyone who attempts to assess the relative prevalence of different types of delinquency, their distribution among various subdivisions of the population, and their temporal trends, has to acknowledge peculiar difficulties. Not only is he uncertain how much of any given type of conduct is being reported and recorded, but also, since criminal statistics at present use legal definitions as the basis of subdivisions, he must recognise that even what is recorded under the same heading is a very mixed bag. He is in the position of an ornithologist who is trying, for example, to map the distribution of wild birds by using reports from people who can distinguish birds only as large or small, aquatic and non-aquatic, migratory or non-migratory.

VIOLENCE

When basing descriptions of the trends and distribution of crime on criminal statistics it is probably safer to use the broader rather than the more precise subdivisions, since at different times and in different areas similar types of behaviour may be classified under different minor subdivisions, but are less likely to be classified under different broad headings. For example, crimes of personal violence which do not involve the death of, or a sexual offence against, the victim are subdivided in the English Criminal Statistics into:

1. attempted murder;
2. felonious wounding; this includes most acts which endanger life, especially shooting or wounding with intent to do 'grievous bodily harm' or resist arrest;
3. malicious wounding; broadly, this consists of inflicting 'grievous bodily harm' without having the intention of doing so;
4. other indictable assault; this is usually an assault occasioning actual but not grievous bodily harm, or an assault accompanied by an attempt at a felony (such as housebreaking);
5. non-indictable assault; usually this consists either of an assault which results in no bodily harm (an assault may consist of the mere threat of force) or of obstructing or offering resistance to a constable.

A domestic brawl in which a husband hits his wife with a hammer could be classified under any of these headings. The choice of heading would be made by the police after their initial enquiries and without any reclassification in the light of the offence of which the husband was eventually convicted; the classification would therefore be determined by the judgement and policy of the police and the more or less accidental features of the crime. Thus the husband who could be proved to have said before hitting his wife 'I am going to kill you' might well be recorded as an attempted murderer; if he kept his mouth shut, or if his words went unheard, he would probably not. If his blow fractured her skull it would probably be recorded as a felonious wounding; if it merely rendered her unconscious, as a malicious wounding, or even a mere indictable assault. If she successfully dodged it, it might well be treated as a non-indictable assault. Moreover, from the clinical observer's point of view it is fallacious to distinguish even murder from crimes of this sort, since often it is mere accident that determines whether an attempted murder succeeds, or whether a blow that was merely intended to inflict serious harm has fatal results.

It has been suggested,[1] for example, that the apparent failure of the English murder rate to rise at the same rate as other crimes of personal violence over the last quarter of a century is at least partly due to the greater skill of the medical profession in saving the lives of victims of violence. That this is possible can be seen from the following table:

TABLE 1 Annual average numbers of reported offences per million inhabitants aged 8 or older (based on Tables A and E of the criminal statistics for England and Wales)

years	murder[2]	attempted murder	indictable woundings
1930–9	3·6	2·2	46
1950–4	3·7	4·0	152
1955–9	4·2	4·2	243
1960–1	4·4	4·8	372

The rate of recorded murders has increased by about 20 per cent, but if these are combined with recorded attempts, the rate for what might be called 'recorded attempts, successful and unsuccessful' has increased by about 60 per cent.

However this may be, the distinction between murder, attempted murder, and lesser crimes of violence is so much a matter of accident and the personal judgement of the police that in assessing trends it is safer to look at broad categories, such as indictable crimes of non-sexual violence against the person.[3]

As Table 1 shows, the increase over the last thirty years in indictable woundings recorded as 'known to the police' has been spectacular. Even when allowance is made for the increase in population, the *rate* appears almost eight times as high as it was before the war.

There are several reasons why this increase should not be accepted at its face value. McClintock[4] calculated that changes in police methods of recording would by themselves have caused an apparent increase of 13 per cent between 1938 and 1960. A much more important factor must be the increased readiness of ordinary members of the public to report such crimes. The wider the margin of unreported crime, the greater the scope for apparent increases of this kind. In districts where fights are an everyday occurrence and antagonism to the police is endemic, acts of violence often come to the notice of the police only when one of the participants reaches

[1] By Dr Harold Ross in a personal communication to me.

[2] Including murder reduced to manslaughter by reason of diminished responsibility.

[3] Non-indictable assaults should be disregarded, partly because we have less information about them (for example, figures for those known to the police are not published) and partly because most of them are rather different in nature from indictable crimes of intentional violence.

[4] To whose *Crimes of Violence* (1963) this section owes several of its observations.

the casualty department of a hospital. McClintock believes that even in 1960 there were many areas where only a fifth or a sixth of the assaults which occurred became known to the police. If so, such areas must have been even more numerous before the rehousing operations of the post-war decade. Moreover, if it is true that the middle-class outlook is being acquired by an increasing number of skilled manual workers, the percentage of the population who regard the police as their natural enemies is probably decreasing.[1] The publicity given to crimes of violence by the press, radio and television may also have persuaded more people that it is their duty to report them. If the margin of unreported offences is as wide as McClintock estimates, such influences could account for a very large apparent increase. We have only to suppose that in pre-war England 10 per cent of minor indictable assaults were reported, and that by the nineteen-sixties 25 per cent were reported, to see how the statistics would show an apparent increase of 250 per cent. We cannot, of course, dismiss the whole of the apparent increase in this way: almost certainly some of it reflects a real trend. But equally certainly the real trend is not nearly as spectacular as the statistics make it seem.

For the natural history of violence in England we must rely almost entirely on McClintock's survey. He observed that, contrary to common belief, Londoners are not more prone to violence than other Englishmen. The rates in other large cities were higher, and rates for the north of England[2] were higher than for the south. Less surprisingly, the age-group most given to violence was that of 'young adults' between 17 and 21, with 'young persons' between 14 and 17 a bad second, although here again part of the difference may be due to unwillingness to report fights between youngsters. An analysis of crimes of violence in London[3] showed that a third were the outcome of domestic quarrels, but almost as many consisted of attacks in the street. A fifth occurred in fights in public houses and cafés; an eighth were attacks on the police. Only 2 per cent were committed with firearms which were being deliberately carried in working order,[4] and only 5 per cent involved knives, razors and other deliberately carried weapons. In over a third of the cases some object ready to hand was snatched up, and in more than half the fists and the feet were used. In nearly four cases out of five it was the first time the offender had been convicted of a crime of violence. But nearly half the offenders had previous convictions for other sorts of offence, presumably in most cases larceny.

A sample of Scottish criminal careers[5] suggests that with each conviction for crime – even *non*-violent crime – the probability that the offender will eventually be convicted of violence increases slightly. But with each conviction for *violence* the likelihood of a further conviction for violence increases more sharply.

---

[1] Although the survey of the Willink Commission on the Police (1962) drew attention to a new phenomenon – antagonism to the police among middle-class motorists.

[2] i.e., north of a line from the Mersey to the Wash.

[3] I have excluded sexual attacks from McClintock's figures, which relate to 1960.

[4] McClintock, however, excludes shot-guns and other firearms used in family quarrels or used as blunt instruments.

[5] See Walker, Hammond and Steer, 1967.

Among men of violence – as among thieves and burglars – unskilled manual workers are over-represented.[1] Often their employment has been intermittent, a few weeks in one job being followed after an interval by a short period of some other kind of work.

Unlike thefts and burglaries, crimes of violence are traced to the offender by the police in nearly nine out of ten cases, presumably because the victim usually knows the identity of his assailant.

Murder. The most reliable source of information about English murders is Evelyn Gibson's analysis of murders committed in the nineteen-fifties.[2] Like many other crimes of violence, they were often the result of domestic disputes. About 30 per cent of adult male victims were killed by wives or relatives, over half the adult female victims by husbands or relatives, and about three in every four victims under the age of 16 are put to death by their own parents or relatives. It is not surprising, therefore, to find that the majority of murderers are suffering either from severe mental strain or diagnosable mental disorder: a third commit suicide before arrest; another third are found to be insane or of diminished responsibility (q.v.) when brought to justice. Only the remaining third are sentenced as mentally normal, and some of these are later found to be disordered. Indeed, even murder by shooting is more typical of the mentally unstable offender than of the professional criminal, for out of sixty-nine murderers who used fire-arms in 1955-60, three-quarters either committed suicide or were declared insane or of diminished responsibility. The types of mental illness usually associated with murder and violence will be discussed in Chapter 4.

Slightly over thirty murders a year were committed by men who not were diagnosed as mentally abnormal. In about 40 per cent of these cases the cause seemed to be a quarrel or violent rage; in another 20 per cent it was robbery or some other form of financial gain. In about 15 per cent the motive was sexual. Rather more than half of these 'sane' male murderers had previous convictions, and of this majority more than half had previous convictions which were confined to offences against property; the others had convictions for violence or sexual crimes or both. Men in their twenties were markedly over-represented, whereas among suicidal and mentally abnormal murderers there was a disproportionate number of older men.[3]

When it is realised that murders in Britain are so few – about four per million inhabitants every year – and that the sane murderer is responsible for less than a third of them, it becomes clear how rare a person he is. His fatal act seldom seems to be premeditated, but more often to be the outcome either of a sudden quarrel or of a situation in which he is surprised or resisted in the course of committing a robbery or burglary. For every such case in which his victim dies there are many more in which he survives. In other words, the typical sane murderer probably differs from other sane men who commit bodily violence only in one accidental respect: his victim's death.

[1] 'Over-representation' is a convenient and precise term. A class is over-represented in a sample if members of the class are more numerous in the sample than their numbers in the whole population would lead us to expect.

[2] 1961. But see also T. Morris and L. Blom-Cooper, 1964.

[3] The same was true of the women.

SEXUAL OFFENCES

Another group of offences in which there has apparently been a spectacular increase is sexual offences; but before examining this trend we should be clear about the nature of the very diverse forms of activity which fall under this broad heading.

Heterosexual Offences. If we exclude bigamy, soliciting,[1] brothel keeping[1] and abortion,[1] which are connected with sexual activity but are not usually classed as sexual offences, virtually all offences in this group are committed by men, and the majority of reported offences are against females. They take three main forms, and in this case the legal boundaries seem to distinguish fairly accurately between three dissimilar patterns of conduct.

'Indecent exposure' – sometimes called 'exhibitionism' by psychologists – is legally defined as 'the exposure of the naked person with intent to insult a female',[2] although the state of mind of the offender must usually be much more complex than this.[3] The Cambridge survey of sexual offenders[4] found that three-quarters of indecent exposers were between 21 and 50 years of age, two-thirds of these being married men, the great majority of whom had children. But among the single men the percentage still living at home with their parents was higher than in the case of other sexual offenders. The usual place for this type of offence is a park, or a street at night: the person chosen is a young girl under 16 in about half the reported cases, but not infrequently the man exposes himself to a group of children. He seldom commits any more serious sexual offence against the girl or woman, and, although sometimes the exposure is accompanied by invitations, if these are refused he does not molest her. The harm done is usually negligible; the offence is often not reported; and the law treats it as being less serious than other sexual offences by classifying it as non-indictable and limiting the maximum penalty to three months' imprisonment.

Indictable Heterosexual Offences. Sexual intercourse with a woman of any age against her will, whether by means of force, fraud or intimidation, is rape. A man who has intercourse with someone whom he knows to be his granddaughter, daughter, sister, half-sister, or mother is committing the offence of 'incest', and if his partner is 16 or older and consents she can also be convicted. An act of indecency which does not amount to sexual intercourse may be an indecent assault if it is done without the female's consent, which a girl under the age of 16 is presumed to be incapable of giving. An act of gross indecency committed with a girl under 14, though it may not be an assault because she has responded to an invitation, can now be prosecuted as 'indecency with a child'.[5] Sexual intercourse with a mentally defective

---

[1] A little will be said about these offences in Chapter 14.

[2] See the Vagrancy Act, 1824, s. 4, under which such charges are usually made.

[3] The need to prove the intent to insult seems to lead to a high rate of acquitta (Radzinowicz, 1957.52).

[4] On which most of the information in this section is based. But see also the valuable nviews with samples of English homosexuals and paederasts in M. Schofield, 1965.

[5] Under the Indecency with Children Act, 1960. The other indictable sexual offences are defined in the Sexual Offences Act, 1956.

woman, or a girl under the age of 16, is an offence, usually known as 'carnal knowledge', and if she is under 13 it is punishable with life imprisonment. With one exception these offences are regarded as serious, and usually punished severely. The exception is carnal knowledge of girls just under 16, an age-limit fixed in 1885 when physical maturity was attained later than it is now. Not only does the law allow a young man under the age of 24 to put forward the special defence that he reasonably believed the girl to be past her sixteenth birthday; even where a youth is unable to offer this defence he is often not prosecuted if he intends to marry the girl. The Cambridge survey found that for one reason or another there was no prosecution in 46 per cent of their cases.

Although some of these offences – rape, indecent assault and incest – can and do involve adult and even elderly women, the Cambridge survey found that in four out of five reported indictable offences the female was under 16.[1] In all but a minority of cases the offender was a considerably older man: in 52 per cent of cases he was over 30, and in 81 per cent he was over 17. At least half of the adult men were unmarried or no longer married. Manual workers, skilled and unskilled, were over-represented among all heterosexual offenders; only about 15 per cent of indecent exposers and 12 per cent of other heterosexual offenders came from white-collar occupations.[2] Of those who were found guilty, only one in eight had previous convictions for sexual offences, usually of the same type, although twice as many admitted the commission of similar offences for which they had not been convicted. A remarkably high percentage, however, had been convicted of other kinds of offence, usually petty thefts or frauds, and in cases of 'carnal knowledge' the percentage was as much as 79.[3] The typical offender against young girls seems, on this evidence, to be a man living a more or less irregular life, committing occasional petty crimes of dishonesty; being deprived – perhaps through his own inadequacy – of sexual relationships with adult women, he turns to some young girl because she is less likely to repel his advances.

Homosexual offences. These consist either of 'buggery' or of 'gross indecency'[4] committed between two men (not two women) in certain circumstances, which have to some extent been re-defined by the Sexual Offences Act, 1967. If, for example, one or both of the participants is under the age of 21, or if coercion is used, or if the act is not committed in private[5],

---

[1] Indeed, in two out of three cases she was under 13.

[2] The Cambridge survey could not use subdivisions comparable to those used in official analyses of the whole population; but it seems likely that at least 30 per cent of the population would fall within their 'groups A & B', which I have called 'white collared'.

[3] In contrast, indecent exposers included fewer (34 per cent) with previous non-sexual convictions, but more (21 per cent) with sexual convictions, usually for indecent exposure.

[4] 'buggery' usually means intercourse *per anum* with man or woman, but confusingly intercourse with animals by man or woman is also 'buggery' in English law. 'Gross indecency' has never been authoritatively defined.

[5] It is not private if, for example, it is committed in a public lavatory or if more than two participate. Otherwise it is for the courts to say what constitutes privacy.

or if it takes place on a U.K. merchant ship between two members of the crew, the act is criminal. 'Importuning', 'procuring' and 'brothel-keeping' for homosexual purposes are also offences.

Like the victims[1] of heterosexual offences, male victims in the Cambridge sample were under 16 in four out of five cases.[2] But where this was so, the tendency for the offender to be an older man was even more marked (94 per cent were over 17, and 57 per cent over 30). As might be expected, the majority of these offenders were unmarried, separated or divorced; but a substantial minority (17 per cent) were married, and almost as many (13 per cent) had children. For at least three-quarters this was their first conviction for a sexual offence, although, as with the heterosexual offenders, about a quarter admitted that they had committed similar offences, and about one in six had been convicted of thefts and other non-sexual crimes.

A much higher percentage of homosexual than of heterosexual offenders in the Cambridge sample belonged to white-collar occupations – 32 per cent compared with 12 per cent. With the possible exception of embezzlement and fraud there is no other group of indictable offences in which non-manual vocations are so strongly represented. Another strongly represented group consisted of 'domestic workers, hairdressers, cooks, waiters, barmen, actors, musicians and artists', who between them accounted for one-fifth of the homosexuals in the sample. Unlike property offenders, these men were on the whole satisfactory employees.[3]

It would be a great mistake, of course, to assume that these offences or the men convicted of them are representative of homosexuals. Quite apart from the unknown number of men whose inclination is homosexual but who have refrained from giving expression to it, the majority of practising homosexuals do not resort to making advances to immature boys or to importuning in public places. Of Westwood's sample of 126 adult male homosexuals collected through non-penal channels,[4] 80 per cent had never had any sort of contact with the criminal law; the rest had been convicted of homosexual offences once (17 per cent) or more often. Only 3 out of the 126 admitted sexual interests in boys under the age of 16, and when this is compared with the fact that 84 per cent of the Cambridge sample of reported indictable offences were against boys of this age, it suggests very strongly that most of the homosexuals who fell foul of the penal system belonged to the very specialised group known as paederasts. Like those who commit the minor offence of importuning, paederasts are said by psychiatrists to be very 'compulsive' in their behaviour – in other words to be unable to resist their periodic urge to act in this way.

Post-war Trends. The apparent increase in the incidence of both heterosexual and homosexual offences has been as spectacular as the multiplication

---

[1] 'Victim' is used here simply to mean the younger partner, and without implying that he was legally or morally innocent.

[2] Indeed 84 per cent were under 16 and 73 per cent under 13. The survey took place, of course, at a time when acts between males of any age were criminal.

[3] Judging from employers' reports to the police.

[4] 1960.

of crimes of violence, with one interesting difference: that the rate of increase of reported sexual offences has slowed down considerably in recent years and has been negligible since 1959. Table 2 shows, in four groups, the rates for the main indictable offences reported to the police.[1] The rates suggest that, even if the increase in population is allowed for, these four groups of offences have multiplied enormously. Reports of incest are

TABLE 2 Trends in sexual offences. Annual average numbers of reported offences per million inhabitants (figures in brackets show the extent of the increase, treating the annual average for 1930-9 as a base of 100)

years	rape and indecent assault[2]	intercourse with girls under 16 or 13	incest	homosexual offences[3]
1930–9	60 (100)	14 (100)	2·5 (100)	26 (100)
1950–4	198	36	6·3	140
1955–9	226	60	7·4	153
1960–1	248 (414)	99 (709)	7·7 (308)	134 (515)

three times as frequent as before the war; of indecent assaults, four times; of homosexual offences, five times; and of intercourse with girls under 16, seven times. There is one important possibility, however, that must be taken into account. The number of sexual offences which are committed without being reported is generally agreed to be very large indeed: Radzinowicz, for example, suggests that not more than 5 per cent of illegal sexual misconduct is revealed.[4] In Chapter 1 ten possible reasons for not reporting an offence were listed, and every one of them may operate in the case of one sexual offence or another. Offences such as incest, homosexual acts between consenting boys, or intercourse with girls under 16 are seldom reported by the participants, but usually by a third party, such as an inadvertent witness, the indignant parent of a pregnant daughter, or the outraged wife or neighbour of an incestuous husband. Often embarrassment, dislike of giving evidence on such delicate topics, concern for the good name of the family, or unwillingness to ruin the career and reputation of the offenders must dissuade these people from telling the police of their knowledge or suspicions.

Even the victims of indecent assaults – most of whom are young girls[5] –

[1] It is unfortunate that the Criminal Statistics do not give rates for reported non-indictable sexual offences, such as indecent exposure or importuning. Numerically insignificant indictable offences such as bigamy, abortion, procuration and abduction are also omitted, but can be found in the Criminal Statistics.

[2] Rape, attempted rape, and indecent assault on a female are grouped together because an act, which in one place or year is charged as one of these, might elsewhere or at another time have been charged as one of the other offences.

[3] For similar reasons, buggery, attempted buggery, and gross indecency between males are grouped together. Non-indictable offences are excluded.

[4] 1957.xv. In the U.S.A., the Kinsey data suggested that only about 6 per cent of sexual offences against young girls were reported to the police: see Gagnon, 1965.

[5] Radzinowicz, 1957.85.

are sometimes inhibited by modesty or irrational guilt from telling anyone what has happened. A child victim may tell her parents, but they may take the view that she will suffer less harm if she is not examined and interrogated by strange doctors and policewomen.

Influences such as these may have been increasingly counteracted in recent years by tendencies to franker discussion of sexual matters and by growing public concern about sexual misconduct. Concern of this kind may itself be traceable to franker newspaper reports of offences, coupled with despondent editorials. Not only may the ordinary member of the public be persuaded into sufficient alarm or moral indignation, but the police themselves may be stimulated into more active enquiries. This is probably the explanation of the trend of reported homosexual offences in the nineteen-fifties. Concern at the prevalence of homosexual behaviour led the Government to set up the Wolfenden Committee with the primary task of reporting on this aspect of the law. The rates of reported offences rose steadily to a peak of 170 per million in 1955, after the appointment of the Committee, but then began to fall. Since 1957, when the Committee recommended in favour of legalising homosexual acts between consenting adults, the reported rate has averaged less than 140 a year, and seems to be slowly declining. The most probable explanation is that the report led to a less censorious attitude on the part of both public and police.

If we suppose then that reported sexual offences are only a fraction of those committed, it seems highly probable that before the war they were an even smaller fraction. The smaller these fractions the larger would be the apparent effect produced by a change of attitude towards reporting. For example, it is unlikely on the most cautious estimate that information about more than one in every 2,500[1] indictable homosexual acts reaches the ears of the police. If this ratio rose to 5 in 2,500 this would wholly account for a five-fold increase in reported offences.

It would be ridiculous to suggest that the increases in Table 2 should be completely explained away on this assumption, which is after all more plausible when applied to, say, homosexual offences between consenting partners than to offences against unwilling women. At least one observation of the Cambridge investigators is more consistent with the supposition that a substantial part of the apparent increase is genuine. Not only are sexual offences rather more frequent in rural areas than in cities and towns, but the increase has been more marked in rural areas.[2] This is not necessarily attributable to rustic degeneracy: it is more likely that the countryside provides both countrymen and city-dwellers with better opportunities for finding victims, and that the sharper increase is due to cheaper and better means of transport. However this may be, London seems to have lower rates for sexual offences, both heterosexual and homosexual, although the latter do seem to be rather more frequently reported in the south of England. Heterosexual offences, like crimes of violence, seem to be decidedly commoner in the northern counties.

[1] One of the estimates quoted by the Wolfenden Committee, 1957.18. It is selected simply because it is the most cautious for the purpose of my argument.

[2] Radzinowicz, 1957.14-.

PROPERTY OFFENCES

Sex offences and crimes of violence, however, are overwhelmingly outnumbered in the criminal statistics by what are sometimes called 'property offences', sometimes 'offences of dishonesty'. The great majority of these are thefts of various kinds, of which over half a million were reported in 1961. Less numerous, but as a rule more profitable to the offender and more resented by the victim, were the 165,000 burglaries, shopbreakings, and other forms of 'breaking and entering', and the 40,000 frauds. In comparison, the 4,000 embezzlements and the 2,000 robberies[1] seem rare events.

Unreported Property Offences. Like sexual offences, thefts and embezzlements have their penumbra of known but unreported cases, although the reasons why they are not reported are different. If the loss is not serious and the prospect of recovery seems negligible, the victim may feel that he would be wasting his time by telling the police about it. Even if he believes that he knows the identity of the thief, his relationship to him may be such that he hesitates to voice his suspicions. Employers who prefer to be on good terms with employees often refrain from calling in the police when the identity of a pilferer is discovered, and simply reprimand or discharge him, as Martin's survey[2] of companies in the Reading area showed. Among the six most recent cases of theft or embezzlement which each company could recall, more than half were not notified to the police, the most frequent reasons being that the result would not have been worth the unpleasantness or publicity, that the offender was regarded as a good worker or 'a decent chap', that it would have been 'a waste of time', or that the loss was not serious enough. Martin found that in many firms a distinction was drawn between 'stealing' and mere 'pilfering'; the latter, which was much less likely to be dealt with officially, was usually distinguished from the former by the value of the goods, and while the borderline was vague some firms even set it above £10. On the other hand, if it is money that is abstracted, this is hardly ever condoned as 'pilfering', however small the amount.

It is most unlikely, however, that changes in the tendency to report property offences will explain the enormous increase in the incidence of officially recorded cases, which can be studied in Table 3. Indeed, it is more likely that employers are readier than they used to be to condone minor thefts, since the present conditions of comparatively full employment make satisfactory employees harder to replace. Moreover, offences such as housebreaking or robbery have always aroused such strong feelings of resentment or alarm that it is most implausible to suppose that the victim would fail to enlist the police on his side.[3]

[1] 'A person is guilty of robbery if he steals and in order to do so . . . uses force on any person or wilfully puts or seeks to put any person in fear of being then and there subjected to force' (s.7 of the Theft Act, 1968).

[2] 1962.75-.

[3] It is conceivable, however, that the growing popularity of insurance against loss through causes such as theft has been responsible for some of the increase in reported thefts, since insurance policies oblige the claimant to report the incident to the police of he wants to make a valid claim.

TABLE 3 Trends in property offences. Annual average numbers of reported offences per million inhabitants aged 8 or older

years	larceny	burglary	robbery etc.	fraud
1930–39	4441 (100)	1086 (100)	6 (100)	432 (100)
1950–4	8320	2359	24	702
1955–9	9267	2681	33	686
1960–1	12631 (284)	3915 (278)	54 (900)	937 (217)

It is much more probable that there really has been a marked increase in the rate of these offences, and while part of the explanation may lie in the psychological and social changes in our population – of the kind which will be discussed in Chapters 4 and 5 – we should not overlook the obvious. This is that the rise in property offences has accompanied a rise in the amount of portable property at risk. L. T. Wilkins has pointed out that the rising graph for 'larceny from motor vehicles' follows very much the same course as the graph for numbers of motor vehicles registered.[1] In other words, the affluent society is a society of opportunity, which includes the dishonest as well as the industrious amongst its beneficiaries.

Unlike crimes of violence, property offences are not traced to the offender in the majority of cases. There are exceptions, such as embezzlement or 'larceny by a servant' where the discovery that an offence has been committed usually makes it obvious who the offender must be. But less than a half of most other forms of theft are cleared up,[2] and in some cases – such as thefts from unattended vehicles – less than a quarter. This does not necessarily mean, however, that more than half of our thieves are never caught, as I have explained on page 13. The thief who tries to make a living by petty stealing has to solve at least one difficult problem, unless he confines his thefts to ready cash: the disposal of his booty for money. Professional 'receivers' are not easy to find,[3] and when found are seldom ready to deal with strangers (they may even report them to the police). Selling the stolen articles to chance acquaintances in public-houses is the petty thief's usual resort, and is almost as risky as it is unprofitable.

Just as employers are often willing to refrain from reporting minor thefts, so police will not infrequently let the reported thief off with a caution. This

[1] Wilkins, 1964.

[2] The 'clearing-up rate' can be estimated roughly from the table in the Criminal Statistics which shows numbers of offences 'known to the police' together with numbers 'cleared up' during the year. Although the latter must include some which were made known in the previous year, some made known in the current year will have been cleared up by the end of the following year, so that for practical purposes they can be treated as comparable. But there are traps: for example, the apparent fact that in 1961 over 80 per cent of 'larcenies from shops and stalls' were cleared up is explained when we realise that shops usually report shoplifting only when they have caught the shoplifter and want him or her prosecuted.

[3] The great majority of the 8,000 odd persons found guilty of 'receiving' in 1961 were friends or relatives who helped thieves, and not persons who were 'in business' as receivers.

practice will be discussed later in Chapters 9 and 10. The great majority of males who are dealt with in this way are teenagers with clean records, but an adult who has neither been convicted nor suspected of previous offences is sometimes simply cautioned. If his offence involves breaking and entering, or the use or threat of violence, he is almost always prosecuted, probably because these are regarded as the methods of the 'professional' criminal.

So far as minor thefts are concerned there is a very marked 'peak age' at which males are much more likely to be detected in such offences than at any other age. Whereas it is the young adult male, about the age of 20, who is most likely to commit a crime of violence, it is the boy of 14, in his last year at school, who is most often cautioned or prosecuted for some form of theft. This can be seen from Figure 1, which shows the rates at which young males were found guilty in 1956 of indictable offences (the overwhelming majority of which consisted of property offences, especially in the early teens). The rates for 1937 are also shown, and in order to eliminate the effect of the general rise in the incidence of such offences both sets of rates have been shown as percentages of the mean rate for all ages in 1937 or 1956 as the case may be. The result is interesting, for it shows that in 1956 the peak was both sharper and later by one year. This is at first sight surprising, since nowadays children reach physical maturity earlier and not later than they did before the war. It is very probable that the explanation is connected with the minimum permissible age for leaving school, which in 1937 was 14 but in 1956 had been raised to 15; in both years the 'peak age' occurred just before compulsory schooling came to an end.[1]

Most boys who are prosecuted for stealing are 'first offenders', at least in the sense that they have not hitherto been found guilty of any offence. But even in 1960 and 1961, when children of eight could be prosecuted, 4 per cent of boys of this age who appeared in court had already, in the few months at their disposal, been found guilty of theft. By the early twenties, the percentage has reached about 50; and from that age onwards there is a roughly even chance that a man convicted of a property offence has at least one similar conviction in his record; if he has, more often than not he has three or more. Nevertheless, even in middle age there seems to be a steady influx into the dock of newcomers with no previous convictions. Some of these have no doubt led virtuous lives until then, but almost certainly the majority have already committed a number of undetected thefts and have simply fallen victims at last to the geometric progression of their chances of being caught.

DRUNKENNESS

The effects of alcoholism, both on the drinker himself and on his family, have focused a good deal of attention on the rising figures for offences of

[1] Another possible explanation, that the apparent shift in the peak is due to changes in police forces' policy of cautioning young thieves instead of prosecuting, cannot be completely ruled out, since the 1937 statistics do not show rates of cautioning. The post-war statistics do, however; and even if the rates for boys cautioned at each age are added to those for prosecutions, the shape of the curve remains much the same. So that while cautioning may be relatively more frequent it is unlikely that it can explain the shift.

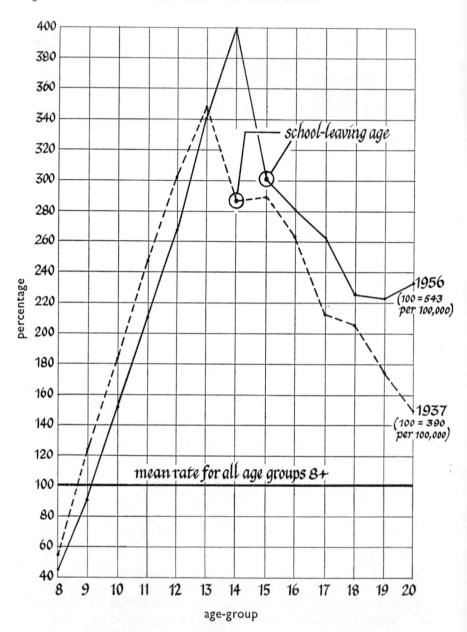

FIGURE 1 *The Peak Age*
Rates at which young males of different ages were found guilty of indictable
offences in 1937 and 1956, shown as percentages of the mean rate for all
age-groups in the year (England and Wales)

drunkenness. It is a non-indictable offence to be found drunk in a public place, and if intoxication is combined with disorderly behaviour it is punishable rather more severely.[1] Official statistics[2] for proved offences of this kind certainly show a definite increase over the last two decades, although it is much less striking than the apparent increases in rates for crimes against the person or against property.

TABLE 4 Trends in offences of drunkenness

years	offences of drunkenness proved, per million of population aged 15 or older	percentage committed by women
1938	1684 (100)	14
1950–4	1533	10
1955–9	1797	8
1960–1	2015 (120)	6

It is worth noticing that the trend is confined to offences by men; the rate for women has been slowly falling. Like violent and sexual crimes, offences of drunkenness are relatively commoner in the industrial north than in the south of England.[3]

How many of these offenders had simply happened to drink more than they could hold for once, and how many were chronic drinkers? Our best evidence is a rather small sample of 151 men, taken by Gath in 1967 from 'drunks' convicted in two metropolitan courts.[4] He found that half were addicted to alcohol in the strict sense, while another quarter found it 'a serious problem'. Fully a third of the sample, and nearly half of the real alcoholics, were Irish. In spite of the tendency of middle-class alcoholics to be saved from the courts by psychiatry or Alcoholics Anonymous, more than a quarter were from white-collared occupations.[5]

---

[1] Licensing Act, 1872, s. 12, and s. 91 of the Criminal Justice Act, 1967.

[2] *Offences of Drunkenness* (an annual Home Office White Paper). Strictly speaking, since these are offences proved against people, they are not exactly comparable with offences 'known to the police'. But while the police turn a blind eye to an unknown number of trivial cases, it is impossible, in the nature of things, that there should be a large number of cases where the police believe an offence of drunkenness to have occurred but cannot identify the offender. In other words, for practical purposes these can be regarded as 'offences known to the police'.

[3] Although Central London has the highest rate of all, it is artificially increased by two factors—the number of pleasure-seeking visitors, and the comparatively low density of residents from which the rate is calculated.

[4] Gath, 1969. His sample is probably more representative of 'drunks' in big English cities than of those in other types of area.

[5] i.e., Registrar-General's Groups I, II and III.

What is more, addiction seems to be commoner in middle age and later life, whereas drunks are relatively most frequent among young men above the age of 20, and it is in this age-group that the recent increase in frequency has been most marked:

TABLE 5 Age and offences in drunkenness

age-group	rate per 10,000 in:	
	1956	1961
18–20	56	82
21–29	54	65
30–59	36	43
60 or older	11	13

It is true that it takes time to acquire an addiction, and that some of these young drunks will no doubt become the alcoholics of the nineteen-seventies. But the great majority will not.

Increases in the incidence of offences of drunkenness have been found to be correlated with upswings in the business cycle,[1] and trends such as these probably reflect the enhanced purchasing power of the male wage-earner, one of whose ways of spending the surplus from his pay-packet is in drinking. It is the young wage-earner, without dependants, who has benefited more than the rest from post-war wage increases, the elderly who have gained least; and the trends in the table reflect the difference.

Yet while most drunks are no more than a minor and temporary nuisance, alcohol seems to play quite an important part in three more serious types of offence. Most widely publicised is its association with dangerous driving; but its role in crimes of violence and sexual assaults on women should not be overlooked. McClintock found that of crimes of violence in 1957 and 1960 one-fifth occurred in fights in public-houses and cafés, while no doubt many of the street attacks took place around closing-time. The peak age for drunkenness is also the peak age for this sort of violence. As for sexual assaults on women, nearly one in four in the Cambridge sample were committed by men who had been drinking, though not necessarily to the point of intoxication. A substantial minority of homosexual advances to adult males also seem to be made by men who have been drinking. But offences against boys or girls are much less often associated with drink.[2]

MOTORING OFFENCES

One of the most interesting fields for study, which has only recently begun to be explored in this country, is traffic offences. As Lady Wootton says, 'In half a century the invention of the internal combustion engine has completely revolutionalized the business of our criminal courts.'[3]

Delinquent motorists overwhelmingly outnumber all other offences: two

[1] By Dorothy Thomas (1925): see Chapter 5, Section A.
[2] Radzinowicz, 1957.98.
[3] 1959.25.

out of every three people found guilty in court are traffic offenders. At least a quarter of their offences – over 200,000 a year – consist of handling a moving vehicle with some degree of negligence or disobedience of the Highway Code.

The number of people killed or injured in road accidents each year is more than ten times the numbers involved in all the forms of assault recorded in the Criminal Statistics. Many of these casualties were due to the victims' own negligence or disobedience of rules; but even if we allow for this by halving the figures, it is clear that anti-social use of vehicles is a much more important source of death, bereavement, physical suffering and disablement than any intentional forms of violence.

Yet the penal system treats motoring offences far less seriously than crimes of violence or even of dishonesty. Almost all kinds of motoring offence are non-indictable: out of the 680,691 people tried for traffic offences in 1961 only 0·2 per cent were tried at higher courts – most of them for reckless or drunken driving. Even in summary courts these offences are distinguished in practice from other non-indictable offences; in the majority of cases the most severe penalty imposable for a first offence is a fine or disqualification from driving. In practice, magistrates imprison less than half of 1 per cent of traffic offenders, but nearly 3 per cent of other adult offenders.[1] Even the penalty of disqualification has been so reluctantly used that Ministers of Transport have gone to the length of making it more or less mandatory for some offences. Moreover, although other offenders – as we shall see in Chapter 10 – are likely to receive heavier sentences if they have already been convicted for other sorts of offence, a previous conviction for a traffic offence is usually disregarded as something quite different. Indeed there have even been suggestions that motoring offenders should not be tried by criminal courts at all, but by a different sort of tribunal.[2]

This tendency to distinguish between motoring offences and other types of delinquency seems to be based on the assumption that the motoring offender is usually a respectable person who has transgressed the law through inadvertence and not intentionally. It is true that inadvertence is the excuse offered by most people accused of illegal parking, speeding, or disobeying traffic signals; and that partly because this defence is so hard to disprove, partly in the hope of making the negligent driver less negligent, the law has been drafted so that even negligent transgressions are offences. This encourages the impression that *most* such transgressions are merely negligent, although it is very doubtful whether this is so.

As for the 'respectability' of English motoring offenders, our only factual information comes from Willett's investigation of 653 convictions for 'serious' motoring offences committed in 1957-9 in one police district of the Home Counties.[3] His data suggest that motoring offenders should be subdivided into at least two main groups: those who drive carelessly or dangerously, and those who disregard the laws requiring them to have

---

[1] i.e., offenders aged 21 or over.   [2] See Fitzgerald, 1962.63.
[3] See Willett, 1964, but also the important re-examination of his data by Carr-Hill and Steer, 1967.

C

licences and third-party insurance. The former seemed to be fairly representative of the motoring population in social class, age, occupation, and type of vehicle. The latter, on the other hand, tended to be young males, usually motor-cyclists, from manual occupations, of whom a high percentage (29 per cent) had previous convictions for non-motoring offences. In other words, a distinction must be drawn between the dangerous and the dishonest driver, and the latter is more likely to have a criminal record. The dangerous driver, on the other hand, is more representative of 'respectable' sections of the population.

Like all the types of crime which we have been considering, motoring offences have increased sharply in numbers since the 1939-45 war. Although, as Figure 2 shows, much of this rise is attributable simply to the greater volume of traffic on the roads, this does not wholly account for the increase after 1950 (when petrol rationing was abolished), for since then offences have multiplied faster than traffic. But some of the remaining increase may well be due to increased police activity (assisted by a greater readiness on the part of the public to report offenders). There is at least one piece of indirect evidence which supports this conjecture: casualties, as the figure also shows, have risen more slowly, so that there are now more prosecutions and warnings which have not arisen from casualty-producing accidents.

OTHER NON-INDICTABLE OFFENCES

Finally, we are left with a miscellaneous assortment of non-indictable offences. Most of them are concerned with infractions of the numerous statutory regulations which have been found necessary in a crowded and industrialised country, in order to protect its inhabitants from threats to health, nuisances, and from destruction of amenities, or in order to collect the state's revenue. In most of these cases the prosecutor is neither the local Chief Constable nor the Director of Public Prosecutions, but a government department, a public undertaking or a local authority. As in the case of indictable offences, the largest single group with any claim to homogeneity consists of various forms of dishonesty, from the evasion of taxes to travelling on public transport without a ticket. It is interesting to observe that convictions for offences against the revenue laws seem to be less frequent now than in the pre-war decade, although apparently they have begun to increase again:

TABLE 6 Trends in revenue offences

years	annual average numbers per million inhabitants
1930–9	905
1950–4	573
1955–9	551
1960–1	757

Most of these consist of failures to buy or renew licences for motor vehicles

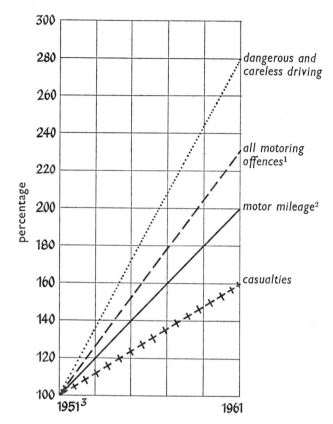

FIGURE 2 *Traffic, casualties and offences on British Roads, 1951-61*

In order to demonstrate the differing rates of increase clearly, figures for 1961 are shown as percentages of the corresponding figures for 1951,[3] and fluctuations in intervening years are ignored. Since the published motor mileage and casualty figures include Scotland as well as England and Wales, it has been necessary to add Scottish motoring offences 'made known to the police' to English and Welsh offences recorded as dealt with by warning or prosecution. Though not entirely satisfactory, this is preferable to comparing British mileages and casualties with English and Welsh offences; and since few motoring offences 'made known' to police are dealt with otherwise than by warning or prosecution the Scottish figures are in all probability comparable. Unfortunately, no published Scottish figures were available for 'dangerous and careless driving', so that the trend indicated for this group of offences relates only to England and Wales.

---

1. Based on the Home Office's Annual Returns of Offences relating to Motor Vehicles and the Scottish Home Department's Criminal Statistics (Scotland), both published by HMSO.
2. Based on the Road Research Laboratory's estimate in 'Road Accidents, 1962' (HMSO).
3. The first complete calendar year after the abolition of petrol rationing in 1950.

GENERAL

This brief survey of the main groups of offences has been deliberately confined to description; explanatory theories will be discussed in Part Two.
But without anticipating this discussion a few general observations can be
made.

First, the types of crime about which most concern is expressed – murder,
violence, sexual offences – are among the least frequent; murder is numerically as insignificant in the criminal statistics as death from anthrax is
among this country's infectious diseases. Table 7 shows the proportions in
which the main types of offences which have been dealt with in this chapter
are represented among men, women and children found guilty in 1961.[1] It
is dominated by traffic offences, which account for nearly two out of three
cases. Of the remaining third, one-third consists of 'property offences', to
which we ought probably to add revenue evasions and most railway
offences, as representing other forms of dishonesty. Next in numbers are
the drunks. Violence is near the bottom of the list and only 1 per cent are
sexual offenders. It is essential, however, to remind ourselves that if all
offences of every kind were conscientiously reported to the police and
successfully prosecuted the proportions would almost certainly differ in two
respects. Property offenders – who in this statistically imperfect world so
often escape detection – would dominate the picture even more; and all the
unknown number of unreported sexual offences would greatly add to that
1 per cent. In this corrected perspective, violence would appear even more
insignificant.

We have seen, too, how at least three types of offence seem to be relatively
commoner in the north of England – drunkenness, violence, and heterosexual offences. (The same may be true, for all we know, of property
offences.) This geographical anomaly must be at least partly attributable to
differences in the distribution of manual workers (especially in unskilled
males) who, as we saw, are over-represented among those convicted of such
offences. What we do not know is whether the anomaly would disappear if
these differences were allowed for; in more concrete terms, whether a
builder's labourer in the north is more likely to behave in these ways than
his counterpart in the south.

A question of some importance is 'What percentage of our population
has ever been convicted of an offence?' Surprisingly, we have no reliable
answer: only a number of very rough estimates, based on indirect calculations and doubtful assumptions. Only one study of an actual sample is
worth mentioning – the analysis by Douglas and others of the careers of
2,402 boys born in Britain in the first week of March, 1946, who were still
traceable and living in this country by their 17th birthday in 1963. By this
time 8 per cent had been found guilty of indictable offences (largely, no

---

[1] It is unfortunately impossible to construct a table of this kind for offences *known to
the police*, since the Criminal Statistics do not give this information for non-indictable
offences. If such a table could be constructed, offences such as larceny, would no doubt
account for a larger percentage of the total (perhaps 20 per cent), since they include
such a high percentage of cases known to the police which do not lead to a conviction.

TABLE 7 Offences in perspective. Percentage of persons found
guilty in English Courts in 1961

traffic offences	61·3
breaking and entering (3·2), receiving (0·8) and larceny (9·3)	13·3
drunkenness	7·0
murder (·001) and other non-sexual violence[a] (1·999)	2·0
sexual offences[b]	1·0
revenue evasions	2·5
railway offences	1·8
breaches of local bye-laws and similar regulations	2·2
malicious damage to property	1·6
miscellaneous	7·3
total 1,152,397[c]	=100

[a] Including non-indictable assaults.

[b] Including soliciting, indecent exposure and other non-indictable offences.

[c] This total represents appearances in court at which a finding of guilt was recorded, and since an unknown number of persons were involved in such appearances more than once in the same year, the figure does *not* indicate the number of individuals involved.

doubt, thefts) and another 4 per cent had been found guilty of, or cautioned for, non-indictable offences: a total of nearly one in every eight boys.[1]

Indirect calculations[2] suggest that after their 17th birthday, at least another 6 per cent of these males will have been convicted once or oftener of an indictable offence. In other words we shall soon be faced – if we are not already – with a population in which one in every seven adult males has been convicted at least once, and some oftener, of an offence of dishonesty, violence or (rarely) sexual molestation; and in certain occupations, chiefly unskilled manual, the ratio will be much higher.

The implications of this are only beginning to dawn on penal administrators. For example, it was found not long ago that out of 38 persons sum-

[1] See J. W. B. Douglas, *et al.*, 1967.

[2] See, for example, Little, 1965. Little used the tables in the Home Office's Supplementary Criminal Statistics which show first convictions for indictable offences by age-groups. By converting these to percentages of the population in each age-group and adding up the percentages he arrived at an individual's cumulative probability of being found guilty of an indictable offence by a given age. For boys reaching their seventeenth birthday his estimate was 10·88 per cent. His method assumes that first-conviction-rates will remain stable at the level which they have reached in the tables used, whereas of course they were lower and will almost certainly be higher at later stages in the individual's lifetime. It also assumes that individuals were correctly shown in the tables as having no previous convictions for indictable offences, whereas it is suspected that this is by no means always so, *and especially in the case of juveniles*. These two factors no doubt account for most of the considerable discrepancy between Little's percentage of 10·88 per cent and Douglas' figure of 8·0 per cent. I prefer, therefore, to accept Douglas' figure for boys aged 17, and use Little's method only to calculate *subsequent* probabilities of conviction.

moned as jurors to the Old Bailey, 4 certainly and 9 probably had convictions serious enough to be recorded at the Criminal Record Office; and an attempt is now made to exclude certain categories of ex-prisoners from jury service,[1] on the assumption that they are likely to be biassed in favour of the accused. But there are other aspects, less easily defined but more important, of this situation. If – as is likely – this high percentage of males who have experienced the penal system 'at the receiving end' is a recent phenomenon, which will increase further, this is bound to have radical effects both on our penal philosophy and on the capacity of the system to cope with the problem.

[1] Section 12 of the Criminal Justice Act, 1967 disqualifies persons who have served prison sentences of five years or more at any time in their lives, and persons who have served sentences of three months or more in the last ten years. For a discussion of the problem see the report of the Morris Committee on Jury Service, 1965.

PART TWO

★

EXPLAINING AND PREDICTING CRIME

[3]

CONSTITUTIONAL

THEORIES

Although the main part of this chapter is concerned with a particular type of explanation, some preliminary warnings are necessary about the sort of explanations that are encountered in this field.

CRIMINOLOGICAL EXPLANATIONS IN GENERAL

In so far as explanations are based on evidence, this may be of three kinds. It may be introspective, consisting of someone's beliefs about the circumstances or state of mind in which they have committed (or, more often, would commit) some delinquent act. Since the introspector is usually well educated, middle-class, and law-abiding, while most offenders, as we have seen, are none of these, this arm-chair psychology is worth little. It is less open to criticism when it is used to suggest plausible connections between variables that have been found to be associated by more reliable methods.

Case-study. Another sort of evidence is based on case study; that is, on the detailed investigation of the history, psychology, and patterns of behaviour of individual offenders. If done with insight and without more than the unavoidable minimum of preconceptions, this is a valuable source of ideas and information which can lead to new explanatory hypotheses. As soon as it is treated as evidence, however, an awkward question arises. How can we be sure that the one or two cases studied are typical of what we are trying to explain?

Statistical Evidence. The study becomes a statistical one as soon as an effort is made to ensure that cases studied are typical. The crudest way of doing so is to study such a large percentage of the individuals in which one is interested that the chances of the sample's being unrepresentative are small. For obvious reasons this is impossible in the field of delinquency. What is more likely to be practicable is to select a sample in such a way that it is unbiased, or, more precisely, is probably not biased in a respect which is relevant to the characteristics being studied. We shall see in this and the following chapters what the chief possibilities of bias are. It is not often appreciated that a well-selected small sample is preferable to 'the big battalions'. For example, Lady Wootton, in her well-known review[1] of twenty-one criminological investigations, refused to consider any in which

[1] 1959.

less than 200 subjects were involved, a criterion which eliminated some valuable studies.[1]

Controls. Let us suppose, however, that a satisfactory sample of some type of delinquent shows that a high percentage exhibit some characteristic, such as overcrowded homes. This observation is valueless until one has made sure that the percentage of overcrowding among non-delinquents (or some other type of delinquent) is lower. This can be done in two ways. Overcrowding rates can be studied for the general population of the area from which the delinquents were selected; if we can assume that delinquents are only a small minority of this population it does not matter that it includes them. A more accurate method, which is likely to detect smaller differences, is to select a 'control sample' of people who are selected from the same area but are known to be non-delinquent. If other variables are known to be associated with overcrowding (for example, having a large family), the control sample should be matched[2] to the delinquent sample in such a way that their effect is minimised.

Significance. This process will reveal either similar percentages of overcrowding in the two groups, or a difference in the percentages. But a difference cannot be accepted as a basis or part of the basis on which to found a theory unless the probability that it has occurred by chance is negligible. This probability can be calculated from the sizes of the percentages and the numbers in the two samples,[3] and is then expressed either as a percentage or as a decimal (for example, $p = 5\%$ or $p = \cdot 05$ which means that the probability of the difference being the result of chance is 1 in 20). The smaller this probability, the more 'significant' the difference, and the more reliance is placed on it. Probabilities which exceed $\cdot 05$ are not usually treated as significant, and most social scientists would not be satisfied with probabilities exceeding $\cdot 01$. A fallacy, however, is often perpetrated when samples show small differences with probabilities exceeding $\cdot 05$: the investigator is apt to report 'no significant difference', and to treat this as if it indicated that delinquents did not differ from non-delinquents in respect of the characteristic in question. Unfortunately it may mean that there *is* a slight difference, which would have been found to be significant at the $\cdot 05$ or even $\cdot 01$ level if the samples had been larger.

---

[1] e.g., Andry, 1960. One of Lady Wootton's other criteria is also open to criticism. She would not consider a report of a study which did not 'contain data on not less than half, or nearly half, the hypotheses under review'. Since she was reviewing no less than twelve hypotheses, her selection was confined to what may be called the 'blunderbuss' type of study, in which a miscellaneous assortment of questions is fired at a large sample of delinquents in order to see what happens. Her criterion automatically excludes studies in which the sample and the questions were designed to test specific hypotheses.

[2] Matching may take the form of 'group matching' in which all that is aimed at is that each of the two samples should contain roughly the same numbers of individuals with families of two, three, four members, and so on. But if more than one variable is involved, a more satisfactory method is 'pair-matching', in which each individual in the delinquent sample is matched to an individual in the control sample who corresponds in respect of all the variables.

[3] For the method of calculation, see any elementary textbook of statistics for social scientists, such as Connolly and Sluckin, 1957.

Hard and Soft Data. The validity of results also depends on the nature of the characteristics being studied. Overcrowding, for example, can be assessed fairly objectively by comparing the number of members of the household with the number of rooms they occupy. Equally important, it can be expressed in a numerical notation, which has the advantage of being unambiguous. In contrast, assessments of such characteristics as 'family discipline' depend to a great extent on the subjective impressions formed by an investigator. Even if descriptions of parental discipline can be reduced to a finite number of categories (for example, 'over-strict', 'lax', 'inconsistent', 'reasonable'), one investigator's notion of what is 'over-strict' might include some cases which another would classify as 'reasonable'. Moreover, if the investigator knows that the family which he is visiting is the family of a delinquent, and knows that faulty discipline is regarded as a likely cause of delinquency, he may tend to classify the discipline as defective in a case in which he would not have done so if he had believed the family to belong to a non-delinquent.[1] When reports of investigations are being examined it is therefore important to consider whether the data are 'hard' (i.e. objectively measurable) or 'soft' (i.e. impressionistic). Sometimes it is possible to increase the validity of 'soft' data by obtaining independent assessments of it from two or more people: if more than one investigator classifies a family's discipline as 'lax', then this classification is more reliable, and reliability is usually accepted as evidence of validity.[2]

Testing a Theory. As we shall see, the exponents of some explanations of delinquency (especially but not only sociologists) often appeal for support to observations which have already been reported. These appeals are legitimate so long as they are not mistaken for tests which *verify* the hypothesis. So many observations have been made, and so many associations established, that it would be difficult to propound a hypothesis for which a little ingenuity could not find some supporting evidence in the literature of psychological or sociological research. In order to test a hypothesis properly it is necessary to deduce from it a prediction that if a study (or experiment) of a certain type were carried out, the result would show a positive, negative or non-existent association between two or more variables; nor is it sufficient to make a pseudo-prediction, that is, to 'predict' what one knows already to have been established, since this knowledge may well have influenced the form of the hypothesis. If we want to test the skill of a water-diviner we are not satisfied if he finds underground water in a bog, or where the map says 'Underground River'; but we are rightly impressed if he finds it where nobody has suspected its existence.

The Democratic Fallacy. Another kind of error is sometimes committed when independent investigations disagree on the same issue. Lady Wootton, for example, noted that out of thirteen investigations which had been con-

---

[1] 'Blind' studies, in which the investigator does not know whether he is dealing with a delinquent or a non-delinquent, are virtually impossible if any conversation is involved, since references to the delinquency are almost unavoidable.

[2] In the human sciences, a measurement is 'reliable' to the extent that repetitions give similar results. It is 'valid' to the extent that it measures something which is independent of the judgement of the observer (and of the observed subject).

cerned with (*inter alia*) the association between delinquency and large families, all but one noted that delinquents tended to come from families with more than the average number of children; and she concluded 'on the whole, it seems that offenders come from relatively large families'.[1] But the single investigation which did not support this conclusion was the one best designed to test it. This was Ferguson's analysis of information about 1,349 Glasgow boys. He took the trouble to subdivide his families of different sizes according to their degree of overcrowding and found that when this was done the association between delinquency and large families had disappeared,[2] while the association between overcrowding and delinquency remained. To arrive at a conclusion by taking a vote, instead of deciding which investigation is best designed to answer the question, is democratic rather than scientific.

Types of Explanation. The explanatory theories which I shall discuss in these chapters fall into two main groups, the 'individualistic' and the 'environmental'. Explanations of the first type envisage the delinquent as an individual who is in some way more prone to delinquency than the non-delinquent, even in the same environment. When explanations account for this proneness they subdivide into two groups, those which attribute it to some inherited or at least congenital feature of the individual's constitution, and those which attribute it to some stage of his upbringing. Environmental explanations, on the other hand, place less emphasis on individual differences of disposition than on differences between the environments of the delinquent and the non-delinquent. Some such theories place the greatest weight on the non-human aspects of the environment, such as the economic climate; others on the human environment, in other words the associates, neighbours, and other acquaintances of the delinquent.

The extent to which any two or more of these theories must be regarded as contradictory depends on whether they are asserted in the 'weak' or the 'strong' form. In the weak form all that a theory of this kind claims is that it is an explanation, or an important part of the explanation, of a sufficiently large number of cases of delinquency to make it interesting. In the strong form the theory claims that it is the explanation, or the most important part of the explanation, of most or even all cases of delinquency. So many strong theories have weakened in the history of criminology that it is now rare to find one stated in this form; but there are examples.[3] When, as is more usual in these disillusioned days, theories are stated in the weak form, it is not easy to be sure whether they are contradictory or merely complementary.

In the rest of this chapter and the next I shall discuss theories which relate

---

[1] 1959.85-7 and 134.

[2] 1952.22.

[3] Thus D. Cressey, 1953, claims to formulate an explanation of embezzlement which is true of all of his 200 cases, and T. R. Fyvel, 1961, explains all teenage offences in all civilised countries as due to 'insecurity'. In both cases this is achieved largely by formulating the explanation so that it can hardly fail to be true of all cases, rather like the fortune-teller's prediction that her client's life will be altered by a fair person of the opposite sex.

criminal behaviour to certain characteristics of individuals. Such theories, which I call 'individualistic', belong either to the 'constitutional' group or to the 'developmental' group, according to the emphasis which they lay on nature or nurture, or in other words on innate or acquired character-istics.

CONSTITUTIONAL THEORIES

Constitutional theories are those which assert that a substantial number of offenders are predisposed to behave in this way because of the physical or mental constitution with which they are born. Theories of this kind, though detectable in earlier folk-lore, received their first scientific statement from the phrenologists of the nineteenth century. Later, the Italian psychiatrist Lombroso was inspired by the new Darwinian theory of human evolution to suggest that persistent criminals were atavisms, that is, throw-backs to an earlier stage of humanity. The best of his evidence, which consisted largely of measurements of the sizes and shapes of the crania of criminals and non-criminals, was presented as scientifically as the instruments and statistical knowledge of his day permitted, and it was not until Goring, the English prison doctor, was able to carry out a more careful and larger series of measurements, with the newly invented statistical techniques of Karl Pearson, that Lombroso was contradicted by real evidence. Later, the dis-covery by Boas[1] and Shapiro[2] that human crania altered in shape from one generation to another as a result of migration from one country to another cast further doubt on the Lombrosian theory; but forms of it lingered on – particularly in the theories of Hootton and Sheldon at Harvard – until the middle of the twentieth century. Today, the evidence for inborn factors which may predispose people to criminal behaviour takes two different forms, and consists of studies of: (1) types of physique; (2) twins.

Physique. There is some evidence for an association between juvenile delinquency and a certain type of physique.[3] Sheldon has evolved a method of classifying different human body-builds. On the hypothesis that in bodily growth one of three types of tissue may come to predominate in him, the individual usually belongs to one of the following 'somatotypes':

1. The *endomorph*, in whom the endoderm, or tissues associated with digestion, such as stomach and fat, predominate. This is associated with the *viscerotonic* temperament, given to food, drink, comfort, company and sleep.
2. The *ectomorph*, in whom the ectoderm, or skin and nervous system, predominate.[4] This is associated with the *cerebrotonic* temperament, given to books and privacy, sensitive to pain, needing less sleep, and producing a youthful and intent manner.

[1] 1912.

[2] 1939.

[3] Although Lombroso's anatomical theories were largely concerned with the cranium, and only with superficial characteristics of the torso, such as hair and tattooing, it is possible to trace the intellectual descent of Sheldon's hypothesis from Lombroso.

[4] Sheldon does not seem to mean that ectomorphs literally have larger brains, although he does mean that endomorphs have larger stomachs.

3. The *mesomorph*, in whom the mesoderm, or bone, muscle and sinew, predominate. This is associated with the *somatotonic* temperament, insensitive to pain and given to movement, adventure and aggression.

Some people, however, seem to belong to a 'balanced' type. In scientific somatotyping, each person is not simply classified under one of these four heads, but is awarded a score of 1 to 7 points on each of the three 'dimensions' – endomorphy, ectomorphy, and mesomorphy. Thus a modified endomorph with a little of the mesomorph about him might be marked 5:1:3, while a balanced type would be 4:4:4.[1]

Although Sheldon himself found evidence that young male delinquents tended to be mesomorphic with a leaning toward endomorphy, his samples and other aspects of his methods were open to criticism.[2] But a more carefully controlled comparison by the Gluecks[3] appears to confirm this finding, as the following table shows:

TABLE 8 Delinquency and somatotypes

somatotypes	percentage of persistent juvenile delinquents	percentage of matched non-delinquents
mesomorphs	60	31
endomorphs	12	15
ectomorphs	14	39
'balanced' type	13	15
N=100%=	495	484

A greater preponderance of mesomorphs among delinquents was found even among the groups of different ethnic origin – for example, when delinquent boys of Italian stock were compared with non-delinquents of Italian stock. Their results also seemed to show that the somatotypes were

[1] Even so, Sheldon had to recognise exceptional types of physique, such as *gynandromorphs*, dysplastic cases with endomorphy in one part of the anatomy and mesomorphy in another, and *gnarled mesomorphs* (chiefly immigrant Italian peasants).

[2] 1949. His delinquents were 200 young males referred by a large variety of social agencies in Boston to the Hayden Goodwill Inn, a sort of free hostel with the aim of salvaging desperate cases. His controls were 4,000 students from six centres of higher education, and were not matched for social class, residential area, or indeed any characteristic. Moreover, the somatotyping consisted of predicting what the youth's score would be when he was full-grown!

[3] 1956. The somatotyping was done by an associate of Sheldon at the Harvard Anthropological Institute, using photographs taken in the prescribed somatotype poses (see Sheldon, 1949), and classifying each boy on the basis of his present physique, instead of attempting to predict his adult physique, as Sheldon had done. 'At no time were the other data of the survey consulted in connection with the anthropological analysis.' This seems to imply that the somatotyper did not know which boys were delinquent and which were controls.

distinguishable by certain temperamental differences, even among the non-delinquents[1]: for example, mesomorphs were less 'sensitive' or 'emotionally unstable'.

Gibbens'[2] study of English borstal boys also disclosed an unexpectedly large percentage of mesomorphs, and somewhat similar temperamental differences between them and the ectomorphs or endomorphs; but he was unable to somatotype his control sample.

Natural Selection of Mesomorphs. This apparently well-established association between mesomorphy and juvenile delinquency raises the question whether it reflects an inherent tendency in mesomorphs to be anti-social; certainly Sheldon and the Gluecks seem to have thought so.[3] Another possibility, however, is that this is an example of natural selection. If for 'mesomorph' we substitute 'a muscular, athletic boy' and for 'juvenile delinquent' we substitute 'a boy who fights, robs and steals', it is easy to see how the mesomorph's physique is the best adapted of the somatotypes to the sort of things that juvenile delinquents do – assault other people, climb walls, run away from the police. Children begin to learn at an early age what they are physically able to do successfully, and what is not their strong point. It would help us to decide between the two explanations – in terms of inherent tendencies or natural selection – if we knew:

1. whether offences that do not require an athletic physique – such as forgery, fraud – also tended to be committed by mesomorphs more often than we should expect on chance; if so, this would favour the theory of inherent antisocial tendency;
2. whether the association between mesomorphy and juvenile delinquency becomes weaker as one confines the sample to younger and younger boys. If so, this would favour the hypothesis that boys gradually learn whether they are physically adapted to crime.

Criminal Parents. Most studies which include the criminal records of parents in their data observe that children with at least one convicted parent are more likely to be delinquent than those without. The frequency of the association between delinquency in children and delinquency in their parents or siblings has suggested the hypothesis that a disposition to 'criminality' is inherited or, more precisely, transmitted from one generation to another through the mechanism of the genes; and investigators have traced the genealogies of families with delinquent members for several generations. Evidence of this kind, however, is obviously inconclusive, since most delinquent children have lived with their delinquent parents or siblings long enough to acquire delinquent ways of life by imitation or some other non-genetic process of transmission. More interesting evidence is provided by studies of the careers of twins.

Twins. Where the genetic transmission of any characteristic is concerned, there are three possibilities. One is that the genetic influence is non-existent,

---

[1] 1962. Appendix E.

[2] 1963.

[3] And, of course, Kretschmer, whose work inspired Sheldon, thought that different body-builds were associated with tendencies to different types of mental illness.

or negligible, in which case the characteristic can be regarded as determined wholly by environment. An example of this is the ability to speak French or any other language: this is determined not by the language of a person's parents or ancestors, but by the language spoken by those who bring him up and teach him. At the other extreme is the possibility that the characteristic is determined so overwhelmingly by one's genes that the influence of environment upon it is negligible, as is the case with eye colour. Examples of this are commoner among physical than among behavioural characteristics, especially in human beings, since learning can modify so many forms of human response. One example, however, of abnormal behaviour which is unquestionably transmitted through the genes is the behaviour which is the symptom of a cerebral disorder known as Huntington's chorea. This never occurs in persons unless a parent or grandparent was affected by it,[1] and no means of preventing its onset by environmental influence has so far been discovered.

It is the intermediate possibility – namely that a characteristic is determined partly by genetic inheritance and partly by environment – that gives rise to controversy. Most children are brought up by their natural parents, so that even some of their physical characteristics are affected to an unknown extent by the same environment as affected their parents. It was found, for example, by Shapiro that even the shapes typical of Japanese skulls underwent detectable changes in the pure-bred descendants of Japanese who migrated to Hawaii,[2] presumably as a result of differences in diet. Behavioural characteristics of parents may be reproduced in children by imitation, to say nothing of more complex reactions. Consequently, investigations which have simply traced the genealogies of delinquents and found them to contain high rates of delinquency are inconclusive.[3] More reliable evidence is provided by the study of twins.

Twins are of two kinds. One kind, known as 'dizygotic', 'non-identical', or 'fraternal', results from the simultaneous fertilisation of two ova by two spermatozoa. Twins of this sort may be of the same or different sexes, and may differ in blood groups; they may resemble each other strikingly, or no more than two ordinary siblings. 'Monozygotic' (or 'identical' or 'uniovular') twins, on the other hand, result from the fertilisation of a single ovum which splits to form two independent embryos. They are invariably of the same sex and the same blood group, their finger-prints are very alike, and they are never as dissimilar in appearance as some dizygotic twins.

A pair of twins in which both exhibit the same characteristic – such as a blood group – are said to be 'concordant' in respect of it; if only one member of the pair exhibits it, they are 'discordant'. Thus 100 per cent of monozygotic twins are concordant in respect of blood group, but a much lower percentage of dizygotic twins are. If the percentage of concordances in respect of any characteristic is significantly higher among monozygotic twins than among dizygotic twins, this is usually accepted as evidence that

---

[1] Except, of course, in the exceedingly rare case of a mutation of the gene.
[2] 1939.
[3] e.g., R. L. Dugdale, 1877; H. H. Goddard, 1912.

genetic transmission[1] is operating as well as environmental influences. Thus studies of twin pairs in which at least one member is schizophrenic have found concordance percentages varying from 67 to 88 among the monozygotic pairs, and much lower percentages, from 10 to 23, among the dizygotics; and this is accepted as very strong evidence of a considerable genetic factor in the causation of that psychosis. Very similar concordance percentages are found among twins with epilepsy (q.v.) of the kind known as 'idiopathic' – that is, without detectable brain damage.

Most investigations of delinquency in twins have proceeded on similar lines, collecting pairs in which at least one twin was known to have been convicted at some time in his or her life, and finding high concordance-rates for the monozygotics and low rates for the dizygotics. An improvement on these is the study by Karl O. Christiansen,[2] based on a follow-up of all twin births recorded in the Danish birth-records from 1881 to 1910. He was thus able to avoid the criticism that concordant twin pairs are more likely to be noticed or recalled than discordant ones; and was also able to cover the complete life-span of most of his pairs, whereas other investigators were content with samples in which most members were still alive. Moreover, he was able to calculate not only the concordance-rate but also the 'twin coefficient'. For example, amongst *all* his male twins the frequency of those convicted of serious crime was about 9·6 per cent. But if a man's twin had been convicted this percentage (i.e. the concordance-rate) was as high as 52·7 per cent. The factor by which it exceeds the general frequency of 9·6 per cent (i.e. × 5·49) is the twin coefficient; and when these coefficients are compared for monozygotics and dizygotics they measure more accurately than concordance-rates the effect of being the monozygotic twin of a convicted man upon one's own chances of conviction. Christiansen's twin coefficients were as follows:

TABLE 9 Christiansen's Twins. Twin coefficients for convictions among Danish twins

Type of twin pair	Serious Offences	Minor Offences	No. of pairs
Male monozygotic	5·49	3·31	67
„ dizygotic	2·28	1·18	114
Female monozygotic	20·76	—	14
„ dizygotic	4·88	—	23

The twin coefficients for monozygotics are much higher than for dizygotics, and this seems to hold for both sexes. Like virtually all the other studies this

[1] This does not imply, as is often assumed, that the absence of differences in the concordance rate proves the genetic factor to be negligible, since even the concordance rate of dizygotic twins may be partially attributable to inheritance. But the lower that rate is, the smaller must be the genetic effect.

[2] Christiansen, 1967

D

suggests that if one is genetically similar to a convicted person one's chances of incurring a conviction are much higher than usual.

The only sample of which this does not appear to have been true was the only sample which was restricted to *juvenile* twins. The Rosanoffs[1] in California found that 93 per cent of their 42 monozygotic pairs were concordant for convictions, but so were 80 per cent of their 25 dizygotic pairs! This can be reconciled with the pattern for adults in several ways. Perhaps the juvenile's environment was so productive of delinquency that most of them gave way to it whether genetically prone or not; perhaps some were convicted for conduct that would not have brought an adult into court; or perhaps a disposition to crime which appears in, or persists into, adulthood is genetically determined to a greater extent, or more often, than the evanescent misbehaviour of childhood.

Studies of 'criminal twins' have been attacked with three sorts of criticism. One[2] points out that it is possible to be mistaken when deciding whether a pair are monozygotic or dizygotic, especially if – as was the case with the earlier studies – reliable tests such as blood grouping are not used. This criticism, however, overlooks the fact that the most likely form of mistake is the inclusion of dizygotics among the monozygotics, which would result in an artificial reduction, not an exaggeration, of the difference in concordance rates. The second type of criticism asserts that the investigators knew when they were investigating a monozygotic pair, and tended to look for, or accept, forms of criminality which they would ignore if investigating dizygotic pairs. Investigators must often be confronted with cases such as those of the Korf twins,[3] of whom one had many convictions for crimes of violence, the other was a chucker-out in a bar. Should they have been classified as concordant or discordant in respect of violence?

The third type of criticism accepts the difference in concordances, but argues that there is a non-genetic explanation. This is that the environmental influences to which monozygotic twins are subject are even more similar than those to which dizygotics are exposed. For example, since dizygotics are more easily distinguishable, their parents' treatment of them may differentiate between them more than it would do if they were monozygotic. This involves the assertion that the whole of the high concordance rate of monozygotics is attributable to environmental influence, and that the failure of dizygotics to exhibit the same high rate is due to the tendency of people, especially their parents, to treat them differently. This is not impossible, but it is not particularly plausible, especially if it has to be used to explain the even wider differences between concordances in the case of schizophrenia, or idiopathic epilepsy; and if it is not extended to such disorders, it seems necessary to explain why not.

A conclusive refutation of this last argument, however, could be provided only by a study of criminal monozygotic twins who had been reared apart from each other. A few such cases are reported in the literature, but not enough for statistical requirements; and it is unlikely that any single

[1] Rosanoff, *et al*, 1934.
[2] See, for example, S. Hurwitz, 1952.104.
[3] Kranz, 1936.124.

investigation will ever be able to collect enough pairs of this sort. J. Shields,[1] however, was able to investigate 44 pairs of monozygotics brought up in different homes for the whole or most of their childhood, and to compare them with 44 pairs of monozygotics who had not been separated in child-hood, and who had been selected so that each pair was matched in sex and age with one of the separated pairs. He was also able to compare them with 32 pairs of dizygotics, 21 reared together and 11 reared apart, although these were not matched for age and sex. Although his study was not con-cerned directly with the inheritance of delinquency,[2] it confirms that there is a marked genetic factor underlying measurable traits of personality, such as extraversion and neuroticism,[3] and of course intelligence.

Thus there is strong but not conclusive evidence based on unseparated twins for a partial determination of 'criminality' by genetic inheritance; and fairly conclusive evidence, based on separated and unseparated twins, for a similar determination of at least two personality traits. The onus of proof therefore seems to lie on those who wish to explain away the higher con-cordance rates for delinquency in monozygotics.

Finally, a rare but interesting type of constitutional abnormality must be mentioned because of its interest to criminologists. The body cells of normal males contain two sex chromosomes, of types known as X and Y, but in rare individuals there are combinations such as XXY and XYY. The presence of an extra chromosome seems to be associated with mental subnormality (for such individuals are over-represented in institutions for the subnormal). Recent studies[4] have suggested that individuals with the XYY combination suffer from some kind of pre-disposition to violence or sexual misbehaviour, and perhaps also to mental disorders; for they seem to be over-represented not only among the populations of some penal institu-tions but also of the special hospitals for dangerous mental patients.

These findings about *some* delinquents do not, of course, justify the crude assertion that a genetically determined predisposition is part of the cause of *all* delinquent behaviour. In any case, they raise the question 'What form does this predisposition take?' Even the most ardent believers in genetic factors must turn, like the sceptics, to examine psychological theories.

---

[1] *Monozygotic Twins brought up apart and together*, O.U.P. (1962).
[2] Only three of his pairs contained delinquents.
[3] These were measured by *self*-rating questionnaires, which practically eliminate any bias of the investigator. Intra-pair correlations were markedly higher for monozygotics than for dizygotics, and very similar for monozygotics reared together and apart.
[4] Which are summarised, with a bibliography, in Medical Research Council, 1967.

[4]

MENTAL

SUBNORMALITY

AND ILLNESS

Psychological explanations can be subdivided into those which regard delinquency as a symptom of mental abnormality and those which treat it as the normal result of the sort of upbringing that is typical of delinquents' families. It seems best to reserve the label 'psychological' for the latter type of theory, and to call the others 'psychological casualty' theories.[1]

PSYCHOLOGICAL CASUALTIES

Some offenders are unquestionably suffering from mental disorders which are recognised as such by psychiatrists,[2] and it is usually assumed that the disorder is an important part of the cause of their delinquent behaviour. There are a few disorders which are so disabling that they actually reduce the probability of the sufferer's committing an offence: an example is the severe defect known as anencephaly, in which the child is born with only the rudiments of a central nervous system.

Subnormal Intelligence. In any population or community there occur individuals whose intelligence and general capacity to look after themselves is sufficiently below that of the remainder to make them noticeable,[3] and a subject of concern. The great majority of these individuals are the result not

[1] The popularity of the unfortunate term 'psychopath', which originally had the wide and philologically correct meaning 'psychological casualty' but has now a narrower one, prevents me from calling them 'psychopathological theories' as I should like to do.

[2] I use 'psychiatrist' to mean a registered medical practitioner whose main occupation consists in treating or caring for the mentally ill, defective or psychopathic, irrespective of whether he has a specialist qualification for this work, or whether he is psychoanalytic in his approach. I reserve 'psychoanalyst' for those who are members of a national association of psychoanalysts, thus excluding 'Jungians', who are known as 'analytical psychologists' and 'Adlerians', who prefer to call themselves 'individual psychologists', and seem to have chosen an apt name. When referring collectively to these and other disciplinary descendants of Freud I shall use the term 'psychotherapists'. For an account of the psychotherapeutic schools, see my *Short History of Psychotherapy*.

[3] The level below which it is noticeable depends, of course, on the level of the intelligence of the majority. But even when the group is actually selected for qualities which include high intelligence, the inevitable variation leads to the same phenomenon; every University has its 'village idiots'.

of any pathological event but simply of the variation which is the effect of the polygenic transmission of intelligence from one generation to another. Characteristics, such as height, which are transmitted polygenically – that is, not through one or two but through a larger number of genes – are found to be distributed in a special way in the population. The distribution is such that the largest group of individuals is that with the mean height, the next largest are groups on either side of the mean, and so on. The result is a symmetrical distribution of the form:

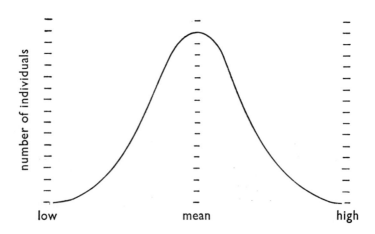

FIGURE 3 *The 'normal distribution' curve*

To the extent that intelligence can be measured by tests, it is distributed in this way, and there is other evidence that most of the variation between the intelligence of individuals is attributable to polygenic transmission. Another factor which is known to be responsible for smaller variations is the stimulation – or lack of stimulation – by parents, siblings and other people, which the child receives during his upbringing; children brought up among animals or deaf-mutes will not attain the level which they would have if reared amongst interesting conversation. On the other hand, apparent intelligence can be lowered by emotional difficulties; even highly intelligent parents may produce this effect by cruelty, frustration or merely neglecting to talk to their children, and some children's scores in intelligence tests improve after psychotherapeutic treatment. Formal education is another important factor; quite apart from its ability to impart the special skills or information which are useful for some intelligence tests – an effect which the devisors of tests try, of course, to eliminate – school can be a source of the stimulation which the child's home often fails to provide.

Just as at one extreme individuals of strikingly high natural intelligence are the products of the natural combination of the effects of a large number of genes, so most cases of noticeably low intelligence are its natural products at the other extreme. A minority of them, however, are the products of specific pathological events. Thus the form of subnormality known as 'mongolism' – from the facial appearance of the child – is probably the effect of an abnormality in the maternal chromosomes; and it occurs with slightly greater frequency in the offspring of elderly mothers. The form known as 'cretinism' is the effect of a failure of the thyroid gland to function with full efficiency, and unlike mongolism it can be remedied if thyroid extract is administered to the child from its early life. A type of subnormality which is inherited by means of a single recessive gene is phenylketonuria; but unlike most inherited types it can be corrected – if it is detected very early in life – by a special diet. Other types are microcephaly, in which the skull is noticeably small, and hydrocephaly, in which it is noticeably large. In general, it does not seem that pathological types of subnormality of themselves predispose the individual to violent or otherwise anti-social behaviour; indeed, mongols and cretins[1] are usually amiable and docile, while most other forms of defect are too disabling to make it easy for the sufferer to commit offences. The difficulty of training them to feed, clothe, relieve, and otherwise look after themselves makes most of them a burden to their families, and their abnormal appearance sometimes alarms the unaccustomed; as a result most of them are looked after in institutions. But as a source of delinquency they are negligible.

What must be discussed more thoroughly, however, is the relationship between non-pathological low intelligence and delinquency.

Intelligence. The impression that delinquents tend to be stupider than the law-abiding, which is still widespread, owes its popularity to two causes. It seems to offer an easy and satisfying explanation of criminality, and one moreover which, like Lombroso's belief in the born criminal, enables us to regard offenders as a different sort of human being. In addition, it seemed to be confirmed by the impressions gained from conversations with criminals in courts and prisons.[2] It even seemed to be confirmed by standardised intelligence tests,[3] at least until it was found that according to these tests an impossibly large percentage of presumably non-delinquent Americans drafted into the army in the First World War were also feeble-minded. As the need was recognised for more and more precautions and improvements, the apparent differences between the average intelligence of delinquents and that of the general population diminished practically to vanishing point.

For example, a person's apparent intelligence depends to some extent on his formal education and on the intellectual level of the people by whom and among whom he has been brought up. It is possible, however, to distinguish, and measure with a certain amount of accuracy, the innate ability which contributes to the intellectual level actually attained[4]. The tests by which this is done are designed so as to be as free as possible – and much more free than the early tests – of items which depend on formal education

[1] Who are in any case becoming quite rare.
[2] Even Goring, 1913, who was so meticulously scientific in his anthropometric investigation, fell into this error.
[3] For a review of the literature, see M. Woodward, 1962; and, for a short history, G. B. Vold, 1958.79.
[4] The minority of psychologists who believe that innate factors are negligible tend to be those who take the same position in the whole nature-nurture controversy.

or even on what was assumed to be 'general knowledge'.[1] This is especially desirable when delinquents are being compared with non-delinquents, since the former's education has often been interrupted by truancy or spells in institutions, and even when not interrupted may have been defective because of their lack of interest, or even because of the inferior quality of the schools in their district.

Another source of illusory difference is the association between intelligence and the parents' occupational status. The lower this is, the lower the intelligence of their children tends to be.[2] Since most offenders also have parents with low occupational status, they cannot be compared with controls which include children from professional or other middle-class families.

Large Families. Since there is also a tendency for children from large families to be of lower intelligence than those from small ones – a tendency which is independent of the relationship between intelligence and occupational status[3] – another possible source of illusory difference is the alleged tendency of delinquents to come from lar ger families. It is true, as we have seen, that this tendency is by no means conclusively proved; and in any case the association between low occupational status and large families means that controls matched in the former respect are likely to be roughly matched in the latter also. But the perfect investigation would undoubtedly be one which also matched delinquents with controls from families of similar sizes.

Age and Intelligence Tests. An intelligence test is a series of questions, problems or tasks of varying difficulty, which has been tried out on a large and representative sample of the population for which the test is intended (there are different tests for adults and children) so that the percentages of similar samples which will achieve a given score can be predicted. A score is usually converted into what is called the Intelligence Quotient (IQ), which in modern tests is a measure of the extent to which it deviates from the average for the large sample on which the test was 'standardised'. Although the IQs of normal adults do not alter markedly (merely declining slowly after the late twenties) appreciable changes can take place in children's IQs within a few years. For this and other more technical reasons[4] it is desirable that delinquents should be compared with controls of more or less the same age. And since the intelligence tests which have been most thoroughly standardised and are most constantly brought up to date are tests designed for children of school age, the best comparison is probably between delinquents and controls of school age. Moreover, a

---

[1] It is difficult to believe that English delinquents sometimes do not know the name of the current Prime Minister, until one reflects that they probably do not talk politics with their friends or families. Do *you* know the name of the English football team's captain?

[2] Vernon, 1960.142, summarises results from English, Scottish, and American surveys: 'One can generalise that children of the upper professional groups usually score 1 standard deviation above the mean, and those of the least skilled labouring groups half a standard deviation below. The latter do not fall so far below as the former rise above the mean because they constitute so much larger a proportion of the total population.'

[3] Vernon, 1960.159.

[4] See Vernon, 1960.104.

comparison based on adult offenders would in most cases be a study of those rather unusual individuals who do not grow out of delinquency or espond to penal treatment.[1]

The numbers of delinquents and controls tested should be large. More precisely, they should be so large that if differences of a few points in mean IQ between delinquents and controls are observed, the probability that this is due to nothing more than chance will be negligible. One would also expect the distribution of IQs among the controls to approximate to a normal curve, although with a mean below 100 (see Figure 3).

As more and more of these precautions were taken, successive investigations found smaller and smaller differences between the average intelligence of delinquents and non-delinquents. Although no investigation yet reported seems to be above all criticism,[2] the one which seems open to the fewest is that of Professor Maud Merrill,[3] whose results can be summarised in the following table:

TABLE 10

IQ	percentage of juvenile delinquents	percentage of non-delinquents
40–69	18·3	10·4
70–9	22·0	16·3
80–9	17·3	24·3
90–109	32·0	40·7
110–149	10·4	8·3
N=100%=	300	300
mean IQ	86·7	89·3

probability of difference ·06

The main criticisms which might be made are:
1. that girls, boys under 12 and over 18, and non-property offenders might well have been omitted, or analysed separately;
2. that an urban area would have been more typical than a rural one;
3. that under the Californian system some serious offenders – especially in the late teens – were not referred to the juvenile court;

[1] These are, of course, an important category from the practical point of view, and it is worth noting that adult property offenders – whether recidivists or not – do not seem to be less intelligent on average than men of similar occupational and educational background. See for example, Marcus, 1956.

[2] Some otherwise excellent studies are ruled out for this purpose because of their method of selecting their delinquents or controls. For example, Healy and Bronner, 1936, deliberately eliminated the duller delinquents before matching the rest with controls; while the Gluecks' 500 juvenile delinquents were deliberately matched with non-delinquents in such a way that the IQs of each pair did not differ by more than 10 points.

[3] 1947.

4. that the occupational levels of the subjects' fathers were not very closely matched. 54 per cent of delinquents' fathers but only 32 per cent of controls' fathers were in semi-skilled or unskilled jobs (but if anything this must have exaggerated the inferiority of the delinquents' IQs).

But these imperfections are less serious than they would have been if the investigation had revealed a substantial difference between the intelligence of delinquents and controls.

There are several points of interest in these figures. The mean IQ of the delinquents is well below the mean for the population as a whole (which should be 100); but so is the mean for the controls. The result is only a small gap between means, with a 1 in 17 probability that this is due to chance. A substantial 10 per cent of the delinquents have intelligences well above 110 – that is, in the top 25 per cent of the population. Indeed, at both ends of the range there are more delinquents than controls; and this wider 'scatter' is consistent with the results of other investigations.[1]

Another interesting feature of the Merrill investigation was that a retest, five years later, of what seems to have been a fairly unbiased sample of the same delinquents and controls[2] seemed to show that while the mean IQ of the delinquents was much the same (85·9 for the sample of 100) that of the controls had increased (92·1 for the sample of 100). This suggests that the tests were to some extent finding out which subjects profited by formal and informal education, and that the controls had meantime profited more, as we should expect.

The slight inferiority of the original IQs of Professor Merrill's delinquents to those of her controls can be attributed to one or more of three causes – chance, the failure to match their fathers' occupational levels more closely, or 'selective detection'; that is, the possibility that higher percentages of the stupider than of the cleverer offenders are caught. Common sense suggests that this must be so, but the only statistical evidence fails to confirm this. Eleanor Glueck found that among her 1,000 juvenile delinquents referred in 1917-22 to the Judge Baker Clinic in Boston, the 30 per cent whose IQs were under 80 did not differ significantly from the cleverer ones either in average age at first arrest, in the average time between first delinquency and first arrest, or in the number of arrests prior to the present one.[3] This does not, of course, show that selective detection of the less intelligent does not occur. At most it suggests that it did not occur in Boston

---

[1] In statistical terms, the distribution of delinquents' intelligence is found to have a larger standard deviation than that of non-delinquents, irrespective of the difference between the means. The same phenomenon appears in the comparison of boys with girls: their means are the same, but the boys have a wider standard deviation.

[2] Merrill, 1947.355. She used both the 1916 Stanford-Binet and the Terman-Merrill 1937 revision of it: both showed a wider gap, though the 1937 revision showed the wider.

[3] 1934. She has not published the actual means, although it is implied that in both groups they approximated closely to the mean age at first arrest and mean age at first delinquency (9½ years) of the whole 1,000. Unfortunately, the 1,000 were not an unbiased sample of all juveniles tried, since they consisted only of those referred to the Clinic for diagnosis and treatment. The Gluecks do not say what percentage were otherwise dealt with.

in the years immediately after the First World War. After all, the extent to which it biases a sample must depend on the percentage of offences which are being brought home to individual offenders at the time. If the percentage is very high, selective detection could not bias the sample appreciably. But if – as in England today – over half of the commonest offences, thefts, are not traced to their authors, the possibility that the uncaught thieves tend to come from the cleverer half cannot be completely ruled out.

Intelligence of Recidivists. There is evidence of another kind, however, which seems to confirm that low intelligence is not an important factor either in producing criminal behaviour or in enhancing the probability of conviction. If it were, we should expect offenders with more than one conviction to be more stupid than those with only one. But several investigations[1] have failed to show a difference of this kind, and indeed one or two found that recidivists tended to be more intelligent.[2]

So far I have been discussing the relationship between low intelligence and undifferentiated delinquency, which means in practice property offences. But if we concentrate on the more marked degrees of low intelligence, and on more specialised forms of offence, at least one association does emerge, namely that between subnormal intelligence and sexual offences. This is illustrated by a comparison between the indictable offences of all male offenders aged 17 or more dealt with by English courts in 1961 and the offences of the 305 males of similar age who were committed to hospital by criminal courts as being subnormal or severely subnormal (see Chapter 12).

TABLE 11 Mentally abnormal offenders and offences of violence or sex

	percentages of:		
offence group	all adult males	mentally ill adult males	mentally subnormal adult males
against property	77	57	54
personal violence	10	25	7
sexual[3]	5	6	32
other	8	12	7
	100	100	100
		(N=252)	(N=305)

The table shows the distribution among four broad groups of the indictable offences which in 1961 led to hospital[4] orders in the case of

[1] Merrill, 1947 (using the sample described above); Anderson, 1958 (a very good sample of 146 boys aged 13 and 14 from a London Remand Home); Marcus, 1956 (adult males in Wakefield Prison).

[2] e.g., Calhoon, 1928.

[3] Not including the non-indictable offence of indecent exposure, another offence to which the subnormal seem prone.

[4] Or in a few cases guardianship orders.

mentally ill[1] or subnormal[2] male offenders, and for comparison the distribution of all male offenders aged 17 or more who were dealt with for
indictable offences. The percentage of subnormal offenders dealt with for
sexual offences is six times as high as the percentage of all offenders.

This over-representation of sexual offences among the crimes of the subnormal is not hard to explain. Men of low intelligence are unable to compete
with their more intelligent coevals in impressing and amusing the opposite
sex, and so find it hard to achieve ordinary heterosexual relations with
women of their own age. Indeed, there is a tendency for the feeble-minded
to consort with the immature simply because they are more at home with
them, and in their search for sexual satisfaction they often use persuasion or
force on children, many of whom do not realise what is happening. Another
possibility is the use of force against an adult woman, or a resort to homosexual behaviour, often learned in boyhood. Prohibitions on certain types
of sexual behaviour have to be learned, but are harder for the subnormal to
learn than the prohibitions on stealing and violence, which their coevals
enforce in a way that they can understand.

On the other hand, there is no confirmation of the belief that subnormal
men are prone to offences of violence. If the sexual offenders are discarded
from both groups, and the percentages recalculated without including them,
the ratios become strikingly similar:

TABLE 12

type of offence	percentage of all offenders	percentage of subnormal offenders
against property	81	79
personal violence	11	10
others	8	11

What is more, the majority of offences by the subnormal, like the majority
of those committed by ordinary offenders, are property offences – pilfering
or damage – which differ only in being less skilful and on the whole more
trivial.

MENTAL ILLNESS

'Mental illness' is a generic name for a large variety of abnormalities. They
can all be described very generally as abnormalities in the sufferer's percep-
tion of his environment or his reaction to it, or in both. Unlike pathological
or non-pathological subnormality of intelligence, they do not usually
become manifest in the child's early years, so that the share of constitutional
and environmental factors in their causation is often more debatable. They

[1] Not including mixed classifications, such as those including psychopathy or those
combining mental illness and subnormality. Subnormality includes severe subnormality.
[2] Since only 8 per cent of the mentally disordered offenders who could not be eliminated were under 17, the comparison is only slightly inexact.

also tend to differ from most forms of subnormality in the way in which they may improve, either spontaneously or in response to treatment.[1] On the other hand, they can occur in individuals who are also subnormal in intelligence.

Mental illnesses can be broadly subdivided into those which are clearly associated with an identifiable cerebral abnormality, and those which are not. These groups are sometimes distinguished by the labels 'organic' and 'functional'.

Some organic illnesses are distinguishable from others in being more frequently associated with anti-social behaviour. Among these is epilepsy. It is possible for the innumerable minute transfers of electric potential which constitute the everyday activity of the brain to be suddenly over-whelmed by what has been likened to an electrical storm. This produces the unconsciousness, convulsions, and cries which are characteristic of the full epileptic fit; but the effects may be milder, so that consciousness is hardly disturbed and convulsions are confined to a few muscles. Epileptic seizures can be induced in the normal brain by special techniques, such as the rapid flashing of a light into the eyes at a critical frequency, which varies from one person to another. In the brains of 'epileptics', however, the electrical 'storms' occur without sensory stimulation. In some cases, the source of these storms seems to lie in a damaged portion of the brain; a frequent site is one of the temporal lobes, which are susceptible to permanent damage from an interruption of the blood-supply, a common accident during a difficult birth. Cerebral infection, systemic poisoning from disorders such as uraemia, and injuries to the brain, can also lead to epilepsy. In other people no clear source of the disturbance can be identified, and the epilepsy is then classified as 'idiopathic'. Studies of twins and other evidence suggest that this type is largely inherited, and it is commoner among those of sub-normal intelligence than in the rest of the population. The disposition to seizures seems to be increased by fatigue or emotional stress. It can be reduced, or even kept in abeyance, by barbiturates and other drugs; where these are unsuccessful surgical excision of an identified 'focus' sometimes abolishes or reduces the frequency of fits.

During the seizure itself the epileptic is usually incapable of co-ordinated movement, so that unless he is driving a car or holding a loaded firearm he seldom harms anyone else.[2] But the seizure may be followed by a condition known sometimes as 'automatism' or 'the twilight state' in which the epileptic may commit what appear to be purposeful attacks upon other people, acts of indecency such as urinating in public, or other unpopular behaviour. Moreover, seizures may be preceded by moods of mounting irritability or depression, in which the epileptic may commit acts of violence with little, if any, provocation. States of this kind may occur without an observable seizure, and are then called 'epileptic equivalents'.

[1] Although a few types of subnormality, notably cretinism and phenylketonuria, do respond to treatment, they do so only if it is administered while the brain is developing, that is, from an early age.

[2] Although such cases are reported – for example, the woman whose automatic sawing motion with the breadknife she was holding at the time of the fit injured her child.

Epileptics are of special interest from the criminological point of view. Even at normal times their brains reveal, under the electroencephalograph,[1] a characteristic type of rhythmical electric activity known as the 'spike and wave'. Similar rhythms can sometimes be observed in the brains of other members of their family, either in their normal resting state or under some physiological stress, although those members may never show any of the other symptoms of epilepsy. Men who have committed assaults are sometimes found to have electroencephalograms with this abnormality, or epileptic relatives, or both; and if so are strongly suspected of having committed their crimes in an 'epileptiform' state, although they have never been known to have an overt seizure.

Examples of other organic abnormalities of the brain which are sometimes discovered in offenders are tumours or advanced syphilitic infection. Encephalitis lethargica in children quite often results in permanent damage to the brain of a kind which seems to deprive them of self-control or regard for others, so that they commit thefts, assaults, acts of cruelty, or sexual misdemeanours. Little can be done except place them in special hospitals, which still contain some of the victims of the epidemics of this disease that followed the First World War.

Acts of aggression are sometimes committed by people who are in temporary states of cerebral abnormality as a result of some kind of poisoning. The commonest example is drunkenness, but there are more inadvertent types, such as oxygen deficiency[2] or hypoglycaemia, a condition which can occur in careless or badly doctored diabetics.

Brain Injuries. On the other hand, brain injuries are probably blamed for criminal behaviour more often than the facts justify, and more often by defence counsel than by psychiatrists or neurologists. Cases are described in which wounds in the head, concussion, or the multitude of tiny injuries in the brain of the punch-drunk boxer, are probably responsible for anti-social behaviour. But where there are no symptoms of damage other than the offence itself, neurologists are sceptical.

Some disorders are attributed to degenerative changes which are common in old age and may begin in middle age. Hypertension and arteriosclerosis may affect the cerebral blood vessels, or the cells of the brain itself may atrophy or degenerate. Certain disorders of this kind – for example Huntington's chorea and Pick's disease – are genetically transmitted by single genes, although unlike most characteristics inherited in this way they do not usually manifest themselves until early middle age or even later.

[1] The electroencephalograph records electrical activity at or near the surface of the brain at points which can be selected. Recordings, called 'electroencephalograms' or 'EEGs', are usually made when the subject is supine and at rest, although sometimes he is stimulated, for example by provocative remarks, to see whether irritation produces any abnormality in the EEG. The EEGs of children, epileptics and people with certain types of brain damage show specific patterns which are not observable in the great majority of normal adults. But some adults with no detectable abnormality of conduct have EEGs with these abnormalities, and the age at which childish rhythms disappear varies greatly from one individual to another.

[2] High-altitude climbers sometimes experience intense irritability, although they do not seem to commit assaults on each other.

Huntington's chorea
Schizophrenie: its main types
MENTAL SUBNORMALITY AND ILLNESS   63

Sometimes the clinical symptoms of the disease are preceded by a phase in which the sufferer begins to behave in grossly anti-social ways for the first time in his life, with the result that he is mistakenly held responsible for his conduct until the clinical symptoms appear.

Psychoses. Of special importance, however, are the disorders which are sometimes called the 'functional psychoses'. These are the disturbances of thought for which no unmistakable physiological cause has yet been demonstrated, and which are still regarded by a minority of psychiatrists as the result of a highly abnormal upbringing.

Schizophrenia. One of the most frequent diagnoses in mental hospitals is 'schizophrenia', although the symptoms and course of this disorder vary so widely that several sub-species are recognised, and it is quite possible that, like 'psychopathy' (q.v.), this category will eventually be broken up into two, three, or more quite distinct disorders. Thus Mayer-Gross *et alii*[1] distinguish four types of schizophrenia. Commonest among young adults is hebephrenic schizophrenia, which seems to consist of a disorder of thought. This is insidious in its onset, so that it may at first be dismissed as neurosis. A promising student may find it harder and harder to concentrate and think logically; he drifts off into vague metaphysical interests. Or he may degenerate into a ceaseless joker: mild hebephrenics have become successful clowns or stage humorists through their ability to exploit their spontaneous silliness. Occasionally, in the early stages of the disorder, there is a sudden flare-up of sexual impulses, or of rage or terror, which may lead to anti-social behaviour. The progress of the disorder sometimes halts spontaneously, more often under treatment. If it is not halted, symptoms such as hallucinations and withdrawal from reality manifest themselves.

In contrast is the catatonic, whose chief symptom is stupor and a resistant, negative attitude to attempts to induce purposive activity. Advanced catatonics will assume bizarre poses and maintain them for long periods. They may occasionally commit impulsive and brutal attacks, for example on doctors or nurses, but since the disorder is so easily recognised and leads so surely to hospital the public is usually protected from them.

Paranoia is the most frequent form among the middle-aged or elderly, and especially among elderly women. The distinguishing symptom is a delusion of persecution which may drive the sufferer to flee into various parts of the country, and eventually to retaliate against his fancied persecutors, as M'Naghten (q.v.) did when he fled to London and then shot the man whom he mistook for the Prime Minister. Often the delusions take a sexual form. A husband or wife will suspect the other spouse of infidelities of the most improbable kind or frequency, and will eventually commit an assault upon the spouse; or an elderly woman may imagine that indecent suggestions are being made to her, often by mysterious means. 'Poison pen' letters are sometimes the work of paranoiacs.

Fourthly, Mayer-Gross distinguishes the 'simple' schizophrenia, without catatonia, hallucinations or delusions, but consisting apparently of a rapidly developing shallowness of emotion, irresponsibility and lack of will-power. He cites the 'solitary solicitor who fell out with all his former

[1] 1960.

Depression & shop-lifting

friends because of his seclusiveness and aggressiveness. For a long time he spent his nights in a brothel with a low prostitute, giving away large sums and munificent presents. He procured the money by fraudulent receipts which he presented to the authorities. At the same time he continued his law practice with relative success. . . .' Women schizophrenics may become prostitutes. More spectacular, of course, is the solitary, quiet schizophrenic who suddenly commits a crime of violence, often involving sexually motivated mutilations, and not infrequently against his wife, mother, father or other relative with whom he is living at the time.

Depression. Another type of psychosis which seems to be associated with offences is depression. This can be a temporary result of the administration of some therapeutic drugs – such as the sulphonamides – or of an illness such as influenza. It may be 'reactive': that is, the response to an occurrence such as a bereavement or a failure in one's career, although we can usually distinguish between grief or disappointment which is normal and that which is excessive in duration and intensity – there is a point at which 'mourning becomes melancholia'. Thirdly, there is the endogenous depression, which seems, as its name implies, to develop from within, unprovoked by any but the slightest changes in the external environment. Some psychiatrists would say that an apparently reactive depression which is more severe or protracted than seems appropriate to the outward occasion for it is really an endogenous depression which has simply been 'triggered off'. The depression may be periodic, improving and relapsing independently of treatment or changes in the patient's environment. The state seems to be most acute in the early part of the day.[1] Women seem to be somewhat more prone than men to endogenous depression, and the older the patient the longer the state seems to last.

Suicidal behaviour is, of course, a frequent accompaniment of depression, and a depressed mother or father, in a state of unrealistic despair over the future of their families, will often kill spouse and children as well as himself. A depressed lover may persuade his beloved into a suicide pact. Some investigators have also found an association between shoplifting and depression among women.[2] The condition is usually treated by drugs or in severe cases by electro-convulsion.

Mania. The contrasting condition of abnormal elation, known as 'mania', is sometimes associated with violence and occasionally other forms of anti-social behaviour. It is less often encountered, perhaps because its milder forms (the 'hypomanic state') are less easily recognised as pathological than are the milder depressions. Stallworthy[3] writes:

What in one person could be his normal state could in another be a definite hypomania. The friends . . . of the man in hypomania will say that his talkativeness and exuberance are quite out of keeping with what for him is normal: sometimes the patient will admit the same. His exuberance and chatter soon make him a nuisance to those about

[1] T. C. N. Gibbens actually says that most depressive murders occur between 6 am and 8 am, presumably Greenwich Mean Time.
[2] e.g., Woddis, 1957.
[3] 1963.90.

him. He is too excited and elated to go to bed at a normal hour. . . .
He wakes up his neighbours at 3 a.m. to tell them a wonderful scheme
for altering their garden; he puts through a person-to-person call to
the Prime Minister to tell him how to run the country. . . . One very
capable solicitor . . . drew all his trust funds to found a grandiose
scheme in France without thought of his responsibility to his clients.
. . . The hypomanic man with a full bladder may, wherever he is, see
no reason for not emptying it. If he sees a comely girl, he may feel it
is an honour for her to see his virility. . . .
If he is thwarted or disagreed with he may be consumed by brief
anger, in which . . . he may be viciously abusive or physically violent.
In acute mania the patient is so noisy, destructive, often obscene . . .
that his insanity is obvious to the most unskilled eye.

Manic 'episodes' may begin with slight depressions, or may alternate with
more acute depressions, in which case they are known as 'manic-depressive'
conditions. They often disappear and reappear spontaneously. Treatment
usually consists of sedation or electro-convulsion.

Psychosis and Violence. Like the crimes of the ordinary offender or the
subnormal, those of the mentally ill are usually 'property offences', as
Table 11 confirms. But whereas sexual offences were over-represented
among the subnormal, it is personal violence that is obviously the special
risk in the case of the psychoses, and especially the schizophrenias, depression or mania.

Neuroses. All or most of the mental illnesses I have been describing would
be classified by most psychiatrists as psychoses, although some would be
doubtful whether depression should be. Those which I am about to discuss
are usually classified as neuroses. Their symptoms never include hallucinations or delusions; their onset is less sudden and definite than that of the
usual psychosis; they are usually attributed to faulty upbringing rather than
to some physiological cause, although it is usually recognised[1] that inborn
susceptibility to neurosis-inducing influences varies from one individual to
another. They usually respond better to psychotherapeutic methods of
treatment than to drugs, although of course tranquillisers are often prescribed by baffled general practitioners in order to relieve the symptoms.

Anxiety. The most frequent type of neurosis is the anxiety state, in which
the apprehension and worry which are normal human reactions to certain
situations become chronic and severe. In some individuals the anxiety is
chiefly focused on their health, and the slightest *malaise* is taken for signs
of cancer or heart disease. In others it centres on their work, their relations
with their acquaintances, or their children's health or conduct. In the most
severe cases the sufferer has to be admitted to hospital. It is only rarely, however, that this kind of disorder leads to a criminal offence; usually the
sufferer is his own victim.

Compulsive Behaviour. People whose behaviour is otherwise more or less
normal may suffer from recurrent impulses or longings to perform irrational
acts; and although this is sometimes associated with a diagnosable psychosis
it is often the only detectable abnormality. Sometimes the compulsion is

---

[1] Even by Freud himself.

E

trivial and harmless, such as the desire to touch walls as one walks beside them, or to make sure again and again that all the doors and windows are locked. Sometimes it takes an anti-social form – for instance, compulsive stealing of more or less useless objects by people who could easily afford to pay for them.[1] Often deviant sexual desires become compulsive, and force the sufferer to expose himself, or make physical advances to small boys. The sufferer seems to be able to resist the compulsive desire at first, but gradually to be worn down until he performs the action; thereupon he feels a feeling of almost physical relief, but often with remorse, self-disgust or fear of the consequences if the act was anti-social.

Hysteria. 'Hysteria',[2] like 'schizophrenia' and 'psychopathy', is a diagnostic category which tends to be overloaded by psychiatrists with cases which are difficult to classify in any other way, and it is very difficult to offer a definition which would not be regarded as inadequate by a substantial minority. With this reservation, it can perhaps be described as a condition in which the person has lost control over some sector of his behaviour. He may, for example, have a hysterical paralysis of an arm, loss of sight or voice. Or his whole body may perform a complex series of actions which in his normal state he would refuse even to think about; the usual example is the soldier whose nerve breaks in battle so that he runs away in an hysterical fugue. Sometimes the person alternates between his normal state and what is called a dissociated state in which his personality seems to be different and he behaves disreputably. When he returns to the normal state he may have little or no recollection of what he did.[3] A third type of case is that of the demagogue, preacher, or confidence man who works himself up so that he believes the fictions he is uttering; sometimes he has other hysterical symptoms as well. If the patient is willing to be treated, most hysterical conditions seem to respond to psychoanalysis or other forms of psychotherapeutic treatment, with or without the assistance of drugs such as sodium pentothal.

Diagnostic Difficulties. The disorders which have been briefly described so far are those which are not only associated to an appreciable extent with anti-social behaviour but are also diagnosed with a certain degree of confidence by virtually all psychiatrists. For several reasons, diagnosis is more difficult in psychiatry than in other branches of medicine. Symptoms fluctuate more in their severity, and may even disappear completely for a time; this is said to be especially likely after some act which satisfies a compulsive urge or after an outburst of psychotic violence. Even mildly subnormal patients may appear more intelligent when they are in situations with which they are familiar. If the patient is subnormal or psychotic, it is not easy to obtain useful information from him about his history, his background or the introspectible aspect of his symptoms. Thirdly, just as more than one physical disorder – for instance,

[1] This used to be called 'kleptomania'.
[2] Which must not be confused with the popular use of the word to refer to spectacular outbursts of crying, laughing, terror, and the like.
[3] Apart from fictional examples, such as Dr Jekyll and Mr Hyde, there are the notorious cases of Sally Beauchamp, described by Morton Prince, and of 'Eve' (Thigpen, 1959).

tuberculosis and peptic ulcer – can be present in the same individual, so the same patient may be suffering both from a psychosis and from subnormality of intelligence; and either subnormality or a psychosis may very well be associated with a neurosis. (Indeed, in some cases the neurosis is said to be attributable to the abnormal difficulties which subnormality or incipient psychosis impose on the sufferer.) Finally, the borderline between disorder and normality is even more indefinite than in the case of physical ailments. Apart from disorders with a demonstrable genetic or physiological origin – such as Huntington's chorea or epilepsy – almost all mental abnormalities have their 'sub-clinical' fringe of cases in which the symptoms are too mild to justify a definite clinical label. This is most obvious where the principal symptom – depression, anxiety, elation – is merely an exaggeration of normal emotional states. But even in the case of schizophrenia many psychiatrists recognise what is called 'the schizoid personality' – withdrawn, unemotional, day-dreaming – as a sub-clinical form. Nevertheless, in spite of all these diagnostic problems, there is now a considerable amount of agreement among British psychiatrists in applying the diagnostic labels which have been discussed. There are two other labels, however, which give rise to even more difficulties, and which are used with much less unanimity. These are the concepts of 'maladjustment' and 'psychopathy', which will be discussed in the following chapter.

[5]

MALADJUSTMENT,

THE NORMAL OFFENDER,

AND PSYCHOPATHY

We must now examine claims that, in addition to anti-social behaviour which results from mental illness, a substantial amount of delinquency should be attributed to faulty development of personality which is the effect of mistakes of upbringing. A complication which sometimes leads to misunderstanding is that holders of such theories often believe also that disorders such as schizophrenia are wholly or largely the result of faulty upbringing, particularly in very early infancy. Such views apart, however, theories of the kind which will now be discussed can be referred to as 'theories of maladjustment', since they all make use of this concept, though sometimes under different names.

MALADJUSTMENT

Most such theories are psychoanalytic in origin, although their parentage is not always acknowledged. When held by psychoanalysts, they tend to be held in the 'strong' form, that is, they are assumed to explain not merely some types of delinquency, or some delinquents of each type, but most, if not all, types and individuals. It is true that psychoanalytic explanations are more frequently offered and accepted for types of offence which are themselves regarded as abnormal, such as sexual offences or cruelty to children; but it is clear that their leading exponents believe them to be essential to the understanding of such everyday crimes as burglary and theft.[1] It is also true that the majority of cases used as evidence or illustrations of the psychoanalytic explanation of ordinary delinquency are children; but most psychoanalysts would say that this is so simply because the pathological nature of delinquency is more obvious, and its causes more easily ascertained, in the case of the young, who are in any case more likely than adult criminals to be referred for psychological investigation.

Psychoanalytic explanations of everyday kinds of delinquency take two main forms. They may seek to explain the actual nature of the delinquent acts; or they may try to account for the development of a delinquent type

[1] See, for example, K. Friedlander, 1947, chapter IV, and E. Glover, 1960.23 & 175, and M. Schmideburg, 1956.

of personality. Thus, for example, repeated thefts by a child may be explained either as attempts to satisfy a need for affection from the owners
of the stolen objects, or simply as manifestations of a personality with a
conscience that is not sufficiently developed to restrain him from satisfying
his desires in anti-social ways. Explanations of the second type, which
modern psychoanalysts seem to prefer to the first (and older) type, often
accept the delinquent acts themselves as not requiring any specifically
psychoanalytic explanation. Examples of what may be called 'behaviour-
specific' explanations are therefore commoner in the earlier literature, but
are sometimes still observable. They may take the following forms:

1. The delinquent behaviour is attributed to a traumatic incident, of
   which the memory, or the emotions appropriate to the memory,
   have been repressed. Thus the behaviour of a 16-year-old boy who
   persistently ran away from home and jobs was traced by Aichorn[1]
   to the repression of grief and horror at the sudden death of his
   mother who had been shockingly mutilated in a factory machine.
   'Traumatic' explanations of this sort, however, belong to the earlier
   phase of psychoanalysis, and would nowadays be regarded as over-
   simplified. Modern psychoanalysts would argue that unless the
   traumatic incident coincided with some powerful emotion in the
   child himself, of a kind of which he felt deeply ashamed, it would
   make little impression on him; on this view, Aichorn's boy must
   have felt that his mother's death fulfilled some half-acknowledged
   wish of his own, so that he was trying to escape from himself.
2. The offence is explained as a symbolic expression of some desire which
   the offender is debarred from expressing more directly, either
   because he dare not or because he is simply too inarticulate. The
   commonest example is the explanation of children's thefts from their
   mothers – especially thefts from the larder – as prompted by the need
   for more affection.
3. The delinquent behaviour can be regarded as a displaced form of
   otherwise natural activity. Thus Friedlander explains the mutinous
   behaviour of a schoolboy towards his teachers as displaced hostility
   to his father, whose place he wanted to take in his mother's
   affections.[2]
4. Repeated offences by individuals are sometimes attributed to an
   unconscious desire for punishment, arising from unconscious guilt
   over feelings (or other acts) which the offender regards as sinful –
   such as masturbation. Glover[3] attaches such importance to this type
   of explanation that he writes '. . . the factors of unconscious guilt, or,
   as it is more accurately expressed, of the unconscious need for
   punishment, is consistently neglected in non-analytical researches. Yet
   here surely is the key to all problems of delinquency. . . .' Glover
   gives no examples, but Friedlander[4] cites the case of a girl who felt
   so guilty about her *undetected* shoplifting that she later committed it
   in circumstances in which detection was inevitable.

Behaviour-specific explanations are most generally based on case histories

---

[1] 1936.43-.   [2] 1947.136.   [3] 1960.302.   [4] 1947.123 & 149.

constructed as a result of psychotherapeutic treatment, which do not lend themselves to rigorous statistical presentation. The fact that successful treatment is often based on the assumptions that such explanations are true is strong but not conclusive evidence in their favour, since

1. such treatment takes a considerable time, during which the symptomatic behaviour might have disappeared either spontaneously or simply because the patient had learned by experience that detection and scandal were highly probable consequences of it;

2. even if it can be shown that it is the treatment which abolishes the behaviour, it is very difficult to show that the feature of treatment which is effective is the verbalised explanation. More and more emphasis is being laid by psychoanalysts on the 'transference'[1] as the most effective feature of a successful analysis.

Nevertheless, many of the case-histories carry a certain amount of conviction, and raise the question: 'What percentage of everyday delinquencies, such as thefts, might be found to lend themselves to this type of explanation if it were possible to apply the psychotherapeutic method to all of them?' I shall return to this question in the next section.

The behaviour-specific type of psychoanalytic explanation, however, is most convincing when applied to behaviour which is itself sufficiently abnormal to suggest that its motivation must be abnormal – for example, when it is used to explain pointless thefts of articles for which the thief has no use. When faced with delinquencies that do not seem to compel us to assume abnormal motives – such as thefts of useful goods or money, or assaults in the pursuit of a quarrel or revenge – psychoanalysts more often employ a logically different type of explanation. This attributes abnormality not to the desire or impulse which prompted the act, but to the personality which did not resist its prompting in the way in which a normal personality would have. Explanations of this type might be called 'personality-specific'. Broadly speaking, they suggest that delinquents suffer from one of the following defects:

1. *Weakness of 'ego'*. In psychoanalytic theory the 'ego' is the part of the mental organisation that controls the ways in which the person seeks to meet the demands of his 'id' or what are sometimes called his 'instinctual drives'. When his hunger, his sexual urges and his aggression dictate his actions without control, as they do in early infancy, he finds the reaction of the environment so unpleasant that he gradually learns to modify his ways of gratifying his instincts; the 'pleasure principle' is tempered by the 'reality principle'. The ability to control desires and impulses, or to exercise foresight and restraint in gratifying them, is called the 'ego'. If at the age when this should be developing the child is treated too indulgently, he fails to develop a normal degree of self-control; and there may be such a thing as a congenital inability to acquire as much self-control as the normal person. Such persons are said to have a 'weak ego'.

[1] That is, the emotional relationship, partly dependent, partly antagonistic, which develops between patient and analyst in the course of successful treatment, and which should itself be eventually reduced to negligible proportions by the end of the analysis.

2 *Weak super-ego.* On the other hand, a child may develop an adequate
   amount of self-control and foresight, but fail to develop normally in
   another way. Some behaviour, whether or not it leads of itself to
   physically unpleasant consequences, is strongly disapproved by
   parents. If their disapproval is impressed on the child at the crucial
   age with sufficient strength and frequency, he does not merely refrain
   from the behaviour, as an older person would, for fear of this disapproval; he comes to disapprove of it himself, and this self-
   condemnation becomes so automatic that he forgets the origin of it,
   and feels what is known as guilt. He has developed the function of
   self-criticism according to an ingrained code of behaviour, which in
   psychoanalytic terminology is the super-ego. In some people this
   function is developed to such a degree that they feel excessive guilt
   over minor transgressions such as failure to pay a bus-fare. Others,
   with what psychoanalysts call a weak super-ego, feel little or no guilt
   over quite serious delinquencies. An under-developed super-ego may
   be the result of lack of parental training at the crucial age or even
   perhaps a congenital difficulty in developing this function.

In crude terms, a person with a weak ego is likely to commit impulsive
delinquencies, without much foresight of the consequences, but unless he
also suffers from a weak super-ego he will afterwards feel remorse. If, on the
other hand, his only defect lies in his super-ego, his delinquencies will be
more circumspect, but he will feel little guilt. Needless to say, however, the
sort of upbringing that results in one is likely to result in the other, so that
many delinquents are diagnosed by psychoanalysts as suffering from both.

3. *The affectionless character.* A child who does not have close physical
    contact during his first few years of life with a person who treats him
    affectionately and can serve as a constantly present object of affection
    does not develop the ability to feel affection for other people in later
    life. Psychoanalysts such as Bowlby believe that the 'affectionless
    character' is the result of temporary or permanent maternal
    deprivation during the early stage of life in which the child is almost
    wholly dependent on this parent, and that this type of personality is
    often associated with stealing.

Psychological theories of this sort can be tested in two ways. One is to
compare the characters of delinquents and non-delinquents, using personality tests in order to eliminate as much subjective bias as possible. The
other is to deduce from the theories testable inferences about the differences
which ought to be observable between the families of delinquents and those
of non-delinquents.

Personality Tests. The variety of personality tests is considerable. Leaving
aside those which do not yield consistent results even when re-applied to
the same sample, there are those which do and those which do not[1] show
significant differences between delinquents and non-delinquents. Those
which do distinguish them, however, lend some support to theories which
use concepts such as ego development and super-ego development. Tests

----

[1] The latter are not necessarily invalid or unreliable, but simply irrelevant for the
present purpose,

which seem to measure impulsiveness and impatience – which seem to be instances of weak self-control – delinquents score higher: in the Porteus maze test, for example, they cut corners and cross lines more often.[1] Tests of cheating or of ability to choose the morally right action in an imaginary situation, which can be regarded as to some extent measures of the strength of the super-ego, show the expected differences between delinquents and non-delinquents. Tests which measure 'affectionateness' do not seem to be reported in the literature.[2]

The second way of testing a psychological theory is to infer that if it is true then the families of delinquents and non-delinquents will differ in some respect that can be confirmed, preferably in terms of hard data. Inferences of this kind are:

1. that delinquency is associated with broken homes (since this would presumably interfere with the formation of either ego or super-ego);
2. that delinquency would be associated with deprivation of parental care (for the same reason);
3. that a higher percentage of only children (or first children or last children!) would be delinquents (because they are more likely to be treated too indulgently by their mothers).

Broken Homes. The often repeated assertion that most criminals come from broken homes needs very close examination. It is true that among the Gluecks'[3] delinquents 60 per cent came from homes which had been 'broken by separation, divorce, death or prolonged absence of a parent'; but so did 34 per cent of their non-delinquents. It is even possible that the absence of a parent may have been a factor which influenced the decision to send many of these boys to correctional schools, in which case part of the difference between 34 per cent and 60 per cent would have to be disregarded. The best British evidence is that of Carr-Saunders *et alii*,[4] not only because their samples of delinquents were not biased by being taken from penal institutions but also because their analysis of the family structure is the most precise.[5] Out of 1,953 delinquent boys and 1,970 non-delinquent controls, 28 per cent of the former and 16 per cent of the latter came from families in which one or both of the natural parents were missing for one reason or another. These percentages are not impressively high, and the gap between them was chiefly accounted for by cases in which parents had separated, the mother remaining in charge (as she almost always did), or cases in which a natural parent was cohabiting with someone who was not a natural parent of the boy, or where his mother was simply dead.[6]

---

[1] Porteus, 1952; Gibbens, 1955.

[2] M. Argyle, in his very thorough review of the literature (1961), was not able to find anything better than tests of cruelty and aggressiveness, or of social perceptiveness – that is, the ability to tell when one is incurring the approval or disapproval of others.

[3] 1950.122.

[4] 1942.

[5] Among his Glasgow boys Ferguson found the delinquency rate only slightly above average where the home had been 'broken by causes other than death'. Unfortunately, he does not subdivide this category, either by causes or by the sex of the missing parent.

[6] Since the figures given in the detailed analysis cover only cases in which precise information could be obtained, they cannot be given as percentages of the total samples.

Parental Care. Most frequently emphasized of all associations is that which is believed to exist between delinquency and the quality of parental care. Not only is this emphasis satisfying to those who take their responsibility for their own children seriously, but it also provides a useful connecting link to explain associations which would otherwise be puzzling. Thus investigators who find an association between large families and delinquency usually explain this by arguing that in large families each child receives less parental affection – or discipline, depending on one's other assumptions – than in smaller families. The quality, however, of parents' attitudes to their children is easily misjudged, especially by an investigator who knows whether they are parents of delinquents. This is the softest of soft data, and there are both motives and opportunities for distortion.

For example, since psychoanalytic theory stressed the importance of babies' physical relationships to their mothers for normal psychological development, investigators such as Bowlby reasoned that where this relationship was most severely disturbed, as it presumably is when the infant is separated from his mother, this should produce marked disturbances in him. When they studied infants who for one reason or another had been placed in institutions they found that they appeared 'emotionally withdrawn and isolated', developing no close ties with adults or other children. Bowlby[1] suggested that '. . . there is a specific connection between prolonged deprivation in the early years and the development of an affectionless psychopathic character given to persistent delinquent conduct and extremely difficult to treat'. So far as delinquency was concerned, however, his own investigations were limited to 44 juvenile thieves who had been referred to the London Child Guidance Clinic because they had already shown signs of psychological abnormality. Moreover, later investigations – including one by Bowlby himself – led to the conclusion that quite apart from delinquency the character defect described by him did not always occur after such physical separation and sometimes occurred without it. This has led psychoanalysts to preserve the hypothesis by amending the definition of maternal deprivation so as to include cases in which the mother, though never absent, was inattentive or otherwise abnormal, and so as to exclude cases in which the child, though separated from its natural mother, was cared for by an adequate substitute.

It is therefore even more imperative than usual to disregard all but the most rigorously scientific investigations. Though none are tree from defects, the least open to criticism appears to be that of R. G. Andry.[2] His delinquent sample of 80 London boys aged 12-15 with more than one recorded conviction for theft excluded other types of offender, boys with very low or high IQs, or with diagnoses of neurosis or psychosis, boys from the middle and upper classes, and boys from broken homes. The non-delinquent controls were carefully selected from schools in a London working-class area with a high delinquency rate, and were 'group-matched' with the delinquents for age, social class and intelligence. All 160 boys were interviewed, and in 38 per cent of each sample the parents were interviewed as well, in order to see how far the boys' impressions of their relationship to their parents tallied

[1] 1951.34.   [2] 1960.

with the latter's. Andry found no evidence for an association between stealing and physical separation in childhood from either parent.[1]

What he did claim to find was that, in comparison with non-delinquents

1. delinquents experience less open and strong love from their parents (especially from their fathers);
2. delinquents experience less adequate communication (both environmental and psychological) with their parents (especially with their fathers);
3. delinquents experience a more tense home atmosphere (to which their fathers contribute a substantial share);
4. delinquents experience less adequate parental training (especially from their fathers);
5. the deviant behaviour of delinquents was less known to and less adequately dealt with by their parents.

These findings were confirmed where the parents themselves were interviewed. The results emphasise the importance of the relationship between boys and their fathers, and suggest that the maternal role in the development of delinquency can be exaggerated.

Sibling Relations. As for the deduction that only children, first children or last children would be more prone to delinquency because they receive more indulgent treatment and so fail to develop normal egos or super-egos, the Gluecks[2] found that among their carefully matched delinquents and controls it was the *non-delinquents* who had higher percentages of only children, first children and last children.[3]

Family Size. Practically all investigators report that delinquents tend to have larger families than controls. Ferguson[1] also observed this association in his sample of Glasgow boys:

TABLE 13 Delinquency and family size

number of children in family	number of boys at risk	percentage convicted between 8 and 18 years of age
1–2	241	7·8
3–4	432	8·1
5–7	437	13·9
8 or more	239	20·0

But he investigated this observation more thoroughly by subdividing large

[1] As he points out (1960.112), his results do not disprove this hypothesis completely They do suggest, however, that whatever harm 'maternal deprivation' does cause in psychological development, it probably takes some form other than teenage stealing. The exclusion of broken homes from the samples was no defect from this point of view, but a virtue, since on the 'maternal deprivation' hypothesis this should be associated with delinquency in the child even where marital relations are good.

[2] 1950.120.

[3] Could this have been because parental indulgence went to the length of saving them from the arm of the law?

and small families into the severely overcrowded and the others, and finding the percentages of delinquents in each group[1]:

TABLE 14 Delinquency and overcrowding

number of persons to a room	number of children in a amily	
	1–4	5 or more
1–2	7·0	6·3
4 or more	11·2	12·2

The result suggests that it is overcrowding and not mere size of family which is associated with higher delinquency rates, and this would explain the varying strengths of the apparent associations between size of family and delinquency rates which are reported by other investigators. This is not to say that overcrowding is proved to be a 'cause' of delinquency (although it could lead to it by driving children out on to the streets). It may merely be a symptom which has a closer connection with the complex conditions producing delinquency than has the number of children in the family.

THE PSYCHOLOGICALLY NORMAL OI FENDER

The psychological theories which I have been discussing have at least one feature in common – the assumption that unless the individual suffers from some abnormality of constitution or upbringing he will abide by the rules of conduct of his community. In other words, they take it for granted that man is naturally law-abiding, and that the exceptions are casualties of one kind or another. An alternative type of explanation is based on the view that man is not naturally law-abiding, but learns to be so, and that delinquents are the exceptions who fail to learn.

The Theory of Ethical Learning. 'Learning', in the sense in which it is used by psychologists, includes not only intellectual learning – by which, for example, we 'learn' geography – but other kinds as well. One of the earliest forms is the learning of motor skills – how to use the muscles of our arms, legs and other organs to achieve our ends. This we seem to do by a process of trial and error that begins in the first few days of life; some trial movements are successful, and bring some kind of satisfaction, others bring nothing, or even pain – for example, the pain of a tumble. Movements that are followed by satisfaction seem to be repeated more often than the other kinds, and are said to be 'reinforced'. A more intellectual form of learning is the experience by which we 'learn' that certain complex patterns of behaviour have consequences that we prefer to avoid; as, for example, we learn not to buy second-hand radios. These forms of learning might be conveniently distinguished by being labelled 'intellectual', 'motor', and 'prudential'.[2]

[1] 1952.21.

[2] There are other types with which we need not be concerned, such as 'perceptual' learning.

Prudential learning is undoubtedly an important factor in rendering some individuals law-abiding. The fact that a large percentage of people do not seem to repeat their offences after their first experience of detection and punishment is strong evidence for this.[1] Not everyone, however, requires first-hand experience of the consequences of detection in order to learn in this way. A combination of intellectual and prudential learning enables many people to observe the consequences of detection in the case of others, and apply these in imagination to themselves. Nor are penal consequences the only ones which are feared: the disapproval of relatives, neighbours, friends, or colleagues at work, which is sometimes lumped together under the word 'stigma', is another potent deterrent.

A more or less intellectual process of this sort, however, will hardly account for the fact that many people refrain from behaviour even when it is exceedingly unlikely that it would have any undesirable consequences for them (and equally unlikely that they mistakenly foresee such consequences). For example, a large number of Europeans have so strong an aversion from personal violence that they could not bring themselves to take part in homicide or flogging even when this is legalised and socially approved in the form of capital or corporal punishment; and this is even true of some people who are themselves in favour of such penalties. A large percentage of men and women have somewhat similar reactions – though perhaps not of the same strength – against stealing, lying, and some forms of sexual behaviour. Most of these reactions can be called 'ethical', since we tend to express them by describing the behaviour that produces them as 'wrong' or 'immoral' or 'unethical'.

Yet the very people who express ethical reactions, when they are old enough to do so, appear to have no such reactions during early infancy; whether we are destined to become moral and law-abiding or amoral and criminal, we all pass through a stage when we appear to be completely lacking in ethical feelings. As soon as the infant has enough strength and motor skill to appropriate his sister's toys, strike her with accuracy, or experiment with her in sexual play, he does so. His later aversion from theft, personal violence and sexual licence seems to be acquired and not innate. The process by which it is acquired can be called 'ethical learning'.[2]

Ethical learning seems to take place at an earlier age than prudential learning. Trasler[3] suggests that the strength of the ethical reactions which a child acquires depends upon the strength of the anxiety aroused in him when he misbehaves or contemplates misbehaviour.[4] Anxiety of this sort

---

[1] See Chapter 12 on the reformative efficacy of penal measures.

[2] C. H. Waddington has pointed out that man's facility for ethical learning, which enables learned behaviour to be transmitted from one generation to another in a way that could not be achieved by the mechanism of genetics, justifies us in calling man 'the ethical animal', since even other primates exhibit it to a much smaller extent (1961).

[3] 1962.III-V. This is the best exposition of the contribution of learning theory to the understanding of delinquency. Although it will be obvious that this section is based to a considerable extent on his book, my terminology and reasoning differ occasionally from his.

[4] Trasler also recognises the effect of 'reinforcing' good behaviour by rewards, tangible and intangible – such as expressions of approval. But he regards the essential element in what he calls 'social conditioning' as being 'avoidance conditioning'.

can be aroused by punishment, such as a smacking or deprivation of toys or food, but seems to be more effective if aroused by the withdrawal of parental approval while the child is of an age to be emotionally dependent upon this approval.[1] It will be even more effective if the parents are able to explain to the child in general terms what sorts of actions they object to. This enlists the aid of intellectual learning in enabling the child to recognise more quickly the possibilities of incurring parental disapproval.

On this hypothesis, people whose ethical reactions are weak should occur as a result of five possible situations:

1. If parents sometimes discipline the child, sometimes do not, for the same sort of misbehaviour, or if one parent does and the other does not; for experiments in producing avoidance reactions by conditioning show that this is less effective if the electric shock, or whatever unpleasant stimulus is used, frequently fails to occur.

Certainly several investigators report that inconsistent discipline is more frequent in the families from which delinquents come than in other families.[2]

2. If children are in some way deprived of a close emotional relationship with their parents (or parent-substitutes) at the age when this is important.

This is confirmed or supported by several studies; the best-designed is that of Goldfarb.[3] He compared children who had been brought up in foster-homes with a matched group who had spent roughly the first three years of life in institutions before being placed, like the others, in foster-homes. The case-workers responsible for the children were asked to complete check-lists of forms of 'problem behaviour', without being told the purpose of the research. Most kinds of problem behaviour – aggressive, dishonest, or emotional – were commoner among the children who had been in institutions; and all of them exhibited some problem behaviour, whereas one quarter of the others did not.

3. If children are reared by parents who do not foster strong emotional dependence on themselves, or who, through doing so, do not make use of this dependence as an instrument of ethical training; who, for example, do not say 'mother doesn't love boys who steal'. In this type of family the parents may disapprove of stealing, lying, assault and sexual misbehaviour and yet be unaccustomed to the use of this emotional technique to discourage it.

Trasler suggests that this kind of upbringing is typical of the families of unskilled manual workers, as described by several British sociologists[4];

---

[1] Trasler says 'There is no theoretical reason why direct punishment should not be as effective in mediating avoidance conditioning in children as it is in animals, but in practice many parents are unwilling to apply a sanction which is severe enough to stimulate an adequate anxiety reaction'. (1962.69.)

[2] S. and E. Glueck, *loc. cit.* R. G. Andry, *loc. cit.*

[3] 1943. The criticisms of such studies by Lady Wootton, (loc. cit., 1959), do less than justice to the care with which they were designed and carried out.

[4] e.g., Spinley, 1953.

and he points out that it is this occupational group whose children are over-represented in penal institutions.

4. If the behaviour against which we expect people to react ethically is very different from the types of behaviour against which they were ethically conditioned by their parents.

Trasler suggests that traffic offences are examples of this situation; since a young child cannot commit them, his parents do not bother to produce in him an ethical reaction to them. Thus we disapprove of traffic offenders in a more intellectual way, and learn prudentially, not ethically, to abstain from traffic offences ourselves. Other examples of this sort might be revenue offences.

5. If the child, though subjected to ethical conditioning of the emotional type, is abnormally unresponsive to this sort of conditioning.

Laboratory experiments by Eysenck and others, while by no means con-clusive, suggest that there may well be inborn differences between individ-uals in responsiveness to conditioning. For obvious reasons the form of conditioning which lends itself most readily to measurement is the con-ditioning of simple muscular movements. For example, if a light puff of air is directed at a person's eyes, he will blink; and if the puff of air is accom-panied by a noise, he will eventually blink involuntarily at the noise alone; but the noise alone will produce this conditioned response on only a limited number of occasions before the response is 'extinguished'. The number of occasions which it takes to establish and extinguish the response varies from one individual to another. This is, of course, a different sort of con-ditioning from ethical conditioning; but there is a tendency for a certain type of personality – the 'extraverted' – to take longer to acquire the blink response and a shorter time to lose it, than the more 'introverted'.[1] There may also be a tendency for offenders in English prisons to be more extra-verted[2] than the population at large. More direct evidence, however, on the 'conditionability' of delinquents – for example, the comparison of rates of acquisition and extinction in carefully matched samples of delinquents and non-delinquents – is clearly needed.

It is important to be clear about the relationship between this account of the genesis of delinquency and the sort of explanations which are offered by the psychotherapeutic, and especially the psychoanalytic, school.

In practice, the delinquents who are referred to psychoanalysts and eventually appear in their case-histories are usually atypical in one of two ways. Their offences may have abnormal features: they may seem pointless – for instance, they may be thefts of objects useless to the thief; they may seem designed to harm someone whom the offender loves; they may be committed in such a way that detection is obviously certain; or they may be connected with deviant sexual desires, such as the theft of women's clothes by men. In the other sort of case, the offence may not present any unusual

[1] Franks, 1957.

[2] Trasler, 1962.87, quoting an unpublished investigation carried out under the direction of the Chief Psychologist to the Prison Commission. But earlier studies yielded no such difference.

features but the offender may be discovered to be conducting himself oddly in other ways – an example being the young shoplifter who also runs away from home; or the offender's personality may reveal abnormalities as a result of interviews or tests: the prostitute may be found to be emotionally attached to another woman. It is this sort of case which the psychoanalytic account seems better designed to explain than does learning theory. Indeed, learning theorists could – and some do – concede that the language of psychoanalysis is more convenient in such cases than the more elaborate groups of words which they would have to use, although this does not mean that learning theory is not applicable to the abnormal offender.

It is when psychoanalysts and learning theorists apply their explanations to the offender who exhibits no obvious abnormalities in his offences, his other behaviour, or his personality that the rivalry becomes a little sharper. Even so, there are types of case in which both schools appear to be merely describing the same process in different language. The psychoanalyst says that the child who is deprived of parental affection and discipline at the crucial age does not develop a sufficiently strong super-ego; the learning theorist says that some of the necessary conditions for ethical learning are absent. Both might point to the same individual as examples of what they mean, and might name the same necessary conditions, such as maternal love and the arousal of anxiety by the threat of its withdrawal.

There comes a point, however, at which the two points of view diverge, and the divergence is so invariable that it may well be inevitable. On the learning theory it is possible for a delinquent to differ from non-delinquents in nothing but his failure to learn – by prudential or ethical learning – not to commit offences. The absence of one of the conditions necessary for ethical learning might not have produced any other difference between him and his law-abiding counterpart. For example, he may be the child of two affectionate parents, never parted from either; and having the normal ability to respond to conditioning. Only one thing may have been lacking – a willingness on his parents' part to threaten the withdrawal of love when he lied, stole or assaulted his sister.

The psychoanalyst, on the other hand, would find it difficult to imagine delinquents who differed from non-delinquents in nothing but their tendency to commit offences. His explanation of the genesis of this tendency would make it inevitable that the delinquents should also exhibit some other differences of personality, some signs of what he would call 'maladjustment'. In this sense he does not believe, while the learning theorist does, in the psychologically normal offender.

If so, the issue has been reduced to a question which might conceivably be answered by empirical investigation. Is it true that all offenders exhibit psychological abnormalities which extend beyond the tendency to commit offences? It might be unfair to the psychoanalysts to point to motoring offenders, income-tax evaders, or similar delinquents, as examples of normal offenders. Certainly learning theory offers a neat explanation of their absence of guilt, as we have seen, while psychoanalysts sometimes offer rather strained descriptions of dangerous drivers in terms of displaced aggression, or even the death-wish. But it would be fairer to restrict the field we are searching to behaviour which most parents undoubtedly discourage in children, such as stealing, and to ask whether there are no psychologically normal thieves.

Answers to this question which are based on offenders referred to psychiatric clinics must clearly be disregarded, since those referred are almost always a selection, and the very reason for selection is almost always that the offender or his offences exhibit some abnormality. Answers based on studies of properly selected samples of inmates of penal institutions are less suspect, but still not entirely satisfactory, not only because the conditions of detention may themselves produce maladjustment, but also because the great majority of inmates of penal institutions are persistent offenders, who have failed to respond to other penal measures and are therefore atypical. It is interesting to note, however, that even in a sample of male recidivists with long careers of crime and imprisonment, D. J. West[1] found 12 per cent in whom neither he (a psychiatrist) nor a psychologist who administered tests were able to find any mental disorder or seriously deviant personality. This makes it likely that among more typical offenders, with fewer convictions, an even more substantial percentage are psychologically normal.

Excitement. Lastly, a psychological aspect of delinquency which has received hardly any attention in serious explanatory theories is the extent to which it satisfies a taste for excitement. Both psychologists and sociologists tend to treat theft, fraud and other crimes of dishonesty as means to an end. Usually the end is assumed to be a conscious and rational one: the acquisition of money or goods which are either wanted for their own sake or easily convertible into money. Where this assumption will not work, psychologists tend to assume that the offence is an indirect way of achieving some end which is not clearly recognised by the offender himself. The child may be 'asking for punishment' to satisfy his guilt, or trying to obtain the attention of a neglectful parent. Some observers of teenage delinquents, however, report that one of the attractions of stealing for them seems to be the risk of arrest. They do it 'for kicks' or for a 'thrill'.[2] Provided that it is not inflated into an explanation of more than some delinquencies this observation should not surprise anyone who is acquainted with adolescents or can recall his own youth. Nor is it necessarily inapplicable to adults, although their crimes of theft, violence or sex usually seem to be prompted by motives which are either more commercial or more pathological, like most adult behaviour. Nevertheless, it has been suggested that some women shoplifters are motivated by the quasi-sexual thrill which they derive from the risk of detection and arrest. Whether this explanation is applied to women shoplifters or adolescent thieves, its importance is difficult to estimate, since the investigator must rely almost wholly on the frankness and capacity for introspection of the offender himself. But inability to measure a factor does not justify complete disregard of it.

[1] West, 1963.
[2] North London police discovered at the end of 1966 that inter-school and inter-class shoplifting competitions were going on at Christmas time in their area (*Daily Telegraph* for 5th January 1967).

F

PSYCHOPATHY

There is a group of offenders for which the explanations offered vary so widely that they could not be properly discussed until the varieties of physiological, psychiatric and psychological accounts had been dissected. This consists of people who are said by some psychiatrists to be suffering from 'psychopathy',[1] and by others from 'personality disorder'. There is, however, much more disagreement between psychiatrists as to the nature and causes of this condition, and over the question whether certain individuals are or are not suffering from it, than is observable over a diagnosis or a definition of, say, subnormal intelligence.

What seem to be common, however, to almost all descriptions of psychopaths, and definitions of their abnormality, are these features:

1. the onset of their abnormality is not observable as is the onset of, say, schizophrenia. It is difficult to point to an age in the psychopath's early life when he was not abnormal. Nor does he improve suddenly, although he may do so very gradually as he approaches middle age;[2]

2. no form of treatment which is regarded as effective in alleviating some other form of mental abnormality has so far had a similar effect upon this condition;

3. the condition itself – unlike most mental illness – does not seem to involve suffering for the psychopath, except as a possible consequence of his behaviour;

4. psychopathic behaviour is not usually as specific as the symptoms of other disorders, such as the compulsive stealing of the kleptomaniac, the delusions of the paranoiac, or the fits of the epileptic. The same individual psychopath may be sexually promiscuous, a thief, a swindler and cruel to his children;

5. on the other hand, it is more definitely associated with breaches of the criminal law and other accepted rules of conduct than are other abnormalities. There are large numbers of idiots, psychotics and neurotics who do not behave delinquently, or even anti-socially.

[1] The word itself is unfortunately chosen. As coined by Koch in the nineteenth century it probably meant 'psychological casualty' – someone whose psyche had suffered damage. Hence Freud's *Psychopathology of Everyday Life* is about minor abnormalities of speech or behaviour. This philologically correct usage is still found in some present-day writers, such as G. B. Vold (1958.109), but in most modern authorities the meaning is more restricted, and excludes other clinically recognisable abnormalities such as the psychoses and neuroses. Some psychiatrists – notably in the United States – confine the term to people whose abnormality includes anti-social sexual conduct, and the term is used in this narrow sense in some States' penal codes. In the penal codes of other States, and in the English Mental Health Act, it is used in the wider sense which includes abnormally aggressive or irresponsible conduct. In the Scottish Mental Health Act, such conduct is also recognised as grounds for compulsory admission, but is not called 'psychopathy'.

[2] D. K. Henderson, 1939, says that psychopathic 'disorders' are 'usually of recurrent or episodic type', but he may simply mean that the *behaviour* which is the symptom is not continuous, as indeed it could hardly be.

In contrast, if the psychopath did not behave anti-socially we might hesitate to label him as such.[1]

The tendency of psychiatrists to use causal hypotheses as a basis for classification is particularly evident in the literature on psychopaths, where subdivisions such as 'the immature psychopath', 'the constitutional psychopath'[2] or 'the impulsive psychopath'[3] abound. This is understandable when the behaviour upon which a diagnosis of psychopathy has to be founded is so lacking in specificity. In such circumstances it is not easy to classify by observable differences. But, if we confine ourselves to typologies which are at least *prima facie* related to observed behaviour rather than supposed causes, psychiatrists appear to encounter at least three distinguishable kinds of psychopath:

1. the aggressive type, which is prone to acts of personal violence, often on slight provocation;

2. the callous type, who feels no remorse for the effects of his behaviour upon others, and seems to have little affection for wife, mistress, child or parents. Some authorities have observed personalities of this kind among men with successful careers in politics, the arts and the professions, where they are simply regarded as being more than usually conscienceless and selfish; and D. K. Henderson classified them separately as 'creative psychopaths';

3. the inadequate type, who seems to drift from job to job, with little perseverance at any task and little planning. He seems to commit petty offences of dishonesty as the easiest means of extricating himself from difficulties, and without much calculation of his chances of detection. He is sometimes described as having charm of manner, which he uses in swindling people or persuading them to employ or marry him.

At the same time, it would seem from psychiatric case-histories and text-books that aggressive psychopaths are not seldom callous as well, that callous psychopaths may on occasion behave like the inadequate type, and so on. Moreover, just as a mentally subnormal individual may or may not also be suffering from some form of mental illness or maladjustment, so any kind of psychopath may or may not also be mentally ill or subnormal.[4] It is therefore far from certain that varieties of psychopathy can be diagnosed in the same way as varieties of influenza, since the number of 'hybrid' or 'intermediate' cases may so nearly equal the 'typical' cases of each type as to leave no real borderline. Indeed, psychiatrists have a tendency to regard psychopaths as simply individuals who exhibit normal traits in an extreme degree. For example, there is a limit to the patience of everyone, although

[1] It is true that D. K. Henderson and others have distinguished a category of 'creative' or 'successful' psychopath. But even so, there is an element of the anti-social in their description of them.

[2] Gibbens, Pond and Stafford-Clark, 1959.114.

[3] R. S. Hodge, 1945.

[4] Of 890 male offenders on whom hospital or guardianship orders were imposed during 1961, 3 per cent were classified as psychopaths who were also mentally ill, while 1 per cent were classified as psychopaths who were also subnormal.

some can keep their tempers better than others: on this view, the aggressive
psychopath is merely at one end of this scale. People also vary in their concern for the feelings of others, and the callous psychopath may simply be
higher on the scale of selfishness than most. The irresponsible psychopath,
too, may simply be at the opposite end of the same scale as the over-
conscientious person. Mayer-Gross[1] even goes so far as to suggest that if
these traits could be measured as height and intelligence can be, they would
be found to have a normal distribution of the same symmetrical kind (see
Figure 3). On this view we should not expect to find either clear-cut types
of psychopathy or specific causes of them. They are merely natural variations, or combinations of variations, from what we regard as usual in the
way of patience, concern for others, sense of responsibility and so forth.

On this assumption – which is quite speculative – psychopathy is no
more a specific disorder than is polygenic feeble-mindedness (with which
it is sometimes associated). A possible, though not the only, explanation
of natural variations of this sort could be based on what I have called the
theory of ethical learning. Pavlovian psychologists suggest that many
psychopaths suffer from a constitutional abnormality, though of a less
spectacular kind than low intelligence: they are simply very difficult to
condition. Lykken[2] compared 12 male and 7 female 'psychopaths', 13 male
and 7 female 'neurotic sociopaths' and 15 'normal' controls, roughly
matched in age, intelligence, and socio-economic background. He found
the psychopaths significantly less responsive to conditioning of a laboratory
type, and less 'anxious' (as measured by a questionnaire).

As we saw, however, a low degree of responsiveness to conditioning is
only one of the possible reasons for anti-social behaviour which are suggested
by the ethical learning theory. Some of the others we need not seriously
consider as explanations of psychopathy. An example is the fact that some
type of antisocial behaviour such as motoring offences are not committed in
our formative years; psychopaths are not so specialised in their anti-social
conduct. More plausible, however, is the suggestion that deprivation of
parental care and affection, either as a result of the physical absence of
parents or as a result of abnormal parents, might be a cause of the callous
types of psychopathic personality, especially if these conditions were present
in an extreme form.

Explanations of this kind, though not in quite the same language, are of
course favoured by psychoanalysts. It is true that, even with their emphasis
on post-natal factors, psychoanalysts who have practical experience of
psychopaths seem compelled to attribute some of their characteristics to
innate peculiarities. Glover, for instance, says 'In the case of psychopathy,
for example, constitutional factors may be assumed to be responsible for

[1] 1960.
[2] See his chapter in Sarbin (ed.) 1961.149. Trasler (1962.58) also suggests this explanation of psychopathy, but with only scanty supporting evidence. The studies he quotes
suggest only that many psychopaths are extraverts and that many extraverts are hard to
condition, which does not necessarily show that psychopaths include an undue number
of people who are hard to condition. Lykken's study is the only one known to me which
really attempts to test the hypothesis.

the following general reactions: tendencies to irritability, excitability and a-rhythmic responses, sensitivity, intolerance of frustration, flight and aggressive reactions, explosive discharge and swings from active to passive. . . .'[1] Like most other psychoanalysts, however, he seems to believe that these predispositions need not necessarily develop into psychopathy, and do so only because it is so difficult to identify, and equally difficult to satisfy, the unusual needs of these individuals in the infantile stage.

At the other extreme, neurologists emphasise the number of psychopaths who appear to suffer from abnormalities of cerebral functioning gross enough to be detectable by the electroencephalograph.[2] Hill, Pond and Stafford-Clark[3] recorded the EEGs of 94 murderers, whom they divided into five groups: those whose murders were unintentional but incidental to an ordinary rational offence, such as shop-breaking; those for which there was an understandable motive; those which they regarded as 'motiveless' or virtually so; those with a 'strong sexual element'; and those committed by persons who were legally recognised as insane. The results were:

TABLE 15 Murderers' electroencephalograms

EEG classification	incidental	motivated	motiveless	sexual	insane
normal	13	22	4	4	7
with abnormality	4	6	14	5	15
of which					
'mild unspecific'	2	3	7	4	9
'severe unspecific'	1	0	4	0	2
'specific, focal, or epileptic'	1	3	3	1	4

The striking feature of this table is the difference between the proportions of normal to abnormal EEGs in the different groups. In groups 1 and 2 (which might be regarded as 'rational' murderers) normal EEGs outnumber abnormal. In groups 3 and 5, however, the reverse is the case, and it is noticeable that the 'motiveless' murderers have fully as high[4] a percentage of abnormal EEGs as the insane; if we remind ourselves that to be legally recognisable insanity has to be quite severe,[5] this is remarkable. The 'sex murderers' occupy an intermediate position. This evidence suggests that

---

[1] 1960.138. Freud himself, of course, believed in variations in innate susceptibility to the disorders in which he was interested.

[2] See p. 62.

[3] See their evidence to the Gowers Commission on Capital Punishment, from which these figures are taken. A later report, including 6 more cases, was published in the *Journal of Mental Science*, 1952. Using a similar classification, J. N. Walton classified the EEGs of 20 murderers, with similar results (*Medico-Legal Journal*, 1963).

[4] In fact, a higher percentage, but of course the numbers are too small to make this difference significant.   [5] See Chapter 13.

some crimes of personal violence, especially those for which the motives are obscure, are committed by people whose brains appear to function with some abnormality. In some cases the abnormality is of the kind which is associated with epilepsy or brain damage, in others it is 'unspecific'.

Abnormal EEGs are certainly not confined to the violent. Not only are they found in a small but substantial (and presumably law-abiding) percentage of the general population, but they appear to occur in samples of ordinary offenders and 'inadequate psychopaths', as was shown by a sample of 72 psychopaths whom Gibbens, Pond and Stafford-Clark compared with 59 prisoners selected as controls.[1] The most that can be said is that abnormalities seem to be most common in the aggressive psychopath, less common in the inadequate, less common in the ordinary prisoner, and least common among non-offenders. Moreover, this investigation included a follow-up of about nine years, which showed that the subsequent records of the psychopaths with abnormal EEGs were no worse than the records of those without abnormalities. Indeed, there were two sub-groups among which an *abnormal* EEG was actually associated with a *better* record: these were the inadequate psychopaths and psychopaths (whether inadequate or aggressive) over the age of 25. While the numbers were small, the association with age is consistent with two independent observations. Abnormal EEGs in the general population are less frequent the older the age group, and epileptics, who have a specific abnormality, tend to 'grow out of' their fits in middle age. It seems probable that the older psychopaths with abnormal EEGs did better in the follow-up because it was long enough to extend into the period during whichthese cerebral abnormalities – whatever they may be – begin to die away, while if the younger ones could have been followed up for, say, another ten years they too might have been found to reform.

What these (and other) studies suggest is not that all offenders diagnosed as 'psychopaths'[2] suffer from some defect of cerebral functioning, but that they include a sub-group which ought not to be classified as psychopaths at all, even on the assumption that this is a useful diagnostic category.[3] It must be appreciated, however, that these studies were carried out in the nineteen-forties and -fifties, when electroencephalographic equipment and interpretation were at a comparatively early stage of development. Numbers in the samples were comparatively small, and the incidence of these abnormalities in the general population only roughly measured.

Finally, we must consider the body of sceptical opinion which in effect demands firmer evidence that there is something which differentiates psychopaths from people who are merely wicked. Questions of this sort are usually asked in the course of arguing whether psychopaths should be

[1] 1959.

[2] However stringent the diagnostic criteria, it seems highly probable that, unless the criteria actually include an abnormal EEG, those diagnosed as psychopaths will include some with apparently normal EEGs.

[3] Perhaps 'encephalopaths' would be an appropriate label, since it would draw attention to the fact that they appear to have some brain defect instead of, or as well as, some 'psychic' defect, and would thus contrast them with 'psychopaths' in whom only defects of personality are observable.

regarded by the criminal law as 'responsible' for their acts or omissions; but it is possible to consider how one should answer the question without becoming involved in the jurisprudential issue. The question assumes that 'being wicked' and 'being psychopathic' are two mutually exclusive states, like 'being tired' and 'being fresh', so that it makes just as much sense to ask 'Is he wicked or psychopathic?' as to ask 'Are you tired or fresh?' It seems much more plausible, however, to regard 'psychopathic' and 'wicked' as belonging to two distinct sets of terms which are no more mutually exclusive than terms dealing with physical beauty and those dealing with physical health. It makes little sense to ask 'Is she ugly or healthy?', and 'Is he psychopathic or is he wicked?' is a similar question. This would not prevent someone who thought in terms of moral wickedness from taking the view that individuals who are classified as psychopathic should not be subject to moral condemnation, or should be subject to a lesser degree of it, just as one might say 'I'm afraid that someone in bad health never looks attractive to me'. In other words, while information as to whether an offender is psychopathic or psychologically normal may affect the moral judgements of people who think in moral terms, the two sets of concepts should not be grafted together and used as a divining-rod.

A more pertinent question is whether labelling someone as 'psychopathic' conveys any useful information at all, especially for penal or psychiatric purposes. Certainly it warns us that his behaviour is not as reliable as that of most other people; and if he is labelled an 'aggressive psychopath' this tells us that he is likely to behave violently with little or no provocation. Much more useful, however, would be a more precise description of his idiosyncrasies: for example, the information that what tends to provoke him is a refusal to lend him money, or jokes about his personal appearance.

Nevertheless, the label might serve a purpose if it told us that the individual belonged to a group whose abnormal behaviour was traceable to a specific cause. As we have seen, however, this is far from being the case. The explanations that have been suggested are varied, speculative and incomplete, and in all probability there are different causes of different, but so far unidentifiable, sub-groups. Admittedly the same may well be true of other psychiatric labels such as schizophrenia, which probably cover several varieties of disorder, each with its own cause or set of causal factors. But labels like schizophrenia or endogenous depression at least convey some idea of what the patient's future is likely to be without treatment, and what sort of treatment will alleviate his condition or arrest its progressive deterioration. One of the distinctive features of the psychopath, however, is his failure to respond to any form of treatment, penal or psychiatric, so that the label gives no more than this negative piece of information. This leaves only the possibility that it gives useful prognostic information, by telling us for example how the psychopath's future career will differ from that of the normal offender.

Unfortunately, the already-cited investigation by Gibbens, Pond and Stafford-Clark casts doubt on even this possibility. Their eight-year follow-up of the careers of 72 men diagnosed as 'severely psychopathic' and 59 ordinary criminals' showed less differences between the two groups than might have been expected. For example, since the number of previous convictions is always strongly associated with the probability of relapse, at least among ordinary offenders, they compared the 24 psychopaths who had less than 5 previous convictions with the 26 controls who had less than 5. The result was strikingly similar:

TABLE 16 Psychopathic offenders' reconvictions

	subsequent convictions					
	0	1	2	3	4	or more
24 'psychopaths'	6	5	5	4	4	
26 'ordinary criminals'	5	7	7	4	3	

As the investigators remarked, 'previous convictions seem to be a surer guide to prognosis than psychiatric diagnosis.'

On the whole, therefore, the term 'psychopath' seems to be a label which obliterates more information than it conveys. The diagnoses of 'personality disorder' or 'behaviour disorder', which are becoming fashionable alternatives, appear at first sight to be more expressive but are being used with no more precision.

6

ENVIRONMENTAL

THEORIES

The theories which I have so far discussed have one feature in common: they look for causes in the individual. Some find these in traits which are attributed to his physiological constitution; some in characteristics which result from his upbringing. Both of these types of explanation, however, are 'individualistic' in the sense that, whether the blame is ultimately laid on nature or nurture, they envisage the delinquent as an individual who is more prone than the non-delinquent to anti-social behaviour even when both live in the same society, with the same temptations and opportunities. In contrast, the group of theories which I am about to describe can be called 'environmental', because they emphasise the part played by the economic, ecological or social conditions in which the delinquent develops.[1]

ECONOMIC THEORIES

It is the environment that must provide the essentials for survival – food and clothing. Scarcity of these provides the most obvious of all incentives for the commonest of all crimes – theft. Since theft was most frequently committed by members of the poorer classes, it was not surprising that nineteenth-century investigators looked for and found evidence to confirm the causal relationship between economic conditions and crime. Correlations were observed between fluctuations in the price of rye (or whatever happened to be the basic cereal of the popular diet) and fluctuations in the rates of offences against property.[2] These correlations were more marked, however, in predominantly agricultural areas, such as von Mayr's Bavaria, and as increasing industrialisation complicated the economic link between the worker and his food the relationship became less clear; moreover, the spread of charitable or official measures to alleviate destitution must at some stage have become an important factor.

Dorothy Thomas,[3] whose study is still one of the most scientific and thorough investigations of the relationship between crime and economic conditions, therefore used more sophisticated indices. From statistics for unemployment, exports, retail prices, railway freight receipts, coal production,

---

[1] It is, of course, somewhat artificial to classify explanations in terms of parental influence as 'individualistic', while treating the influence of people outside the home as 'social' and therefore as 'environmental'.

[2] The classic studies are those of G. von Mayr, and W. Woytinsky's application of the method of product-moment correlation to his data.   [3] 1925.

provincial bank clearings, pig iron production and blast furnaces in operation she constructed a 'British business cycle' for the sixty years 1854 to 1913. When the effect of the secular, or long-term, trends had been allowed for, the cycle appeared as a series of wave-like fluctuations measuring from seven to nine years between peaks. Comparing these with various social statistics[1] she found, for example, that at the prosperous stages in the cycle the marriage-rate and the birth-rate were higher, while during the lean years admissions to poor-houses, suicides, and illegitimate births tended to rise; divorce and emigration, on the other hand, seemed to have no correlation with the business cycle. In the field of delinquency, she found that prosecutions for drunkenness (like other indices of the consumption of alcohol) increased with prosperity, while burglary and other forms of 'breaking and entering' showed a strong tendency to increase in the lean years; ordinary larcenies showed a weaker tendency of the same sort.[2]

Similar, or even stronger, correlations were observed by A. F. Henry and J. F. Short[3] between burglary or robbery and downswings in the short-term business cycle in two samples of cities in the U.S.A. during the period 1929 to 1941, and 1946 to 1949.

Unemployment. Since most crime, however, is committed by city-dwellers in the wage-earning occupations, who are especially vulnerable to the most definite type of economic set-back, namely unemployment, one would expect to find particularly strong correlations between property offences and unemployment among the wage-earning age-groups. The best study of this seems to be that of D. Glaser and K. Rice,[4] who correlated arrests by age-groups with unemployment rates in Boston, Cincinnati, Chicago and the U.S.A. as a whole, for periods varying from 20 to 25 years between 1930 and 1956; they distinguished between property offences, crimes against the person, and a group of misdemeanours consisting of drunkenness, disorderly conduct, and vagrancy. In Boston and Cincinnati[5] they found positive correlations varying from 0·56 to 0·91[6] between the national unemployment rate and arrests by the police for all three types of offence in the age-groups between 21 and 45, and somewhat lower correlations in the older age-groups.[7]

[1] By product-moment correlations.

[2] Vold (1958.178-) dismisses Dr. Thomas' correlations as 'equivocal'. She took the trouble to see what happened when, instead of merely calculating correlations for synchronous fluctuations, she correlated the business cycle with the crime-rates and other social statistics of one, two and three years later. She found that in most cases a three-year time-lag converted a negative into a positive correlation. Vold's criticisms seem to overlook the fact that this is what one would expect if three years were nearly half the length of the cycle.   [3] 1954. App. V.   [4] 1959.

[5] Whose statistics, for various reasons, are preferable to those for Chicago or for the U.S.A. as a whole.

[6] All significant at the ·001 level of probability.

[7] Among the age-group 10 to 17, on the other hand, they found *negative* correlations. These were too weak in the cities to reach an acceptable level of significance; but in the U.S.A. as a whole, at least so far as property offences and crimes against the person were concerned, they were strong enough to be significant at the ·01 or ·001 level of probability. Glaser and Rice suggest the explanation that unemployment keeps fathers at home where they in turn keep their teenage sons out of trouble.

Observations such as these, however, have been overshadowed by the more spectacular long-term trends of both economic conditions and crime, in which a steep and steady rise in the standard of living of practically all social classes in Western Europe and the Americas has been accompanied by a steep and steady rise in the rate of crimes, including all forms of property crime.

It would be naïve, however, to conclude from this phenomenon that economic adversity is not, or is no longer, an important stimulus to property crimes. It is true that the man who steals to keep himself and his family alive is more likely to be found in a society with such a low standard of living that many of its members are only just able to survive, as was the case in some of the rural areas from which the nineteenth-century economists drew their correlations between theft and the price of cereals. The higher the standard of living rises above such a level the less frequent will be 'stealing for survival'. But as the objective standard rises, so does the subjective; a family that in 1900 would have been content with full bellies, warm clothing and a dry room to sleep in now feel that a radio or even a television set is another necessity of life. If so, it is not difficult to see why economic recessions, even in an affluent society, should be accompanied by increases in the property crimes, and especially in those of the 'breaking in' type which yield the highest returns: the reason may well be that any fall in a standard of living, however high, is felt as hardship. It is noticeable that all the twentieth-century studies cited in this section have found this type of property crime to be linked to periods of recession from comparative prosperity.[1]

Such reasoning, however, is not sufficient to explain why a steep increase in property crimes should take place during a period of more or less full employment, with no appreciable economic recession, as it seems to have done over the last fifteen years in Britain. Unless one abandons economic reasoning for some other type of explanation at this point, it seems necessary to argue that what can be called the 'subjective standard of living' rises not merely at the same rate as the objective standard, but faster. This is not implausible. It is not difficult to find features of the affluent society which seem almost designed to achieve this. The intensive advertising of consumer goods, and the use of hire-purchase schemes to market them, are obvious examples. Mass media of news and entertainment, and the increasing mobility of wage-earners, gives them a closer acquaintance with more expensive ways of life, and probably stimulates a desire for them.

Opportunity. Another aspect of increasingly affluent societies, however, is the increasingly frequent opportunities which they provide for crimes of dishonesty. The more cars there are, the more there are to steal, or to steal from. Wilkins has pointed out that thefts from unattended vehicles has followed much the same rising curve as the numbers of vehicles registered.[2]

---

[1] Indeed, Henry and Short (1954, *loc. cit.*) observed high correlations between the downswings in the U.S.A.'s business cycle and (1) the suicide-rates of *white* males of working age (especially middle-class males); (2) the lynchings of negroes by white males. They link these, by an elaborate psychological theory, to the frustration engendered or intensified by a recession from prosperity.   [2] 1964.

Moreover, the more property people have, the less care they take to protect it.

Opportunity is undoubtedly part of the reason for other variations in the distribution of offences. Theft is proportionately much rarer in rural than in urban areas; and whatever one may believe to be the differences between the morality of the countryman and the city-dweller, the impossibility of shoplifting where there are no shops must not be overlooked.[1]

Opportunity is also the most probable explanation of most seasonal variations in crime rates. Burt[2] analysed nearly a million offences committed by adults in the decade 1900-1909, and observed marked peaks in the summer months for violence against the person, suicide, and sexual crimes, while there were much less marked peaks in the winter months for property crimes. He went to the length of correlating the rates with recorded temperatures, daylight, sunshine, and rainfall for each month, and found that the first three at least of these factors were strongly correlated with such crimes, but showed negligible correlations with forgery. The explanation is almost certainly that theft and housebreaking are facilitated by the long nights of winter, while months of daylight and sunshine, when women and children are found (or can be lured) out of doors, offer more chances to the rapist or seducer. Forgery, on the other hand, is an all-weather pursuit. (It is true that nineteenth-century continental criminologists offered physiological explanations of these phenomena[3]; and certainly the summer peaks for personal violence and suicide are less easy to explain in terms of opportunity.) Juvenile delinquency varies with the day of the week, especially during school terms: Sunday is a day not of rest but of misbehaviour.[4]

TOPOGRAPHICAL ASPECTS

Another aspect of the non-human environment whose association with delinquency was at one time the subject of considerable study is topography. Not only is crime proportionately more frequent in urban areas, but it is more frequent among the residents of some parts of towns than among the residents of other parts. In his study of Chicago in the nineteen-twenties, Shaw observed that the highest rates occurred in areas near the centre of the city where the buildings were being allowed to deteriorate and the population was declining; and that these had been areas of high delinquency-rates for at least a quarter of a century, in spite of changes in the national, racial, or cultural composition of their populations. Because these areas occurred between the commercially active city centre and the more attractive residential areas to which those families who could afford it were migrating, he called them 'interstitial'. Inspired by him, studies of other American

---

[1] In 1961, 'crimes' were reported to the police at a rate of 35·4 per 1,000 of population in Glasgow, whereas in the Shetland Islands the rate was only 2·3 per 1,000. 'Crimes' consist largely of theft or housebreaking. When the rates are compared for 'offences' – many of which are minor creations of modern welfare or revenue legislation – the differences are much less striking: 51·1 per 1,000 in Glasgow, 15·4 in the Shetlands.

[2] 1944.161-.

[3] See, for example, S. Hurwitz's summary (1952.247-).

[4] Burt, loc. cit., 159-.

cities found similar distributions of delinquency.[1] The ecological school themselves – as Shaw and his followers have rather imprecisely been labelled – did not regard the physical surroundings of the slums as directly responsible for delinquency, but believed that they were causally associated with a social disorganisation which promoted it.

Rehousing. Nevertheless, one of the hopes which has motivated the massive rehousing operations of post-war Britain, and no doubt of other countries, has been that the removal of delinquents' families to better homes further from the opportunities and temptations of city shops and offices, would at least reduce delinquency-rates. I know of no properly planned investigation of this aspect of rehousing, and the most relevant evidence is provided by Ferguson's analysis[2] of 1,349 Glasgow schoolboys who left school in January 1947. Of these, 960 lived in privately owned properties, ranging from 'residential, and good working-class' to slums, while 389 lived in local authority housing schemes, built for the most part between the wars. Fortunately for the investigators' purpose at least, Glasgow's policy had been to rehouse families from their slum-clearance areas in special housing schemes. The table below shows the percentage of boys with known convictions from each type of residential district:

TABLE 17 Delinquency and housing areas

type of district	number at risk	percentage of boys between 8 and 18 years old with convictions	
		at least 1	2 or more
residential and good working class	188	6·9	2·6
fair working-class	381	9·1	4·9
bad working-class	252	14·2	6·3
slum	139	22·3	8·6
local authority's slum clearance houses	142	21·8	7·7
other local authority houses	247	6·8	0·8
	1,349	12·2	4·8

85 per cent of the boys rehoused from slums had lived in their local authority houses since they were 8 years old, some of them all their lives.

The most striking feature of the table is the similar percentages of delinquency among the boys who were still living in slums, and those whose families had been rehoused from slums, in the great majority of cases six or more years before. It is true that the Glasgow housing schemes have never been renowned for their amenities; so that a passionate town-planner could argue that the effects of modern neighbourhood planning upon behaviour

[1] C. R. Shaw, 1929 and C. R. Shaw & H. D. McKay (edd.), 1931.
[2] 1952.17-.

have not really been tested. But the difference between the squalor of the Gorbals and even the unimaginative hygiene of the rehousing schemes was so great that it should have had some effect. Until Ferguson's is superseded by better evidence, we must proceed on the assumption that the physical nature of one's residential area makes a negligible contribution to one's delinquency. 'Men, not walls, make a city.'

THE HUMAN ENVIRONMENT

We come now to theories which stress the part played by what can be called 'the human environment'.

Differential Association. The simplest of these is E. H. Sutherland's 'principle of differential association'. Criminal behaviour, in his view, is neither inherited nor spontaneously adopted, but learned from other criminals by conscious communication within intimate personal groups. Not only are techniques learned, but also what Sutherland called 'definitions'[1] favourable to the violation of the legal codes. In other words, the robber is a man who has learned from other robbers not only how to rob but also to regard the law that makes robbery a crime as something to be broken without shame. While Sutherland recognised that a person's 'prior life experiences' played a part in determining his attitudes to law-breaking, he clearly thought that the main reason why the robber flouts the law is not a general distortion of his character by his upbringing, but a specific association with people who lead him, by word or act, to feel that robbery is not really reprehensible:

> *The specific direction of motives and drives is learned* from definitions
> of the legal codes as favourable or unfavourable. In some societies
> an individual is surrounded by persons who invariably define the legal
> codes as rules to be observed, while in others he is surrounded by
> persons whose definitions are favourable to the violation of the legal
> codes. In our American society these definitions are almost always
> mixed, with the consequence that we have culture conflict in relation
> to the legal codes.
>
> A person becomes delinquent because of an excess of definitions
> favourable to violation of law over definitions unfavourable to violation
> of law. This is the principle of differential association. . . .

Although he employs the word 'learning', Sutherland's theory must be clearly distinguished from the theory of what I have called 'ethical learning', as expounded, for example, by Trasler. Trasler's delinquent needs no associates to tell him that law-breaking is not reprehensible; Sutherland's does, and is therefore a theory of human environment while Trasler's is an individualistic theory of upbringing.

In its original form this theory assumed that psychological differences between individuals were irrelevant, and it is the crudity of this assumption which has been most strongly attacked. If Sutherland really believed that it was simply the numerical excess of contacts with law-breaking persons over contacts with law-abiding persons which turned someone into a delinquent, and that each contact of either kind could be simply counted as if it were of

---

[1] 1955.77-.

equal effectiveness, then he laid himself open to awkward questions. For example, how is it that prison staff or probation officers, who are in frequent contact with criminals, do not themselves become criminals more often than they do? Clearly it is necessary to modify the theory – as Cressey did[1] – to give weight to 'the prestige of the source of a criminal or anti-criminal pattern and emotional reactions related to the association'. Since convicted offenders have little prestige for prison staff or probation officers, association with them has a negligible corrupting influence. But this leads to the question why one source or associate should have more prestige or emotional impact than another; and the answer to this presumably lies either in the psychological theories I have discussed or in the more elaborate sociological accounts which I am about to discuss.

We should not altogether dismiss differential association as a sterile hypothesis. Not only is it the most probable explanation of the way in which property offenders acquire their techniques, but in quite a few cases it probably explains why delinquency, which has to be accounted for in more elaborate ways, should have taken the *precise form* which it did take. In more concrete terms, the psychological, economic or sociological explanation of an individual's delinquency often stops short of explaining why he became a burglar rather than a robber; and the answer must often be that his associates happened to specialise in one or other form of property offence. But this merely illustrates the life-cycle of so many criminological hypotheses, which begin with the observation of the obvious, generalise it into a principle, and are eventually reduced again to a statement of the limited truths from which they originated.

Culture Conflict. Another example of this life-cycle is the 'culture-conflict' hypothesis. Sociologists who observed that crime is sometimes the result of the imposition of the ethical rules of one type of society upon a society which behaves in accordance with different rules have generalised this into a 'strong' theory. There is no doubt that when one type of society forcibly imposes its codes of conduct on another – as usually happens when a nation of European origin colonises territory elsewhere – there is a period, often spanning several generations, before the subordinated society abandons its own rules in favour of the new ones. Cannibalism, the suicide of widows, the stoning of adulteresses, and the exposure of unwanted children are all practices which, though regarded by one society as ethically unexceptionable, or even in certain circumstances obligatory, have been discountenanced and punished by a conquering society.

Sub-culture Conflict. Observations of this sort have prompted sociologists to look for similar conflicts of ethical attitudes within societies of the European type which are not amalgams of recently conquering and conquered cultures. Although such societies are more homogeneous, and although the great majority of their members have grown up under, and come from families which have grown up under, the same code of criminal law, nevertheless sociologists are able to detect in them 'sub-cultures' whose ethical attitude to this code, or parts of this code, is either one of very luke-warm support or one of covert opposition. These sub-cultures may consist

[1] For example, in his revision of Sutherland's *Principles of Criminology, op. cit.*

of immigrant or other racial minorities, such as negroes in the U.S.A., West Indians in England, or Irish in Glasgow. On the other hand, their members may be distinguishable not by their ethnic or geographical origins, but by some other characteristics: for example, residence in certain parts of cities or membership of groups such as gangs, school classes, or clubs.

Gangs. Some sociologists strengthen this argument by pointing to groups which seem to exist for the very purpose of committing crimes more efficiently. One of the most spectacular features of the American way of life is – or was – the existence of 'organised crime' in the form of illegal gambling facilities, 'protection', large-scale brothel-keeping, drug-trafficking, or bootlegging; and the large, well-armed gangs which seemed to engage in these operations with relative impunity. More recently, a great deal of attention has been paid to juvenile gangs in New York which seem to exist simply in order to fight each other.

As evidence, however, for the theory of sub-cultural conflicts, gangs are of doubtful value. In the first place, not all countries with high and increasing crime-rates seem to have numerous and well organised gangs. In Britain, for example, there may be a few adult gangs in the largest cities devoted to lucrative robberies and burglaries; but it is very hard to be sure that they would not be more accurately described as temporary associations of criminal acquaintances for the purpose of single 'jobs'. Criminal gangs among teenagers, though much publicised by the press in the nineteen-fifties, are even more probably a dramatisation of their real patterns of association. P. D. Scott,[1] for example, was able to distinguish at least four types of groups among his London delinquents:

1. 'adolescent street groups' whose members 'admittedly sometimes get into trouble, but not usually as members of these groups, which in the great majority of cases bear no more relation to the actual offence than would any youth club . . . which the individuals happened to attend together . . .';
2. 'fleeting casual delinquent associations' of boys who are not close friends, but who on one occasion carry out some spontaneous delinquency together; these are uncommon, and the boys concerned tend to be psychologically immature or abnormal;
3. 'groups of friends or siblings' whose usual activities are not delinquent. This is the commonest type of group offence. Although the groups have leaders and perhaps a nucleus of 'regulars', membership is not controlled or subject to initiation procedures. 'It is quite possible . . . for some . . . members to abstain from the occasional delinquent activities without losing face . . . a situation . . . unthinkable in a gang.';
4. 'loose anti-social groups', of very anti-social children or youths 'unhappy and disturbed in relation to their homes and to society as to be careless of the consequences of their actions, often hoping to be removed from home, and regularly looking for . . . delinquent openings in an . . . unplanned manner. . . .'

These groups are not only rarer but also smaller than the newspapers,

[1] 1956.

fiction or American experience suggests; seldom do they seem to include more than four, five or perhaps seven at any one time.[1]

Indeed, there have been suggestions that gangs are no longer as important a part of the American scene as they used to be; or even that the so-called 'gang warfare' of New York teenagers is much less organised than press descriptions imply.[2] However, that may be, what is certain is that most instances of most types of offence are not carried out by groups that could be called gangs by even the most liberal interpretation.

Immigrants. The contribution of immigrants to delinquency has been studied less closely in Britain than in the U.S.A., where concern about the effects of immigration became widespread much earlier in this century. Surveys, however, by the Immigration Commission and the National Commission on Law Enforcement in 1911 and 1931 suggested that the crime-rate was *lower* among first-generation immigrants than among the general population (presumably because they were afraid of being repatriated); it was their American-born children who exceeded the national rate. Immigrants from some countries are, of course, likely to have ways of life which either infringe the criminal law directly (as drug-peddling does) or outrage their indigenous neighbours, and so provoke violence.

Nevertheless, while conquered societies, racial minorities, immigrants, and delinquent gangs may suggest the notion of sub-cultures with norms which are in conflict with those of the main culture, and may even serve as analogies which help to make the notion clearer, they are not evidence in favour of 'culture-conflict' as an explanation of everyday delinquency. But if we search among expositions of the theory for straightforward evidence, all that we find are examples of rather special kinds of crime inspired by membership of rather special kinds of groups. Vold,[3] for example, cites the imprisonment of conscientious objectors, violence between employers and employees in industrial disputes, between racial minorities and segregationalists, and of course between gangs. What is really required, however, is evidence that a majority or a substantial minority (depending on whether the theory is propounded in a strong or weak form) of everyday offences of theft or personal violence can most plausibly be explained in these terms.

The over-representation of certain socio-economic groups among most categories of offender cannot be said to be strong support, since explanations in terms of ethical learning or economic conditions will fit this fact equally well. Nor is it plausible to regard so enormous and heterogeneous a group as 'social classes IV and V' – which is scarcely more than a demographer's diagram – as something which forms and maintains delinquent norms of conduct not only without efficient media for communicating them, but actually in the face of extremely influential mass media – newspapers, radio, television – which discountenance them.

More relevant is evidence that delinquency is not merely frequent in 'working-class areas', but especially frequent in comparatively small neigh-

---

[1] Scott refers to one group of type 4 which seemed to be part of some sort of group involving about 15 boys.

[2] See S. Yablonsky, 1959.

[3] 1958.207-.

G

bourhoods within these areas. Numerous investigators[1] have found that the addresses of the adult and juvenile delinquents of a given city tend to cluster in certain streets, or in groups of one or two adjoining streets. Although these streets often consist of deteriorating or even abandoned houses, they may occur in properly maintained housing schemes. The economic status of their inhabitants, though it tends to be low, and may contribute to their thefts and robberies, may equally well be an effect rather than a cause of careers interrupted by dismissals and imprisonment. These delinquent neighbourhoods are small enough in size to make informal communication of norms possible, and even plausible, and since they cannot be explained in terms of factors which affect wider topographical areas or occupational strata – for example, in terms of fluctuations in unemployment, or of working-class methods of child-rearing – they offer some support for the theory of sub-cultural norms. Unfortunately there is another possible explanation: that individuals who are already criminally inclined tend to find homes in these streets; they may be attracted by the prospect of under-standing, tolerant neighbours, by cheaper rents or by landlords who 'ask no questions'. Such hypotheses cannot apply to delinquent streets in local authority housing schemes, since new tenants are allocated to houses according to official policy; but it is often official policy to concentrate troublesome families, or families from troublesome slum streets, in selected streets of housing schemes; and none of the studies I have been able to trace seem to exclude this as a possible explanation of delinquent neighbourhoods in housing schemes.

Let us assume for the sake of argument, however, that there is some evidence which fits the theory of deviant sub-cultural norms more neatly than it fits other explanations. There is at least one point at which the theory, as I have so far described it, seems incomplete. What still remains to be explained is how deviant norms come into existence and persist in the face of so many kinds of discouragement – explicit disapproval in mass media of communication, deterrence by penal measures, and temporary elimination of influential delinquents by imprisonment or its equivalents.

Where a culture contains the remnants of a conquered society, or a racial minority, norms peculiar to these groups are usually traceable to earlier stages in their history: the use of drugs such as marijuana was and still is socially respectable in some societies. In some cases the deviant norms may have been the result of antagonism between these groups and other members of the culture which now incorporates them. It is not surprising that antagonism towards immigrants produces aggressive behaviour among their able-bodied males. But when we turn to the delinquent behaviour of ethnically homogeneous societies some more elaborate explanation has to be found.

Anomie. Some of the explanations offered are still historical. The ethics of the 'pioneer' or 'frontiersman' of early American history have been blamed for the financial dishonesties of Wall Street, and the Sicilian Mafia for the uninhibited vendettas of Chicago gangsters. Most sociological

[1] Apart from the Chicago School (Shaw, McKay, *et alii* . . . *loc. cit.*), see Miss Jephcott's study of 'Radby' and T. Morris's study of Croydon (1957).

explanations, however, of the existence of deviant sub-cultural norms make use of the concept of 'anomie', originally imported into sociology by Durkheim, and developed by R. K. Merton. The theory points out that modern societies of the Western European type differ from mediaeval ones – and from a diminishing number of contemporary Asian and African ones – in the extent to which individual members can alter their status. In feudal or caste-systems a man's status is determined within narrow limits by the 'station in life' into which he was born. If he were born the son of a Saxon peasant, or of a menial *sudra* in India, it was out of the question for him to become a merchant or a priest: so much so that it was only the exceptional man who even entertained the thought of improving his position. In contrast, modern societies not only contain few formal barriers to advancement[1] but have ideologies and even mythologies[2] which emphasise the possibilities of it; the slogan is no longer 'every man to his station' but 'equality of opportunity'. Indeed, in some societies this emphasis on the individual's chances of improving his status has become an implication that this is expected of him; so that if he does not try to 'get ahead' he may well incur disapproval. To this extent, enhancement of status might be said to be a goal which these societies actually force upon individuals.

Merton[3] points out that societies differ in the relative emphasis which they place on the importance of achieving the goals they prescribe and on the importance of adopting only institutionalised methods. At one extreme, a society may be so obsessed with the latter that the goals themselves are virtually or literally forgotten, and all that matters is that the individual's conduct should be correct. The ritualised way of life in pre-twentieth-century China or under the Hindu caste-system, at least as described by Western sociologists, are examples. At the other extreme are societies in which the emphasis is on the achievement of the goal, and the means of achieving it are distinguished not so much by their correctness as by their technical effectiveness. The whole range of attitudes between these two extremes can be illustrated by competitive games. Some people regard it as more important to play a 'good straightforward game' of bridge or golf than to win it; others are so intent on victory that they take any chance of gaining an advantage by hook or by crook. From this point of view, cricket and fly-fishing, with their ritualised and technically ineffective procedures, are highly institutionalised sports, while mountaineering or American football are much less so.

In a society with strongly prescribed goals and sharp distinctions between institutionalised and unorthodox means to them, the individual can adjust himself in four different ways.[4] He can accept both goals and the approved means to them; Merton calls this 'conformity'. He may accept the institu-

---

[1] Sometimes called 'upward social mobility'.

[2] Ranging from the Tale of Dick Whittington to the biographies of politicians and captains of industry, and novels such as *Room at the Top*.

[3] 1957.

[4] As Merton himself does, I am putting on one side the fifth solution, which he calls 'rebellion' – the solution which seeks to substitute changes in the goals and perhaps also in the institutionalised means to them.

tionalised means, but despair of achieving the goals and therefore renounce them; this is 'ritualism', the solution not only of disillusioned clergy but also of members of bureaucratised organisations, who find it so hard to get anything done that they concentrate on correct procedure. The individual may even renounce both goals and approved means, as vagabonds and beatniks do; this is 'retreatism'. But the most frequent form of adjustment, next to conformity, is 'innovation'; the goals are accepted and striven for, but institutionalised means are discarded in favour of unorthodox ones.

It is this last way of adjustment which, in Merton's view, accounts for crime. American society, he argues, places a high premium on economic affluence and social ascent for all its members, yet contains large groups of people whose lack of formal education and financial resources makes it exceedingly difficult for them to attain these ends by legitimate means. A few take refuge in ritualism or retreatism, but the normal solution is innovation, and where material wealth is concerned innovation means fraud, embezzlement, blackmail and theft.

> It is only when a system of cultural values extols, virtually above all
> else, certain *common* symbols of success *for the population at large*
> while its social structure rigorously restricts or completely eliminates
> access to approved modes of acquiring these symbols *for a considerable
> part of the same population*, that antisocial behaviour ensues on a
> considerable scale.[1]

Merton himself stopped more or less at this point, and it was left to his followers, notably Cohen, Cloward and Ohlin, to attempt the task of working out in detail why different individuals choose different types of solution in the dilemma which Merton described.

Cloward and Ohlin[2] suggest that if the frustrated aspirant belongs to one psychological type – the type that has been called 'intropunitive' – he blames himself for his failure to reach his goal by legitimate means, and either becomes mentally ill or takes to solitary crime. If he belongs to the 'extrapunitive' type, which blames the environment, he joins a group of people who share this kind of attitude – in other words, an antisocial group. The sorts of antisocial group available for joining depend on the nature of his neighbourhood. If it is a stabilised area, where the roles of police, criminals and local politicians are clearly defined and understood by all concerned, he will have no difficulty in finding an ordinary criminal gang to join – that is, a gang existing chiefly to commit lucrative property offences. But if the neighbourhood is an unstable one, with no fixed and recognised patterns of this kind, and perhaps an immigrant population trying to find their place and role in it, he is more likely to find a conflict group, that is, a fighting gang, to join. If he is one of those unfortunates whose strict moral code will not allow him to join a thieving or fighting gang, as the case may be, he joins what Cloward and Ohlin call a retreatist group, whose members find satisfaction and status in extracting 'kicks' from jazz, alcohol, drugs, sex, or combinations of these.

It is a rare individual, however, who can do without the approval of any of his fellow men; and even those who are impelled to adopt means to their

<hr />

[1] *loc. cit.*   [2] 1961.

goal that are officially disapproved will choose, if they can, means that have the approval of at least some minority. Moreover, the most effective of unorthodox means – such as safe-blowing – usually have to be learned from others (as Sutherland observed), and usually require the co-operation of others. For these reasons, thieves tend to form associations with each other, and to develop a modified code of morality which allows them to replace the forfeited approval of society at large by a mutual respect for each other's observance of their own code. Thus many thieves seem to have unwritten codes which prohibit stealing in certain circumstances. J. B. Mays[1] believed that among his Liverpool teenagers only a pathological boy would steal from his own home, or from a small shop in his own street; but large stores and public undertakings were fair game. Another device by which the property offender seems to retain his self-respect is his disapproval of sexual offenders; they are 'real criminals', ostracised and even beaten up by other prisoners.[2]

By reasoning along these lines, Merton and his followers supplemented the theory of deviant sub-cultural norms with an explanation of the way in which a modern society may actually generate the strains that lead to the formation of these deviant norms in the groups which are subjected to the strains.

Their account has the advantage over earlier sociological explanations of being plausible when applied to the largest group of crimes – acquisitive offences. It is also consistent with several observations which seem to be true of such offences not only in the U.S.A. but also in most Europeanised countries:

1. while acquisitive offences – and most other types too – are most frequently committed by people who are at the lower end of the economic ladder, they increase rather than diminish in frequency as the material standard of living of the whole society, including its poorest groups, improves. Acquisitive crimes, such as fraud and embezzlement, are not infrequent among the better-off;

2. most thieves – and other offenders – are badly educated and have unsatisfactory records of employment; in other words, they have made little use of the institutionalised means to the goal of affluence. It is true that the reason may well have been disinclination rather than genuine obstacles, but this does not alter the fact that they seem to find institutional means abnormally hard to adopt;

3. individuals who are unorthodox in their means of achieving one sort of goal – for example, economic gain – might be expected to be unorthodox in achieving others, such as sexual satisfaction. This seems to be so; cohabitation and promiscuity seem to be commoner among thieves than among the law-abiding. But unorthodoxy must be limited to the means, and must not extend to the sexual goal. One

[1] 1954.
[2] Merton himself paid too little attention to this step in the explanation of sub-cultures with deviant norms, and it was left to followers such as Cohen, Cloward and Ohlin. Unfortunately they concentrated on the easiest phenomenon to describe – juvenile gangs. To some extent, therefore, I have improvised in this paragraph.

must not be a homosexual or a sexual molester of little girls if one
wants to be accepted in the world of prison.

Merton's explanation has several merits. Unlike other culture-conflict
theories in terms of the human environment, it applies to societies which
have no recent history of conquest, faction or large-scale immigration.
Unlike explanations in terms of recessions or business cycles, it applies to
controlled economies with comparatively full employment, of the kind
which has been exemplified by post-war Britain. Unlike explanations in
terms of psychological casualties it becomes more and not less plausible as
crime in such societies becomes (or perhaps is recognised as being) endemic.
For although it is not impossible to believe that a large minority – or even a
majority – of a population are psychological casualties, the larger the percentage of people who are classified as casualties the larger will be the
fraction of this group who will be found to be law-abiding; in other words,
the weaker will become the association between being a psychological
casualty and being a delinquent.

Even the ethical learning theory, which is designed to offer an explanation
of normal acquisitive crime on the part of men who are the products of an
upbringing which is common among the families of unskilled manual
workers, is inferior to Merton's account in at least one respect. People
without deeply instilled revulsions from stealing and violence appear to
undergo a later process of what I have called prudential learning, and to
refrain from crime through an appreciation of the risks and consequences of
detection. The ethical learning theory is not designed to answer the question
why, among men with similar upbringings (including brothers from the
same family), one man will act in accordance with prudential learning,
another not. Merton's theory would suggest that this could happen because
the former was fortunate enough to find, or be helped to find, or be trained
for, a better legitimate means of acquiring money, pleasure and status – for
example, in concrete terms, better employment.

On the other hand, the intellectual attractions of a theory must not be
confused with the evidence for it. It is possible, as we have just seen, to
select several observed phenomena which are consistent with Merton's
theory; but, as I pointed out in my introductory discussion[1] of types of
evidence, so many associations of different sorts are recorded in the
literature that it is not difficult to assemble a small collection to fit almost
any intellectually plausible explanation. In such a situation a rigorously
scientific approach would insist that 'off-the-peg' observations are not confirmation of a theory, which may well have been designed (consciously or
unconsciously) to fit them; and that what is required is a test designed to
confirm or refute the theory. In a test of this kind the theorist should deduce
from his theory that if he performs an experiment of a certain kind he will
either get a certain result or not; and that if he does not the theory is false,
or at least in need of modification.

It is sometimes argued that so stringent a requirement places the sociologist under a disadvantage in comparison with the psychologist. For the
psychologist thinks in terms of causal variables which are attributes of

[1] On p. 43.

individuals or at most small groups of individuals, while the sociologist's causal variables are attributes of much larger units – sub-cultures, societies or even civilisations; and the psychologist is therefore able to manipulate his causal variables in an experimental way which is denied to the sociologist. But this oversimplifies the difference. The psychologist may be interested in variables, such as different methods of child-rearing, which are just as impossible to manipulate, though for different reasons. In situations such as this the nearest approach to an experimental manipulation that is open either to psychologist or sociologist is what may be called experimental selection; that is, the selection of samples of individuals in such a way that one sample has been exposed to the causal variable in one form while other samples have been exposed to it in other forms. This is what psychologists do when they select samples of children who have been brought up in institutions and compare their delinquency rate (or any other characteristic) with that of children brought up by their own families. Similarly it is open to the sociologist who offers explanations of delinquency in individuals to select samples which have been exposed to different forms of the causal variable in which he is interested. It is true that the criteria which he would have to specify for the selection of his samples might well be more numerous and difficult to satisfy than those of the psychologist, and might sometimes be harder to specify in quantifiable terms (although psychologists' criteria too are often made quantifiable only with great ingenuity). But this does not mean that we are setting the sociologist an impossible task.

Until sociologists have accepted these standards of evidence and produced studies which comply with them, it might be thought a waste of time to carry the discussion of causal factors further. We have still to consider, however, not only the relationships which are logically possible between explanations of delinquency, but also the uses to which they can be put; and these will be the subject of the next chapter.

7

EXPLANATION

AND

PREDICTION

The explanations which I have outlined in the four previous chapters are
of six kinds:

A. Individualistic explanations in terms of
  1. inborn differences between delinquents and non-delinquents,
     whether congenital or hereditary;
  2. maladjustment resulting from faulty upbringing;
  3. weak ethical learning as a normal result of working-class ways of
     child-rearing.

B. Environmental explanations in terms of
  4. economic conditions;
  5. deteriorating urban areas;
  6. sub-cultures with unofficial codes of conduct.

To what extent should these six types of explanation be treated as con-
flicting rivals? In the first place, to what extent are they contradictory? I
have already pointed out, for example, that *some* psychoanalytic accounts
of the development of personality in delinquents look very like some parts
of the ethical learning theory; there seems to be what might be called an
'overlap of meaning'. Another example of such an overlap can usually be
found between explanations in terms of deteriorating urban areas and those
in terms of sub-cultures with deviant norms; it is very rare to find anyone
stating the former without some references to the attitudes and codes of the
inhabitants. But such overlaps should not be exaggerated; it is possible to
state each of the six types of theory in such a way that it does contradict
each of the others. For each theory emphasises the causal importance of a
different sort of variable. Hence it implies that even if in the case of a given
individual the variables emphasised by each of the other theories were
found to be at a level which is within normal limits for non-delinquents, the
individual would be delinquent if the variable emphasised by the theory in
question were *not* within normal limits.

But though they may be essentially contradictory, hypotheses may avoid
conflict if they are offered as explanations of different groups of observations.
For example, if psychoanalysts limited themselves to the explanation of
sexual offences and irrational stealing, while sociologists limited them-

selves to property offences with a rational economic motive, there would be no conflict.

Suppose, however, that two or more theories with little overlap of meaning are put forward to account for the same sort of offences – such as theft. There seems at first sight to be another way in which they might avoid conflict. I have already pointed out that it is possible for each to be stated either in a 'strong' or a 'weak' form. In the 'strong' form, a theory claims to explain most (or even all) of the cases in question; in the weak form it merely claims to explain some. It is only when two or more theories claim to explain 51 per cent or more of the observations that they are in conflict; if none – or only one – does so, conflict seems avoidable. Reasoning in this way, a psychoanalyst and a sociologist might agree that while many thieves stole because of their early relationships with their fathers, another substantial fraction did so simply because they belonged to a delinquent subculture; one of them might even allow the other to use the word 'most', although this is unlikely.

Conflict could still arise, of course, if the pair of them were presented with a selection of individual thieves and asked to decide in each case whether maladjustment or sub-cultural influences were primarily responsible. In some individuals the symptoms of maladjustment might be so marked that the sociologist would concede the importance of that factor; in others they might be so hard to detect that the psychoanalyst would leave them to the sociologist. There would probably, however be a third group of individuals in whom the psychoanalyst would diagnose a moderate degree of maladjustment, and ascribe their delinquencies to it, while the sociologist would argue that they were maladjusted merely by the psychoanalyst's standards, which the sociologist might go on to classify as 'middle-class'; and he would claim that what seemed to the psychoanalyst the symptoms of maladjustment were endemic in the sub-culture from which the thieves came.

Theoretically, it should be possible to resolve differences of this sort. If a sample of men from the same sub-culture who were known to be law-abiding were carefully matched with the sample of thieves, then from the psychoanalyst's assumptions maladjustment should be found to be either more frequent or more intense – and preferably both – among the thieves.

When we are trying to estimate the comparative importance of different factors in the generation of delinquency, it is obviously better to investigate the incidence of these factors among the same samples of delinquents and controls than to compare the findings of different investigations, each concerned with a different factor or group of factors, and using its own separately selected sample and controls. A few investigations have attempted this, with varying degrees of success.[1] All unfortunately were unable to overcome certain difficulties. Some variables – such as family size – are hard data, leaving little room for subjective error, but the classification of factors such as 'family discipline', even into such broad categories as 'strict', 'lax' or 'inconsistent', depends very much on the investigator's standards and even on the circumstances in which he finds the family when he visits. Moreover,

[1] S. and E. Glueck, 1950; T. Ferguson, 1952; Carr-Saunders, Mannheim and Rhodes. 1942.

factors of the kind which sociologists regard as important – norms, value-systems, goals, and so forth – do not lend themselves even to the crude sort of measurement which is possible in the case of domestic or psychological variables.

Nevertheless, to the extent that investigators have found it possible to measure the incidence or intensity of psychological, domestic and social factors in the same sample of delinquents and controls, the result is not so much to eliminate some of the factors studied[1] as to reveal weak positive associations between delinquency and a large number of factors, constitutional, psychological and social.

Results such as these have led to what is sometimes called the 'multiple-factor' assumption. This may, however, take two forms, and it is not always clear which of these is in the mind of a given criminologist at a given moment.

The 'Peculiar-Factor' Assumption. It is possible to cling to the assumption that a single factor has predisposed each individual to commit his offences, by supposing that there are different sub-groups of offenders, each with its own type of predisposing factor but not differing from non-offenders in respect of any other variable. As an imaginary example, it can be suggested that there is a sub-group whose only abnormality lies in the form of parental discipline under which they were brought up, while in the case of another sub-group the only variable that is outside normal limits is the criminality of their current associates. It is not logically essential to this interpretation that the sub-groups should be distinguishable in any other characteristic – for example, that one should consist of property offenders, the other of men of violence – although if this proved to be so it would strengthen the interpretation. This descendant of the 'single-factor' assumption might be called the 'peculiar-factor' assumption.

The 'Factor-Interaction' Assumption. The alternative interpretation of modern studies such as those cited is based on the 'factor-interaction' assumption. This is that, however one sub-divides offenders, it will be found in many cases that no single variable is outside the limits which are observable in the case of non-offenders, and that the abnormality lies in the combination of moderate deviations from the average in two or more variables. Thus it is theoretically possible that in samples of offenders and non-offenders the worst cases of poverty and lax parental discipline might both be found among the non-offenders' families, and that the only feature which distinguished the offenders' families might be the combination of both poverty and lax discipline in the same family.

A rough attempt to explore the fact or-interaction assumption has been made by the Gluecks, using data from their dossiers of 500 delinquent and 500 non-delinquent Massachusetts boys.[2] They observed that whether or not certain personality traits in their boys – such as high intelligence – were associated with delinquency, those who exhibited these traits were more

[1] Although this occasionally happens; Ferguson's results suggested that the apparent association between family size and delinquency was an illusion resulting from an association between overcrowding and delinquency; see p. 76.
[2] 1962.

likely to be delinquents if their family environment exhibited certain characteristics – such as faulty parental discipline. From such observation they inferred that 'certain sociocultural circumstances operate as catalytic agents in the delinquency of children possessing certain character traits regardless of whether these traits are in themselves neutral as regards criminogenesis. . . .' Although the nature of their data, and the levels of significance which they were prepared to accept render their actual conclusions doubtful,[1] their attempt is a step in an interesting direction.

THE FUNCTION OF EXPLANATION

At this point – if not before it – we should pause to consider the purposes of causal studies. A purpose which has motivated a great many searches for scientific explanation is the intellectual satisfaction which success provides, not only to the searchers but also to interested onlookers. From a purely utilitarian point of view, this justification of causal studies gives them the status of a spectator sport, although of a kind usually regarded – at least by middle-class intellectuals – as superior to football.

In the field of delinquency, explanations have undoubtedly been used to provide intellectual satisfaction. They have also at times been used to support or induce a moral attitude to the delinquent, as, for example, when they are made the basis for a deterministic exculpation of the individual. His upbringing, his associates, the high unemployment which prevailed in the years immediately after he left school, are aggregated into an explanation of his thefts in which moral choice is not an item. In this way, the results of causal studies can be built into an argument against a retributive attitude to penal measures. More rarely, the supporters of retributionism sometimes point to case histories in which none of the variables whose connection with delinquency has been established seem to be present, and regard these as evidence for a residual factor, roughly corresponding to sin. I am concerned not with the logic of either use, but simply with the fact that in the field of penology scientific explanation is sometimes applied to this unusual end.

Most modern justifications of science, however, seem to appeal at some stage to the profit-motive. In the penological field, causal investigations could have two obvious applications.

Remedies. One obvious function of causal studies is to suggest remedies for delinquent behaviour once it has manifested itself. Certainly they sometimes fulfil this function. Delinquency attributed to mental disorder often ceases when the disorder is treated, although success of this kind is more frequent where the disorder is a well-marked psychosis than where it is diagnosed as compulsive or maladjusted behaviour or as psychopathy. Epileptics may be prevented from the violence which sometimes precedes or follows their fits by giving sedatives which avert the fits. Reasoning in this way the staffs of approved schools and other institutions often try to remedy the deficiencies of a delinquent's upbringing by supplying the con-

---

[1] Most of the family characteristics were assessed impressionistically by a social worker, while most of the personality traits were assessed as a result of an interview with a psychiatrist. The number of associations studied was so large that a substantial and unidentifiable group of them is likely to have been the result of pure chance.

sistent discipline, or the understanding and affection, which that upbringing seems to them to have lacked.

The problem of assessing the remedial efficacy of penal measures will be
discussed in Chapter 12. The point which is relevant here is that penologists
are sometimes in danger of assuming that the remedy for a social evil must
consist of attacking the cause. This fallacy probably originates in the
analogy of medicine, but of medicine at a stage which that technique has
now outgrown. Doctors are certainly happiest when they can eradicate a
virus, remove a diseased appendix, or set a bone, but often they have to be
content with treatment which compensates for, rather than removes, the
cause of the disorder; and sometimes they even choose such treatment in
preference to attacking the cause, as when they decide against excising a
peptic ulcer. In psychotherapeutic medicine, which is a closer analogy to
penal treatment, practitioners are beginning to recognise that while they
may know the cause of a disorder with a fair degree of certainty, it does not
always follow that it can be directly attacked. The effects upon a very
young infant of a seriously abnormal parent – such as a sadistic mother –
may be almost impossible to remedy. Certainly the longer the cause persists
and the older the child when treatment first begins, the harder is the psychotherapist's task. Even if there is some hope of eventual success by methods
directed at the cause, there may be methods of the compensatory type which
are quicker, more effective and less wasteful of highly trained manpower.
Thus, although bedwetting in children seems to be associated with separation from parents, it is often easier to remedy by conditioning techniques
than by psychotherapy.

In the field of penology both causal and compensatory attempts at treatment can be observed. The older methods – deterrence and the temporary
or permanent elimination of the offender – are compensatory. For some
time past, however, it has been regarded as more scientific, as well as more
humane, to apply causal techniques. For example, the emphasis of most
psychological explanations upon the importance of parental attitudes to
children has suggested that those in charge of juvenile delinquents –
whether on probation or in approved schools or elsewhere – should try to
supply the deficiencies of the parents, and provide a reliable and kindly
figure to whom the delinquent can form an attachment and from whom he
will receive consistent discipline and a pattern of conduct on which he can
model his own. Theories which emphasise the importance of the delinquent's associates and of possibilities for orthodox achievement of his goals
have supported measures which separate him from his friends at school or
on the street corner, or which include placing him in a 'steady' job with a
room in a carefully supervised hostel.

It would unquestionably be unscientific to neglect to experiment with
causal techniques. It would be equally unscientific, on the other hand, to
assume that they are bound to be more effective than compensatory
methods. As we shall see, such evidence as it is possible to obtain suggests
that the situation is not nearly so simple as that.

Prevention. It also seems reasonable to expect causal investigations to
point to measures which would reduce the incidence of delinquents or their

delinquencies. Genetic studies suggest that eugenic measures would yield some benefit, though it is only in the rather specialised group of epileptic and psychotic offenders that the yield would be more than negligible. Psychological studies suggest that parents – especially in the families of unskilled manual workers – should be the targets of propaganda on the principles of child-rearing, with considerable emphasis on the role of the father, consistent (rather than stern) discipline, and the use of the child's emotional dependence as an instrument of ethical training. Studies of social factors suggest that measures such as rehousing are likely to reduce delinquency only if they are applied so as to break up slum communities and separate their members altogether from their old haunts and neighbours; that fluctuations in unemployment levels and wage rates are to be avoided for this, if no other, reason; and that raising the school-leaving age may raise the rate of delinquency for those who are kept at school against their inclinations. These are merely examples of conclusions which might conceivably be drawn from some of the observations I have mentioned. But preventive measures which are applied to the whole population or to large sections of it are unlikely to have spectacular effects. It seems reasonable to assume that if more intensive techniques could be applied to the minority which is likely to become seriously delinquent they would achieve more.

PREDICTION

Partly in this hope, partly because of the complications of causal hypotheses which I have outlined, some penologists have in recent years begun to abandon causal thinking for what is known as the 'predictive' approach. Historically this was first used in an attempt to distinguish between penitentiary inmates who were likely to keep out of trouble if released early on parole and those who were unlikely to do so, and some of the major advances in the technique – notably by L. T. Wilkins[1] – have been concerned with the subsequent conduct of already convicted offenders. Another use of the technique, however, which is likely to become increasingly important, consists of attempts to identify future delinquents among unconvicted juveniles with sufficient accuracy to justify the application of special social measures to them; the first successful use of prediction in this way was achieved by the Gluecks.[2] These two uses can be distinguished by calling the former 'relapse-prediction' and the latter 'delinquency-prediction'.

In either case, although confusion has been introduced by the increasing refinement of the arithmetical methods used and the intrusion of some rather muddled ethical doubts, the rationale of prediction is simple. Among any group of individuals, no amount of information will enable us to say with certainty that this individual or that will in the future commit an offence. But information about the past behaviour of individuals with similar characteristics, if it is analysed to the best advantage, will enable us to separate our group into sub-groups of which different percentages will commit offences, or in other words into sub-groups whose members have different probabilities of doing so.

[1] 1955.   [2] 1959.

The following example shows the simplest kind of prediction. Out of twenty boys who left school in 1963, let us suppose that half were convicted of larceny within a year. In addition to this information, only one other fact is known about each boy – whether he had a job to go to when he left. Our information can then be tabulated thus:

convicted		unconvicted	
a.	no job	k.	a job
b.	no job	l.	a job
c.	a job	m.	a job
d.	no job	n.	no job
e.	no job	o.	a job
f.	no job	p.	a job
g.	a job	q.	no job
h.	no job	r.	a job
i.	no job	s.	a job
j.	no job	t.	a job

Clearly, having a job to go to is strongly associated with keeping out of trouble. More precisely, if the boys are sorted into the ten with a job and the ten without, only two of the former got into trouble, while eight of the latter did. If, with no more information than this, we were simply told that a given boy *had* a job to go to, and were asked to guess whether he got into trouble or not, obviously our best guess would be that he did not; if we were unlucky he might be one of the two with jobs who *did* get into trouble, but we would have an 8 in 10 chance of being right.

Suppose that we are now presented with a different group of twenty boys who have just left school and are told no more about each than that he has or has not a job to go to. We are asked to predict which will and which will not get into trouble within a year. All we can do is to use the information from the first sample, and say that fewer of those with jobs to go to will get into trouble than of those without jobs. If both our samples had been much larger – say 200 or 2,000 instead of 20 – we might go further and predict that something like 20 per cent of those with jobs and 80 per cent of those without would get into trouble. Almost certainly, the actual percentages would be a little more or less; but the larger the numbers in both samples the smaller the error would be.

But if predictions are to achieve sufficient accuracy to be of practical use, they must in fact be based on many more items of information about each individual. As soon as we have to deal with two or more items, however, the arithmetic becomes more complicated. Suppose that we know not only whether each boy had a job to go to but also whether he had ever played truant at school:

convicted

a.	truant; no job	f.	not truant; no job
b.	truant; no job	g.	truant; a job
c.	truant; a job	h.	not truant; no job
d.	truant; no job	i.	truant; no job
e.	truant; no job	j.	not truant; no job

unconvicted

k.	not truant; a job	*p.*	not truant; a job
l.	not truant; a job	*q.*	not truant; no job
m.	not truant; a job	*r.*	truant; a job
n.	truant; no job	*s.*	truant; a job
o.	truant; a job	*t.*	not truant; a job

It will do us no good to sort them out twice, once into those with and without jobs, and once into truants and non-truants; we need some way of sorting them which combines both pieces of information. The simplest method, which was actually used by early predictors, is to give each boy one point for having a job and one for being a non-truant, and then sort them out according to the number of points:

number of boys with	*number convicted*
no points: 6	5
one point: 9	5
two points: 5	0

This enables us to sort the boys into three groups, each with a different rate of conviction; and the accuracy of our guesses has been slightly increased, since we can guess that any boy with no points was convicted with only a 1 in 6 chance of being wrong, and we can say with complete certainty that any boy with two points was not convicted. If this rough formula is applied to a new sample, and used to predict convictions, it will be slightly more accurate than the first. It has the defect, however, that it does not make the best possible use of our information. For it gives equal weight to having a job and being a non-truant, whereas a glance at the information shows that truancy distinguishes less markedly between the delinquents and the non-delinquents than does having a job: 6 out of 9 non-truants kept out of trouble, but 8 out of 10 with jobs were also unconvicted. We should do better if instead of giving one point for each we gave points in those proportions – for example, only 6/9 or 0·7 for being a non-truant, and 8/10 or 0·8 for having a job (or 7 points and 8 points if we wanted to avoid decimals). This would enable us to draw better dividing lines between the sub-groups:

number of boys with	*number convicted*
0 *points:* 6	5 = 83%
7 *points:* 4	3 = 75%
8 *points:* 5	2 = 40%
15 *points:* 5	0 = 0%

In practice, the information obtainable consists of larger numbers of variables, but each have rather weak associations with conviction. In order to extract out of this information the most accurate divisions into sub-groups more refined formulae have been used by L. T. Wilkins; but the aim of the technique remains the same – to sort individuals into sub-groups between whose conviction rates there is the greatest possible difference.

Relapse Prediction. These methods are fairly successful in predicting reconviction rates of sub-groups of known offenders to whom some form of penal treatment has been applied. The classic example is the formula derived by Wilkins from his sample of ex-borstal boys. When applied to a later sample this formula discriminated between different probability sub-groups slightly *more* effectively than it had done in the case of the original sample:

TABLE 18 Validating the Borstal prediction formula

probability sub-group	percentage not reconvicted within 3½ years	
	in original sample	in later sample
A	87	81
B	67	68
X	not predicted	not predicted
C	34	33
D	13	0
	N=385	N=338

Relapse prediction can be put to several practical uses. It can be employed, as it was by its American inventors, to identify individuals who can be discharged early from institutional custody with a low risk of committing further crimes. It could be used to identify those with the highest chances of relapse in order to subject them to measures which for one reason or another – they might be too costly – cannot be applied to the whole group.

Alternatively, relapse prediction can be used in testing the comparative efficacy of different penal measures. As we shall see in Chapter 12 one of the difficulties of this task is to eliminate the effect of other variables associated with higher or lower reconviction-rates, and this can be achieved to a certain extent by incorporating them in a prediction formula, and comparing the reconvictions of similar probability sub-groups after differing penal measures. Thus Wilkins used his formula to compare the efficacy of short and long stays in closed and open borstals:

TABLE 19 Prediction used to compare results

probability sub-group	percentage not convicted within 3½ years after leaving			
	'open borstals'		'closed borstals'	
	long stays	short stays	long stays	short stays
A+B	60	86	67	67
X	55	67	58	54
C+D	40	37	27	30

Taken at their face value,[1] the percentages suggest that, however high the

[1] In fact, there are objections to Wilkins' use of *his* prediction formula for this purpose. It was designed to use the minimum number of variables with the maximum combined power of discrimination among the sample *as a whole*; but it is possible that a variable which was discarded from the formula because it did not add materially to this discriminatory power would in fact have discriminated between boys likely to benefit and boys not likely to benefit from this regime or that. For example, although he found that the judgements of staff had a low predictive value when applied to the sample as a whole, it is conceivable that they could tell which boys would benefit from open borstals.

H

probability of reconviction, the actual rates are lower after a stay – preferably a short stay – in an open borstal.

It seems likely that this use of relapse-prediction will eventually be developed into a method of selecting the type of sentence which has the highest probability of deterring or otherwise reforming an offender with given characteristics.[1]

The Limitations of Relapse Prediction. Such uses, however, have certain limitations which it would be dangerous to ignore. The power of a prediction formula to discriminate between probability sub-groups depends on the similarity between the sample from which it was derived and the sample to which it is being applied; as the similarity lessens so it weakens, although it may not altogether disappear. Thus, for example, the power of Wilkins' formula is less when it is applied not to borstal boys but to ordinary prisoners; and it has been found that even when applied to borstal boys its power has decreased with the lapse of time since the original sample left borstal.[2]

Ethical Objections. A different sort of limitation arises from popular distrust of statistical methods of arriving at decisions, especially when these have important effects upon the lives of individuals. To some people it is an objectionable notion that the choice between probation, a fine, or imprisonment for an offender, or the determination of the time which he spends under supervision or in prison, should be made not by another human being but by a multiple regression equation. In some cases the objection seems to be that the equation cannot be as sensitive as a human arbiter to individual differences between offenders. To this the supporters of predictive methods could reply that if the criterion is the accuracy of discrimination, investigation shows that even experienced human beings are inferior to mathematical formulae in this respect, probably because they are unable to give different weight to each of a comparatively large variety of factors.[3]

What ought to be conceded by the supporters of prediction is that since the factors which their equations take into account are necessarily those which appear *frequently* in offenders' dossiers, it is not always illogical to suspend the application of such an equation in the occasional case in which a really unusual factor appears. If Wilkins' borstal equation is again taken as an example, there are three logical groupings of factors:

1. those which were expressly taken into account:
      drunkenness;
      prior offences resulting in a fine;
      prior offences resulting in prison or approved school;
      prior offences resulting in probation;

---

[1] Something of this sort was probably in the minds of the Streatfield Committee on the business of the Criminal Courts when they recommended that judges and magistrates should be provided with a 'sentencers' handbook' (1961.86).

[2] See Little, 1963.

[3] An impressive collection of evidence on this subject will be found in Meehl, 1954. Wilkins himself found his predictive method superior in accuracy to the judgements of borstal governors and housemasters, as expressed in their written reports on individual inmates, although to do the latter justice it is doubtful whether they intended their reports as forecasts of reconvictions.

not living with parents;
home in an industrial area;
length of the longest period in any one job;
2. those considered in Wilkins' analysis, but excluded because they did
not add appreciably to the discriminatory power of the equation, for
example:
   age at first conviction;
   family structure at time of current offence;
   whether the offence was committed by a gang,
   and if so whether the offender was the leader;
3. those which were not considered in the analysis, either because the
data were not available for enough cases (for example, the result of a
Rorschach test), or because they were in any case unlikely to occur
in more than a small fraction of cases – for example, illiteracy.

Let us imagine a borstal classification centre which is under instructions
to use Wilkins' equation in allocating boys to different types of borstals. In
what sort of case is it logical to allow the classifiers to ignore or modify the
advice of the equation in the light of a known factor about an individual boy?
Clearly not if the factor appears in group 1, since in that case the equation
already takes it into account. Nor would it be logical to do so if the factor
belonged to group 2, since that would imply that its predictive value was
greater than that of at least one factor in group 1, in which case it would have
been in group 1. But there would be no such illogicality in allowing a factor
in group 3 to override the advice of the equation, provided
(a) that there is some *a priori* probability that it is associated with
    response to penal treatment;
(b) that it is unlikely to be closely linked to a factor which already
    appears in group 1 or 2;
(c) that this is done only occasionally, and not regularly.

   Some critics also appear to assume that the use of predictive methods
deprives human beings of any spontaneous role in the treatment of
offenders. In fact it is exceedingly doubtful whether it is practicable or
desirable to allow predictive methods to modify the day-to-day relations
between offenders and the staff who are in contact with them. In the first
place, knowledge of an offender's chances of reconviction may alter the
attitudes of staff towards him in an undesirable way: although Wilkins
showed that his borstal governors and housemasters were unwarrantably
optimistic about the future careers of their boys, those careers might have
been even worse had the boys not been handled by optimistic staff.
Secondly, even if predictive methods did show that a certain type of relationship between staff and offenders yielded the best results with a given type of
offender, it is unlikely that staff could successfully introduce artificial and
self-conscious variations into their manner towards individual offenders,
and in any case such variations might be resented. It seems more practicable
to allow predictions to decide between different regimes – or different types
of probation officer – for different sorts of offender, but not to allow predictions to dictate strained modifications of the spontaneous attitude of
penal staff towards individuals.

A third criticism is directed at the apparent disregard of predictive methods for causal relationships. For example, a discharged prisoner's chances of reconviction vary both with his type of personality and with the frequency of his previous convictions, but we assume that there is a much closer and more direct causal link between his personality and his relapse than between his previous convictions and his relapse. Yet it will almost certainly be found that his previous convictions are a more effective predictor of his chances of future conviction. This does not in fact weaken the assumption that there is a close causal relationship between personality and reconviction; conversely it does not justify any assumption that there is some mysterious and hitherto unsuspected causal link between a conviction in 1961 and reconviction in 1965. The explanation is that at present our most accurate index of the sort of personality traits that increase a man's chances of conviction is not a psychological description, nor even a score on a psychological test,[1] but simply the frequency of convictions. Thus the causal chain that links the predictive variable of previous convictions to the predicted variable of reconviction is an indirect one, and has as its middle link the offender's personality; yet the latter, though closer to reconviction in the causal chain, is of less use as a predictive variable because it cannot yet be quantified with enough accuracy.

This example illustrates several points about predictive procedures. They must select the quantifiable in preference to the unquantifiable variable, and, where both are quantifiable, the more closely associated variable. Yet if the result were the selection of a variable whose nature made it difficult to imagine what sort of causal link could account for its association with the predicted variable, we should rightly be worried lest the association turned out to be due to some chance factor. If, for example, we found that the offenders who had the lowest subsequent reconviction rate were those who were most heavily in debt,[2] we should hesitate to use this as a predictive variable until we had constructed some plausible explanation. When it occurs to us that substantial loans are seldom granted by banks or credit companies without investigation of the borrower's circumstances and antecedents, it begins to seem likely that the extent of a man's debts might be a good index of the sort of background that is likely both to satisfy bank managers and to predispose him against future offences.

Moreover, causal thinking is not only unavoidable but actually desirable when we are *selecting* data as potential predictive variables; for example, when we have to decide whether it is worth calculating the association between baldness and recidivism. In other words, while the final selection of variables for the prediction formula should be made on mathematical criteria, the original collection of data must – if it is to be finite – be based on some sort of causal assumptions. It is true that the use of fast computers will soon make it practicable to calculate the predictive value of any set of variables that is likely to be recorded about any substantial sample of human beings; the limiting factor will then be the amount of detail that

---

[1] Even if test scores were more accurate, they are less often available for a given offender than his previous convictions; and this is likely to be true for some years to come.

[2] This is said to have been observed by investigators in the U.S.A.

human beings can be persuaded to record about each other. But this merely shifts the point at which it is necessary to decide what data could conceivably be useful, and this decision involves causal thinking.

Delinquency Prediction. When instead of predicting relapse among known offenders we try to predict first delinquency among non-offenders, new difficulties arise. First, in comparison with the variables associated with reconvictions in detected offenders, the variables that have to be used when the sample consists of non-offenders[1] are less satisfactory. Variables such as previous convictions are easy to quantify, and are comparatively immune from distortion by subjective judgement. In contrast, the variables which are most useful in predicting first delinquency are such that they are not easy to quantify, and have to be assessed impressionistically. The Gluecks analysed their data about 500 delinquent and 500 non-delinquent Massachusetts boys in order to find out which variables would have most efficiently separated the sample of 1,000 into groups with high and low probabilities of becoming delinquent. They found that tests of intelligence and educational achievement, though they provided quantified information, were of less use than personality traits, as assessed partly by psychiatric interview and partly by the Rorschach test; and that these in turn were less accurate as predictive variables than were impressions of the boy's family atmosphere gained as a result of visits by their investigator, and analysed under five headings:[2]

1. father's discipline of the boy;
2. mother's supervision of the boy;
3. father's affection for the boy;
4. mother's affection for the boy;
5. the cohesiveness of the family.

Even these variables, however, have two disadvantages. First, they are less accurate in their predictions than the variables used to predict reconvictions in detected offenders. This is partly due to the fact that in a random sample of non-offenders only a small minority will eventually become offenders, so that any formula which will correctly identify a large percentage of the future offenders will also label as probable offenders a substantial number of individuals who, in the event, do not become delinquent. Among detected offenders, on the other hand, the fraction who are eventually reconvicted is much nearer half of the sample, which makes it easier to find a formula that will separate them into groups with smaller minorities of 'incorrectly'[3] grouped individuals.

The Gluecks inadvertently misjudged the accuracy of their prediction formula, as a result of selecting their sample so that it consisted of delinquents and non-delinquents in equal proportions; if they had made it representative of the general population of boys – by ensuring that, say, 20

[1] Or, more precisely, non-offenders and an unknown fraction of undetected offenders.

[2] 1959.

[3] Strictly speaking, of course, there is no such thing as an 'incorrect' grouping of an individual; it is inherent in the method that groups will contain minorities who in the event do not conform to the probability assigned to them. Otherwise we should be dealing not in probabilities but in certainties.

per cent were delinquents instead of 50 per cent – they would have found their prediction formula less accurate.

Part of the reason for the lower predictive accuracy of delinquency-prediction formulae as compared with relapse prediction formulae, however, lies in the nature of the predictive variables themselves, which, as we have seen, can be assessed only impressionistically. For example, when paternal discipline is classified as over-strict, lax, inconsistent, or satisfactory, this is done by an investigator who actually has the family under observation for comparatively short periods – that is, while he is visiting the home; during his visits the atmosphere is bound to be a little artificial, and indeed, the boy's father may appear strict simply through his anxiety that his children should not be a nuisance to the visitor. If the investigator relies on the mother's descriptions of her husband and his relations with his son, these may be either too charitable or too uncharitable.

In these circumstances it is remarkable that the Gluecks managed to devise a formula which proved as accurate as theirs did. In one test, for example, out of a total sample of 650 boys, none of them as yet delinquent, who were followed up in the Cambridge-Somerville Youth Study[1], 100 were selected whose records included the data required by the Glueck formula. A panel consisting of a psychiatrist and two penal administrators had already predicted, after protracted discussions of all the data available for each boy, whether he would turn out to be delinquent or not. Mrs Glueck was given only the five items of information required for her formula. The results were as follows:

TABLE 20 Prediction versus human judgment

boys who were eventually	actual outcome	of which there were correctly predicted by	
		Mrs Glueck	panel[2]
delinquent	20	18	18[2]
non-delinquent	80	73	47[2]

Thus, while Mrs Glueck did not correctly identify a higher percentage of the future *offenders*, she was much better at identifying those who would keep out of trouble, for she labelled as future offenders a total of 25 boys, and was wrong in 7 cases, while the panel labelled no less than 51 boys as future offenders and were wrong in 33 cases.

The second disadvantage which has to be faced by delinquency-prediction methods is the nature of the investigation that is required to obtain the necessary data. A visit by a trained investigator to every family is just practicable when the method is applied to a sample, but if it were to be applied to the population in general, or even to families with boys in high delinquency areas, the cost in terms of money and scarce personnel would be enormous. Moreover, if it were applied to families in which no delin-

[1] See Powers and Witmer, 1951.
[2] These are in fact the best scores of individual members.

quency had yet manifested itself, it would be strenuously opposed as an invasion of privacy.

If delinquency-prediction is to be put to a practical use, it must find some sort of data which can be collected by means that are not open to these objections. There is one part of the social services with which practically every able-bodied child is brought into contact before the age at which delinquency usually appears – namely, the school; and at school he is under the observation of teachers for considerable periods. D. H. Stott has therefore experimented in Glasgow with a questionnaire which can be completed by teachers about individual pupils. Since the questionnaire confines itself to behaviour that is observed by the teacher, it does not entail objectionable enquiries. Stott's sample – 404 boys on probation and 415 non-delinquent controls of the same age and from the same schools – was similar in size and composition to the Gluecks'; but he took the added precaution of calculating how well his predictive formula would work if applied to the general population of Glasgow boys, in which only a minority become delinquents. He estimated that if he used a formula which would correctly identify 74 per cent of the future delinquents, he would incorrectly identify an even larger number who would not become delinquents; if he were content with identifying 60 per cent of the future delinquents he would incorrectly identify roughly the same number of non-delinquents.[1]

This illustrates an important point: that the practical application of predictive methods compels us to come to a decision in which arithmetic is of little help. If we are going to subject likely delinquents (or likely recidivists) to some sort of measure to which the rest of our population is not to be subjected – and this is the main point of prediction – we must decide how many people are to be subjected unnecessarily in order that we shall be sure of applying our measures to a large enough percentage of the people for whom they are necessary. In situations where the consequences of failing to apply measures are very serious and the measures themselves are not too drastic, we accept a high percentage of what can be called 'unnecessary applications', as, for instance, when we quarantine people who have been in contact with smallpox or rabies. When the consequences of failure to apply it are less serious, or the measures very drastic or expensive, we become more concerned about the possibility of unnecessary applications; we do not automatically disqualify epileptics from driving motor cars. If the people we are dealing with have already committed offences and are thus subject to compulsory interference, we are less concerned about the possibility that we are applying measures to some who do not need them; we are prepared to use predictive methods to determine when they are to be released from detention, although we know that a substantial percentage of those whom we detain longer would not in fact have been reconvicted.

If it is a question of applying some preventive measure to a group of children whose score on a prediction table indicates that only about 50 per cent will become delinquent, we are apt to be very impressed with the high percentage who will be unnecessarily – some would say 'unjustly' – sub-

[1] See Stott, 1960; it seems possible that the selectivity of his formula might be improved by using a more refined system of weighting.

jected to the measure. Certainly if the measure itself is unpleasant, either for the child or his family, the opposition which it will arouse will probably defeat the object in any case. This is a valid tactical objection, for example, to any supervisory measures which appear to stigmatise children as delinquents. But there are less authoritarian and obtrusive expedients; school welfare staff can usually find a good excuse for visiting such children's families, and if the situation there seems unsatisfactory trained social workers may be able to establish sufficiently friendly relations with one of the parents to be able to influence them. Attempts can be made to interest the children themselves in carefully chosen spare-time activities. Measures of this kind may be open to the objection that they are costly in terms of money or skilled manpower, but hardly to ethical or tactical objections.

PART THREE

★

THE SYSTEM OF DISPOSAL

8

AIMS AND

ASSUMPTIONS

The task of describing the penal measures of a society, and the aims which these are intended to achieve, should be attempted with as much scientific objectivity and detachment as the task of describing its offenders. It is rendered slightly easier by the fact that those who order or carry out penal measures do so subject to laws which, unlike those who incur penal measures, they tend to obey. The result is that a description of what may be called 'the law of disposal' is a fairly accurate though limited description of what takes place, and it can be supplemented by numerical descriptions of sentencing practice, such as those which can be extracted from the annual Criminal Statistics. More difficult is the interpretation of the present-day aims of the penal measures applied. Is imprisonment meant to be a deterrent to imitators, an opportunity for long-term reform of the individual, or simply a form of elimination for the protection of the public? Occasionally the statutes themselves are explicit: for instance, the purpose of the sentence of 'preventive detention'[1] was 'to protect the public'. But that is not the last word. Certainly it is a guide to a court when considering sentence; it must even place a limit on the extent to which the executive allocate preventive detainees to establishments with deliberately relaxed security. But it does not prevent them from attempting to combine this aim with the reformation of the individual; and in their published statement of policy and practice[2] the Prison Commission said 'Although the preventive detainee is deemed *ex hypothesi* to be incorrigible by any method of penal treatment, it is both right and necessary that the system should be such as will, so far as possible, fit him to lead an honest and industrious life on discharge.' This illustrates the need to take note not only of the explicit aims of the statute, but also of any published statements of policy in the carrying out of the measures. For this purpose statements by Home Secretaries and other Government spokesmen during the passage of penal legislation are valuable, but may become out of date as experience in the application of the act modifies policy. Moreover, they are almost always designed to steer the frail bark of the Bill between the clashing rocks of the retributive-deterrent and the humanitarian-remedial philosophies, with the result that they are often less precise about the aims of the penal measures than are the carefully drafted publications of the Advisory Councils or their Departments. For this reason I have generally preferred the latter.

[1] and of the 'extended sentence' which has replaced it: see Chapter 14.
[2] 1960.

A source which must not be neglected is the growing literature of critical descriptions of the way in which penal measures – usually institutional measures – are administered, some written by penal reformers, others by offenders with a talent for autobiography. They are a valuable antidote to the official descriptions of the ways in which committees or departments think or hope the measures are applied. But like all antidotes they too are dangerous if absorbed in sufficient quantity. In almost all cases the author is at best waving the banner of some kind of reform, and at worst revenging himself for his own experiences. Since the number of people who can gain first-hand experience of prison or probation is limited, this kind of literature is valuable as experience at second hand; but it must not be mistaken for scientific description.

In attempting to answer the question 'What form do penal measures take?' I shall therefore deliberately rely as much as I can on official descriptions, not because these are unbiased, but because the best way of finding out what someone *thinks* he is doing is to see what he himself says, and not what someone else says. When attempting to answer the question 'What is our underlying philosophy of punishment?' I have had to range more widely, since official statements tend to skirt this controversial, almost political, subject; and, while I have given first place to professional or semi-professional philosophers, I have not scorned the utterances of Home Secretaries and Lord Chancellors.

PRIMITIVE AND SOPHISTICATED PRINCIPLES

Our assumptions about the nature of both crime and punishment tend to be so deeply ingrained that we are apt either to overlook them completely or, if we notice them, to treat them as axiomatic. It is sometimes instructive to compare the characteristics of sophisticated penal systems with those of more primitive societies, as we did in Chapter 1 when considering the scope of the criminal law; and it may be useful to approach the aims of penal measures in the same way.

Liability. In most primitive systems the offender is liable to penal measures in circumstances which sophisticated codes would treat as partly or entirely excusing him. Examples are cases of self-defence, provocation, infancy, insanity, accident, or mere absence of intention, all of which operate at certain points of the British and other European systems so as to protect the accused from the measures to which he would otherwise be subject. A system of 'absolute liability', in which the person who was physically responsible for the harm caused to another person is subjected to the appropriate penal measures whatever his excuse, seems barbarously inhumane to us. It is worth noting, however, that the British practice is not wholly consistent at this point. Under modern statutes there are whole groups of offences for which the accused is liable to the penalty even if he committed them unknowingly or by accident. Numerous examples are provided by legislation intended to prevent the sale of harmful foodstuffs, or to enforce traffic rules. In these cases it will not help the accused to show that he did not know the food to be adulterated or that he was unaware he was disobeying a traffic signal. Nor is ignorance of the existence of a law an excuse, even if the law is recent or the offender a foreigner. The justification for these inconsistencies is that otherwise it would be so easy for the accused to excuse himself that the prohibition would be unenforceable. In other words, the principle that liability should not be absolute holds good so long as it is not inconvenient.

There is a similar limitation by expediency in the case of insane offenders, many of whom are excused from the measures by the penal system proper, only to be detained in mental hospitals; a practice usually regarded as justified by the principle of 'social defence', which will be discussed later in this chapter.

Vicarious Punishment. Another principle which sophisticated penal codes try to apply is that of 'no vicarious punishment'. In many primitive societies retaliation or redress which for some reason cannot be imposed on the offender himself may be imposed on other members of his family, or is even imposed on both the offender and his family. In medieval England the confiscation of felons' property, which often rendered their families destitute, operated as vicarious punishment. The principle, however, that the penalty should as far as possible affect only the offender is now firmly established, and where this is impossible because of the nature of the penalty, efforts are made to minimise the effect on others. For example, though imprisoning a husband or father may penalise his wife or children, the State tries to ensure that they are maintained and cared for. It is true that the law relating to such matters as the management of public-houses or certain offences by employees of companies sometimes makes the employer liable to penalties incurred by the acts or omissions of his servants. Moreover, as Glanville Williams has pointed out, collective punishments have been imposed on towns and villages in Malaya, Kenya, Aden and Cyprus in order to induce members of these communities to help in the detection and suppression of violent crimes.[1] Coming nearer home, we shall find that if a fine is levied on a juvenile offender the court may – and sometimes must – order the parents to pay it, presumably on the assumption that they could have brought up the child better, or will do so in future.[2] These exceptions, however, merely demonstrate that the principle of 'no vicarious punishment' is not absolute, and is sometimes modified, either by expediency or by other principles.

Double Penalties. Another feature of unsophisticated systems which sometimes appears harsh is the imposition of two or more distinct penalties for the same offence. Felons used not only to suffer death or transportation, but also the forfeiture of property and – if they were not executed – the loss of civil rights. The modern British system, however, though its penalties are milder, by no means excludes the doubling of measures. Fines and imprisonment are usually regarded as alternatives, but for many offences both a fine and imprisonment can be imposed. Disqualification from driving can be coupled with a fine or imprisonment.

Irrevocability of punishment. A feature of almost all penal systems, both primitive and sophisticated, is that once a penalty has been ordered for an

[1] 1961.266.
[2] See Chapter 10.

individual offender it tends to be regarded as irrevocable. This principle is no doubt derived from the retributive conception of punishment: if a penalty is imposed as retribution for a past act, then it should presumably be as unalterable as the act. We shall see how limited is the time within which a court can alter the sentence which it has pronounced, and how after that time only an appellate court can do so, and this, too, within a limited time. Otherwise the law treats the sentence as irrevocable, and an extra-legal device, the royal prerogative of mercy, has to be invoked where the consequences of this seem too objectionable to be borne: for instance, to remit a sentence imposed on someone who is later discovered to be innocent. Some modern types of penal measure, such as probation, are deliberately devised so as to allow modification in the light of the offender's subsequent conduct; but the very necessity for such devices emphasises the underlying assumption of irrevocability.

Unofficial Penalties. Quite apart from combinations which are expressly provided for by the law itself, offenders may suffer other penalties of which the law takes no cognisance. For example, a conviction for certain offences will cost a civil servant his job and his pension; and others may deprive a medical practitioner of his place on the register. In 1963 three professional footballers who had been fined by a criminal court for bribery in connection with the deliberate losing of matches were suspended for life by the Football Association Commission from playing in professional football. Sometimes measures of this kind can be justified on the grounds that the nature of the offence makes it likely that the offender is unsuitable for his type of employment, as when a doctor is convicted of drunkenness in some form; but sometimes the reason seems to be simply that the employing organisation wants to protect its reputation by repudiating the employee. Finally, unless the offender belongs to a neighbourhood in which his offence is regarded tolerantly, he is bound to suffer from a certain amount of social disapproval, which may amount to ostracism. Indeed, this is often stronger if he has been imprisoned than it would be if he had merely been fined or put on probation. Even a trial followed by an acquittal often leaves the offender under considerable suspicion by neighbours and acquaintances; the Scottish verdict of 'not proven' seems almost designed to do so.

AIMS OF PENAL MEASURES

The greatest differences, however, between primitive and sophisticated systems are to be observed in the penal measures themselves and can be found both in the aims of the measures and the techniques used to achieve them. Before these differences are examined it is necessary to draw a distinction between original and contemporary aims. The original aim was what the inventors of a measure intended to achieve by it; the contemporary aim is what its present-day supporters hope that it achieves. Thus the original aim of compelling an offender to compensate his victim may have been to secure justice or – a more practical aim – to prevent the latter (or his sympathisers) from causing further harm to the community's manpower, property or peace by revenging himself in kind. However that may be, those who would like to see this form of penalty used more widely today base their argument on the claim that it has a reformative effect upon the offender.

Another obvious distinction is between aims, original or contemporary, and effects. Some of these may be foreseen and intended, in which case they are part of the aims; or they may be merely foreseen and acceptable, as is the stigma imposed by public conviction. On the other hand, some effects are simply foreseen and deplored, such as the deterioration of a prisoner's relations with his wife and family. Fourthly, some effects are simply not foreseen at all, as happened when the imposition of the death penalty for trivial offences in the eighteenth century caused juries to acquit thieves in the teeth of the evidence. It is, of course, impossible in the nature of things to discover and analyse all the indirect and unforeseen effects of a penal measure; but it is possible – and most desirable – to identify the most obvious and frequent ones and to see to what extent they are compatible with the effects intended by the current supporters of the measure.

Redress. In most primitive penal systems great importance is attached to undoing the harm caused by anti-social actions. Stolen property must be returned or paid for; families of murdered men or raped women must be compensated. In some systems it is only if these rules are not observed that retaliation is permissible or that the penal system proper may be set in motion by an appeal to authority.

Sophisticated systems, in contrast, pay little attention to this aim. It is true that an employer who detects an employee in pilfering or embezzlement sometimes forbears to inform the police on the understanding that his loss will be made good; and occasionally in the court itself a defendant is heard to plead in mitigation that he has restored all or some of the money or goods. Indeed, the court itself may, instead of fining or imprisoning an offender, discharge him or put him on probation with an order to compensate his victim for the loss or the injury. But this method is usually reserved for minor offences against property by offenders with clean records and of course the ability to pay; the majority are dealt with on other principles. Property owners of today rely on insurance and not on the penal system to make good their losses, and only rarely does one bring a civil action against a thief.[1]

Victims of personal violence can seldom hope for compensation from their attackers, not because the latter cannot be identified (they usually can) but because they are almost always without the funds to make adequate payment. Moreover, although the victim's injuries may reduce his ability to look after himself for the rest of his life, he is hardly ever insured against this contingency, which is much less frequent than theft or fire; indeed, only a few insurance companies offer a policy of this kind. The late Margery Fry and her supporters pointed out that our modern penal system was so concerned with punishing or reforming offenders that it ignored the needs of the victim, and they argued that the State was under an obligation to compensate him. Though not accepting the principle that the state is liable

[1] In 1963, however, at Lincoln Assizes, a watchmaker was awarded compensation of £410 against two men convicted of stealing jewellery from him.

for the injuries of victims,[1] the Government has yielded to public demand and established a scheme of financial allowances for the victims of certain crimes.[2]

Retaliation and Retribution. One of the least sophisticated reactions to offensive behaviour is the infliction of loss or suffering on the offender. When this is inflicted by the aggrieved person without invoking the law it is called 'retaliation'. When the infliction is appropriate according to a publicly accepted code it is known as 'retribution', by which the users of the notion seem to mean 'justified retaliation'.[3] Historically speaking, retribution was one of the main aims of early penal methods, and, even when people become able to draw a clear distinction between codes of morality and codes of criminal law, many would still regard it as an essential element of punishment. Indeed, some would argue that punishment which does not include retribution among its aims is not 'punishment'.

Retribution as a Distributive Principle. Even people who believe that the objectives of penal measures should not include retribution (but should be confined, say, to the reformation or discouragement of the offender himself, or the deterrence of potential imitators) may not completely dispense with the notion of retribution. They argue that since even the mildest of reformative measures – such as probation – involves a degree of interference with the privacy and liberty of the individual that must be to some extent objectionable to him, the question whether society has a right to subject him to such measures should still be decided on retributive grounds; in more concrete terms, we have no right even to put a man on probation until he gives us the right by breaking the criminal law. Professor H. L. A. Hart calls this 'retribution in the distribution of punishment'.[4]

Quantitative Retribution. Others would add that retribution should be applied (in addition, or instead) as a principle for limiting the severity of penal measures; for example, that while the aims of imprisonment might be confined to reformation and deterrence, its length and its unpleasantness should not exceed what is retributively appropriate. Lord Longford[5] writes:

---

[1] The 'principle' rests on several rather forced lines of reasoning. One is that the State has failed to fulfil its function of preserving order when a crime is committed; but if it has done its best should it be liable for what no state has ever succeeded in wholly preventing? And if it should, why should it not also be liable for crimes against property? Another argument is that by preventing private citizens from carrying weapons the State prevents them from defending themselves; but presumably this does reduce the total incidence of serious injuries, and in any case children and old ladies cannot use pistols or flick-knives. A third argument is that by imprisoning the assailant for the protection of society the state prevents him from earning money to meet the victim's claim; but few assailants have substantial earnings at the best of times. A sounder justification would be simply that state compensation is desirable on humanitarian grounds and that public sympathy for victims of crimes of violence has created the opportunity for this step forward.
[2] See the Home Office's White Paper 'Compensation for Victims of Crimes of Violence', 1964 (Cmnd. 2323), and the annual reports of the Criminal Injuries Compensation Board.
[3] Most modern retributionists would probably add that it is also necessary that the offender should recognise the reason for the infliction.   [4] 1959.10.   1961.61

'Retribution, in short, provides a justification for *some* punishment, and sets a limit to the amount of punishment justifiable. But deterrence and reform are the main factors which society should take into account in deciding how far society should exercise its right of punishment when passing sentence.' This form of the retributive principle, too, is exemplified in the English penal system, which not only fixes statutory maxima for fines and terms of imprisonment in the case of most types of crime, but also allows courts of appeal to reduce or alter the form of sentences on the grounds that they are excessively severe. The fact that the Scots system places no such limits on the sentencing powers of the High Court is no sign of a different penal philosophy, for its sentences too can be reduced on appeal. The Scots leave it to the court to decide what is retributively appropriate, and merely limit the sentencing powers of the lower courts: the tariff, like that of a Highland taxi, is invisible, arbitrary and incommunicable, but none the less operative.

There is, however, no extant statute which makes it obligatory that a court should determine a fine or a sentence of imprisonment by considering what is retributively appropriate, although there are, as we shall see, certain special types of sentence where the clear implication is that they should not.

In the chapters which follow it will therefore be necessary to refer to retribution in three senses:

1. *retaliatory retribution,* meaning the intentional infliction of an appropriate amount of suffering according to some code upon an offender who is capable of recognising that the suffering is intentionally inflicted because of his offence;
2. *distributive retribution,* meaning the intentional restriction of penal measures to persons who have committed offences (and who fulfil any other conditions regarded as necessary to make them liable to such measures);
3. *quantitative retribution,* meaning the limitation of penal measures which have aims other than retribution so that they do not exceed a degree of severity which is considered appropriate to the offence (and, on some views, to the offender).

Social Defence. Although all civilised criminal codes – and many primitive ones as well – are built up around the principle of distributive retribution, it is sometimes argued that a more rational principle would be what is called 'social defence'. This would allow measures such as supervision or detention to be applied to individuals on the ground not that they had committed a serious offence but that they were likely to commit one. The advantage claimed for this principle is that it would prevent some of the offences now being committed, and thus reduce the sum of harm caused to the community.[1] It would not of course exclude from penal measures persons who had actually committed offences, since, as we have seen, the commission of an offence would be one of the most reliable indications of a tendency to commit such offences. But it would include people who seemed

[1] 'Social defence' is thus logically derivable from Bentham's penal philosophy, although not advocated by him.

I

likely from their behaviour or their circumstances to commit a serious[1] crime: for example, the man who brandishes a knife whenever he loses an argument might be prevented or discouraged by detention from eventually stabbing his opponent, while the man whose wife has left him for a lover might be supervised until any desire for reprisals had abated.

Such a system would, of course, have to overcome not only strong pre-judices in favour of distributive retribution, but also inherent difficulties, such as the increased percentage of the population which would have to be subjected to supervision or detention.[2] What is interesting, however, is the fact that even a penal system which is so strongly linked to the principle of retributive distribution as is the British system should have some features which can be justified only as forms of social defence.

Under our 'social procedure', which is described in Chapter 10, a child under the age of 17 may be placed under compulsory supervision, or even removed from his home and sent to an approved school, without being found guilty of any offence, if a court is satisfied that the child is not receiv-ing proper care and guardianship from his or her parents and is falling into bad associations, or is exposed to moral danger or is beyond control. It is true that in such cases the child may very well have committed offences which have not been detected, or with which the police have decided not to charge him; but the procedure can be, and is, invoked in cases where this is not so. Persons over 17 are immune from 'care, protection and control' proceedings, but may be compulsorily admitted to hospitals for the mentally ill or subnormal if their mental condition seems to warrant this and if it also seems necessary in the interests of the patient's health or safety or for the protection of other persons. Some people who are dealt with in this way have committed offences, such as minor assaults, thefts, or sexual offences; but others have not, and are merely considered to be very likely to do so. Although children dealt with under social procedure may find themselves in the same approved schools as children found guilty of offences, and adults may be detained in the same mental hospitals as psychotic or defective offenders, these forms of control do not seem to be regarded as breaches of the principle of retributive justice in the distribution of penal measures, since they are classed not as 'penal measures' but as measures of social protection.

Even within the penal system proper there are one or two traces of social defence. Thus a man who has behaved in an unusually quarrelsome way, but has not yet committed or provoked an assault, may be charged before a magistrate with unlawfully conducting himself in a noisy, disorderly and turbulent manner 'against the peace', and may be 'bound over' for a period, on pains of forfeiting a 'recognisance' of a certain sum of money if he does not 'keep the peace'. A manual written by a police training officer says, 'This charge is useful where the breach of the peace does not amount to any other

---

[1] It would be possible, but ridiculous, to extend the argument to cover all kinds of offence.

[2] But we must allow for the possibility that we could deduct from our present prison population, for example, people whose crimes were of such a nature that they are most unlikely to repeat them: domestic murderers are an instance.

offence. . . . It is particularly appropriate where the disorder is likely to continue or recommence unless action is taken'.[1] Again, the Prevention of Crimes Act, 1871, and the Vagrancy Act of 1824 made it possible to arrest and charge men who were found in possession of housebreaking tools at night without lawful excuse, or men with a record of theft who loitered with felonious intent in places of public resort. Nor was such legislation confined to our apprehensive forebears, for the Prevention of Crime Act of 1953 made it an offence to have with you in a public place an article made or adapted for causing personal injury; and the penalty may now be as much as two years' imprisonment, or a fine of £200, or both. But since the criminal law is supposed to apply penal measures only to someone who can be shown to have committed an offence, it was necessary to define as offences situations which, in reality, merely make it very probable that an offence will be committed.

Deterrence. Many forms of penal measure were originally designed with the aim of deterring either the offender himself or potential imitators from committing another offence of the same kind. In most cases it is assumed that what discourages others from imitating the offender's example also discourages the offender himself from a repetition; but since there are obvious exceptions – for example, the death penalty, the punishment of the insane and the imprisonment of the destitute – it is necessary to distinguish the two aims under such labels as 'individual' and 'general' deterrence.

Techniques of Deterrence. The more sophisticated the penal system the less often its deterrent measures take the form of physical violence. Capital punishment is applied to a decreasing number of crimes, and in jurisdictions where it is still applied more and more grounds are discovered for exempting individuals from it. The scope and severity of corporal punishment are also reduced. The infliction of bodily suffering is replaced by the mulcting of money or goods, the withdrawal of civil rights, or the restriction of liberty by incarceration. The loss of liberty is aggravated by the physical discomforts and inconveniences of prison, the separation from families and friends, and the monotony of food, work, and recreation. In the early stages of prison development these are deliberately imposed additional deterrents. In England it was a principle of the system of poor-law institutions that life inside them should be less tolerable than life outside, in order that people should be discouraged from relying on their support, and this 'principle of less eligibility' was adopted as part of the philosophy of imprisonment.[2]

The deliberately deterrent aspect of the prison regime continued to be emphasised in the nineteenth century: Du Cane, the first Chairman of the new Prison Commission, described it succinctly as 'hard fare, hard labour and a hard bed'. Even as late as 1923 an Annual Report of the Prison Commissioners said 'The prison day should be hard, but the object is not mere [*sic*] severity. It should be interesting, but the object is not to make it

[1] J. D. Devlin, 1961.86.

[2] Cf. Bentham '. . . saving the regard due to life, health and bodily ease, the ordinary condition of a convict doomed to punishment, which few or none but individuals of the poorest class are apt to incur, ought not to be made more eligible [i.e. 'preferable'] than that of the poorest class of subjects in a state of innocence and liberty.'

pleasant.' It was at this period, however, that a rival point of view began to secure official recognition. There was a school of thought which held that incarceration was sufficiently deterrent (or retributive, according to one's precise point of view) without the intentional addition of an unpleasant regime The dictum of a Prison Commissioner of the nineteen-twenties, Alexander Paterson, that 'men are sent to prison as a punishment, not for punishment' was intended to discourage deliberate severity in the treatment of prisoners, and is now a slogan of the newer generations of prison officers.[1]

This cannot, however, wholly rid life in prison of deterrent features of two kinds. One is the deliberate intensification of discomforts and inconveniences by a minority of subordinate staff who either are temperamentally out of sympathy with the official policy or have been provoked by the behaviour of prisoners. The other is the imposition of restrictions for administrative reasons which is almost inevitable in any large organisation. For example, the 'rationing' of prisoners' outgoing and incoming letters is now defended not as a deliberate intensification of their deprivation of freedom, but on the grounds that there is not enough staff to censor them.

It is interesting to note, however, that deterrents which have been eliminated from the penal system sometimes linger in the disciplinary codes of institutions. Corporal punishment as a penal measure has been totally abandoned in Great Britain since 1948, but is still permissible for inmates of remand homes and approved schools. Solitary confinement and the 'hard fare' of Du Cane are no longer a prescribed feature of any sort of prison sentence, but short periods of 'cellular confinement' or 'restricted diet' can still be ordered for breaches of prison rules.

The other forms of sophisticated deterrent need little comment. The mulcting of money or goods usually takes the form of a fine. The withdrawal of civil rights is hardly used in the British penal system, in contrast to that of France, for example.

Elimination. Another unsophisticated penal measure deals with the offender by eliminating him, permanently or temporarily, from the community. Outlawry, transportation, and banishment are the most obvious examples, and survive in the vestigial form of the deportation of alien offenders. Indeed, deportation can also occur in unofficial forms. I have seen an English magistrates' court discharge a petty thief on the understanding that he would go back to his home town, Glasgow. (Capital punishment, though it certainly has the foreseen and accepted effect of elimination, has usually been regarded as justified by the aims of retaliatory retribution or deterrence.)

Prophylaxis. The sophisticated form of elimination, however, is detention in an institution under humane conditions which are designed with a view

---

[1] The idea was not a new one: a pamphlet of 1818 by Fowell Buxton (cit. Fox, 403) said '. . . where the law condemns a man to jail, and is silent as to his treatment there, it intends merely that he should be amerced of his freedom, *not that he should be subjected to any useless severities.* This is the whole of his sentence and ought to be the whole of his suffering. . . .' But it was another century before this was officially endorsed.

to security rather than deterrence or reform. Thus the express aim of 'extended sentences' in the British penal system is 'the protection of the public'; and in the case of many mentally subnormal offenders all that can be done to prevent them from repeating their crime is to detain them under comfortable but regulated conditions in one of the special hospitals (q.v.). The general justification for this is sometimes called 'social prophylaxis'. Under some systems, notably the Danish, it has been used to justify the voluntary castration of repeated sexual offenders.

REFORMATION

The more sophisticated a penal system the more emphasis is placed by those who operate it upon the aim of reforming the offender. During the early stages of the system, its designers and operators are content with individual deterrence. It is sufficient if the measures applied to an offender are so disagreeable that the recollection of them fortifies him against the temptation to repeat his offence or commit any other kind. There are two historical views of what happens next. On one account, it is discovered that there are some offenders who are not deterred however unpleasant the penalty. On another view, the development of humanitarian feelings to include criminals places limitations on the unpleasantness of the treatment to which it is thought right to subject them, so that the percentage who are deterred is reduced. On either view, it becomes necessary to widen one's aim and look for ways of altering the character of undeterrable offenders so that they withstand temptation, or, if one is very ingenious or hopeful, so that they are no longer tempted.[1]

A further stage is reached when those who operate the system extend their aims so that they are trying to make a former offender not only law-abiding but also less anti-social in ways which are outside the scope of the law. For example, they may try to make him less unkind to or neglectful of his wife and children. When this is attempted because he is more likely to become law-abiding if he values his family more, then it is simply a subtler effort to make him law-abiding.[2] But when it is attempted for its own sake, as it often is, then it represents what is probably the most ambitious form that the reformative aim can take. It is probable that this was what the Gladstone Committee intended in 1895: 'prison treatment should be effectually designed to maintain, stimulate, or awaken the higher susceptibilities of prisoners and turn them out of prison better men and women, both physically and morally, than when they came in'. Whether this statement is ambitious or merely ambiguous, it has been adopted as an article of faith by the prison administration of today.[3] Moreover, there is an increasing

---

[1] If anyone doubts that any penal measure is ever so ambitious, it can be pointed out that the castration of sexual recidivists is practised in some countries, and that in this country it is permissible to administer oestrogens to a sexual offender, with his consent, in order to remove his sexual desires.

[2] If, on the other hand, the justification offered is that his children are less likely to become offenders if he becomes a 'good family man', this is coupling reformation with prevention.

[3] Prison Commissioners, 1960.1.

number of probation officers, prison staff and after-care workers who feel that it is both legitimate and in some cases attainable.

It is worth noting, however, that the adoption of reformation as an aim of punishment has not been completely unanimous. In 1895 the Chairman of the Prison Commission and his supporters tried to convince the Gladstone Committee that the State had neither the right nor the obligation to attempt the prisoner's reformation.[1] Nor has this school of thought entirely perished, for as recently as 1954 C. S. Lewis argued that 'To be "cured" against one's will and cured of states which we may not regard as disease is to be put on a level with those who have not yet reached the age of reason, or those who never will; to be classed with infants, imbeciles, and domestic animals. But to be punished, however severely, because we have deserved it, because we "ought to have known better", is to be treated as a human person made in God's image.'[2] His point of view, however, had its ambiguities: for example, he did not make it clear whether he would allow a convicted murderer his own choice between the indignity of reformation and the dignity of hanging.

Techniques of Reformation. As soon as the aim of reformation is extended beyond individual deterrence, theories about the way it is to be attained begin to multiply. The variety of these theories and the rapidity with which fashions in them change is a sure index of the failure of any one of them to yield spectacular results. At least five varieties of technique can be distinguished.

Solitude. The assumption that reflection in *voluntary* solitude leads to regeneration can be traced back to the cell of the eremite or monk. From this it was a short step to the belief that *compulsory* seclusion could also be beneficial: a thirteenth-century Pope advised his bishops that 'while prison is recognised as proper for the custody of offenders and not for their punishment, we see no reason why clerics under your authority who have admitted or been convicted of offences should not be committed by you to prison, either for life or for a time, whichever seems best to you, in order to complete their penance'.[3] The secular jails of medieval England, constructed chiefly for the 'custody of offenders and not for their punishment', made hardly any use of the solitary cell, and although solitary confinement was advocated in the eighteenth century by Bishop Joseph Butler, it was left to another religious movement, in the Quaker State of Pennsylvania, to reintroduce it. Blackstone and Bentham favoured it, the latter explaining in graphic detail how 'the mind of the patient is by this means reduced to a gloomy void', and thus rendered receptive to better ideas.[4] He recognised, however, that prolonged treatment of this sort would produce madness or apathy, and advocated only short periods of it. Nevertheless, the theory died hard, especially in the minds of churchmen: Sidney Smith tried – but failed – to persuade Peel to introduce it.

[1] See Grünhut, 1948.248.
[2] 1954.
[3] '. . . ad paenitentiam peragendum' (Boniface VIII, cit. Grünhut, 1948.11).
[4] *Principles of Penal Law*, p. 425. The whole passage is oddly reminiscent of modern descriptions of 'brainwashing'.

Indeed, it was probably architectural problems and unwillingness to incur the expense of rebuilding the jails, rather than consideration for the prisoners, which restricted the introduction of solitary confinement to one or two suitably constructed local jails and the first convict prisons. However that may be, the 'separate system' which was eventually adopted for the English convict prisons of the nineteenth century was a modified form of solitary confinement under which the prisoner did not communicate – in theory at least – with his fellow-convicts, even at work or exercise, but only with warders and chaplain. Where work or exercise had to be taken 'in association', the 'rule of silence' was supposed to be enforced. By this time a new justification had been devised – as so often happens with penal measures – and the system was claimed to serve the less ambitious purpose of preventing the more inveterate criminals from contaminating the novice. In effect this was a disillusioned inversion of the ecclesiastical theory: if segregation did not help imprisonment to make men better, at least it prevented them from being made worse. Even as late as 1895 the Quaker-led Howard Association still favoured separation and was opposed to increased association between prisoners.

Towards the end of the nineteenth century, the separate system was replaced by the classification of prisoners into categories as a means of reducing contamination.[1] Even so, the 'rule of silence' at work was enforced until the nineteen-thirties. Its origin had been forgotten, and it was probably employed as one of the minor inconveniences which enhanced the deterrent effect of imprisonment. Even today talking is still prohibited on some occasions in prisons, and 'exclusion from associated work' is used as a deterrent to discourage breaches of discipline.

Homily. Another notion which is religious in origin is that offenders can be improved by direct moral instruction. Fielding and Howard thought that regular prayers, reading from the Bible, and the appointment of chaplains were essential ingredients of a reformative jail. Since many nineteenth-century prison reformers were inspired by religious ideals, it is not surprising that this point of view gained ground. Nonconformists, and especially Quakers, were at first more active than the Church of England, but when prison chaplains were appointed to the convict prisons, compulsory attendance at worship became part of the regime, and the Established Church began to play a more direct part. It took many years of discouragement to bring home the realisation that only the suggestible or hysterical offender was affected by direct exhortation, and that even in those cases the success might be only temporary. Chaplains and lay visitors were compelled to resort to more and more indirect means of winning the co-operation of prisoners, and the more tangible benefits of prison welfare work are attributable to this diverted effort.

Outside the prisons the Church of England Temperance Society laid the foundations of the modern English probation service when in the eighteen-seventies it appointed 'missionaries' to the London police courts to take charge of minor offenders – many of them chronic drunkards – whom the courts were willing to entrust to the missionaries' care instead of sentencing

[1] See pp. 157-61.

to imprisonment. For this reason the early probation service and its methods had a strongly religious flavour. Many probation officers were parish priests and ministers who added this to their pastoral duties, and it was not until the increasing use of probation led to the creation of a corps of full-time officers that the religious approach began to be replaced by secular notions.

Industry. The earliest of these secular notions was that of reclamation through industry, which, in contrast to the theories of reclamation through solitude and reclamation through homily, does not seem to be derivable from religious doctrines. It is traceable to the foundation of the bridewells and houses of correction to cope with that phenomenon of the sixteenth century, the rapid increase in 'rogues and vagabonds', whose common characteristic was not so much serious crime as an idle and disorderly way of life. The chief feature of the institutions to which they were committed was therefore hard work, which was intended partly to pay for their keep, but partly also to turn them into sober and self-supporting citizens. The distinction, however, between houses of correction and the jail as a place of mere custody gradually disappeared, and with it the tradition of useful labour. The tradition was revived in the last years of the eighteenth century, when the threatened end of transportation made it necessary to draw up plans for convict prisons in this country. But that was an age of deterrence, and the Hard Labour Act of 1779 was merely designed to ensure that life in prison should be as full of drudgery as existence in the plantations of Virginia. A century later it was being proclaimed by Du Cane that work in his prisons should be 'hard, dull, useless, uninteresting, monotonous labour', although later in his sentence the prisoner might earn the privilege of being placed on useful work. One of the most important of the changes recommended by the Gladstone Committee of 1895 was the abolition of unproductive labour (although with the cautious words 'wherever possible') and the development of productive industries, especially gardening, farming, and land reclamation.

The practical difficulty of providing enough useful work to fill a prisoner's day is still one of the unsolved problems of our large local prisons. There is no doubt about the importance which is attached to it in the philosophy of the modern Prison Commission:

> A prisoner's work must always be in certain ways the basis of his
> training. It should fill the greater part of every week-day, and his
> response to it and to the conditions in which he has to do it may well
> have much effect on his response to other forms of training. If for no
> other reasons, it should therefore be purposeful and interesting enough
> to enlist his willing co-operation. It should also enable him to acquire
> or maintain the habit of regular and orderly industry, and where he
> needs to learn a trade, so that he can earn an honest living when he
> goes out, he should be so taught.[1]

It is interesting, however, to see that the justifications offered for this emphasis on work are still very varied. A discussion of 'The purpose and value of work in prisons' in the report of the Advisory Council on the Employment of Prisoners[2] contains traces of most of the reasons which

[1] 1960.23.   [2] 1961.

have been offered in the last four hundred years for making prisoners work:

 ... Work may be a punishment to a lazy prisoner. Where this is so we do not deprecate it. ... Prisoners should be required to work neither more nor less hard than is expected of honest citizens. ...

 ... The fundamental reason why prisoners should work is that every person should make the best contribution he can to the community; secondly, suitable work, if properly organised, is a most valuable part of a prisoner's training; thirdly, prisoners represent a considerable labour force which ought not to be wasted. ...

 ... An excellent way [of training prisoners in social relations] is to provide useful, satisfying work and reasonable industrial conditions in which a good working relationship can be established between prisoners and the prison staff. ...

Activity. Akin to the theory of reclamation through industry is the notion that physical exercise is not merely advisable to counteract the ill-effects of incarceration but probably conducive in itself to moral improvement. This idea was adopted from the nineteenth-century English public schools by the borstals which were modelled on these establishments. Great emphasis was – and to some extent still is – laid upon strenuous games and other forms of physical recreation for young males,[1] partly on the assumption that this uses up energy which would otherwise be devoted to less desirable activities, partly with the object of giving the boys interests which might outlast their sentence. The use of hard exercise has been carried even further in the post-war detention centres. These were to some extent inspired by the military establishments of the same name, whose regimes were unashamedly deterrent. Physical training of the gymnastic type alternates with productive manual work to fill the boys' day. That the effect is still at least partly deterrent is recognised by those responsible; but another aim is to induce boys to take a pride in developing their hitherto unused physical powers, and so respect qualities other than those of the urban delinquent. A third claim is that the discipline involved in organised activity under orders is also beneficial; this too has a military origin.

All three of these justifications – diversion of energy, deterrence and the inculcation of physical self-respect – can be discerned in the Prison Commissioners' description of physical education at detention centres:

 Instruction is progressive, and boys are encouraged to take an interest in their physical development and athletic achievement. The sessions also provide an outlet for high spirits and soon become an enjoyable part of the training. Organised team games at week-ends play their part in helping disorderly youths to become orderly. ...

 ... The first fortnight is probably very hard for every boy; most are away from home for the first time and in addition are physically flabby and unused to the high standards demanded of them at the centres. But ... the boys soon begin to take pride in their various

---

[1] Girls' borstals, however, seem to set less store by this form of activity, partly, no doubt, because most of them have been simply fitted into wings of adult prisons, partly because the girls themselves are less enthusiastic about organised sport.

forms of achievement; the effort demanded from them is irksome to those who most need it and is an incentive to qualify for the earliest date of release.

Environmental Manipulation. Since the reformation of character was regarded in Victorian England as more or less synonymous with the saving of the soul, and thus as something to be attempted through religious instruction, it was inevitable that secular efforts should concentrate at first on material influences. Poverty provided an obvious incentive to the most frequent form of crime, and we have seen how economic explanations had their prime in continental Europe towards the end of the nineteenth century. The relief of poverty was therefore an obvious measure of prevention, and Victorian social workers were usually occupied in doling out food, clothes, and money, although their religious outlook still showed itself in their practice of seasoning alms with moral advice, and of distinguishing between the 'deserving' and the 'undeserving' poor. The charitable societies which formed themselves round each prison to aid the discharged prisoner were similarly concerned with his material situation, and used their funds to provide him with clothing, money, sometimes tools for a trade, and less often the employment itself.

Although, as we shall see, modern social workers rely on other skills as well, the manipulation of the delinquent's environment is still one of their techniques. The probation officer who finds a hostel and a job for a probationer or discharged prisoner, or the children's officer who tries to arrange the rehousing of a 'problem family', is doing exactly this.

Psychotherapy. Since the First World War, however, a new influence has gradually pervaded not only many forms of penal treatment, but most forms of social work in general. This is the realisation that direct homily and personal example were not the only means by which one human being could influence the conduct of another. As we have seen, psychotherapeutic techniques devised by Freud, and the hypotheses which he founded on them, suggested a new approach to the causation and treatment of delinquency. They gave rise to the 'psychological casualty' hypothesis, which regards delinquency, or much of it, as a symptom of maladjustment originating in early relationships between the child and his parents. This was, fundamentally, the most optimistic theory that had so far been offered, since it was at first assumed that maladjustment of this sort could be rectified by supplying in the delinquent's present what had been lacking in his past. The effects of 'repression' should be undone by a 'permissive' regime.[1] The damage caused by an oppressive or an absent father could be repaired by supplying a well-chosen 'father-figure'.

The first country to adopt psychoanalytic ideas with enthusiasm was the U.S.A. or more precisely Massachusetts, where Worcester College invited Freud to lecture in 1909. The Judge Baker Clinic which opened in 1911 in Boston was one of the first places to which apparently normal children were referred by the criminal courts for psychological investigation: psychological *treatment* was a slightly later development. In the nineteen-twenties

---

[1] As in Aichorn's famous school (1936: *Wayward Youth*) and other educational establishments.

a popularised and diluted form of psychoanalysis gained widespread acceptance not only among American psychiatrists but also among social workers, teachers, and ministers of some religious denominations. British social workers, who had hitherto relied largely on environmental manipulation mixed with direct advice, had for some time felt the need for some more potent weapon, and welcomed the psychotherapeutic approach.

In England, the influence of psychoanalytic ideas is especially evident in the outlook of probation officers, whose training in post-war years has laid great emphasis on them. Modern psychoanalysis stresses the importance of the 'transference', that is the temporary emotional dependence of the patient on the analyst which seems to be essential to successful treatment; and the modern probation officer is trained to pay a great deal of attention to the establishment of a similar relationship with his probationer, which will greatly strengthen his influence over him.

A more recent innovation of psychotherapeutic origin is what is called, not altogether appropriately, 'group counselling'. One of Adler's contributions to psychotherapy had been the discovery that the exaggerated or abnormal reactions of neurotic patients to their personal difficulties can often be more effectively altered by discussions among themse lves under the guidance of a psychotherapist than by têtes-à-têtes between individual patients and the psychotherapist himself. In California, where 'group psychotherapy' quickly became popular, teachers at San Quentin penitentiary noticed that prisoners liked to use classes for discussions of irrelevant but emotionally important subjects; and the classes were deliberately developed into what was called 'group counseling'. As it is now used in British borstals and prisons the method consists essentially of regular discussions between small groups of inmates, in the presence and under the leadership of a member of the staff. Members of the group may freely discuss almost any aspect of the institution, their own offences, and their difficulties, both 'inside' and 'outside', without fear of disciplinary action; the most that the staff may do is to intervene when discussions take an undesirable turn.[1] As with group psychotherapy, members have to rely on each other to treat the content of the discussion in confidence, and gradually they come to do so.

OTHER AIMS

Public Satisfaction. An important influence in the shaping and modifica‾ tion of penal measures is undoubtedly public sentiment. This may take the form of dissatisfaction with measures which seem retributively excessive – for example, hanging for theft – or inadequate as a deterrent – for example, the forty-shilling fine for soliciting in the street. It may express itself in sympathy for a particular category of offender – for example, the insane, children, women, people with dependants, men with 'good war records'; or in antagonism towards other categories, such as immigrants, negroes, 'teddy boys', 'profiteers', 'professional criminals'. Its main impact is upon legislators, especially elected legislators, and upon the lay sentencers in the

---

[1] For example, plans for attacks on inmates or staff, or for escapes. Discussions of Individuals who are not present are also discouraged.

lower courts.[1] Although few legislators would concede that to satisfy the public was one of the aims of a penal system, they would probably point out at the same time that an electorate which thinks in terms of retribution, deterrence, and permanent or temporary elimination sets a limit to innovations which are primarily reformative or supervisory in their aim. Again, while magistrates would not agree that their sentences are intended to satisfy local sentiments, it is not uncommon to hear one justify his sentence by arguing that 'people around here have been getting very alarmed by the recent increase in this type of offence'. Even a Home Secretary sometimes advised the commutation of a death sentence 'in deferrence to a widely spread or strong local expression of public opinion'.[2]

There are nevertheless people who argue that the punishment of offenders has the function of satisfying some emotional need[3] of the man in the street;[4] this has been described sometimes as the need to find a scapegoat for a society in which such things are allowed to happen, sometimes as a reaction against the disowned desire in oneself to do likewise. In assessing such arguments it is necessary to be clear about the meaning of 'function'. If it is used to include 'conscious aim',then it is very difficult to find any convincing example of a modern penal measure adopted with the conscious aim of satisfying public opinion. If, on the other hand, it simply means 'foreseen or unforeseen effect', then the argument is more plausible but less sensational. Few legislators would deny that they foresee the satisfaction or dissatisfaction that is caused by the removal, introduction or modification of a penalty, or that these are tactical considerations which affect the timing or presentation of the legislation. Nor would many judges or magistrates deny that they have experienced public dissatisfaction both as the foreseen and as the unforeseen effects of a sentence. Those who are both introspective and honest would even admit that this is a consideration which sometimes weighs with them.

There is, however, a subtler form of argument which seeks to relate the aims of penal measures to public opinion in a particularly respectable and even dignified way. Like most subtle arguments this is most often heard in discussions of the death penalty. In his memorandum to the Royal Commission on Capital Punishment, Lord Denning wrote:[5] 'Punishment is the way in which society expresses its denunciation of wrong doing: and in order to maintain respect for law it is essential that the punishment inflicted for grave crimes should adequately reflect the revulsion felt by the great majority of citizens for them.' It is clear both from the nature of the argument and from Lord Denning's words that it is applicable not merely to punishment for murder, but to the function of penal measures in dealing

---

[1] Professional judges are more insulated from it, partly because they do not have other occupations to bring them into contact with non-legal opinion, partly because their status discourages direct criticism of their sentences, except occasionally from newspapers.

[2] See the report of the Royal Commission on Capital Punishment, 1953.

[3] Usually regarded as unconscious; see M. Balint, 1957.

[4] To be distinguished from the man on the top of an omnibus; the latter is appealed to by lawyers, the former by leaderwriters.

[5] 1953: minutes of evidence, 9th day, para. 1.

with any 'grave crimes'. It seems to mean that an offender should be dealt with by the order of a criminal court in a way sufficiently terrible to express society's moral condemnation of his offence. What is not clear is whether society's 'expression' is regarded as a deliberate instrument for influencing some group of persons – for example, its own potential or actual criminals – or simply as satisfying society's need for expression, much as individuals use a ritual act or ejaculation.

The Royal Commission themselves interpreted the argument as an instrumental one:

> ... the deterrent force of capital punishment operates not only by affecting the conscious thoughts of individuals tempted to commit murder, but also by building up in the community, over a long period of time, a deep feeling of peculiar abhorrence for the crime of murder. 'The fact that men are hanged for murder is one great reason why murder is considered so dreadful a crime.' This widely diffused effect on the moral consciousness of society is impossible to assess, but it must be at least as important as any direct part which the death penalty may play as a deterrent in the calculations of potential murderers. It is likely to be specially potent in this country, where the punishment for lesser offences is much more lenient than in many countries, and the death penalty stands out in sharper contrast.[1]

It is clear, however, that the argument has sometimes been used in what we might call the 'ritualistic' form; for example, by a Home Secretary when resisting the Death Penalty Abolition Bill:[2] '. . . in executing the capital sentence the State pronounces the moral judgement of society on murder.'

The Humanitarian Principle. The aims which have been discussed so far consist of positive objectives which penal measures have been intended to achieve. One of the most important influences, however, in penal thinking has been what might be called the negative principle of humanity, which sets a limit on moral or emotional grounds to the form, severity, or duration of penal measures. It is logically distinct from the principle of quantitative retribution, since even a penal system in which all measures were devised solely for social prophylaxis, general deterrence, and individual reformation – or any combination of these – without any thought of a retributively appropriate limit, could still be criticised on humanitarian grounds. Thus the protection of the public might seem to require the lifelong incarceration of a violent offender if all risk of his repeating his crimes were to be eliminated; but the humanitarian principle would assert that there is a stage at which the risk becomes small enough to be outweighed by the suffering thus inflicted upon him. Even if the regime of a detention centre could be shown to be a highly successful deterrent, there would still be critics whose objection to it is that it inflicts too much misery upon adolescent males. Humanitarian sentiments have, of course, been responsible for much of the opposition to the death penalty, although they often find expression in practical arguments designed to question its penal efficacy. They have prompted

[1] 1953.20.
[2] In the House of Commons on 16th February 1956. The Home Secretary was Gwilym Lloyd George.

most of the ameliorations of the prison regime in this century – far more than have been suggested as means of reforming the offender. Even those who attempt to think in purely scientific or administrative ways about penal methods cannot afford to disregard it as a factor which limits the scope of experimentation.

OTHER ASSUMPTIONS

Another phenomenon in which scientific penologists should be objectively interested is the way in which some aims are regarded with a greater degree of moral approval than others. Among those directly involved in the British penal system, whether as legislators, theorists, administrators, or practitioners, it is undoubtedly reformation in its most ambitious sense that receives the greatest degree of respect. Thus a probation officer or prison governor who said that he would be satisfied if his charges never broke the law again would run the risk of being told that he was taking too limited a view of his job. He would, however, enjoy more approval than, let us say, the warden of a detention centre who said that all he tried to do was to make life there so unpleasant that his youths took care to keep out of trouble thereafter. Retribution is an even less fashionable objective, although probably the lowest place would be allotted to pure elimination, especially if used to justify capital punishment: 'To take an extreme example, the most effective method of dealing with anti-social conduct would be to inflict capital punishment in every case: this policy alone gives 100 per cent guarantee against recidivism.' In the eighteenth century this argument might have been seriously used, for example by the Rev. Dr Madan. Today it is used by Lady Wootton[1] as a moral *reductio ad absurdum*. As for the aim of consoling the victim of a crime, or satisfying public opinion, it would be unthinkable to declare either of these as a main objective: but, as we have seen, it is permissible to justify redress as beneficial to the offender, and the death penalty as a symbol of the condemnation of the offence. These changes in the current moral values attributed to penal aims may account for the fact that while penal techniques develop slowly, the justifications offered by their supporters change much more rapidly.

'*Ambiguity*' of Aim. One of the features of penal systems – and especially the British – which make it very difficult to divine the intentions of the legislature, to interpret the sentencing policy of courts or to discuss either without misunderstanding, is the multiplicity of justifications which can be offered for any one type of measure. Most of the kinds of sentence which are about to be described can be justified by appealing to at least two of the aims which have been discussed. The death penalty can be regarded as achieving retaliation, retribution, general deterrence, or elimination. The only aims which it can hardly be claimed to achieve are redress and the reformation of the individual.[2] Imprisonment can be regarded as achieving

[1] 1959.253.
[2] Although some churchmen believe that the prospect of execution assists in the spiritual regeneration of murderers to such an extent as to provide a justification for capital punishment. This argument was used by the Bishop of Durham during the debate on this subject in the Convocation of York (15 May, 1962). Describing his

retribution, temporary elimination, general and individual deterrence and reformation,[1] but hardly redress. Fines can be regarded both as retribution and as general and individual deterrents. It is not easy to find a positive penal measure which is free from what might be called this 'ambiguity of aim'. At first sight orders to pay compensation or damages seem unambiguous; but recently, as we have seen, there have been attempts to extend their use on the ground that they assist the reformation of the offender.

Even our methods for dealing with mentally abnormal offenders are partly corrective and partly eliminatory, although we may prefer the more civilised adjectives 'remedial' and 'prophylactic'.

Nor are probation or other supervisory measures entirely unambiguous, although at first thought we should say that their aim was purely reformative. But it is sometimes argued that the main aim of a probation or supervision order is not only to alter the attitudes of an individual but also to provide him with a prophylactic environment for a period during which he will 'settle down' or 'grow out of it'; and certainly some forms of probation – such as the probation home or hostel (q.v.) – are consistent with this. If so, probation is both reformative and prophylactic in its aims.

Indeed, perhaps the only measures which can be claimed as unambiguous in the British system is that of conditional discharge – and perhaps the Scottish deferred sentence (q.v.) – of which the aim might be described as entirely individual deterrence of a mild kind.[2] But these are trivial exceptions, which underline the difficulty that we shall later encounter in guessing what the actual aim of a court was when it pronounced any other type of sentence.

Flexibility. Another striking feature of the British penal system is its flexibility. Unsophisticated codes tend to prescribe a given penalty for a given offence with considerable rigidity; indeed, until as late as the nineteenth century the main features of the English system were the severity of its penalties and the rigid simplicity with which they were applied. In contrast, French and Italian judges in the eighteenth century had such freedom that there was a reaction against both the barbarity and the arbitrariness of these sentences. Beccaria[3] wrote: 'There is nothing more dangerous than the common axiom "the spirit of the laws is to be considered" . . . we

---

interview with a condemned man he said: 'Then began, in the short time at my disposal – less than a week – the most wonderful reclamation and conversion that I have ever seen. . . . If ever I have seen a man fit for his Maker and for all eternity, it was that man. If he had been given a life sentence, it would have been a continuance of prison life, to which he was already accustomed, and no conversion might well have occurred. . . .' The argument seems to be based on the pessimistic assumption that life after death is eternal and that spiritual improvement in the course of it is unlikely.

[1] Note that I am not asserting that all these aims are actually achieved, or achieved in all or any cases; this illustrates the importance of distinguishing aims and effects.

[2] It is certainly the only example of a deterrent measure which nobody could regard as retributive, except in the matter of distribution. It can hardly be regarded as reformative except to the extent that deterrence is reformative. It is not prophylactic, hardly supervisory (although sometimes Scottish courts defer sentence in order to see how the offender will react to informal supervision or whether he will try to make restitution) and seldom involves redress.　　　[3] 1764, Pt. IV.

see the same crime punished in a different manner at different times in the same tribunals. . . .' The solution adopted by revolutionary France and introduced to other countries by the Napoleonic Code was one of rigid prescription. Both in England and in France it was the effect of this inflexibility upon the willingness of juries to convict offenders that led to the third phase of penal philosophy, the era of 'individualisation'.

Individualisation. Originally, the principle of individualisation[1] was that if the punishment is to be appropriate in a retributive sense this cannot be achieved by prescribing different punishments or amounts of punishment for different offences, however minute the gradations of offence; the punishment must be modified to fit the culpability of the offender. In ecclesiastical courts the canon law had for centuries encouraged the searching of the sinner's heart to ascertain the exact degree of his moral culpability. When first propounded, therefore, as a principle for the secular criminal code, individualisation meant simply the mitigation of retributive penalties in the light of extenuating circumstances, such as the youth or extreme old age of the accused, the strength of the temptation to which he was inferred to have been subject, the selfishness or altruism of his motives, and other factors which could be regarded as reducing his blameworthiness. It was in this spirit that the French code was gradually modified in the latter half of the nineteenth century; the objective was a *retributive* flexibility.

In contrast, the principle on which greater flexibility was introduced into English law appears to have been one of *reformative* individualisation. It was the early experiments in rudimentary forms of probation in New England and later in Britain which persuaded courts to refrain from imprisoning young delinquents, unofficially at first but eventually with statutory recognition. Magistrates, and later the higher courts, were allowed to discharge offenders or demand recognisances from them if they seemed likely to reform under supervision. As we shall see, this process has now reached a stage at which, with very few exceptions, a court faced with an offender has a more or less free choice between imprisonment,[2] probation, a fine or some form of discharge, and the limits on its freedom are upper and not lower limits.

Between this flexibility and the arbitrariness which Beccaria condemned there may seem to be only a short step. But the system is saved from arbitrariness by several differences. One is the upper limits imposed (whether in the name of quantitative retribution or of humanity) on the amount of fines or the length of institutional or supervisory sentences. Even within these limits restraint is also imposed by the effectiveness of the machinery for appealing against sentence. Another difference, although admittedly it is a comparatively recent development, is the extent to which British courts are obliged or encouraged to take professional advice on the individual case before passing sentence; and this will be discussed in the chapter on sentencing.

---

[1] Salleilles (1898) says that the word was first coined in 1869, by Wahlberg's 'Das Prinzip der Individualisirung in der Strafrechtspflege'.

[2] Or its juvenile equivalent.

[9]

MEASURES

FOR ADULTS

This chapter, and those which deal with the disposal of juveniles and mentally abnormal offenders, are concerned with the limitations imposed by law not only on courts' use of the various penal measures but also on the way in which these measures are carried out. The considerations which seem to influence sentencers and the problem of assessing the effectiveness of such measures will be discussed in Chapters 11 and 12.

In all these chapters I have attempted to achieve simplicity and clarity by sacrifices of different kinds. Comprehensive phrases such as 'parents or guardians', 'children or young persons' have been avoided by the following conventions:

'parent' includes 'guardian' except where the context makes this non-sense;

'he' includes 'she'; the law of sentencing makes few distinctions between the sexes, but a separate chapter deals with the special features of penal measures as applied to females;

'adult' means a person who has attained the age of 21 and is presumed to be mentally normal (a separate chapter deals with the mentally abnormal);

'young adult' means a person between his 17th and 21st birthdays;

'young person' means someone between his 14th and 17th birthdays, as in modern statutes;

'child' means someone who has not yet attained his 14th birthday;

'juvenile' means 'young person or child', as in 'Juvenile Court'.

'England' includes Wales, but not Scotland, Northern Ireland, the Isle of Man or the Channel Islands. 'Britain' means 'England and Scotland'. Some of the differences between English and Scots law in the field of sentencing are interesting, and are briefly described in the text or footnotes; otherwise it can be assumed that differences, if any, are minor. 'Home Secretary' should be translated into 'Secretary of State for Scotland' and 'Home Office' into 'Scottish Home and Health Department' when Scotland is concerned. The peculiarities of Northern Ireland, the Channel Islands and the Isle of Man have been left to antiquarians. Except where it is otherwise indicated, statistics refer only to England and Wales

K

Abbreviations. The following abbreviations are used for the most frequently cited statutes (others are cited in full):

CYPA 33, 69	*Children and Young Persons Act, 1933, or 1969*
CYP(S)A 37	*Children and Young Persons (Scotland) Act, 1937*
CA 48	*Children Act, 1948*
CJA 48, 61, 67	*Criminal Justice Acts of 1948 or 1961 or 1967*
CJ(S)A 49, 63	*Criminal Justice (Scotland) Act, 1949 & 1963*
MCA 52	*Magistrates Courts Act, 1952*
SJ(S)A 54	*Summary Jurisdiction (Scotland) Act, 1954*
MHA 59	*Mental Health Act, 1959*
MH(S)A 60, 64	*Mental Health (Scotland) Act, 1960, 1964*

PRONOUNCING SENTENCE

The judgement or sentence of the court is decided upon by the presiding judge, the recorder or magistrates, and not by the jury (if any), although the jury can supplement their verdict with recommendations for mercy, and not infrequently did so in cases of capital murder. The sentence is pronounced orally, in the presence of the offender and the public; if the judge or recorder wishes to alter his sentence he can do so only if the assizes or quarter sessions, as the case may be, is still in session, and again he must do so in open court. A magistrates' court cannot alter its sentence after it has risen.[1]

Almost every penal measure imposable by criminal courts is discretionary, in the sense that the court is not obliged by law to impose that particular measure. A few types of offence incur mandatory penalties, which the court has no choice but to order; the most important examples are:

1. murder, which automatically incurs the sentence of life imprisonment;
2. certain traffic offences, which incur disqualification from driving, although some narrowly defined exceptions are allowed.

THE PREROGATIVE OF MERCY

The extent to which the law treats the sentence as irrevocable has already been mentioned in the previous chapter. This irrevocability is to some extent compensated by the constitutional device called the royal prerogative of mercy, which in effect allows the Home Office to interfere with sentences in exceptional cases. In theory, this part of the royal prerogative is based on the assumption that the sovereign is the law-giver, and thus the only person who can interfere with the operation of the law. In practice it survives because it is a safety-valve, allowing the sentencing system to preserve the rigidity which is presumably essential to its function as a deterrent, while permitting interference in cases where this rigidity provokes wide resentment. It makes it possible for the offender whose conviction was unjust but cannot be undone to receive a 'free pardon'; or for a dying or gravely ill prisoner to be released to his home.

---

[1] In Scotland, a summary court can alter its sentence at any time 'before imprisonment has followed on it', but cannot pronounce a 'higher' sentence than the original one.

The prerogative is exercised by the Queen's signature on a document presented to her by the Home Secretary. In theory she can reject his advice, or act on her own initiative: in practice the sovereign has not succeeded in doing so since the days of George IV. The Home Secretary in his turn is usually acting on the advice of his civil servants, to whose notice the case has been brought by the press, by the defendant or his representatives, by the court or by a custodial institution (capital cases, however, are automatically investigated with a view to a possible reprieve). The Home Office have to steer a careful course between several dangers. They must not act as a court of appeal (although they have not infrequently reprieved murderers on the ground that there was a 'scintilla of doubt' about their guilt); nor must they react to every campaign against an individual's sentence. On the other hand, they must not allow the law to take its course in circumstances which would lead to campaigns for the abolition of a normally sound provision. The extent to which the use of this device has anticipated legislation is seldom realised; an example was the tendency to reprieve young murderers, which was eventually ratified by statutes fixing minimum ages for capital punishment. An extra-legal safety-valve of this sort seems to be an integral part of all civilised penal systems.

OBSOLETE PENALTIES

The British penal system no longer includes penalties which consist in the deliberate infliction of bodily harm. The amputation of limbs died out in the Middle Ages. Whipping, which has become progressively less popular (even for schoolboys) since the last decades of the nineteenth century, was finally prohibited as a sentence in 1948, and as a disciplinary measure in prisons in 1967, although it is still permissible, under safeguards, for boys in approved schools and remand homes. Castration and sterilisation, which in some systems can be more or less imposed upon certain sexual offenders, are not allowed. The death penalty for murder was suspended for five years in 1965,[1] and the suspension was made permanent in 1969. Although it continues in theory to be the penalty for treason, certain forms of piracy and arson of the royal dockyards, only the first of these now figures in modern prosecutions, and then only in time of war.

RESTRICTIONS ON SENTENCES

In all but a few cases the court has a choice between several courses. It has no choice in sentencing a person convicted of murder, who must receive 'life' imprisonment.[2] This distinction between murder and all other forms of personal violence (for which the court has a wide choice of sentences) is traceable to eighteenth-century legislation designed to make sure that murderers did not escape capital punishment, and attempts have been made to justify it on the grounds that the burden of choosing between life and

[1] By the Murder (Abolition of Death Penalty) Act, 1965. But note that it is still the penalty for certain forms of murder in the Channel Islands and the Isle of Man.

[2] It may, however, recommend a minimum period for which he should be detained: but see p. 148.

death should not be borne by the court, an argument which vanishes when 'life' is substituted for death. There are other mandatory sentences, however, for which the justification is more rational. Courts are more or less obliged, for example, to disqualify drivers convicted of driving motor vehicles when unfit through drink or drugs, because experience showed that many magistrates would otherwise fail to use this power. With these exceptions, mandatory penalties are rare and unpopular (witness the abolition of mandatory imprisonment for driving while disqualified). On the other hand, most penalties are subject, as we shall see, to restrictions on their use, and this is especially so in the case of imprisonment.

PRISON

A sentence of imprisonment may be imposed by any criminal court, subjec to certain limitations and exceptions:

Type of offence: Many minor offences cannot be dealt with in this way, such as carelessly riding a bicycle, behaving in a disorderly manner in a public library, or committing some other breaches of the peace. Some minor offences can be punished with imprisonment only when the offender has already been convicted of the same offence, for example driving a motor vehicle without due care and attention.

First offenders: An English magistrates' court, and a Scottish court of summary jurisdiction, cannot imprison a first offender without stating its reasons for the opinion that no other method of dealing with him is appropriate. A 'first offender' is someone who has not been convicted since his 17th birthday of an offence punishable with imprisonment; and in Scotland it also includes a person whose last conviction for such an offence occurred more than ten years before.[1]

Age: As we shall see in the next chapter, there are certain ages below which offenders cannot be sentenced to imprisonment.

Life Imprisonment. For murder the sentence must be one of imprisonment for life, the effect of which is that the date of the prisoner's release is decided by the Home Secretary. A few 'lifers' do spend the rest of their lives in prison; at the other end of the scale one is occasionally released within the year (as 'mercy-killers' occasionally have been). In the nineteen-fifties the modal period for the detention of lifers was nine years, but that was a period when most lifers were murderers who had been reprieved from hanging because of extenuating circumstances. Now that lifers luded murderers who would formerly have been hanged, detention beyonncnine years will become more frequent. The Murder (Abolition of Death ᴊenalty) Act, 1965, allowed judges, when sentencing murderers, to declareꟼ e minimum period for detention which they recommend to the Home Secretary. In practice they do not usually make such a recommendation; when they do, it has no binding effect upon the Home Secretary, although it is bound to have some weight in his consideration.

Life imprisonment may be imposed by higher courts for a number of

[1] First Offenders Act, 1958: First Offenders (Scotland) Act, 1960, as amended by cj(s)a, 63. But the case of *Vassall* v. *Harris* ([1964] *Criminal Law Review*, 322) shows how perfunctory the court's consideration of the alternatives may be.

other crimes, such as manslaughter, infanticide, abortion, or rape. In practice, however, prison sentences for such offences are almost always determinate. Murder apart, it seems to be the policy of the Court of Appeal's Criminal Division that life sentences should be confined to cases in which not only is the offence itself 'grave' enough to justify a very long sentence, but also the offender's offences or previous history shows that he is mentally unstable and likely to repeat his crime, with specially injurious consequences to others (as sexual offences or crimes of personal violence may have).[1]

Each case is reviewed by the Home Office soon after trial, and a few released early. The rest are reviewed after four years, and some then go to Local Review Committees, who review all cases after not more than seven years. Whatever their view, the case then goes to the Parole Board, and if its recommendation is favourable the Lord Chief Justice and the trial judge (if available) are consulted. The Home Secretary is not bound by the judges' advice, but can order release only if the Board so recommend, although even then he does not have to.[2] Most lifers are told their release date a year in advance.

Determinate Sentences. For most offences the sentence under English law must, if it is one of imprisonment, be for a stated period which does not exceed the maximum permitted by the statute. For 'hybrid' offences (q.v.) a lower and a higher maximum is fixed, according to the mode of trial; and if the offence is an indictable one for which the accused consents to be tried summarily, there is a general limit of six months on the sentence which a magistrates' court may impose.[3]

In Scotland, practically all the more serious crimes and many other frequent crimes and offences are contraventions of the common law, and are not set out in statute. The position of statutory offences is the same as in England, but in the case of common law crimes and offences the length of imprisonment is limited only by the powers of the court. Since the High Court's powers of imprisonment (or fining) for common law crimes are unlimited, and since almost all serious offences are still common law crimes in Scotland, the High Court could thus impose an indeterminate sentence for most of the crimes which it tries. In practice it seldom pronounces 'life' sentences except in the case of murder (for which this is mandatory) and for some cases of culpable homicide, the Scottish equivalent of manslaughter. As in England, other serious crimes usually receive determinate sentences. In proceedings on indictment a Sheriff may impose not more than two years. When sitting as a summary court he may not impose more than three months in common law cases, although for certain specific offences or in certain circumstances he may impose more.[4] Other courts of summary jurisdiction – burgh and justice of the peace courts – have higher powers for some specific statutory offences but are limited in common law cases to sixty days' imprisonment.

[1] See, for example, the Court's remarks in *R.* v. *Hodgson,* [1968] *Criminal Law Review,* 46.   [2] CJA 67, s 61.   [3] MCA 52, s. 19.
[4] For example, SJ(S)A 54, s. 8, as amended, allows sentences of six months for certain offences when preceded by at least one previous conviction for a similar offence.

Minimum Length of Sentence. Unlike many other systems, British criminal law does not lay down any effective minimum for the length of an ordinary sentence of imprisonment, although it does in the case of certain special types of custodial treatment, such as borstal training (q.v.). A magistrates' court, however, cannot impose less than five days' imprisonment,[1] although they may order detention for up to four days in a police cell;[1] this limitation prevents the time and manpower of prisons from being wasted on the reception, medical examination, and equipment of men who have to be discharged almost as soon as this process is complete. Instead, magistrates' courts have the power to order the more or less nominal detention of an offender in the court precincts or in a police station for the rest of the day on which he was sentenced, as one of the mildest punishments short of absolute discharge.[1] These powers can be used only for offences punishable with imprisonment.

The term of imprisonment begins on the day on which it was imposed by the court; but an exception is made for the offenders sentenced by assize or quarter sessions after being committed in custody for trial or sentence by a lower court, and their sentences are reduced by the length of the period in custody.[2]

Consecutive and Concurrent Sentences. If more than one sentence of imprisonment is imposed on the same offender, either on the same occasion or before the first has expired, they may be either concurrent or consecutive. If concurrent, they are deemed to begin on the same day, so that the time spent in prison is no longer than the longest of the sentences; the only practical effect is that if one but not both of the sentences is quashed on appeal the offender remains in prison. If the sentences are consecutive, the second begins as soon as the other expires, and the offender is not released between them.[3] If the charges on which a man receives two or more sentences arose out of what was in reality one and the same offence, the sentences should be concurrent.[4] The aggregate of consecutive terms of imprisonment for offences of the same category may exceed the legal maximum for a single offence of that category,[5] but if imposed by a magistrates' court may not exceed six months,[6] or, in the case of indictable offences tried summarily, twelve months.

Length of Prison Sentences. Table 21 shows the cumulative percentages of the different lengths of sentences of prisoners received by English and

---

[1] MCA 52 ss. 107, 109, 110. Higher courts are not prohibited from imposing nominal sentences of imprisonment, and in 1961 six men and two women were sentenced to prison for one, two, three or four days.

[2] The Criminal Justice Administration Act, 1962, s. 17. Scots law allows no such reduction.

[3] *Castro* v. *R.* [1881], 6 App. Cas. 229.

[4] This statement, and the rest of this paragraph, does not apply to Scotland, where, for example, consecutive sentences of an inferior court must not together exceed the sentence which it could have imposed for a single offence (*Maguiness* v. *MacDonald*, [1953] J. C. 31).

[5] *Castro* v. *R. cit. supra*; *R.* v. *Greenberg*, [1943] K.B. 381.

[6] MCA 52, s. 108, which allows certain exceptions to this rule.

Scottish prisons in 1961. The distribution is remarkably stable: a similar table for 1960 shows almost identical percentages for men, and only small differences for women. In England, the commonest prison sentence is one of six months, which accounts for 16 to 17 per cent of all sentences on men; the next most frequent is one of three months, which accounts for 14 to 15 per cent. Two-thirds of all men's prison sentences are for six months or less. A false impression of the frequency of longer sentences is gained from analyses of the prison population at any given time; thus while only 2·7 per cent of sentences imposed in 1961 were for more than three years, 17·8 per cent of the daily average male population of the prisons were serving such sentences.

The distribution of Scottish sentences is markedly different. Whereas two-thirds of men's sentences in England are for six months or less, two-thirds in Scotland are for two months or less, and sentences of more than seven years are very rare. Part of the explanation is that because of differences in the procedure for dealing with fine-defaulters (q.v.) a larger percentage of them go to prison for short terms in Scotland.[1] Another factor is that the sentencing powers of the sheriff courts and magistrates' courts, which are responsible for the great majority of the sentences of imprisonment, are more limited than those of the English quarter sessions and magistrates' courts. Nevertheless, the practical effect is that Scottish prisons have to cope with an even higher 'turnover' of short-term prisoners, and a correspondingly smaller percentage of prisoners with medium and long sentences, than their English counterparts.

The extended sentences which can be imposed on certain recidivists are discussed in Chapter 15.

Temporary Release. Sentenced and civil prisoners (including preventive detainees and corrective trainees) can be granted short leaves of absence from their prison at the Prison Department's discretion. Leave of this kind is given, for example, to enable a trustworthy prisoner to attend the death-bed or funeral of a close relative; untrustworthy prisoners may be allowed to attend under escort instead. A prisoner who wishes to marry in order to legitimise a child which is likely to be born before the expiration of his sentence is usually released in charge of an escort. Home leave for about five days towards the end of medium or long sentences is now regularly granted to quite a number of prisoners in order to enable them to prepare their minds for the circumstances in which they will be living after release, and so ease the difficult process of adjustment. Prisoners who are serving sentences of three years or longer in training prisons (q.v.) are considered for two periods of home leave in the last twelve months of their sentence, while prisoners who are serving at least two but less than three years are considered for one period of leave.

Remission. Prisoners with determinate sentences are granted a remission for 'industry and good conduct'. The formula for calculating the amount of remission is prescribed in rules by the Home Secretary, and since early in

---

[1] A difference which has since been reduced by the new procedure in the Criminal Justice (Scotland) Act, 1963.

the Second World War has been one-third of the sentence. Exceptions are:
1. Prisoners who forfeit part or all of their remission for offences against prison discipline. Loss of remission is a punishment which may be awarded by a Governor or a Visiting Committee.
2. Prisoners serving sentences of forty-five days or less. The rule is that remission must not reduce the actual period of imprisonment below thirty-one days. There is therefore no remission from a sentence of thirty-one days or less, and a reduced remission from sentences of thirty-two to forty-five days.

Courts must not normally take into account the likelihood of remission when deciding upon the length of a sentence: although it is impossible to be sure that a sentencer is not doing so, his sentence could be the subject of an appeal if his remarks showed that he was. If, however, the purpose of the sentence is 'treatment or reform', the Court of Appeal now regards it as proper to take remission into account: a wide loophole indeed.[1]

Prisoners with indeterminate sentences can sometimes hasten the date of release by good behaviour, but cannot know the extent to which they are doing so. Quite frequently – in 83 cases in 1961 – the prerogative of mercy is invoked to grant a special remission 'as a reward for information given or assistance rendered' and in a few cases – 19 in 1961 – to remit the rest of the sentence of a prisoner who is very seriously ill.

RELEASE ON LICENCE

To be distinguished from ordinary remission (which is the prisoner's right unless he has forfeited it as a result of a disciplinary award) is release on licence, to which no prisoner has a right, and for which only certain categories, defined by statute, are eligible. Again unlike release on remission, release on licence is conditional, the conditions being specified in the licence, and while the licence is in force the ex-prisoner is liable to recall for any breach of the conditions.

The eligible categories are:
1. *Prisoners serving 'life' sentences.* These are *eligible* for release at any date, and their cases are reviewed at regular intervals by the Home Office. The licence remains in force until the end of the ex-prisoner's life, although eventually all conditions may have been deleted from it, in which case his recall is most unlikely;
2. *Recidivists serving 'extended sentences'* (see Chapter 15). They are *eligible* for release on licence at any time after they have served one third of their sentences. If (as is likely in most cases) they are not released before the date on which they become entitled to ordinary remission, release on licence can be substituted: in either case the licence is in force until the end of the sentence. As a third, but unlikely, possibility, they may simply be released on remission, without a licence.
3. *Prisoners who have served at least one third or twelve months of an ordinary sentence, whichever is the longer.* Their licences remain in force until the dates on which their remission would have been due.

[1] See *R. v. Turner*, [1967] *Criminal Law Review*, 118.

TABLE 21 Lengths of prison sentences. Cumulative percentages of
sentences of different length imposed on men and
women received into prisons in 1961.[1]

| length of sentence[2] | England | | Scotland |
	men	women	men[3]
1 to 6 days	0·2	0·4	2·7
1 week or less	2·7	5·2	4·5
2 weeks or less	7·3	13·7	10·2
3	8·6	16·3	23·8
4	12·4	21·8	24·2
1 month or less	20·6	37·7	44·5
2 months or less	29·5	52·7	67·7
3	46·0	72·3	78·9
6	67·1	86·3	91·0
9	73·6	90·0	93·3
12	82·5	94·6	96·3
18	89·0	97·2	97·5
2 years or less	93·5	98·3	98·9
3	97·2	99·6	99·3
4	98·5	99·7	99·6
5	99·5	99·9	99·8
6	99·7	99·9	99·9
7	99·8	99·9	(8 men)
8	99·9		(1 man)
9	99·9		
10	(17 men)		(1 man)
12	(2 men)		(1 man)
13	(1 man)		
14	(3 men)		(1 man)
15	(4 men)	(1 woman)	
19	(1 man)		
20	(2 men)	(1 woman)	
21	(1 man)		
22	(1 man)		
25	(1 man)		
42	(1 man)		
total received (=100%)	37,383	2,419	11,582

[1] Excluding corrective trainees, preventive detainees, 'lifers' and
court-martial prisoners, but including fine-defaulters. Consecutive
sentences are added together.

[2] Ignoring the possibility of remission.

[3] Scottish sentences on women prisoners are not shown: in 1961
they numbered only 768, and the longest was for 18 months.

4. *Prisoners who were under the age of* 21 *when sentenced and who are serving a sentence of at least* 18 *months.* Like prisoners serving extended sentences they may be released on licence after one third or twelve months of their sentence, whichever is the longer, or be released on licence instead of receiving remission (the licence in either case remaining in force until the end of the sentence) or – again an unlikely possibility – receive ordinary remission, without a licence.

5. *Persons dealt with as juveniles under the provision for those convicted of grave crimes* (see Chapter 10 under 'Imprisonment'). Like 'lifers' they may be released on licence at any time, after consultation with the judge who tried them and the Lord Chief Justice. The licence remains in force until the end of their 'sentence' if this was a determinate one, otherwise for the rest of their lives (although eventually all express conditions may be deleted from it).

As a means of exercising some control over the Home Office's power to release on licence the Criminal Justice Act of 1967 was amended during its passage through Parliament to provide for a national Parole Board, and so as to allow the Home Secretary to set up Local Review Committees. The Parole Board must include someone who has held judicial office, a psychiatrist, a person with knowledge or experience of the supervision or after-care of ex-prisoners, and a person who has studied the causes of delinquency or the treatment of offenders (the first British attempt at a statutory definition of a criminologist). The Local Review Committees, of which there is one for each prison consists of the prison Governor (or a Deputy Governor representing him), a member of the Visiting Committee or Board of Visitors (q.v., later in this chapter), a probation and after-care officer, and an independent member without any official connection with the prison service or probation and after-care service. The task of the Local Review Committees is to review the cases of eligible prisoners in their prison and report to the Home Office on their suitability for parole. If the Home Office consider a prisoner suitable, they must obtain the agreement of the Parole Board before releasing him[1]; and if he is a 'lifer' or belongs to category 5 the Home Office must also 'consult' (but not necessarily obtain the agreement of) the Lord Chief Justice and the judge who tried the prisoner (if he is available). The Parole Board may also advise the Home Office about the conditions attached to licences and other matters connected with release on licence or the recall of prisoners on licence. The experience of the first 18 months of the system suggests that 20 to 25 per cent. of the population of sentenced prisoners are eligible for parole, but that of those eligible about 7 per cent. refuse to be considered, and only about 17 per cent, are recommended for it on first review, although another 3 per cent. or so are recommended on second review.

[1] In practice, every case in which a Local Review Committee recommend parole is referred to the Parole Board, although this does not oblige the Home Office to act on their advice.

About 4 per cent. of those paroled have been recalled. An ex-prisoner on licence can be recalled, and his licence revoked

1. on the recommendation of the Parole Board;
2. by the Home Office without consulting the Board if the need seems urgent (but they must later refer the case to the Board, who can recommend immediate release);
3. by a higher court which has convicted him of a further offence punishable with imprisonment.

The normal grounds for revoking the licence are a further conviction for an offence serious enough to be punishable with imprisonment, or a breach of one of the conditions of the licence. Normally, the licence will require him to be under the supervision of a specified probation department; to report on release to an officer of that department; to keep in touch with him as instructed by him; and to inform him of any change of address or loss or change of job. The licence also includes a general requirement that the parolee should be of good behaviour and lead an industrious life. Although sometimes ridiculed as a paper attempt to enforce virtue, this has more point than is usually realised; for it makes it permissible to recall a parolee who, though he has neither been convicted of further law-breaking nor infringed the instructions of the licence or of his supervisor, is nevertheless behaving in such a way that he seems likely to break the law before long. In practice, however, it is invoked only as a last resort.

Prison Administration. Prisons are the direct responsibility of the Home Secretary, who through the Prison Department of the Home Office builds, owns, staffs, and administers prisons, borstals, detention centres, and remand centres.[1] The great majority of prison staffs consist of the uniformed grades of Prison Officers. Recruits to the basic grade spend a month at the prison nearest to their home before being sent to Wakefield or Leyhill for two months' training, during which a considerable number are rejected; even after training they are 'on probation' for a year, during which they can be rejected as simply unsuitable. Later, they can specialise – for example, as Hospital Officers. They are eventually eligible for promotion to Senior Prison Officer, Principal Officer and Chief Officer. Principal Officers and Chief Officers can be selected for the Assistant Governors' training courses, where they are mixed with direct entrants, an increasing percentage of whom are university graduates, usually in the social sciences. Assistant Governors can be promoted to Deputy Governor and Governor, and Governors are from time to time appointed to administrative posts in the central department, which thus consists of a mixture of staff with prison experience and civil servants with experience in the police, criminal, children's or other divisions of the Home Office. Professionally trained staff – chiefly Prison Medical Officers, Prison Psychologists and Welfare Officers – are recruited through the Civil Service Commission.

[1] But not police cells, approved schools, remand homes, attendance centres, children's homes, or the 'special hospitals' (q.v.), although the experimental attendance centres for young adults are directly staffed and run by the Prison Department (see Chapter 10).

Prison Rules. The personalities and training of individual members of the staff[1] probably have more effect than any other factors upon the atmosphere and morale of a prison. The design of prison buildings, which in most cases belongs to the nineteenth century, imposes many limitations which neither staff nor prisoners want. There are, however, two formal codes which also influence the prisoner's life. The best known is embodied in the Prison Rules, which are statutory instruments, published and on sale. They prescribe such matters as the amount of remission which can be earned, the type and quantum of punishments that can be awarded for breaches of discipline, and the rights of the different classes of prisoner. To a great extent their function is to guarantee certain protections to the prisoner against arbitrary treatment. They are made by the Home Secretary, who must lay a draft before Parliament, for discussion if members demand it.[2] Thus while only legislation could alter the maximum length of prison sentences imposable by courts, the Home Secretary could increase or reduce the period which the typical prisoner actually spends in prison, by altering the standard amount of remission for good conduct and industry.

Standing Orders. All prisons, however, are subject to Standing Orders, which are not published, although extracts from them are given to each prisoner on his 'cell card'. They deal with matters of detail, and can be altered by the Governor, but cannot run counter to the Prison Rules.

Visiting Committees. Another protection for prisoners is the visiting committee[3] which must be appointed for each prison. Members of these committees must pay frequent visits to the prison, and the committee itself must meet once a month at the prison. They must have free access to all parts of the prison and every prisoner, and must be allowed to see him, if they want, out of sight and hearing of prison officers. The more drastic awards of punishment can be ordered only by the visiting committee and not by the Governor, and if a prisoner is reported for certain offences, such as assaulting an officer, the case must be referred by the Governor to the committee, unless he dismisses it outright. Visiting committees are sometimes asked by the Home Secretary to hold inquiries into complaints about the management of their prison.[4] Members of visiting

---

[1] As in the army, it is often the personality of the senior staff who have entered through the basic grade which is the most important. The Chief Officer, like the Company Sergeant-Major, has a much greater effect on the prisoner's day-to-day life than has the Governor.

[2] Unlike some statutory instruments, they are not subject to negative or positive resolution, which means that the Home Secretary is not bound by any Parliamentary decision to alter an unpopular draft. In practice, however, he would almost certainly do so.

Strictly speaking, prisons to which prisoners may be committed direct by a court have 'visiting *committees*' appointed by local quarter sessions and justices, while other prisons, borstals and detention centres have '*boards* of visitors' appointed by the Home Secretary.

[4] See, for instance, the Percy Report of 1963 (Cmnd. 2068). It is doubtful whether members of the Visiting Committee or Board for the institution in question are the best people to hold such an inquiry. Not only are they usually on very good terms with the senior staff; they may also be investigating a state of affairs which indirectly reflects on their own effectiveness.

committees should not be confused with prison visitors; the latter are simply individuals allowed by the Governor to visit specified prisoners who seem likely to benefit from the contact.

Types of Prison. Prisons are distinguished as 'local' or 'training', and as 'Category A, B, C' or 'open' – terms which will be explained in the course of the next few pages. In addition prisons and borstals – or parts of them – specialize in providing facilities such as psychiatry. Almost all local prisons still consist of Victorian buildings, conveniently situated for their primary function of producing prisoners quickly in court, but otherwise out of date. The Prison Department, though handicapped by the difficulty of securing enough funds, has in recent years managed to embark on a considerable building programme, which has already provided several new training or specialist establishments. The rising prison population, however, has so far meant that this effort has provided new accommodation without re-placing the old.

Local prisons accommodate practically every kind of prisoner (civil, un-tried, remanded for sentence, stars, ordinaries, young prisoners, and recidivists at certain stages of 'extended sentences') at the outset of their stay in prison, and some of them for the whole of their stay (for example, short-term ordinaries). Although local prisons are the most over-crowded and least well equipped for work or recreation, many prisoners find them more congenial than regional or central prisons because their friends and families find them easier to visit, and because the constant movement of prisoners in and out brings a daily supply of gossip and new faces. Special local prisons receive short-term stars and ordinaries (q.v.) and civil prisoners; most of these are open prisons (q.v.).

As a result of a successful experiment in north-eastern England, prisons are now being organised into regional groups, each of which will eventually have at least one prison of each kind (with the possible exception of highly specialised institutions such as psychiatric prisons).

The Classification of Prisoners. Prisoners are sorted into a number of classes for which different prisons or parts of prisons are reserved. The objectives of the system of classification are:

1. *That persons in custody who have not been found guilty of a criminal offence should not be denied certain privileges which are denied to convicted prisoners.* The Prison Act, 1952, s. 47, requires that there shall be rules for the special treatment of persons awaiting the result of appeals and of unsentenced prisoners.[1] Under the Prison Rules, untried prisoners are separated from convicted prisoners, but may associate more freely amongst themselves; they may wear their own clothing, have food and drink sent in from outside, pay for their cells to be cleaned, correspond more freely with friends or legal advisors, and abstain from prison work unless they want to take part in it. Appellants and convicted prisoners awaiting sentence have only a few privileges designed to assist them in preparing for their appeal or appearance before the sentencing court. Untried and unsentenced

[1] 'Fine-defaulters', however, are treated as sentenced prisoners.

prisoners are kept in ordinary local prisons as near as possible to their place of trial. 'Civil prisoners' who have been imprisoned for non-payment of debts or contempt of court are allowed their own clothing, receive more frequent letters and visits than convicted prisoners, but must eat prison food and do prison work; they are often sent to local open prisons.

2. *That prisoners who are criminally sophisticated should be separated from those who are not.* Until 1964, the Prison Rules required the separation of prisoners under 21 years of age ('young prisoners'), those who were serving their first sentence ('stars'), and others ('ordinaries'), in order to protect the unsophisticated offender from the influence of the experienced criminal. Numerous exceptions had to be made to this rule (for example, because some 'ordinaries' would clearly benefit from being treated as 'stars') and the 1964 Rules allow prisoners to be classified 'having regard to their age, temperament and record, and with a view to maintaining good order and facilitating training.' At present, however, the broad distinctions between 'y.ps.', 'stars', and 'ordinaries' are still the main basis of segregation.

3. *That among convicted prisoners those sentenced to special measures should be differently treated in certain ways.* This principle should probably be regarded as obsolescent, although not yet completely obsolete. Prisoners under sentence of death used to be completely segregated, and watched night and day. Preventive detainees and corrective trainees (q.v.) used to receive special treatment, but both categories have now disappeared, and 'extended sentence' prisoners (q.v.) are treated like any others with long sentences. People imprisoned for seditious offences are still entitled to many of the conditions of unconvicted prisoners (see 1. above); but the Sedition Act is rarely invoked nowadays.

4. *That different prisoners need different degrees of security in their custody.* On the assumption that imprisonment fails to achieve its objective whenever a prisoner escapes, security is one of the main pre-occupations of the system. In 1965 some 2 per cent of the daily average population of males escaped; but if those who were deliberately allowed to live or work in 'open' conditions are excluded the percentage was about 0·4 per cent. Most escapers are recaptured or surrender themselves within a few days or weeks, having done no serious harm; their punishment is a substantial loss of remission. In 1966, however, a series of escapes by criminals who were regarded as dangerous (including Blake the spy) led to the Mountbatten Report[1] and a considerable tightening of security. The Report recommended that prisoners be classified into four categories:

A. those whose escape would be highly dangerous to the public, the police or the security of the State;
B. those for whom the very highest security is not necessary, but for whom escape must be made very difficult;

[1] 1966, Cmnd. 3175.

c. those who cannot be trusted in open conditions, but lack the ability or resources to make determined attempts at escape;

d. those who can reasonably be trusted to serve their sentences in open conditions.

Prisoners in category A go to prisons or wings of prisons with stringent security precautions. Category B prisoners cannot be sent to certain 'closed' prisons where strict security would be incompatible with the regime. Category C can be placed in any ordinary closed prison, but only Category D may go to open prisons. In ordinary closed prisons men who have attempted to escape wear uniforms with yellow patches, and are not allowed to move about the prison without escort.

In spite of the security campaign of 1966, however, the long-term trend in the prison system is towards the relaxation of security. Even the Mountbatten Report recognised that it is not sufficient to classify prisoners according to the likelihood of their escaping: it is more important to consider how much harm they would do if they did escape. By 1965 as much as 17 per cent of men serving prison sentences were doing so in open prisons.

In open prisons prisoners live without restraining walls or locked doors, and some are allowed to go out to work in surrounding farms or villages with very little supervision. Certain types of prisoner are, with occasional exceptions, not allowed to graduate to them:

(a) *men with long sentences and previous prison experience*; although some of the former may graduate to an open prison near the end of their sentences, the incentive to escape is usually too great;

(b) *prisoners who have committed serious offences of violence or sexual assaults;* if these were not excluded, local communities would be much less helpful towards open prisons than they are;

(c) *prisoners with homosexual tendencies which are likely to make them 'dangerous in an open community';*

(d) *stars who are regarded as bad escape risks* because of emotional instability or for other reasons.

5. *That if prisoners who deliberately resist authority and subvert discipline are segregated the staff can treat the remainder less strictly.* They thus have a better chance of establishing good relations and allowing other relaxations of discipline which may not only make prison life pleasanter but also more beneficial. It is for this reason that a small number of prisoners are eventually classified as 'recalcitrants' and sent to special wings.

6. *That the sexes must be segregated.* There are separate prisons, or wings of prisons, for women prisoners, and strict rules about the presence of male officers or prisoners in them. Historically the reason for this was the abuse of female prisoners by male warders or prisoners. More will be said about women's prisons in Chapter 14.

It is noticeable that the principles I have outlined so far are negative; each one is simply designed to counteract some unintended and undesirable effect of imprisonment. In recent years, however, there have been signs of the application of a principle intended to enhance any positive influence which imprisonment may have upon its subjects:

7. *That different types of delinquent personality respond to different types of regime.* This is one of the important assumptions upon which the borstal classification (q.v.) of youths into mature and immature, sophisticated and unsophisticated, is based. In adult prisons the best example is the deliberate policy of making up the population of some training prisons largely from stars but with an admixture of ordinaries who seem likely to respond to the special regime. A more specialised example is the attempt to apply psychotherapeutic techniques to prisoners whose offences seem to arise from abnormalities of personality. The difficulties of doing so in the atmosphere of an ordinary prison have led to the establishment of special wings at prisons such as Wakefield. More recently still, an entire prison has been designed and built at Grendon for offenders who, though not sufficiently abnormal to justify transfer to a mental hospital, are likely to benefit from psychiatric treatment and a regime adapted to this.[1]

Feltham serves a similar purpose within the Borstal system.

Numbers and Classification. Obviously, the more prisons there are the more subdivisions are possible. If it is decided to have more subdivisions than prisons, different wings of the same prison must be devoted to different purposes. Although this is what is done it is not entirely satisfactory, because staff are moved from one wing to another to fill gaps caused by sick leave or holidays or mere short-handedness, and they carry the habits of one wing over to the other. The alternative, however, is to have a large number of very small prisons, which increases the number of staff required per prisoner, and other 'overheads'.[2]

Consequently, the classification of minority groups is almost inevitably cruder than the system I have just described. Women offenders, for reasons which will be discussed in Chapter 14, are relatively much less numerous, and in 1961 there was only one in prison for every thirty men. Half of the 900 women prisoners were either in Holloway or in Manchester prisons.

Another relatively small group is the Scottish prisoners, for whom there is a separate prison system, administered by the Scottish Home and Health Department It comprises only nine prisons, one of them devoted largely to women. In 1961, out of a daily average population of 2,300, two-thirds were in the two prisons in Glasgow and Edinburgh. Scotland has only one small open prison, and no psychiatric prison, and the service would be improved by amalgamation with the English system.

After-care. To what extent imprisonment achieves its *intended* effects is a question that will be discussed in Chapter 12. Whatever the answer, there seems to be general agreement about the nature of at least some of its *side-effects*: loss of one's job, impaired capacity for work, estrangement from one's family, the formation of criminal associations and ways of thinking

---

[1] See chapter 13, on mentally abnormal offenders.

[2] In 1965 the average annual cost per inmate for all the Prison Department's institutions was £780 (for detention centres it was £898, for borstals £841, for remand centres £840 and for prisons £757). See the Estimates Committee's 11th Report (1966-7), p. viii.

Admittedly it is often too readily assumed that these misfortunes are attributable to a prison sentence, and that before it the prisoner was a model worker, husband and father. I know of no investigation which makes a genuine attempt to measure the side-effects of incarceration. Nevertheless, one of the major developments of recent years has been the emphasis on what is known as 'after-care', a form of social work which is very largely an effort to counter-act these side-effects.

'Voluntary after-care', which the ex-prisoner is not obliged to accept, must be distinguished from the compulsory supervision to which certain categories must submit. Supervision is compulsory for all ex-prisoners on licence (q.v. *supra*) and also for prisoners who were under 21 when sentenced to less than eighteen months imprisonment; they are released when their remission (if any) falls due, but like detention-centre inmates (q.v. in Chapter 10) are under supervision for a year afterwards. The supervisor is normally a probation officer of the same sex. Most probation departments, however, are making use of some 1200 unpaid 'associates' to supplement their professional supervision by befriending the ex-prisoner.

The formal conditions of the licence have already been mentioned. In practice, whether the ex-prisoner is on licence or not, the probation officer's main concerns are his prospects of steady employment and his relations with his family. Officers of the Department of Employment and Productivity visit prisons to help with the finding of jobs. Probation departments have contacts with employers who are willing to give steady work to ex-prisoners, although some prisoners prefer to find their own jobs ((for example because they do not believe that they can conceal their record from fellow-workers if the employer knows it).

As for family relationships, there is certainly evidence (which will be mentioned in the chapter on recidivists) that prisoners whose contacts with their families are poor are more likely to be reconvicted.[1] An excellent study of prisoners' relationships with their wives (by Pauline Morris, 1965) confirms that most prisoners' marriages, and especially those of recidivists, were showing signs of serious strain before imprisonment, and suggests that if a marriage was even moderately harmonious it will not usually be broken by a single prison sentence, only by a series of sentences. The scope for successful marital conciliation is thus unlikely to be large, and in any case a probation officer must think hard about the interests of the family as a whole before deciding to use them as an instrument of rehabilitation. On the other hand, Mrs Morris' investigation disclosed a considerable need for material aid to relieve real poverty among prisoners' families during their sentences.

The days or weeks immediately after release, when the ex-prisoner has not yet begun to earn money and has not yet settled down in a home, are said to be the time when he is especially likely to commit another offence. His first visit to a public-house may lead to trouble with the police; or his first wage-packet may seem so far off that he steals in order to raise ready money. Efforts are made to ensure that he is not destitute during this critical period. If his sentence was for more than four years he receives a

[1] See the chapter on recidivists.

L

complete new outfit of clothing; otherwise he is dressed in the clothes in which he entered, with any deficiencies made up to a reasonable standard. He is given his fare home, and a sum of money for subsistence. If he has nothing to live on until he begins to earn, he is given a document to show to the Department of Health and Social Security, who will keep him from destitution in the interval. Unless he has been able to keep up his National Insurance contributions during imprisonment – and few prisoners do – he is given a new insurance card.[1] Prisoners serving more than three months who are willing to accept help in finding work are interviewed by officers of the Department of Employment and Productivity. The prison welfare officer, who is a member of the reception board that interviews each prisoner at the beginning of his sentence, tries to find out whether he has any domestic or other problems that will make it difficult for him to settle down after release; if so, an effort is made to straighten them out, unless the prisoner prefers nothing to be done.

To help long-term prisoners to adjust themselves to the difficulties that they face on release, voluntary lectures and discussions are held in some prisons. For the last few months of their sentences prisoners serving a sentence of more than four years may be selected for pre-release hostels. These are managed by the Prison Department, and are annexes of ordinary prisons which segregate the 'hostellers' from the other prisoners; in some cases the hostels are completely outside the prison. The prisoner goes out unescorted by day to work at a job which has been found for him, and which he can keep after release if he wishes to. The fact that he is a prisoner is concealed if possible from his fellow-workers, but is, of course, known to the employer, who must communicate at once with the prison if the 'hosteller' fails to arrive at work at the right time. After work he is free to visit his family or friends, subject only to the requirement that he must be back in the hostel by 11 p.m.; and he can get leave to spend the week-end at home.

Half-way Houses. The pre-release hostels, however, are at present reserved for a relatively small number of carefully selected long-term prisoners. A need which has only recently been recognised – although it was pointed out by Bentham – is post-release hostels in which prisoners – whether under compulsory supervision or not – can spend the awkward period of transition between custody and freedom. Indeed for some recidivists the only chance of keeping out of prison seems to lie in more or less permanent residence under the tactful but vigilant management which a good hostel of this kind can provide. The Home Office now gives grants to organisations which provide places in hostels for ex-prisoners.

SUSPENDED PRISON SENTENCES

The court which passes a prison sentence may suspend it; that is, may add an order that it is not to take effect unless during what is called 'the

---

[1] This practice is often criticised as making it obvious to employers where he has been. It is defended on the grounds that discharged servicemen, hospital patients and British subjects returning from abroad receive similar cards. It would be possible to stamp prisoners' cards during their sentence at the country's expense, but this would be criticised (by a different body of opinion) on the principle of 'less eligibility' (q.v).

operational period' the offender commits another offence punishable
with imprisonment and as a result a court orders the sentence to take
effect. The operational period is specified in the original order, and
must be not less than one year and not more than two years. The sentence
itself must not be more than two years in length. If its length is six
months[1] or less then the court is *obliged* to suspend it unless one
of a number of conditions are satisfied. (It is not obliged to, but *may*,
suspend the short sentence if the offence involved an assault, a threat
of violence, the possession or use of firearms or other weapons, or
indecent conduct toward a person under the age of 16; or if the offender
had originally been put on probation or conditionally discharged for
the offence or was subject to a probation order or conditional discharge for another offence; or if the court is passing a sentence of
immediate imprisonment for another offence; or if the offender is serving,
or has ever served a prison or borstal sentence, or been already subject to
a suspended sentence.)[1]

If the offender is again convicted of an offence punishable with imprisonment during the operational period, the suspended sentence does
not automatically take effect: it does so only if a court so orders.
Normally it must so order if it knows that he is subject to a suspended
sentence. But if it states its reasons for thinking that 'it would be unjust
to do so in view of all the circumstances which have arisen since the
suspended sentence was passed, including the facts of the subsequent
offence', it can take one of three other courses. It can substitute a
shorter prison sentence; it can continue the suspension for a further
period, which must not be longer than three years from that date;
or it may simply make no order at all. In any event, it can also sentence
him for the latest offence. If it passes another prison sentence it can
order the suspended sentence to take effect as soon as the other has
ended, or it can make the two concurrent. If the suspended sentence was
passed by a higher court a magistrates' court cannot decide whether it
is to take effect or not, but must either commit him to a higher court or
inform the higher court which passed the suspended sentence of his new
conviction.

One of the aims with which the suspended sentence was introduced in
England[2] in 1967 was the reduction of the number of offenders sent to
prison for short periods: hence, in particular, the mandatory suspension of
sentences of six months or less unless the offender seems likely to do personal
harm to someone, or has already failed to respond to an actual or suspended
sentence. Table 21 shows that in 1961 two-thirds of all the sentences
imposed on men, and 86 per cent of women's sentences, were of six months

[1] But note that the Home Secretary can make two important changes by subordinate
legislation. He can order that (with the exceptions mentioned) any sentence of *twelve*
months or less must be suspended. He can also order that the exception for offenders
who have already been subject to actual or suspended sentences shall apply only to
sentences passed within a specified period before the offence in question. The period
specified, however, must not be less than three years.
[2] But not in Scotland.

or less. The first year of suspended sentences – 1968 – saw a sharp drop in sentences of six months or less, although some of course must only have been postponed. The figures also showed that some suspended sentences were being used instead of fines and probation orders.

FINES

Although fines are the least spectacular of penal measures, they are numerically the most important, certainly the cheapest, and by no means the least effective (see Chapter 10). Over a million of them are imposed each year for indictable offences, motoring offences and other non-indictable offences. Indictable offences apart, eleven out of every twelve offences are dealt with by fines.

An adult can be fined for any offence for which the penalty is not fixed by law.[1] For all but a few offences[2] the amount of the fine is limited by statutory maxima,[3] and in Scotland also by general limits on the amounts of fines imposable by courts of summary jurisdiction.[4] Some statutes allow a person to be both fined and imprisoned for the same offence, and if convicted of more than one offence at the same appearance he may be fined for one and imprisoned for another. A fine cannot, however, be combined with a probation order or conditional discharge.[5]

In fixing the amount of a fine, courts are expected (and lower courts are required) to take into consideration, *inter alia*, what they know of the offender's means.[6] Since fines are frequently used, however, it is difficult for courts to make thorough inquiries into a person's means; and indeed their power to exact information is limited. Fines for traffic offences (which account for three quarters of all fines) tend to be fixed according to locally agreed rules of thumb, with little regard to the offender's earnings; but since most such fines are small the hardship which they cause is probably not great. It has been suggested, however, that a more rational system for determining the amount of fines could be devised on the lines of the Swedish 'day-fine' system. A 'day-fine' is the amount which, in the court's view, the offender can spare from his day's earnings by exercising great economy; and the number of day-fines which he must pay is fixed by the court in the light of the gravity of the offence. Even in Sweden, however, the majority of fines are fixed without invoking the day-fine system.

---

[1] i.e. for offences other than murder, high treason, piracy with violence and setting fire to Her Majesty's ships or arsenals.

[2] e.g. forging a passport, certain corrupt practices, and carrying an offensive weapon in a public place.

[3] The maxima for a large number of offences, which had become out of date as a result of the declining value of money, were revised in the 3rd schedule for the Criminal Justice Act, 1967.

[4] £150 for Sheriffs without juries and Stipendiary Magistrates, £50 for Justice of the Peace Courts, Burgh Courts and Police Courts. But statutes, especially recent ones, sometimes lay down other limits for such courts in the case of certain offences.

[5] At least in England: see *R. v. Parry* [1951] 1 K.B. 590; *R. v. McLelland* [1951] 1 All E.R. 557.   [6] See *R. v. Brook* [1949] 2 K.B. 138.

Another problem is the enforcement of fines. The usual practice is to ask the offender, when imposing the fine, whether he can pay there and then. If not (and he can be searched if the court so orders) he can ask for time to pay, and for permission to pay in instalments. The traditional sanction is imprisonment for default, but this is now discouraged by a number of limitations. Although higher courts must still, when fining, fix a term of imprisonment (not exceeding 12 months) to be served in default, this must not result in the immediate imprisonment of the offender unless he seems to have the means to pay forthwith (but does not), or appears unlikely to remain long enough at a 'place of abode' in the United Kingdom to enable payment to be enforced by other means, or is being sentenced to a term in prison or a detention centre, or is already serving one. Otherwise the higher court delegates enforcement to the appropriate magistrates' court.[1]

Magistrates' courts, on the other hand, must not even fix the term of imprisonment when imposing the fine, but (with the same exceptions) must wait until the offender defaults, and then (unless he is already serving a prison or detention centre sentence) must inquire into his means in his presence. Unless the offence itself is punishable with imprisonment and the offender seems able to pay forthwith, they must try – or at least consider – all other means of enforcement and must come to the conclusion that they are inappropriate or unsuccessful before they are allowed to commit him to prison. The periods for which they can do so are severely limited, ranging from seven to ninety days, according to the amount of the fine. On the other hand if there has been any change in his circumstances which would justify remitting all or part of the fine, they can do so (but only with the consent of a higher court if the fine was originally imposed by that court).[1]

The other means of enforcement are attachment of earnings, a warrant of distress and a money payment supervision order. The first involves an order which enables the fine to be recovered from the offender's employer and deducted from his earnings.[2] A warrant of distress authorises the seizure of the offender's money and goods.[3] A money payment supervision order places the offender under the supervision of a suitable person, usually a probation officer, until the fine is paid or it is clear that this method will not succeed.[4]

In prison a fine-defaulter is classed as a 'star' or 'ordinary' like other sentenced prisoners. Because his term is a short one he usually remains in a local prison, but may be sent to an open prison. He is entitled to the normal remission (if his term is long enough); and if he decides after all to pay the fine, or part of it, he can obtain release at once or after he has served the fraction of his term which corresponds to the unpaid part.[5]

Even before the Criminal Justice Act, 1967, compelled courts to take even more care before sending fine-defaulters to prison, the numbers who went to prison represented less than one per cent of persons fined. These

[1] See CJA 48, s. 14, and CJA 67, ss. 44-7.
[2] CJA 67, s. 46.
[3] MCA 52, ss. 64-6.
[4] MCA 52, s. 71
[5] MCA 52, s. 67(2).

offenders were often chronic drinkers, or had already been to prison for other reasons, so that in their case prison could not be expected to be an effective sanction.

Fines without Trial. Following examples abroad, the Road Traffic and Roads Improvement Act, 1960, introduced what is known as the 'fixed penalty prodecure'. This gives a person detected in a minor traffic offence the opportunity of paying a prescribed sum of money (usually £2) instead of being prosecuted, although he can choose the latter course if he prefers it. The procedure applies only to areas specified from time to time by the Home Secretary at the request of the local police authority, and only to breaches of the lighting requirements for stationary vehicles or to parking offences. A notice is given to the offender (either personally or by fixing it to his vehicle) by a constable or traffic warden. By paying the 'penalty' (which is strictly speaking not a 'fine') to the local justices' clerk the offender 'discharges any liability to conviction' for the offence.[1]

The fixed penalty procedure was instituted to save the time of both police and courts. Most offenders too prefer it not only because the penalty is less than the maximum fine for the offence but also because they avoid an appearance in court and a conviction. Its extension to some other traffic offences has been promised by the Government,[2] and there is no obvious reason why it should not be applied to minor offences of some other kinds, such as failure to have radio or television licences.

PROBATION

Instead of sentencing an offender a court may make an order known as a 'probation order', which places him under the supervision of a probation officer for a specified period. The only offences which cannot be dealt with in this way are murder and the other rare crimes for which the penalty is fixed by law. Otherwise, the court is merely required to have regard to the circumstances, including the nature of the offence and the character of the offender, and if it comes to the conclusion that this is an 'expedient' method of dealing with him may adopt it.[3] Although it is often regarded as a 'second chance' for a first offender, over a quarter of those placed on probation in 1961 had been on probation before, some of them three times or more. It is even used for serious offences such as attempted murder, especially if there is evidence of a moderate degree of mental abnormality,[4] or some extenuating circumstance. If the offender has ceased to be a child, he cannot be placed on probation without his consent; but since the alternative would almost certainly be a fine or imprisonment he seldom refuses. The specified duration of the order must be not less than one nor more than three years; over half the orders in the case of adults are for two years, and over a quarter for three.

[1] See s. 80 of the Road Traffic Regulation Act, 1967, which is a consolidation of this among other enactments.

[2] See para. 33 of the White Paper *Road Safety – a Fresh Approach* (Cmnd. 3339 1967, H.M.S.O.)

[3] For the statutes governing probation, see CJA 48, ss. 3-6, 8, 11, 12 and Sch. I & V: CJ(S)A 49, ss. 2-13 and Sch. I-III.   [4] See Chapter 13.

Probation Officers. Probation officers, unlike prison staff, are the employees not of a central department but of local committees of magistrates,[1] who are responsible for appointing and paying them, and providing them with offices, equipment, and clerical staff. The supervision of probationers is only one of the officer's functions; equally important are the after-care of discharged prisoners and borstal boys, matrimonial conciliation work with couples considering divorce or separation, and – perhaps the most important of all – the preparation of reports on offenders to assist courts in considering their sentence.[2] The work of probation departments is supervised by the Probation Inspectorate of the Home Office, and the selection of applicants who seem suitable for training as probation officers is done with care, although the shortage of fully trained applicants at present compels some probation committees to appoint officers who have not undergone the full process of selection and training. There are different courses of training, of varying lengths, for candidates of different ages and educational levels. A probation officer is not confirmed until a year (sometimes two years) after he has entered his first post, during which his work is subject to particularly close attention from his own Senior or Principal Probation Officer.

Combining Probation with Other Types of Sentence. Since the Act (s.3) states clearly that the court places an offender on probation 'instead of sentencing him', probation cannot be combined with, say, a fine or – as some people would like – a short sentence of imprisonment. The Act, however, did not say what was to happen if the offender was dealt with at the same time for more than one offence; and until 1958 there were a number of cases in which courts did impose a Borstal or detention centre sentence for one offence, and a long probation order for another offence, so that when the offender came out he would still be subject to it. In the case of *R. v. Evans*,[3] however, the Court of Criminal Appeal held that while the Act did not expressly prohibit this, it was contrary to the spirit and intention of the Act, and that there was the further objection that the probation order could not be effective until the offender was released. In Scotland there was a similar decision in 1964.[4]

There is nothing, however, to prevent courts from fining an offender for one offence and putting him on probation for another, as many do. Moreover, even if the offender is found guilty of only one offence, the Act explicitly allowed probation to be combined with permission to any other person to give security for his good behaviour. It also allows probation to be combined with an order that the offender should pay damages for injury or compensation for loss caused by his offence, but does not allow this to be

---

[1] In 1966 there were 84 'probation committees' in England. In theory there is one for each petty sessional division (in Scotland, for each county and large burgh), but the advantages of probation departments with substantial staffs, under the supervision of senior officers, have led to combinations of areas, a process which has been accelerated as a result of the recommendations of the Morison Committee (1962).
[2] See Chapter 11.   [3] [1958] 3 All E.R. 673.
[4] In *Downie* v. *Irvine* [1964] *Scots Law Times* at 205.

made a requirement of the order itself, so that failure to pay is not a breach of the order.[1] In 1960 about one in every eleven probation orders was combined with orders to pay damages or compensation.

The Probation Order. Higher courts are free to word a probation order as they please, but a form of probation order is prescribed which courts may use.[2] It contains the following requirements, although a court may delete, modify or supplement any of them:

'1. to be of good behaviour and lead an industrious life;
2. to inform the probation officer at once of any change of residence or employment;
3. to keep in touch with the probation officer in accordance with such instructions as may from time to time be given by the probation officer and, in particular, if the probation officer so requires, to receive visits from the probation officer at whatever address is stipulated.'

The English order merely names the petty sessional division in which the offender lives or will live; and the effect is that he is supervised by an officer assigned to that division by the probation committee.[3]

Two optional requirements are expressly mentioned by the Act:
1. the offender should live in a certain place; this is included if the court has considered his 'home surroundings' and concluded that he is more likely to keep out of trouble if he lives elsewhere. Often the probation officer is able to suggest suitable lodgings. This requirement is more frequently imposed on juveniles than on adult probationers, only about 2 per cent of whom are subjected to it;
2. he should submit to treatment for his mental condition. This is frequently imposed on adults, and will be discussed more fully in Chapter 13.

Breach of Probation Order. If the probationer fails to comply with any of these requirements, the probation officer may bring him before a magistrates' court, which may either fine him an amount not exceeding £20, or deal with him for the original offence (or, if the probation order was made by a higher court, commit him to that court to be dealt with). In practice, probation officers have to use their judgement as to whether they should treat a breach of the order in so formal and drastic a manner.

Although the probationer is strictly speaking convicted[4] of his offence, his conviction must be disregarded for the purpose of any statute which

[1] In Scotland, where there is no corresponding provision, some courts do make reparation a condition of the probation order.

[2] The Scottish form is in the statute, and obliges all courts, higher and lower, to include at least the requirements (1) to be of good behaviour; (2) to conform to the directions of the probation officer as to conduct.

[3] Scottish courts are required to name the probation officer himself. The Morison Committee could see no advantage in this.

[4] In Scotland, only superior courts proceed to a conviction before placing an offender on probation or discharging him; summary courts do so after the charge has been proved and without convicting. But this does not prevent a probation order or a discharge in summary proceedings from being laid before the court *as if* it were a previous conviction.

imposes (or allows or requires the imposition of) any disqualification or disability upon a 'convicted person'. This prevents, for example, a court from withdrawing someone's driving licence for an offence for which it has placed him on probation.[1] The conviction is also deemed not to be one for any purpose other than the proceedings in which the probation order was made[2]; so that, for example, it could not be counted towards the number of previous convictions needed to render an offender eligible for corrective training.[3]

NOMINAL MEASURES

Absolute or Conditional Discharge. Unless the penalty for the offence is fixed by law, any court may dispose of the offender by an order for absolute or conditional discharge. In order to do so, it must have considered 'the circumstances, including the nature of the offence and the character of the offender', and come to the conclusion that it is 'inexpedient' to inflict punishment and that a probation order is not appropriate. If the discharge is absolute no further steps can be taken against the offender under the criminal law, although he may, of course, be sued under civil law if he has caused injury or damage. If the discharge is conditional – and most of them are – he is discharged subject to the condition that if he commits another offence during the specified period – which must not exceed three years – he will be liable to be sentenced for the original offence. Other conditions – for example that the offender returns to his own country – are occasionally imposed, but are improper and unenforceable. The conviction of a discharged offender is disregarded to the same extent as that of a probationer. Absolute discharges are used in a variety of circumstances. The offender may be technically guilty, but morally innocent (for example, because he was excusably unaware of the statute which he infringed. He may be very young – or old. He may be under some mental handicap or disturbance which is not sufficiently severe to justify the court in requiring him to be treated. It may be obvious that the shock of his appearance in court is all that is required to punish or correct him. Conditional discharges seem to be used when, in somewhat similar circumstances, the court is not quite so confident that the offender will not offend again.

Recognisances. For any offence except murder, a court can order an offender to enter into a 'recognisance' – that is, a recorded contract – to keep the peace and be of good behaviour. The effect is that he is liable to surrender a specified sum of money if he fails to keep to the terms of the recognisance. When imposing a recognisance the court may also ask for some other person to act as 'surety', in which case that person also forfeits a

---

[1] This protection is lost, however, if an offender who was seventeen or older at the time of the offence is later brought back to court and sentenced for it as a result of his subsequent misbehaviour.

[2] Or, of course, any subsequent proceedings arising out of the offence for which he was placed on probation; see CJA 48, s.12.

[3] *R.* v. *Stobbart* [1951] 35 Cr.App.R. 125. No doubt courts will apply the same principle to 'extended sentences' (q.v.).

specified sum in the event of a breach of the recognisance. In the case of certain offences[1] this method can be combined with any other permissible punishment; otherwise it seems to be used instead of passing sentence. Unlike probation or discharge this procedure does not have the effect of requiring the conviction to be disregarded.[2]

Scotland. A Scottish court may discharge an offender absolutely (which under summary procedure means that he has been found guilty but not 'convicted'), or admonish him, or defer sentence. An admonition is simply a reprimand which carries conviction. A deferred sentence is the Scottish equivalent of a conditional discharge. The court announces that it will defer sentence for a period (usually a year): at the end of this period the offender's conduct is reported on by a probation or police officer, and the court decides upon its sentence in the light of this report. The legality of this procedure has now been placed beyond doubt by a Scottish statute,[3] but attempts by English courts to defer sentence have been severely criticised by the Court of Criminal Appeal.[4]

CAUTIONING

Although this chapter is primarily concerned with the means by which criminal courts are able to dispose of adult offenders, we should not forget the semi-formal method of dealing with them known as 'cautioning'.[5] English[6] police forces have considerable freedom in deciding whether to prosecute or not. They are obliged by law to report certain serious offences to the Director of Public Prosecutions, but otherwise may exercise discretion. Sometimes the decision whether to report a minor breach of the law is taken by a constable, who may simply admonish the offender without formally reporting the incident; but if an offence is formally reported, and an identifiable individual is suspected of being the culprit, the decision whether to prosecute is taken by a senior officer. Sometimes he concludes that the evidence is too thin to offer a reasonable prospect of a conviction, and abandons the idea of prosecuting for this reason. If the offence is not serious, shows no signs of professional criminality, and has been committed by

---

[1] See the Coinage Act, 1936; the Malicious Damage Act, 1861; the Offences Against the Person Act, 1861; the Forgery Acts, 1861 and 1913.

[2] *Jephson* v. *Barker & Redman, Times Law Report* [1886], 3, 40.

[3] CJ(S)A 63, S.47.

[4] *R.* v. *Wall,* [1957] 41 Cr. App. R. 97; *R.* v. *West,* [1959] 43 Cr.App.R. 109.

[5] In some areas, and especially in Scotland, this practice is referred to as a 'police warning', which is both more expressive and less confusing. The confusion arises because of the use of 'caution' to refer to the stage in the interrogation of a suspect when the police remind him that what he says may be used as evidence; and to increase the confusion 'caution' is used by Scottish courts as the equivalent of the English 'recognisance'. Nevertheless, since the term 'cautioning' is in official use in England – for example in the Criminal Statistics – it would be pedantic to avoid it here.

[6] Scottish police forces also have a certain amount of freedom in deciding whether to report an offence to the public prosecutor (the local Procurator Fiscal), who in turn has some discretion in the matter of prosecuting, and may issue a warning (or instruct the police to do so.)

someone with a blameless record (especially if he or she is very young or very old), the senior officer may decide to let the offender off with a warning. Some police forces have a list of the sort of cases in which this is permissible. This is a frequent method of dealing with traffic offences which have not caused personal injury. A formal caution for a traffic offence is usually delivered in writing, whereas in the case of other sorts of offence it is almost always delivered orally, but is recorded. An offender who wishes to maintain and vindicate his innocence is not, of course, obliged to accept a caution, and may prefer to plead not guilty in court; but few exercise this right.

In 1961 nearly a quarter of a million cautions were administered to motorists. Other non-indictable offences by adults are sometimes dealt with in this way (about 7 per cent in 1961). A small percentage of indictable offences by adults (3 per cent in 1961) were regarded as trivial enough to be dismissed with a police caution. Most of them were probably thefts of small value, or committed by men or women with no criminal record and a respectable background. The most important use of this method is in the field of juvenile delinquency, and more will be said about this in the next chapter.

The proportions in which the measures described in this chapter are used by English courts can be studied in Table 22. These proportions are not quite static, however, and post-war trends in the use of different measures will be discussed in Chapter eleven.

POSSIBLE DEVELOPMENTS

It is worth considering the directions in which the measures which have been outlined in this chapter might develop in the future, and what new features might conceivably be introduced. It need hardly be said that there will be many technical developments. New designs for prisons, improved methods of administering them, the extension of the open prison and the pre-release hostel to a larger percentage of the prison population, are obvious examples. Other possibilities include innovations in techniques of handling probationers or of allocating them to the most suitable probation officer. But there may also be formal changes in the type of measure which is permissible.

Semi-detention. An innovation which might well be imported from Europe is some form of 'semi-detention', that is, some form of custody which is not so complete as to prevent the offender from retaining his job and maintaining some sort of relationship with his family. At present our nearest approach to this type of custody is to be found in the pre-release hostel, where selected long-term prisoners are allowed to go out to work and to spend their leisure at home in the last stage of their sentence. But in Belgium, for example, a similar system has now been developed further by allowing certain offenders to be sentenced to 'semi-detention'. Under this sentence, the prisoner is allowed to leave prison in order to carry on his normal work, but must return to it after working-hours, and spend the whole week-end in custody. Another sentence of a similar kind is 'week-end custody', under which the offender spends the working week at his home and place of work, but reports to the prison each week-end. On the assumption that loss of job and the deterioration of family relationships are among the undesirable effects of imprisonment, it seems logical to experiment with this solution in the case of offenders who have a record of steady employment and a stable family life, and whose offences are not too grave. Clearly there is little point in applying it to those without such advantages at stake; and it would be necessary to segregate those under 'semi-detention' from those serving ordinary sentences. But the experience of other countries does not suggest that the difficulties are insuperable.[1]

Indeterminate and Semi-determinate Sentences. It would be possible to make much more use of the indeterminate or semi-determinate prison sentence than we do at present. An indeterminate sentence is one of which the length is left completely to the discretion of the executive; at the moment this is done only in two rare types of case in Britain. For murderers a 'life' sentence, which is in effect indeterminate, is at present mandatory. For certain other offences it is discretionary, but used in only a handful of cases each year. A semi-determinate sentence is one of which the maximum length is fixed by the sentencing court, but from which the prisoner may be released, conditionally or unconditionally, by the decision of the executive; under some systems the court may also specify the minimum period which he must spend in prison. Semi-determinate sentences are confined in this country to young offenders: as we shall see in the next chapter, borstal training and approved school orders are in effect short semi-determinate sentences with fixed maxima and minima; and a juvenile under the age of 17 who is convicted of a very grave offence can be placed at the disposal of the Home Secretary for a period specified by the court.

It has been suggested by Professor Cross[2] that all prison sentences of more than six months should be semi-determinate, with a maximum fixed by the court within the limits allowed by law, but with a minimum of six months fixed by law.[3] Within these limits the prisoner could be released on licence by the Prison Department when his progress justified this.

Suppose – argues Cross – that a man has been convicted of a serious sexual offence. The judge sentences him to five years' imprisonment. He receives treatment in prison and after two years a competent doctor considers that the chances of a repetition of the crime have been sufficiently reduced to render the prisoner's release a safe risk from the point of view of the general public. What penal principle would be infringed if the prisoner was released? The original sentence would have served its purpose of deterring others; the odium attaching to the offence has likewise been reflected in the sentence, and society has been protected by the cure of the criminal. All that can be said against . . . release is that the prisoner would not have

---

[1] See, for example, the article by P. Cornil in *Revue de Droit Penal et de Criminologie*, April 1963, 'Les Arrêts de fin de semaine et la semi-detention'.

[2] 1962.

[3] The point of the minimum is simply to oblige the executive to detain the prisoner at least slightly longer than they would have had to do if his sentence had been of six months or less.

TABLE 22 Methods by which offenders of both sexes aged 21 or older were dealt with by English courts or police in 1968

method of dealing with the offender	indictable offences		non-indictable offences	
	Assizes and Quarter Sessions	Magistrates' courts	Magistrates' courts	
			non-motoring	motoring
	%p	%p	%p	%p
absolute discharge	n	1	1	1
conditional discharge	3	13	3	n
recognisance	n	n	1	–
probation	10	8	1	n
fine	11	53	90	98
suspended sentence	21	14	2	n
immediate imprisonment	53	8	2	n
hospital order	2	n	n	n
otherwise dealt with	n	4q	n	n
total dealt with by courts	24,488as	117,830a	262,751a	818,425a
cautioned by police	5,889a		16,903a	272,061a

a Since individuals may be dealt with more than once in the same year, these figures represent occasions and not individuals

n Negligible: i.e., less than 0·5%

p Since percentages are given as whole numbers, they do not always total 100 per cent

q Nearly all committed to quarter sessions for sentence

s Including persons sentenced at higher courts after conviction at lower courts

received the punishment he deserved, but I do not think that deserts are the kind of things that can be measured in terms of the length of a prison sentence. . . . Another case in which it is highly desirable that the period of imprisonment should be indeterminate is that of the 'exemplary' sentence. . . . Many people feel uneasy about this way of using one individual as an example. . . . Their scruples might well be diminished if it were only the size of the maximum sentence that were exemplary.

This proposal is of particular importance because it leads almost inevitably to the question 'To what extent should the courts continue to perform the function of sentencing as well as the function of ensuring a proper trial of guilt?' I shall return to this question in the chapter on sentencing.

An equally well-argued case, however, has been put forward by Mr Bottoms in Cambridge[1] for a system of standardised semi-determinate prison sentences for adults. On the assumption that – some persistent and serious offenders apart – all sentences should be long enough to make training possible, he proposes

    a. that all sentences of less than six months should be abolished:

    b. that courts should have a choice between three types of 'training sentence'–

        short: from 6 months to 2 years;

        medium: from 2 to 4 years;

        long: from 4 to 7 years;

        but that the periods actually served by each prisoner should be decided by the executive in the light of his progress.

    c. that there might be a longer type of sentence for persistent offenders or those who commit serious crimes.[2]

The introduction of parole is a step in the direction of semi-determinate sentences, just as the mandatory suspension of short sentences (even with liberal exceptions) is a step towards their abolition. All such systems, however, – including Cross' and Bottoms' – have to face an important difficulty: that they require prison staff to decide if and when the prisoner has been reformed. To do so from his behaviour 'inside' is notoriously difficult (It is easier to do so from his previous career, as the parole system to some extent does, but this weakens the case for leaving the decision to the executive). Experience of the borstal and approved school systems suggests that staff tend instead to adopt a more or less uniform estimate of the stage at which the 'typical' inmate becomes ripe for release, and use this as a rule of thumb. This is especially likely if the institution has a system of 'stages' or 'grades' through which well-behaved inmates must pass. Even so, some form of semi-determinate sentence seems preferable to one which allows – indeed compels – the court to decide the date of a man's release years in advance.

  [1] See his article 'Towards a custodial training sentence for adults' in (1965) Criminal Law Review, October and November.

  [2] This raises a different sort of problem, which is discussed in Chapter 15.

YOUNG

OFFENDERS

MODIFICATIONS OF THE SYSTEM

The system described in the last chapter is modified in a number of respects when it is applied to young offenders. Most of the formal modifications are limited to juveniles, with whom most of this chapter is concerned: but a section at the end deals with young adults. There seem to be eight important differences:

1. We saw in Chapter 1 that private citizens not infrequently refrain for various reasons from reporting even adult offenders to the police; and this tendency is even stronger where the offender is a child. The more trivial the delinquency, the younger the offender and the more severe the penalty is imagined to be, the less likely it is that the law will be invoked. Historically this must be the oldest way of tempering the wind of the law, although we have not always realised that it needed tempering in the case of the young.

2. Even if a child is reported to the police, they may well decide to take no more than informal action, and simply 'caution' him: in 1966 more children of 10 were cautioned than prosecuted for indictable offences. More will be said about this practice in the next section of this chapter.

3. For hundreds of years the law itself has protected very young children, in at least one way, from the punishments awarded to adults. Children under what has come to be known as 'the age of criminal responsibility' are conclusively presumed to be incapable of being guilty of any offence, on the ground that they cannot have a 'guilty mind'. Until the nineteen-thirties this age was 7 under the common law, at least for felonies. It was then fixed by statute at 8 for all offences. In England it was raised to 10 in 1964, but continues to be 8 in Scotland.[1] What is more, in England but not in Scotland children between the age of criminal responsibility and their 14th birthday sometimes receive protection from a rebuttable presumption that they are 'incapable of guile'; in other words, it is for the prosecution to produce evidence that they knew they were doing wrong. In practice, however, this rule is often ignored, and the Ingleby Committee thought that it should be abolished.[2]

[1] At least in theory: see pp. 196-7 and p. 199, where the main Scottish differences are explained.

[2] 1960.36. The legislation, however, which followed their report did not embody this recommendation.

4. It is possible for an offender under the age of 17[1] to be dealt with under what may be broadly called a 'social' procedure instead of criminal procedure. This procedure, which is discussed in the next section of this chapter, is designed for children who are in some sort of danger – whether of having their morals corrupted, or of being the victims of violence, neglect, or sexual offences; but since the situations in which these dangers arise are also associated with delinquency in children, not a few of the children dealt with in this way are also known or suspected to be offenders. The closest analogy to this form of social defence, in the case of adults, is the compulsory admission to guardianship or hospital of a mentally abnormal person.

5. Even when a young offender is dealt with under criminal procedure, and is not acquitted for lack of a 'guilty mind' or some other reason, certain penal measures which can be applied to adults cannot be applied to him, or can be applied only with modifications. (These restrictions and modifications are described in detail in the section on penal measures in this chapter.) Moreover, whether he is dealt with by social or by criminal procedure, the court is under a general statutory obligation, when disposing of him, to 'have regard to his welfare, and shall in a proper case take steps for removing him from undesirable surroundings, and for securing that proper provision is made for his education and training'.[2]

6. The measures which the court can order in the case of juveniles and adolescents give those who are to apply them more discretion in deciding, for example, on the period for which the measure should be applied. Thus, release from borstals and approved schools is in effect at the discretion of the executive within limits imposed by the statute and not by the court; and juveniles who are subject to a 'fit person' order can be allowed to go home 'on trial' as soon as the Children's Department considers this wise.

7. Efforts are made to protect juveniles both against the indirect legal consequences and against the stigma of conviction by a criminal court. The words 'conviction' and 'sentence' must not be applied to juveniles tried summarily; instead the terms 'finding of guilt' and 'order made upon a finding of guilt' are used.[3] This seems, however, to be no more than a verbal safeguard against the stigma, since it does not protect a juvenile from being treated as having been convicted or sentenced if, for instance, he is later convicted of an offence carrying a higher penalty for a second or subsequent conviction; and in any case it does not apply to juveniles convicted on indictment – that is by higher courts. In this chapter and elsewhere it would be cumbrous to avoid the use of 'conviction' and 'sentence', which are therefore used in defiance of the 1933 Act.

On the other hand, some protection against the legal consequences of an early conviction is conferred by several other statutes. Convictions or

[1] In Scotland, 16.
[2] CYPA 33, s. 44; CYP(S)A, 37, s. 49.
[3] CYPA 33, s. 59, as amended; CYP(S)A 37, s. 63, as amended.

findings of guilt before the age of 21 must be disregarded in determining whether an adult offender is eligible for an extended sentence of imprisonment (q.v.), or whether he is a 'first offender' and so imprisonable only if the court finds special reasons for this sentence.[1] Convictions or findings of guilt before the age of 14 must be disregarded 'for the purpose of any evidence relating to an offender's previous convictions' in any criminal proceedings after his 21st birthday.[2]

8. Juveniles, but not young adults, must normally be tried by special magistrates' courts, known as 'juvenile courts'. There are exceptions to this rule:

(i) a child or a young person charged with homicide must be tried by a higher court[3];

(ii) a young person charged with an indictable offence may refuse to be tried summarily[4];

(iii) a court may decide that a young person charged with an indictable offence should be tried on indictment, and if a child is charged jointly with him that both should be tried on indictment[5];

(iv) a charge made jointly against a juvenile and an adult *must* be heard in an ordinary magistrates' court[5];

(v) if an adult is charged at the same time with aiding, abetting, causing, procuring, allowing or permitting the offence, the charge *may* be heard in an ordinary magistrates' court[5];

(vi) if the juvenile is charged with aiding, abetting, causing, procuring, allowing or permitting an offence with which a person aged 17 or older is charged at the same time; or with an offence arising out of circumstances which are the same as or connected with those giving rise to an offence with which a person aged 17 or older is charged at the same time, the charge *may* be heard in an ordinary magistrates' court[6];

(vii) if an ordinary magistrates' court realises in the course of criminal proceedings that the person involved is a juvenile it is not debarred from completing the proceedings.[5]

These exceptions, however, are rare, and in any case other sorts of criminal court have the power to remit a juvenile whom they have found guilty of any offence other than homicide to a juvenile court for disposal.

To be dealt with by a juvenile court confers a number of advantages:

1. The public are not admitted: those present are usually confined to the parties to the case, members and officers of the court, and representatives of the press, although other people with a professional interest – such as child care or probation officers in training – can be admitted

---

[1] First Offenders Act, 1958; First Offenders (Scotland) Act, 1960.

[2] CYPA 63, s. 16. This rule has not yet been adopted in Scotland; but the 'ten-year rule' introduced by CJ(S)A 63, s. 17 (see p. 148), removes some of the need for it.

[3] MCA 52, s. 21.   [4] MCA 52, s. 20.

[5] CYPA 33, s. 46.   [6] CYPA 63, s. 18.

M

with the court's permission. The press are not allowed to report the offender's name, address or school, or any other particulars likely to identify him, or to publish a picture of him, without the permission of the court or the Home Secretary, which can be given only if it seems to be 'appropriate' in order to avoid injustice.[1]

2. The procedure is a simplified form of summary procedure laid down in rules made by the Home Secretary.[2] The court, for example, must explain the proceedings to the juvenile offender, and help him to cross-examine witnesses. If he is not legally represented – and few are – his parents must be allowed to help him in conducting his defence. The parents may be required to attend if the court thinks it desirable.[3]

3. Except in trivial cases, the court must have a report – usually supplied by a probation officer or children's officer of a local authority – on the juvenile's general conduct, home surroundings, school record, and medical history; and if it does not have this it should allow time for the preparation of a report by remanding him. The importance of these social enquiry reports is discussed in Chapter 11.

4. The court must sit either in a different building or room, or at different times from those used for the trial of adults, in order to avoid mixing juveniles with adults in waiting-rooms and other places.

5. The constitution of the court is intended to ensure that the magistrates who sit in it are selected from the local bench as 'specially qualified' for this work, although the only special qualification which is prescribed is an age under 65.[4] At each sitting the magistrates must include at least one man and one woman,[4] and must not number more than three.

In Scotland, although legislation allowed juvenile courts to be set up, this was, in fact, done in only four areas; elsewhere ordinary courts of summary jurisdiction sat on special days as a juvenile court, and were governed by roughly the same safeguards and rules of procedure as an English juvenile court. Their powers, however, were in some cases slightly wider: for example, a sheriff or stipendiary magistrate could impose borstal training on a young person of suitable age, whereas an English juvenile court which considers borstal training appropriate could only commit the offender to quarter sessions, who may or may not act accordingly. In any case, however, the system is being re-organised on the lines described on pages 196 and 197.

[1] In the past some courts have used the power as an additional penal measure. Thus in 1960 the Glasgow stipendiary magistrate, dealing with a boy who had earlier received press publicity through stowing away on a transatlantic aeroplane, allowed the press to identify him as a boy who had stolen money from his mother. 'This boy,' he is reported to have said, 'needs to be brought back to earth. In view of the widespread publicity it would be advisable to expose the whole business to the public.'

[2] The Summary Jurisdiction (Children & Young Persons) Rules, 1933.

[3] CYPA 63, s. 25.

[4] Although even to this there can be exceptions: see the Juvenile Courts (Constitution) Rules, 1954 (S.I. 1954 No. 1711).

NON-CRIMINAL PROCEEDINGS

In this section I shall describe briefly the ways in which delinquent, or potentially delinquent, juveniles may be dealt with officially and yet without being prosecuted in a criminal court.

Cautioning. The practice of cautioning by the police, which was mentioned in Chapter 9, is very frequently applied to the juvenile offender. Roughly a quarter of indictable offences by boys under 14 – which usually means thefts – end in a caution. The younger the child the more probable this is: before the age of criminal responsibility was raised from 8 to 10, children of 8 were more often cautioned than prosecuted. Sometimes the warning is simply delivered by a constable as soon as he observes or traces the offender; in which case it may or may not be recorded as a caution. On other occasions his report is followed by a more formal visit to the child's parents, or an invitation to them to bring the child to the police station, and a formal caution is administered.

The extent to which cautioning is used as a method of dealing with young offenders depends on the policy and instructions of each Chief Constable, and varies remarkably from one police area to another. In London, for example, a formal caution is rare, except in the case of bicyclists' offences, which are, of course, the juvenile equivalent of motoring offences. Otherwise, the offender is either informally warned by the constable or prosecuted.

At the other extreme a number of police forces[1] have developed this practice into what are usually called 'juvenile liaison schemes'. These take different forms, but the essential feature of each is that a child who is detected in a minor offence which seems slightly too serious to be dealt with simply by an informal warning may be placed under police supervision for a period which may be as much as a year. Most schemes do not accept juveniles who have passed their 14th birthdays, those who have already been detected in offences of dishonesty, those whose offences involve violence or 'breaking and entering' (which is regarded as a sign of criminal sophistication), those who do not admit their offence, or those whose parents will not co-operate; such cases are usually prosecuted. Under some schemes the supervision is done by police officers – some of them women – who have been specially selected and trained for the work, and who devote virtually all their time to juvenile offenders; in other police forces it is simply one of the functions of the officers assigned to that district. The police may – if the parents consent – enlist the co-operation of the child's school and other agencies.[2]

[1] By 1962, Liverpool, Leeds, Huddersfield, Birmingham, Bristol, Birkenhead, Bradford, South Shields, Blackpool, West Ham, Manchester, Halifax, and Cardiff; and in Scotland, Greenock, Coatbridge, Perth, Kilmarnock, Paisley, Stirling, and Clackmannan.

[2] For descriptions of the Liverpool and other schemes, see *The Police and Children* published for Liverpool City Police, 1962, and J. A. Mack, 'Police Juvenile Liaison Schemes' in the *British Journal of Criminology*, 1963.

'*Care, Protection or Control.*' The gradual raising of the minimum age of criminal responsibility, together with an increasing tendency to apply what has been called the principle of 'social defence' to the young, has conferred more and more importance on what I have called 'social proceedings' to distinguish them from criminal proceedings. Although these now take place almost invariably in juvenile courts, and are regulated by statute,[1] they developed out of the jurisdiction of the Chancery Court over the persons and property of infants who were deemed unable to look after themselves. This jurisdiction, which rests on the common law, has not been abolished, but in practice nowadays its exercise is usually confined to cases in which the child is an heir to wealth, or his well-being is threatened through the divorce of his parents, or similar circumstances; and even in this field it is increasingly regulated by statute. Where the child seems in danger of being the victim of a crime, or of circumstances which may lead the child himself into a criminal or even socially undesirable career, the usual procedure is to seek a decision from a juvenile court that he is 'in need of care, protection or control'.[2] This decision enables the court to order one of a number of measures, most of which are very similar to those which can be ordered as a result of prosecution. These will be described later in this chapter; for the moment we must examine the social grounds on which a child can be dealt with in this way.

The children's department of a local authority, a police constable, or an officer of the National Society for the Prevention of Cruelty to Children must[3] bring a child before a juvenile court if they have reasonable grounds for believing him to be in need of care, protection or control. Their grounds may be of several kinds:

1. that the juvenile is not receiving such care, protection and guidance as a good parent may be reasonably expected to give, *and* in addition (i) that he is falling into bad associations or exposed to moral danger; or (ii) that the lack of care, protection or guidance is likely to cause him unnecessary suffering or seriously to affect his health or proper development; or (iii) that he has been the victim of a sexual offence or an offence involving bodily injury, or lives in the same household as the victim or perpetrator of an offence of this kind against a juvenile;

2. that he is beyond his parents' control.

Parents themselves can no longer bring a child before the court on the ground that they cannot control him, but can ask the local children's department to do so, and if it refuses can ask the juvenile court to direct them to do so.[4] This procedure was designed to avoid a situation in which a child would have to listen to his parents giving evidence against him in court (since this might well embitter him towards them), and to ensure that children's

---

[1] CYPA 33, as amended; CYP(S)A, 37, as amended.

[2] CYPA 33, ss. 61, 62, as amended by the CYPA 63; CYP(S)A 37.

[3] Unless satisfied that this would not be in his interests, or that someone else is about to take proceedings.

[4] CYPA 63, S. 3.

departments would be in touch with 'beyond control' cases at an earlier stage, with some prospect of dealing with them in such a way as to avoid proceedings in court.

Truancy. Persistent absence from school is usually regarded not only as something which will itself prejudice the child's future, but also as an indication that the situation in the child's home is in some way unsatisfactory. The child's mother, for example, may be ill, or may have deserted the home; she may be keeping the child at home to help her; or she may simply be neglecting to wake, clothe, and feed him in time. On the other hand, he himself may have developed a dislike of school, because he is bullied, or has difficulty in keeping up with the class, or simply prefers some other sort of activity. Usually investigation by the school attendance officer – often known now as the 'school welfare officer' – discloses a state of affairs which can be put right without the intervention of the court. Sometimes, however, it is necessary to prosecute the parents,[1] and this can be done if the child is of compulsory school age, which at present is roughly between its 5th and 15th[2] birthdays. The prosecution is brought by the Education Authority, and the statute provides for certain defences – for example that the child was ill, or unavoidably prevented from attending. The child himself cannot be prosecuted, but the court can direct the education authority to bring him before a juvenile court. This can be done whether or not the parents have been convicted, and the education authority can do so even if not directed. The juvenile court can deal with the child *as if* he has been found to be in need of care, protection or control, although in strict law he has not.

The later sections of this chapter will deal with measures which can be applied by criminal courts as a result of prosecution. It is important to realise, however, that many of these measures may be applied as a result of social as well as criminal procedure, and while there are one or two which are confined to offenders, most of the others are applicable to either group with only minor, sometimes merely nominal, differences. In brief, a juvenile court which has to deal with an offender or a person in need of care, protection or control:

1. may commit him to the care of a local children's department or other 'fit person' (q.v.) in either case;
2. may order him to be sent to an approved school in either case;
3. may place him under the supervision of a probation officer. Under social procedure this is done by means of a 'supervision order', and the supervisor need not be, but usually is, a probation officer. Under criminal procedure the order is a 'probation order' and the supervisor must be a probation officer. Otherwise the consequences are much the same, and the effect of recent legislation has been to make them even more similar; both measures are therefore described together in the next section.

[1] Under the Education Act, 1944, ss. 39 and 40 in most cases; but under s. 40 and s. 10 of CYPA 33 in the case of vagrants whose way of life prevents their children from receiving a proper education.
[2] In the case of certain children needing special education, the 16th birthday.

It is true that a fine can be imposed only under criminal procedure. But if the offender is a child (that is, under 14) it is the parents who *must* normally[1] pay it, and if he is a young person they *may* be ordered to pay it; and under social procedure they may be ordered to enter into a recognisance to exercise proper care and guardianship of the juvenile, which means the forfeiture of a sum of money if they fail to do so. There are institutions – borstals, detention centres, and attendance centres – to which only offenders can be sent; but approved schools and remand homes can receive juveniles under either procedure.

'*In Care.*' It is important to appreciate that children under the age of 17 may be 'received into care' by the children's department without proceedings in court. This can be done if the child is lost, or has been abandoned, or has no parents, or if they are prevented from looking after him properly by illness or some other cause; but it can be done only if intervention by the children's officer is necessary in the child's interests. Intervention of this sort is seldom against anyone's wishes, since the parents are usually either missing, irresponsible, or so desperate that they welcome help. But a children's committee of a local authority can by resolution assume parental rights over the child if the parents are dead, or have abandoned him, or are unfit to have care of him.[2] If a parent objects within a month, the resolution lapses unless the children's department take successful steps to have it confirmed by a court.[2] A person cannot be received into the care of a local authority after his 17th birthday, or remain in care after his 18th birthday, although he can continue to receive help voluntarily from the children's department.

A juvenile received into care in one of these ways is usually placed in one of the children's department's own 'Homes'. Unless he is likely to be in care for only a short time, or there is some other good objection, it is the duty of the local authority to find him a foster-home with a suitable family if they can do so, and about half the children in care at any one time are being looked after in this way; the rest have to be cared for in homes managed by the children's department or by charitable organisations. A small minority, whose parents consent to adoption (or are dead or untraceable), are adopted, usually as a result of arrangements made by adoption agencies. Children's departments are required by statute to supervise any voluntary organisation in their areas which acts as an adoption agency; they may also function as adoption agencies themselves, and many do so.

In addition to these functions, children's departments now have a duty to do what they can to prevent situations in which children will have to be taken into care. This involves for example assisting households in which the mother is unable to cope with all the responsibilities of a large family. It is impossible to estimate the number of cases in which this preventive function

[1] CYPA 63.
[2] Children Act, 1948, ss. 1, 2 as amended by the CYPA 63. These sections (which also apply to Scotland) make it clear that a parent may be regarded as unfit to have care of the child because of permanent disability, mental disorder, habits or mode of life, or persistent failure without reasonable cause to discharge the obligation of a parent.

of children's departments acts as a substitute for the formal action which might otherwise be taken to deal with delinquency in these households.

There are, of course, other social services which intervene in the lives of children, and often in circumstances which make it probable that the children concerned are delinquents or potential delinquents. Voluntary societies receive and care for children for much the same reasons as do children's departments. The National Society for the Prevention of Cruelty to Children investigates reports of unnecessary suffering by children in their own homes. Education authorities' medical services and child guidance clinics examine schoolchildren whose behaviour suggests that they are psychologically maladjusted. In many cases these children are neither delinquents nor potential delinquents but simply the unfortunate victims of people or circumstances. Nevertheless, these measures amount to officially recognised intervention in situations which may involve or give rise to antisocial behaviour, and they should not be completely overlooked in any description of the penal system, however brief.

Some idea of their relative importance may be got from the following figures for 1961[1]:

1. found guilty of an offence[2]   105,043
2. cautioned by the police[2]   35,672
3. dealt with by order of a juvenile court under social
   procedure   19,473
4. received into care of a children's department[3]
   (excluding 'fit person orders' under (1) and (3))   43,000
5. received into care of voluntary societies[4]   4,800[5]
6. cases dealt with by the National Society for the
   Prevention of Cruelty to Children[3]   40,445
7. 'ascertained' as maladjusted by local education
   authorities   1,843

These figures demonstrate the frequency with which the police and the criminal courts impinge on the lives of juveniles, in comparison with other forms of intervention. Fortunately, of course, the effect of intervention by police and courts is much less drastic: as we shall see, it means removal from

---

[1] The figures in this table include an unknown number of children who were dealt with in more than one of these ways (or more than once) during the year; and because of this 'overlap' it would be fallacious to add them up.

[2] These figures exclude motoring offences (which are infrequent in this age-group) but include other non-indictable and all indictable offences. They include an unknown number of juveniles who were found guilty or cautioned more than once during the year.

[3] These figures relate to twelve-month periods which end later than the end of 1961.

[4] Excluding cases 'dropped' (462), or 'brought before juvenile courts' (488); virtually all the latter are represented under item (3). Some of the cases involve more than one child.

[5] This is a very rough estimate, made by dividing the number in care of voluntary societies by three (the average number of years which children spend in care of such societies). Children placed with voluntary homes by children's departments are excluded, since they are included in (4).

home in only a minority of cases, whereas most of the other forms of intervention involve removal. But in terms of frequency alone the penal system is clearly the most important single social service for the young, although workers in other 'social services' might not like to hear it called one.

PENAL MEASURES

In this section I shall deal with the measures which can be ordered by a court which has found a juvenile guilty of an offence. Usually this happens in a juvenile court, but as we have seen there are exceptions. Moreover, a juvenile court which considers that the case calls for a borstal sentence must commit a young person who has reached the age of 15 to quarter sessions for sentence, since only a higher court can order borstal training. There is one measure which only a lower court can order – attendance at an attendance centre. But with these exceptions the measures which I am about to describe can be ordered by higher or lower courts.

Discharge. Like an adult, a juvenile can be found guilty but be discharged, absolutely or conditionally.[1] As an alternative, one of his parents may be ordered to give security for his good behaviour[2] by entering into a recognisance (q.v.). A conditional discharge is a very common method of dealing with young offenders: fully a third of indictable offenders under 14 and a quarter of indictable young persons were disposed of in this way in 1961.

Fines and Other Payments. A magistrates' court, which in the case of juveniles usually means a juvenile court, is subject not only to the general limitations on its power to fine which were summarised in Chapter 9, but also to several other limitations when fining juveniles. It cannot fine a child more than £10,[3] or a young person more than £50.[3] Higher courts are subject only to general limitations, and not to these. But if the offender is a child, any court *must*, and if he is a young person it *may*, order his parent to pay, unless it is satisfied that the latter cannot be found or did not conduce to the commission of the offence by neglecting to exercise due care of the juvenile. The same limitations apply to payment of compensation, damages, costs or forfeitures ordered by criminal courts.[4] Parents who default in payment can be dealt with as if the offence had been theirs. Juveniles who default can be sent to a remand home for not more than a month, and in England (but not Scotland) defaulting young persons may be committed to a detention centre.[5] If a juvenile (or young adult) is found on admission to an approved school, detention centre or borstal to have an unpaid fine hanging over his head, this is often not enforced, on the grounds that it would increase the offender's difficulties when he is discharged. A defaulter under the age of 21 must not be committed to prison (or the equivalent) by a

---

[1] In Scotland, a deferred sentence is the nearest equivalent to a conditional discharge; see p. 169.

[2] CYPA 33, s. 55; CYP(S)A 37, s. 59.

[3] CJA 61, s. 8 (In Scotland the only limits are those which apply to fines levied on adults.)   [4] This is not so in Scotland.

[5] Subject, of course, to the maximum periods of detention allowable for non-payment of fines of different amounts, which are fixed by MCA 52, Sch. III, and SJ(S)A 54, s. 49.

magistrates' court unless payment under supervision has first been tried or has been decided to be impracticable.[1] Otherwise, the infliction of pecuniary penalties on juveniles and young adults is governed by the law applying to adults.

Probation. Since probation developed mainly as a penal measure for the young, the legislation governing its application was drafted with them in mind, and there are only a few modifications which apply to special age-groups. Unlike an adult, a child need not be asked to consent before a probation order is imposed on him, and in Scotland, where his consent at any age is required, the Morison[2] Committee thought that the law should be made the same. A juvenile can simultaneously be placed on probation and entrusted to the care of a 'fit person'.[3] In England a probationer who fails to comply with the requirements of his probation order may be sent to an attendance centre (q.v.) if he is within the proper age limits, instead of incurring a more severe penalty; and if he is dealt with in this way the court is not obliged to revoke the probation order.[4]

Approved Probation Homes and Hostels. Like adult probationers, juveniles can be subjected to requirements that they reside at a specified address, and this can be a special hostel or home approved by the Home Secretary for this purpose. 'Approved probation hostels (or homes)' are run by voluntary organisations, some religious, some secular, with financial help and inspection from the Home Office. Probation committees have no power to provide their own hostels, but in several areas have prompted the formation of bodies to provide them. In a probation hostel the residents have left school, and go out to work or to further training; probation homes are for young offenders over school age but under the age of twenty-one, who are in need of even closer supervision during their everyday life. In 1966 there were only 27 hostels[5] for males, with about 500 places.

Supervision Orders. Very similar to a probation order is the supervision order which can be imposed upon a juvenile as a result of social procedure.[6] This makes him subject to the supervision of a person, who is almost always a probation officer, for any period which the court may specify up to the same maximum as that of a probation order – three years. Like a probation order, it can have conditions of residence or mental treatment attached to it, and the juvenile's parent may be ordered to enter a recognisance to exercise proper care and guardianship. Like a probationer, the juvenile under supervision can also be committed to the care of a fit person. If his response to supervision is unsatisfactory he can be brought before a juvenile court again, and sent to an approved school or committed to the care of a fit person. Unlike probation, a supervision order can be imposed on children under the minimum age of criminal responsibility: in 1966, 27 per cent of the 1,592 boys placed under supervision in England were below the age of 10.

---

[1] MCA 52, s. 71; CJ(S)A 63, s. 25.
[2] 1962.4.
[3] CYPA 33, s. 57; CYP(S)A 37, s. 61.
[4] In Scotland there are no attendance centres.
[5] For girls there were 15, with less than 300 places.
[6] CYPA 33, s. 62; CYP(S)A 37, s. 66.

But supervision is not reserved, even in practice, for the very young; 31 per cent of the boys were between their 14th and 17th birthdays.

'Fit Person' Orders. Juveniles dealt with either as offenders or under social procedure can be committed to the care of a fit person.[1] Occasionally the fit person is a relative or some other private person, but usually responsibility is placed on the children's department of a local authority; 98 per cent of the fit person orders dealing with boys in 1961 took this form. The children's department cannot refuse this task,[2] though it must be given the opportunity of making 'representations' before the order is made. It is supposed to board him out with carefully selected foster-parents, unless this is not practicable or desirable. Since such children are often troublesome to manage, it is usually even more difficult to find suitable foster-homes for them than for other children in the department's care. Gray and Parr[3] found that in a sample of 71 offenders dealt with by fit person order in 1956 only 11 per cent were 'boarded out', the rest being sent to institutions of various kinds, especially local authority homes (27 per cent) or homes for maladjusted children (14 per cent).

In view of the fact that it means the removal of a child from his natural home, the limitations on the use of a fit person order are surprisingly few. Under criminal procedure it can be imposed only on juveniles over the age of criminal responsibility, and only for offences for which an adult could be imprisoned; but under social procedure there is no minimum age – 24 per cent of the 2,068 boys entrusted to fit persons in 1966 were under 10 – and no limitation beyond those entailed by the procedure. The order remains in force until the juvenile attains his 18th birthday; it may therefore mean that the rest of his childhood is spent in a children's home. The children's department has the rights, powers, and liabilities of parents. A conscientious department is on the watch for improvements in the juvenile or his natural home which would justify them in asking the court to restore him to his family, and as they may allow him to be under the charge of a parent or relative, they can experiment with this in view. A substantial percentage of Gray and Parr's sample of offenders under fit person orders were at home 'on trial'. Modern children's homes, organised into separate subdivisions for 'family groups',[4] can be very much happier places than the pre-war 'orphanages'. A good foster-home, if the juvenile is fortunate enough to be sent to one, may well come to be regarded by him as his natural home. But in the hands of a large and impersonal department, or of a large and impersonal institution for children, the juvenile not only has a poorer chance of proper care, but also a poorer chance of being restored to his family as a result of conscientious social work.

Attendance Centres. Attendance centres are a post-war innovation intended 'to vindicate the law by imposing loss of leisure, a punishment that

---

[1] CYPA 33, ss. 57, 62; CYP(S)A 37, s. 66.

[2] Unless the juvenile is, or is to be, subject to a probation or supervision order at the same time.

[3] 1957. Among *non*-offenders dealt with by fit person orders, the percentage boarded out was much higher – 34.

[4] The sizes of these 'families' tend to be Victorian rather than modern.

is generally understood by children: to bring the offender for a period under discipline and, by teaching him something of the constructive use of leisure, to guide him on leaving the centre to continue organised recreational activity by joining youth clubs or other organisations'.[1] The loss of leisure is imposed by requiring weekly attendance at the centre, usually for two hours on several consecutive Saturday afternoons, which are spent in physical training, alternating perhaps with some sort of instruction in handicrafts, under the charge of a police officer. The Home Secretary is responsible for providing the centres, but uses local police forces as his agents.[2] Since the only other penal measure which the police administer nowadays is detention for up to four days in police cells – a minor punishment for adults – this is unusual. Another exceptional feature of attendance centre orders is that they can be imposed by magistrates' and juvenile courts, but not by higher courts, although the latter have the power to discharge offenders whom they convict.

An attendance centre order can be imposed for an offence for which an adult could be sent to prison, for a breach of the requirements of a probation order, or for defaulting in the payment of a fine or similar payment. McClintock[3] found, however, that in practice it was used in the following ways:

1. without any other penal measure   48%
2. for breach of a probation order   3%
3. for a fresh offence during probation   22%
4. jointly with a probation order for another offence   21%
5. jointly with a fine for another offence   5%
6. following detention in a remand home for another offence   1%

The offender himself must be between his 10th and his 21st birthdays, and must not previously have been sent to prison, borstal, a detention centre, or an approved school. The court must have been informed by the Home Secretary that a centre for offenders of his class or description is available; and in practice no centres have been opened for girls, or in rural areas, and only one experimental centre has been opened for young male adults.[4] There are, however, 59 centres for boys between their 10th and 17th birthdays, in the cities and large towns of England, and boys who live within easy travelling distance of them can be sent to them.[5] Two thirds of the centre are in school premises lent for the afternoon by the local education authority; the remainder are more or less evenly distributed between police buildings, youth clubs, halls, and other places. In Scotland the idea of attendance centres has not found favour, and the innovations introduced by post-war legislation did not include them.

---

[1] Ingleby Report, 1960.90.

[2] Except in the case of two centres (at Hull and Reading) which are run by local authorities, and the experimental centre for young adults at Manchester, which is run by the Prison Department of the Home Office.   [3] 1961.

[4] In Manchester, run by the Prison Department of the Home Office.

[5] CJA 61, s. 10, provides that the centre must be reasonably accessible, having regard to the boy's age, the means of access, and other circumstances.

The attendance centre order itself fixes the time of the boy's first attendance, and the number of hours for which he is to attend, which must normally be twelve.[1] The times and the number of occasions for his subsequent
attendances, however, are fixed by the officer in charge of the centre, and he
is told of them at his first visit. The times must not interfere with school or
working hours; he cannot be made to attend more than once on any day, or
for more than three hours at a time. In practice the times of attendance are
always on Saturday, and usually in the afternoons; and while it is not
unheard of for the normal twelve-hour order to be spread over twelve
Saturdays, most centres spread it over six. Many of these, however, open
only on alternate Saturdays, so that in a typical case the boy would attend
for two hours every second Saturday over about three months. Younger
boys – usually those under 14 – are often made to attend at different times
or different Saturdays from older boys. The regimes vary, but usually[2]
include:

1. an inspection of the boys for cleanliness and tidiness of dress;
2. physical training;
3. 'fatigues', such as cleaning the centre, cutting the grass, or chopping
   wood;
4. some kind of handicraft or instruction in a practical subject, such as
   first aid.

Breaches of discipline are dealt with by admonition, temporary segregation,
more disagreeable tasks, extension of attendance by reducing the hours
from two to one on each day, and in extreme cases by bringing the boy back
to court to be sentenced for his original offence. If a boy fails to attend, the
police make immediate enquiries at his home. Corporal punishment is
not permitted.

INSTITUTIONS FOR JUVENILE OFFENDERS

There are four kinds of residential institution to which a young offender can
be committed – a remand home, an approved school, a detention centre,
and a borstal. He cannot be sent to any of them as a penal measure unless
he has been found guilty of an offence for which an adult could be punished
with imprisonment. He can be sent to an approved school if he is found to
be in need of care, protection, or control, and to a remand home for several
other reasons, which will be explained in due course. The minimum age for
committal to an approved school is 10 (with exceptions); in the case of a
detention centre it is 14; and in the case of borstal it is 15.[3] Committal to a
remand home as a penal measure is now intended to be limited to children
between their 10th and 14th birthdays, but in an area where there is not yet
a detention centre for young persons they can still be sentenced to detention
in a remand home.

---

[1] If he is under 14 the court can specify less if twelve seems excessive; it can also
specify any number between twelve and twenty-four if twelve seems inadequate 'having
regard to all the circumstances'.

[2] See McClintock, 1961.35.   [3] 16 in Scotland.

Borstals and Detention Centres. Borstals and detention centres, like prisons, are owned, staffed, and administered by the Prison Department of the Home Office. The buildings are usually conversions of country mansions, military camps, and other similar establishments of a kind to be found in rural or semi-rural areas. Most detention centres and borstals are designed for security, with perimeter walls or wire; but some borstals and one detention centre are 'open'. The staff consist of prison officers, assistant governors, and governors, selected from the prison service as likely to be in sympathy with the aims of the borstal or detention centre regimes. Prison officers working in borstals do not wear uniform, but plain clothes – usually a tweed jacket and grey trousers.[1]

Both types of institution, though conceived at very different dates,[2] were originally intended as alternatives to imprisonment for adolescents specially selected by the courts as likely to benefit from a somewhat different regime. The intention of the borstal system was summed up by the Home Secretary's white paper of 1959[3]: 'Borstal is essentially a remedial and educational system, based on personal training by a carefully selected staff. Its development since the Act of 1948 has been mainly in the extension of vocational training in skilled trades and of education in its widest sense. . . .' The same white paper described the purpose of detention centres: 'Detention centres were intended by Parliament to provide a sanction for those who could not be taught to respect the law by such milder measures as fines, probation and attendance centres, but for whom long-term residential training was not yet necessary or desirable. . . .'

The age range for borstal is now from the 15th[4] to the 21st birthday, and for detention centres from the 14th to the 21st birthday. If the offender is under the age of 17 the court must not sentence him to borstal unless its opinion is that no other method of dealing with him is appropriate, and if it sentences him to a detention centre he goes to a junior one. The object of these restrictions is to protect as many juvenile offenders as possible from contamination by young adults.

Offenders can be sent to borstals or detention centres only for offences

---

[1] Governors and assistant governors do not wear uniform in prisons either.

[2] The principle of borstal is traceable to the Gladstone Commission's report of 1895: '. . . By way of experiment a Penal Reformatory to be established under Government management. The court to have power to commit to this reformatory offenders above 16 and under 23 for periods not less than one year and up to three years with a system of licences graduated according to sentences . . . .' After experiments at Bedford and Borstal Prisons, a special sentence of 'borstal detention' was recognised in the Prevention of Crime Act, 1908, and amended to 'borstal training' by the Criminal Justice Act, 1948. Detention centres, on the other hand, owed their inspiration to the military detention centres of the Second World War. They were provided for in the Criminal Justice Act of 1948, and the first was opened in 1952 for boys between their 14th and 17th birthdays.

[3] *Penal Practice in a Changing Society*, p. 9.

[4] Until CJA 61, s. 11, came into operation, the 16th birthday. The minimum age was lowered because it was found that some boys who were being sent to senior approved schools (for boys of 15 or over) were so difficult to deal with that they would have been more suited to borstal. In Scotland the minimum age is still 16, and likely to remain so.

for which adults could be imprisoned.[1] Only a court of assize or quarter sessions can pass a borstal sentence, but a magistrates' court – including a juvenile – court can commit an offender whom it has convicted to quarter sessions with a view to a borstal sentence, which quarter sessions is not bound to pass. All types of court can make a detention centre order.[2]

The length of a borstal sentence is not determined by the court; the offender is released between six months[3] and two years from the beginning of his sentence, and the date is decided upon by a board in the light of reports on his progress by the staff. The board's decision has to be ratified by the Board of Visitors and the Prison Department. The sentence is thus semi-determinate, since it has a fixed minimum and maximum, and unlike a prison sentence it is not reduced by any forfeitable remission. The average length of stay is just under sixteen months.

For two years after his release the offender is subject to compulsory supervision, with the sanction of recall for six months or until the end of the two years, whichever is the longer. The decision to recall him is made by the Prison Department, and not by a court. If recalled, he is usually sent to a special borstal, and not to his former institution. The supervision is the responsibility of the probation service; but one or two after-care hostels have been established for borstal boys.

A stay in a detention centre, on the other hand, is meant to be short but strenuous. The staff of the centres feel strongly that if they are to achieve the best effect the boys' programme must be carefully planned so that they can aim at passing through various stages and grades at roughly the same time after admission. The statute recognises this to the extent of providing a standard sentence of three months for juveniles who are sent to detention centres, but in England (not Scotland) exceptions are allowed[4]:

1. a higher court can order any period from three to six months;
2. a fine-defaulter can be sentenced to any period between one and six months for which an adult could be sent to prison. (Fine-defaulters cannot be sent to detention centres in Scotland.)

Detainees can earn remission of one third of the sentence.

After release, the detainee is subject to compulsory supervision for twelve months, with the sanction of recall (at the Prison Department's discretion) for one month or two months if he earns full remission on a

---

[1] Although it is possible for an approved school boy who absconds or whose continuation at the school would be 'ineffective for . . . his own reformation or detrimental to . . . other persons therein' to be transferred to borstal on the order of a magistrates' court (CJA 48, s. 72; CJA 61, s. 16); so that a boy sent to an approved school under social procedure occasionally ends in borstal.

[2] In Scotland a justice of the peace court or a burgh court presided over by a lay magistrate is unable to impose borstal training, or to send an offender to a detention centre.

[3] He can be released earlier if he is the subject of a special direction from the Home Secretary, but this is rare.

[4] CJA 61, ss. 4-7.

six-months sentence. Unlike the ex-prisoner or ex-borstal inmate, he cannot be recalled more than once.

Classification. Apart from the subdivision of detention centres into junior centres for boys between their 14th and 17th birthdays, and senior centres for those between their 17th and 21st birthdays, there is no system of classification; a boy is sent to whichever senior or junior centre has been assigned to the sentencing court. So long as precautions are taken to ensure that detainees are physically and mentally fit for the strain of the regime,[1] there would be little point in a more elaborate process of classification for what is essentially a short-term sentence.

Borstal inmates, on the other hand, undergo classification at one of the two prisons which function as allocation centres, where reports on their social, psychological, educational, and vocational characteristics are prepared by psychologists, experienced housemasters, and other staff. Apart from offenders with physical and mental handicaps, who go to two special borstals, they are subdivided chiefly according to their psychological maturity – to which their age is only a rough guide – and the extent to which, from their outlook and previous records, they are likely to abscond if allocated to an open borstal.

Approved Schools.[1] Approved schools, unlike prisons, borstals, and detention centres, are managed not by the Prison Department but in most cases by voluntary boards of managers,[2] although roughly one in four are now provided by the children's committees of local authorities. State control over their regimes is exercised in six ways:

1. through Approved School Rules made by the Home Secretary, and circulars of guidance issued by the Home Office;
2. through inspection and advice by Home Office inspectors;
3. through financial control: the Home Office provides almost half of their income[3];
4. through the Home Secretary's power to give directions on matters of policy[4];
5. through the Home Secretary's power to add managers appointed by him to any *voluntary* board of management[4];
6. in the last resort[5], through the Home Secretary's power to withdraw the statutory approval without which the school could not receive children committed by the courts.

[1] The most up-to-date book on this subject is by G. Rose, 1967.
[2] Many of these boards can trace their origins far back into the nineteenth century, when the first 'reformatory schools' for offenders and 'industrial schools' for children in need of care or protection were founded by philanthropic organisations. Their constitutions often embody religious aims or other specialised traditions. The distinction between reformatories and industrial schools was abolished in the nineteen-thirties (CYPA 33; CYP(S)A 37), since when it has been possible to commit children found to be in need of care or protection to the same schools as those found guilty of offences.
[3] The rest is met partly from the charitable endowments of the school, now in many cases negligible, partly from contributions which the parents are ordered to pay by the court, but chiefly from payments at fixed weekly rates by local authorities.
[4] A new power conferred by CJA 61, and CJ(S)A 63.
[5] CYPA 33, s. 79; CYP(S)A 37, s. 83.

An approved school order can be made by a higher or lower court. If it is made after the offender is found guilty of an offence, the offence must be one for which an adult could be punished with imprisonment (q.v.); but it can also be made if the juvenile is found to be in need of care, protection or control, or beyond control of his parents, or fails to respond satisfactorily while under a supervision order or 'fit person' order.[1] In 1966, about 3 per cent of the 4,770 males committed to approved schools had been the subject of social procedure, although many of them no doubt had previously been detected in offences, and even more must have committed offences.

Normally a child under 10 is not sent to an approved school. Not only is it now impossible for a younger child to be found guilty under criminal procedure, but even under social procedure the court is debarred from applying this measure to a child under 10 'unless for any reason . . . the court is satisfied that he cannot suitably be dealt with otherwise'[2]; and in 1966 only 6 boys under 10 were dealt with in this way. With minor exceptions,[3] only someone under 17 can be sent to an approved school, although he can be kept there – or recalled to it – after that age in circumstances which will be explained later.

Approved schools are subdivided into 27 senior schools for boys over compulsory school age on committal, 29 intermediate schools for those between their 13th birthday and school-leaving age, and 30 junior schools for the younger boys. Like borstal trainees, most approved school boys pass through classifying centres where after observation, interviews and psychological tests they are allocated to a suitable school. There are, however, two important limitations to this system. Almost all Roman Catholic boys are sent to one of the senior, intermediate, or junior schools provided by Orders of that religion; only in exceptional cases – for example, of marked mental abnormality – do they pass through the classifying system.[4] Secondly, at times when the schools are filled to capacity it is often the existence of a vacancy rather than any psychological assessment which is the deciding factor.[5] There are, however, schools which specialise in boys of low intelligence, boys of superior intelligence, and boys who have been so troublesome that they have to be segregated in specially secure units of one or two schools. With the exception of this last type of school, they are all 'open' institutions, at least to the extent that they are not surrounded by high walls or fences;

---

[1] CYPA 33, ss. 66, 84 (as amended). In such cases young adults aged 17 (but not more) can be sent to approved schools.

[2] CYPA 33, s. 44; CYP(S)A 37, s. 49.

[3] See footnote 2.

[4] The approved school order must state the juvenile's religion, and must when practicable allocate him to a school for persons of his religion (CYPA 63, s. 8). The managers of a school are permitted to refuse admission to anyone not of the religion for which the school is intended.

[5] In Scotland, there are no classifying schools. Since there are only 15 approved schools for boys, classification by age and religion usually leaves at best a choice between two schools, and the choice falls on the nearer school to his home if it has a vacancy. There are, however, schools which specialise in boys of low intelligence, boys who create trouble or are persistent absconders, and boys specially selected as suitable for a short stay.

but in most schools exits are carefully locked at night, and boys may leave the buildings only at certain times and with permission.

Nevertheless, official statements emphasise that these are educational and not penal establishments. Much of the day is devoted to lessons; even in schools for boys over 15, vocational training is interspersed with efforts to repair the gaps in their elementary education. Outdoor sports, camping, and in some schools sailing are cultivated. Boys are entitled to short holidays at home with their families, unless their homes are for some special reason unsuitable or the boy has forfeited his entitlement by breaking rules. Schools are subdivided into houses, staffed so far as possible by non-teaching staff who are not responsible for the boys' formal activities, in the hope that they will be able to take a closer, less disciplinary interest in the psychological difficulties of individual boys in their houses. This is the ideal, and many schools fall considerably short of it, partly through shortage of properly selected and trained staff, partly through the persistence of traditional attitudes, especially in schools with a strong religious bias of one kind or another.

Like a borstal trainee, an approved school boy cannot be released in his first six months without the consent of the Home Secretary[1] but must be released on or before a certain date, in this case three years from the date of the order. There are, however, important exceptions. If the boy is still under 15 at the end of the three years, he can be kept until four months after reaching that age; in other words, he can be made to complete his schooling in an approved school. The other exception is the boy who has already passed his 16th birthday before the date of making of the order; he can be kept until his 19th birthday. In practice, it is the younger boy, under 13 on committal, who is likely to spend longer at an approved school, probably because he is made to finish his education there; only a few boys over school age spend more than two years before release, and a small number are released in the first six months, especially from one school which specialises in boys who seem to need only a short stay. The date of release is decided by the managers, in most cases on the recommendation of the staff.

After-Care. For two years after his release, or until he is 21, whichever is the earlier, an approved school inmate is under the compulsory supervision of the managers, who can recall him to the school, but cannot detain him there when he has reached his 21st birthday. For a further period[2] they can 'cause him to be visited, advised and befriended or give him assistance. (including financial assistance)', but they are not obliged to do so and he is not obliged to accept. The actual work of approved school after-care is done by persons selected by the school managers. For some closely populated areas 'approved school welfare officers' have been specially appointed for this purpose, but since the ex-inmates of any given school are scattered throughout the country it is virtually impossible for the welfare officers themselves to keep the close contact that is required and, for this or other

[1] On the other hand, the Home Secretary can direct managers who seem to be detaining a boy too long to release him at any time during the currency of the order

[2] Which ends three years after the end of the period for which he could have been detained in the school, or when he reaches the age of 21, whichever is the earlier.

N

reasons, in practice a local probation officer or children's officer is usually asked to do this.[1]

Remand Homes. Remand homes are provided and staffed by the children's departments of some local authorities,[2] but also serve the areas of adjoining smaller authorities. They serve a variety of purposes, only one of which is the reception of children committed to them by the court as a penal measure. A juvenile of any age up to his 17th birthday may find himself in a remand home for one of several other reasons:

1. that he has been found by the police to be the victim of ill-treatment, neglect, a sexual offence, a crime of violence, or one or two other special offences;
2. that he is waiting to be brought before a court as in need of care, protection, or control, or as not responding satisfactorily under supervision;
3. that he is awaiting trial for an offence and the police are unwilling to release him until then, usually for fear that he will disappear.
4. that he has been found guilty by a court which has remanded him in custody for medical, psychiatric or social reports before deciding what to do with him;
5. that he has been made the subject of an approved school order, and is awaiting allocation to a vacancy;
6. that he is awaiting transfer to a mental hospital.

As a result the population of remand homes is as miscellaneous and transient as that of a local prison; they are as it were the 'pending trays' of the juvenile courts. They cater for a wider age-range than any other penal institution for juveniles. Their use for short periods of punitive detention has therefore been restricted in recent years. Originally any juvenile could be sentenced to not more than a month in one for any offence for which an adult could have been punished with imprisonment. With the advent of junior detention centres for boys between their 14th and 17th birthdays, English courts were instead obliged to send boys of that age-group to those centres as soon as one was opened for their area. One result, however, was that detention centres had to receive boys who had incurred only a few weeks of detention through defaulting in the payment of a fine; the Criminal Justice Act, 1961, therefore made an exception in the case of defaulters, and obliged those who had to serve a term of a month or less to be sent to remand homes as before.

Consequently the use of remand homes as a penal measure varies from area to area. In the diminishing number of areas which still lack junior detention centres for boys, the remand home is used for boys between their 10th and 17th birthdays. In those with junior detention centres it is used tor boys between their 10th and 14th birthdays, and for fine-defaulters

---

[1] The system of approved school welfare officers was criticised by the Ingleby Committee, and the Advisory Council on the Treatment of Offenders has recommended that their work should in future be done by local probation and child care departments (1963.57).

[2] Remand homes were originally provided by local police forces, but criticisms of this system caused responsibility for them to be transferred to local authorities in 1932.

between their 10th and 17th birthdays who have to serve a month's detention or less. For all these categories detention as a penal measure can be used only in cases where an adult could be sent to prison,[1] and the period of detention must not exceed a month. Unfortunately this limitation does not prevent juveniles from spending longer periods in remand homes while on remand or awaiting vacancies in approved schools.

Several factors combine to make remand homes the most difficult sort of penal institution to run satisfactorily. The children in them are very diverse in their ages and their circumstances; delinquents are mixed with the victims of cruelty, neglect, or sexual offences. The periods for which they are in the remand home are usually short, and constantly interrupted by visits to clinics for diagnosis, or to courts for decisions or further remands. The children have not recovered from the shock of what is usually their first removal from home. In most cases, therefore, the staff can hope to do little more than ensure that the child is well fed, cleansed of dirt and vermin, treated for neglected physical disorders, and given healthy recreation mixed with a little education.

It is hardly surprising that detention in a remand home is now little used as a penal measure. Out of the 53,789 boys dealt with summarily for indictable offences in 1966, only 362 were punished in this way; 297 of these were under 14 years of age. Higher courts seldom make use of this method, even in the rare cases in which they deal with children. The undesirability of mixing children who have been committed as a punishment with those who have not is obvious, and it cannot be long before this is made impossible. It may be longer, however, before these establishments cease to be used for juveniles who are waiting for vacancies in approved schools.

The most ambitious function which a remand home can try to serve with any hope of success is that of an observation centre. Although a court which remands a child for diagnostic purposes usually has in mind clinical examinations by psychiatrists and psychologists, the staff of a residential institution, who have to look after the child day and night, have better opportunities than any clinician for observing his reactions to adults and other children. The wise psychiatrist or psychologist will always ask the remand home staff for their observations and impressions, although the latter are not always selected or trained to make use of their opportunities, and their reports may lack the professionalism that impresses.

Imprisonment. In order to prevent contamination by adult prisoners, neither a higher nor a lower court is now allowed to sentence a juvenile to imprisonment either directly or in default of payment of a fine, a recognisance, damages or costs.[2]

This principle applies even to young murderers. Anyone who appears to the court to have been under the age of 18 when he committed a murder must be sentenced not to life imprisonment, but to be detained during Her

---

[1] CYPA 33, s. 54.

[2] CJA 61, s. 2: MCA 52, s. 107: CJ(S)A 49, s. 18. A 'young person', however, of 14, 15, or 16, who is too 'unruly or depraved' to be remanded to a remand home may be remanded to prison during the period before trial or between trial and sentence (see Chapter 11) if no remand centre is available.

Majesty's Pleasure. The place and conditions of his detention and the date of his release are decided by the Home Secretary.[1] A very similar statute applies to a juvenile under 17 who is convicted of an offence for which an adult could be sent to prison for fourteen years or more: for example, inflicting grievous bodily harm. If the court considers that none of the other measures at its disposal is suitable, it must sentence him not to imprisonment but to be detained 'in such place and under such conditions as the Secretary of State may direct'.[1]

In practice, such juveniles are sent by the Home Secretary to borstals, to approved schools, institutions for the mentally abnormal, and only if they are unsuitable for such institutions to young prisoner's wings of prisons. Those detained during Her Majesty's pleasure are released when the Home Secretary, in the light of reports on them, thinks that this should be done. Those detained for a specified period may also be released before the end of it if the Home Secretary thinks fit, but some are detained for the full period, especially if this is short. Except for this last group, who must be released unconditionally, they are subject to the conditions of a licence, which expires at the end of the specified period of detention. The terms of the licence resemble those of the adult's licence.

Scotland. Some differences between England and Scotland have already been mentioned – the embryonic state of juvenile courts, the absence of attendance centres and classifying centres for approved schools and the lower age of criminal responsibility in Scotland, although fundamentally the two systems are based on similar principles. In 1968, however, a radical reorganisation was begun.[2] Its main features are to be:

1. Each large burgh and county will have 'Children's Panels' of laymen with suitable experience (and some specially provided training). Each Panel will be served by a full-time, salaried 'Reporter', who will control the initiation of proceedings.

2. A child under 16 will be brought before the Panel instead of a court if he seems to the Reporter to need some compulsory form of care for one of the reasons specified in the Act. The Crown will retain the right to prosecute children under 16 for breaches of the criminal law, but will invoke it only in exceptional cases.

3. The panel will decide what compulsory treatment or training the child needs, so far as possible after efforts have been made to render this acceptable to his family. The measures open to it will be more or less those open to a juvenile court at present, but will not include fining, punitive detention in a remand home (which will be abolished) or a hospital or guardianship order under the Mental Health (Scotland) Act, 1960 (see Chapter 13).

4. If, however, the child or his parents dispute the alleged facts in the first place, or later wish to appeal against the treatment or

---

[1] CYPA 33, s. 53 as amended; CYP(S)A 37, s. 57, as amended.

[2] In the Social Work (Scotland) Act, 1968, which was based on the recommendations of the Kilbrandon Report (1964, Cmnd. 2306), but with some important differences.

training chosen by the Panel, the case will be referred to the Sheriff Court.

5. Responsibility for providing the necessary supervision, residential care and reports to the Panel will be undertaken by the 'Social Work Department' of the local authority, a new department which will absorb the functions of the Children's Department, the Probation Department and other welfare departments (other than the Health Department).

6. The Panel will be kept informed of the child's progress by the Social Work Department, and in any case will review the arrangements made for each child at least once a year. (It can be required to do so by the parents if three months have elapsed since the last review.)

7. Once the child has reached the age of 16, however, only an ordinary criminal court will be able to deal with him, and then only for infringements of the criminal law, although there will be minor exceptions.

These provisions will virtually abolish the distinction between criminal and social proceedings for children under 16. Since prosecutions of children below that age will be rare, the minimum age at which a person will be liable to be found guilty of an offence will in effect be raised to 16, although in theory it will still be 8.

YOUNG ADULTS

The position of young adults – that is, those between their 17th and 21st birthdays – differs in several ways from those of both juveniles and older adults. They cannot be prosecuted in juvenile courts, or dealt with under social procedure, or received into care by children's departments. They cannot be sent to approved schools or remand homes.[1] They cannot be made the subject of supervision orders or fit person orders, although an order made before they were 17 may remain in force until they are 18. Their parents cannot be fined or ordered to give sureties as a result of their offences. They can be sent to an attendance centre if one is available, but only two experimental attendance centres have been opened for this age-group.[2]

On the other hand, efforts are still made to prevent them from being sent to prisons where they may be contaminated by adult offenders. Neither a higher nor a lower court may sentence a person under 21 to imprisonment (even if he is no longer a first offender) unless it reaches the conclusion that no other method of dealing with him is 'appropriate'; and before coming to this conclusion it must consider information of the kind usually provided in probation officers' reports.[3] Moreover, it was the intention of the Criminal Justice Act, 1961, that no court should be able to send anyone under 21 to prison except in those rare cases in which it decided that only a

[1] Although (i) if sent at 16 they can be kept until 19; (ii) if while they are 17 they are still subject to a fit person or supervision order, they can be sent to approved schools.

[2] Unlike junior attendance centres they are run by the Prison Department of the Home Office (see the Prison Commissioners' annual report for 1962).   [3] CJA 48, s. 17.

sentence of three years or longer will fit the case. All shorter sentences should take the form either of committal to borstal (which in effect means deprivation of liberty for some period between six months and two years in length) or of detention centre orders (which for this age-group may mean a period of three to six months). Thus the type of institution to which the young adult was committed would depend largely on the length of sentence which the court wished and was able to impose – short sentences to be spent in detention centres, sentences of medium length in borstals, and long sentences in special wings of prisons.

There were to be exceptions. Occasionally, a court has to sentence a young offender who is already serving a sentence of imprisonment, from which he may have escaped or been released on licence; in such cases the court is allowed to impose a prison sentence of whatever length seems appropriate, although it is debarred from sending him to a detention centre or borstal. Again, if the young adult has already served a borstal sentence, or a prison sentence of six months or more, a court is not forbidden to impose a prison sentence of eighteen months (not three years) or more, if it prefers this to a borstal or detention centre order.

In any case, the need for more detention centre vacancies has delayed the abolition of the short prison sentence as an alternative, although medium-length sentences have been replaced by borstal training.

'*Young Prisoners*'. Young adults who are sentenced to imprisonment are classified as 'young prisoners',[1] and are then allocated to the special prisons or parts of prisons reserved for this class. Those with sentences of more than three years go to Wakefield, unless they are regarded as 'hardened or depraved', in which case they are sent to one of the other prisons until they are old enough to be sent to an adults' central prison, at the age of 21. Young prisoners with shorter sentences go to Lewes, which takes those 'of the better type', or to a wing of Liverpool prison, or, if they seem suitable for an open prison, to Thorp Arch. Those with sentences of only a few months remain in the young prisoners' sections of local prisons, unless they are fortunate enough to qualify for Thorp Arch. These young prisoners' wings must be one of the least satisfactory features of our prison system. The more successfully they are insulated from the life of the main prison the drearier these small communities become: but the less insulated they are the greater is the risk of the 'contamination' which they were created to prevent. We shall see in Chapter 14 that women prisoners present a similar problem.

Prisoners who were under the age of 21 when sentenced are released on licence. If their sentences are for eighteen months or more,[2] they become eligible for release on licence after twelve months or one-third of it, which-ever is the longer, like ordinary prisoners. If they are made to serve until their remission would have been due, they are released on licence instead, and the licence is in force until the end of the sentence. If their sentences

---

[1] Unless regarded by the Governor as too sophisticated, in which case they are classified as 'stars' (q.v.).

[2] For the position of those under indeterminate sentences, however, see the section in the previous chapter headed 'Release on licence'.

AGE AND THE PENAL SYSTEM

This table compares the child's position under the present English system, the Children and Young Persons Act, 1969, and the new Scottish system

At the age of	Under present English system	Under 1969 Act when fully in operation	Under Scottish system
8	This age no longer has any significance	No change	He becomes liable to prosecution, although social proceedings will be much more usual
10	He becomes liable to prosecution	An offence will become an occasion for social proceedings	—
14	He becomes a 'young person', eligible for a detention centre, and to be fined instead of his parents	He will become liable to prosecution in certain prescribed circumstances	—
15	He becomes eligible for borstal training (and is no longer compelled to attend school*)	Of no significance, (except as regards 'school-leaving age', which will eventually be raised to 16)	—
16	(He becomes able to marry with parental consent. Consent to sexual intercourse becomes valid)	No change	He ceases to be liable to social proceedings* (He can marry with or without parental consent, and consent to intercourse) He becomes eligible for borstal, for a detention centre or for a young offenders' institution
17	He ceases to be liable to social proceedings, or to be triable by a juvenile court*; becomes eligible for imprisonment if court thinks nothing else suitable	No change	—
18	Any 'fit person' or supervision order imposed earlier lapses	Will be raised to 19 for certain 'care orders'	Compulsory supervision under social proceedings lapses (if not terminated earlier)
19	He can no longer be detained in approved school, unless after recall		—
21	He can no longer be sent to any institution for young adult offenders	No change	As in England

* with minor exceptions.

are shorter than eighteen months, they are released when their remission becomes due, but are on licence for twelve months, as if they had been released from a detention centre.

Scotland. The Scottish Advisory Council on the Treatment of Offenders[1] rejected the proposal that courts which were considering a custodial sentence for a young adult should be limited to a choice between a medium-length sentence in borstal and a short term in a detention centre.[2] They thought that there were cases in which sentences for other terms (including terms shorter than the three-month minimum for detention centres) would be appropriate and that the court should have discretion to impose such terms. On the other hand, they thought that all offenders under 21, even those sentenced to long terms, should certainly be separated from older prisoners. They therefore recommended that there should be a third type of institution for young adults, a 'custodial centre'. To those institutions should go young adults for whom the detention centre and borstal sentences were inappropriate or who were not suitable for these forms of training, and such short-stay groups as fine-defaulters and civil prisoners. No special limitation should be placed on the length of 'custodial' sentences.

Scottish courts thus have a somewhat different choice when imposing institutional sentences on young men, and rather more freedom than English courts, although the institutions themselves are less varied.[3] They may send him to a detention centre for three months,[4] although if he has already been in a detention centre or borstal, or been sentenced to a prison or young offenders' institution for two months or more they must have special reasons for doing so. They may send him to borstal if their powers[5] allow this and he has not already been in a borstal; as in England this means a term between six months and two years in length. Thirdly, they may simply sentence him to 'detention in a young offenders' institution' for any period to which their powers would allow them to send him to prison. Fine-defaulters in this age-group can be sent only to a young offenders' institution. The young offenders' institutions are parts of local prisons, and it is not yet clear whether they will be able to achieve more than mere deprivation of liberty and segregation from older and more sophisticated offenders. On the other hand, the existence of a third type of institution should certainly enable detention centres and borstals to concentrate on their training programmes without the trouble of inmates who (either because of their term of detention or for other reasons) cannot be subjected to the normal regime. As in England, those discharged from any of these three types of institution are subject to compulsory supervision.[6]

[1] 1960.

[2] In most cases the possibility of a sentence of three or more years' imprisonment does not arise, since few young adults are sentenced by the High Court.

[3] See CJ(S)A 63, ss. 1-9.

[4] The period is fixed by statute, which allows no exception and no consecutive sentences.

[5] Only justices of the peace and burgh courts presided over by lay magistrates cannot do so; stipendiary magistrates, like sheriffs, can.

[6] With some differences: for example, compulsory supervision after a borstal training lasts for only one year in Scotland, not two.

GENERAL

Standards of Management. The wide variation in the outlook, training, and experience of the staffs of penal institutions for young offenders, together with the diverse assortment of organisations responsible for their management, makes it even more important than in the case of prisons that the regimes in them should be controlled by rules. There are special sets of rules for each of the types of institution described in this chapter, including children's homes; all of them are made by the Home Secretary, and all of them are published. Like the Prison Rules they are largely designed to protect the inmates against arbitrary punishments, other forms of ill-treatment, neglect of health or welfare, and to ensure at least a minimum standard of care. Among the most important parts of each set of rules is that specifying the permissible punishments, since experience has shown that the staffs of penal institutions can be consciously or unconsciously inhumane in devising methods of dealing with misbehaviour. Corporal punishment is not allowed in borstals or detention centres, and is strictly controlled in approved schools, remand homes and children's homes; and the infliction of any sort of punishment must be recorded. Another method of dealing with misbehaviour which needs careful control is that of confining a boy in a 'separation' or 'isolation' room. This is sometimes the only humane way of dealing with a teenager who has gone 'berserk'; but it can reduce younger boys to terror, and there are strict limits on the age-groups which can be dealt with in this way, and the length of time for which they can be kept alone.[1] All institutions which are not directly administered by the Home Office are visited by Home Office inspectors.

Transfers. In spite of the consideration which courts must give to reports from probation officers, local authorities, remand centres, or prisons, before sentencing juveniles and young adults to penal institutions, it is occasionally found that an offender is quite unsuitable not only for the individual approved school or borstal to which he has been allocated by the classification system, but for any institution in that category. The Home Secretary is allowed to order the transfer of such offenders in the following circumstances:

1. a borstal trainee under the age of 18 can be transferred to an approved school; but transfer from an approved school to borstal can be ordered only by a magistrates' court;

2. a young prisoner who is under the directions of the Home Secretary as a result of murder or some other crime punishable with imprisonment for fourteen years or more can be transferred to an approved school;

3. any other young adult who is serving a sentence in prison[2] can be transferred to borstal after consultation with the court which passed the sentence;

---

[1] Other precautions are that the boy must not be left in the dark, or without something to occupy him, or without regular visits from the staff.
CYPA 33, s. 58; CJA 61, s. 16; Prison Act, 1952, s. 44.

TABLE 23 Young males dealt with by English courts for indictable offences in 1966

method of disposal	aged 8-13 JC	aged 14-16		aged 17-21	
		JC	A and Q	MC	A and Q
	%p	%p	%p	%p	%p
absolute discharge	3	2	n	1	n
conditional discharge[r]	25	16	6	8	3
probation	32	27	27	14	21
fine	20	33	8	57	13
'fit person' order	2	1	–	NA	–
attendance centre	11	10	NA	n	NA
remand home	1	n	–	NA	NA
approved school	6	8	9	NA	NA
detention centre	NA	2	26	7	16
borstal training	NA	1[b]	20	4	30
imprisonment	NA	n	n	3	12
committed to quarter sessions for sentence	–	n	NA	5	NA
other methods of disposal[o]	1	1	3	1	4
Numbers (=100%)[p]	21,635	32,154	794	38,790	6,453

JC Juvenile Courts (a negligible number of cases tried at MCs cannot be excluded)
MC Magistrates' Courts
A and Q Assizes and Quarter Sessions
NA Not applicable to this age group or type of court
n Negligible number, representing less than 0·5%.
b Strictly speaking, committed to Quarter Sessions with a view to this sentence
o e.g., as mentally abnormal, or as deportable.
p Since percentages are given as whole numbers, they do not always total 100 per cent
r Including a few recognisances.

4. a borstal trainee whom the board of visitors report to be 'incorrigible, or . . . exercising a bad influence on the other inmates' can be transferred to prison.[1]

The broad effect of the statutes in each case is that the offender simply finishes his sentence in the institution to which he is transferred, and is not kept longer than he could have been if not transferred.[2]

The Courts' Use of Measures. Table 23 shows the ways in which young adults and juvenile offenders were dealt with by higher and lower courts in

[1] Including a 'young offenders' institution' in Scotland.
[2] Indeed, if transferred from prison to borstal he may be discharged sooner than he could otherwise have been.

1966. It is noticeable that the most common measures are fines, probation and – for the younger age-groups – conditional discharge. For young men dealt with by higher courts, however, the most usual sentence is borstal training. It must be remembered, however, that these figures do not distinguish between offenders who were making their first appearance in a criminal court and those with previous convictions. Courts do not usually, for instance, send 'first offenders' to detention centres, approved schools or borstals. Nevertheless substantial minorities of the inmates of these institutions have no previous records. One of the curious features of our sentencing code is that it requires courts to think twice before sending adult 'first offenders' to prison, but not before sending a 'first offender' under the age of 21 to one of these institutions. The underlying assumption of the First Offenders' Act, 1958 was that prison is more likely to corrupt than improve the typical first offender; but the same is probably true of penal institutions for juveniles.

THE CHILDREN AND YOUNG PERSONS ACT, 1969

In 1968 Parliament was presented with the Government's latest proposals for reform, in the White Paper 'Children in Trouble'.[1] Its main proposals, now embodied (with some amendments) in the Children and Young Persons Act of 1969, were that

1. It should no longer be possible to prosecute a child between his 10th and 14th birthdays for an offence; but it should be possible to bring him before a juvenile court as in need of care and control if the offence indicates that he is beyond parental control, or if his parents are not providing adequate care, protection and guidance. In most cases, however, the offender should be the subject of unofficial action by the local authority or police;
2. Proposal (1) should apply also to 'young persons', but it should be possible to prosecute a young person if a member of the juvenile court panel consents; his consent should be given, however, only if certain circumstances (to be prescribed in regulations) are present[2];
3. For these age-groups, probation orders should no longer be distinguished from supervision orders. Supervision should be by the local authority in the case of a child, and by the local authority or probation department, as the court decides, in the case of a young person;
4. Local authorities should develop new forms of 'intermediate treatment' – i.e., involving short periods away from home – for use in

[1] Cmnd. 3601, April, 1968. This supersedes the White Paper of 1965, 'The Child, the Family and the Young Offender', whose proposals resembled those which have now been accepted in Scotland, but were so strongly criticised in England that no attempt was made to legislate on the lines proposed.

[2] Examples of circumstances suggested in the White Paper (Appendix A) were: homicide and other serious offences; offences of types causing much public concern; offenders for whom a simple deterrent, such as a fine, seems appropriate; offenders with whom action not backed by a court order seems unlikely to succeed. The Bill, however, was amended during its passage so as to dispense with the consent of a magistrate.

conjunction with supervision in some cases; and these should replace
attendance and detention centres for children and young persons;

5. Children and young persons needing more prolonged treatment away
from home should be placed in the care of local authorities (so that
approved school orders as such should cease to be made, and borstal
training for young persons will eventually be superseded);

6. Local authorities should be responsible for developing a comprehensive system of 'community homes'[1], to be planned by joint committees
of local authorities, although their plans should be subject to the Home
Secretary's approval. The plans should allow, but not compel, the
participation of voluntary bodies which provide schools[1] or homes.

The formation of these joint planning committees is already under way,
and most of the rest of the Act will be brought into force in the autumn of
1970, although for the time being it will remain possible for children and
young persons to be prosecuted as at present. When the entire system is in
operation it will embody some important innovations so far as England is
concerned. The minimum age for criminal prosecution, which has climbed
by small, hesitant steps from 7 to 10 over the last third of a century, is now
to be raised to 14; and prosecution is to be replaced by social proceedings
or unofficial action by penal agents. There are even to be restrictions on the
prosecution of young persons, including a rather interesting innovation,
the limitation of prosecution by regulations, and in the light of considerations which are not legal in nature. The grounds for care or control proceedings are to include the commission of an offence[2] (although this by
itself will not be a sufficient ground). As for what subsequently happens to
the juvenile, the gradual transfer of control from court to penal agency is
carried one stage further. Apart from such measures as the binding over of
parents, the main choices open to courts will be supervision by the local
authority or committal to its care. It is true that the court will still decide
whether supervision should include 'intermediate treatment' (i.e., short
periods away from home); but this is clearly due to a vestigial mistrust of
the penal agency. Finally, the untidy system under which some institutions
are provided by local authorities, some by the Prison Department, some by
voluntary bodies and some even by the police is to be replaced by one in
which all types of institution will be the responsibility of regional groups of
local authorities: an administrative reform which will not guarantee an
improvement in the institutions themselves, but may well lead to it.

[1] including the present 'approved schools'.

[2] Except, it seems, where the child is under 10. The reason for this exception is
presumably that 10 is the present minimum age at which a child can be found guilty of
an offence, and that the idea of such a minimum age dies hard. Yet it hardly follows
that offences should not be taken into account in *social* proceedings simply because
the child is under 10.

PART FOUR

★

SENTENCING

THE

SENTENCING

PROCESS

The system described in the last two chapters allows the sentencing courts a remarkable degree of freedom. With a few exceptions, they have a choice between an institutional or supervisory sentence, a fine or a discharge (absolute or conditional); *mutatis mutandis*, they have as much, if not more, latitude of choice if the offender is a juvenile. Thus a man convicted of manslaughter or attempted murder may receive anything from a life sentence to an absolute discharge. Statutes do not normally tell the sentencer what aims – retributive, prophylactic or reformative – should govern his choice. Nor, beyond the limitations on fines and prison sentences which are determined by the offender's age, type of offence, and previous convictions, do statutes specify the considerations that should weigh with the sentencer.

OFFICIAL INFLUENCES

As we saw in Chapter 8 this flexibility is regarded as justified by the principle of individualisation, although the ambiguity of aim which is a feature of most penal measures makes it hard to know whether a given sentencer is applying this principle retributively or reformatively. The freedom of sentencers, however, is by no means as great as it was between the wars, and is being increasingly restricted by two unobtrusive but none-the-less effective influences.

Pre-sentence Reports. One of these influences is professional advice. Courts are encouraged to consider reports on the histories and background of any offender if it is at all likely that they will subject him to institutional or supervisory measures. The police themselves usually provide the court with information about his 'antecedents', which usually means his record of crime, education and employment.[1] The court may also have received a probation officer's 'social inquiry report', which deals with the man's

---

[1] It may also include his 'domestic and family circumstances, his general reputation and associates': see the Court of Criminal Appeal's practice direction in (1966) 50 Criminal Appeal Reports, 271 ff. In Scotland antecedents are supplied by the procurator fiscal, who may or may not include information other than the offender's previous convictions. In both countries information about previous convictions which are not considered relevant may be omitted at the discretion of the prosecution.

character, personality, social and domestic background, record at school (including approved schools), attitudes and habits at his last job, and his future prospects of employment. If any of this information suggests that he may be mentally abnormal, a good probation officer will arrange for a psychiatric examination, unless this is already being done by the defence or the prison medical officer. Section 57 of the Criminal Justice Act, 1967 gives the Home Secretary the power to *oblige* courts to consider social inquiry reports before passing a custodial sentence on prescribed categories of offender; but so far he has merely issued *advice* on the subject.[1]

Prison Governors' Reports. If the accused has already served a sentence in prison, borstal or detention centre, the prison service is likely to have useful information about his physical and mental health and behaviour. Prison governors now provide the courts with reports as a matter of course on an accused person who is eligible for borstal training, if he has already served a sentence in a prison, borstal, or detention centre. In other cases they do so only where they think that they have something valuable to contribute – as they may have, for example, if the accused has been in custody while waiting for his trial or if they are asked for a report. In some circumstances courts are obliged to obtain and consider reports from governors; for instance, before they take the exceptional step of imposing a detention centre order on someone who has already experienced borstal training or a prison sentence of six months or more.

There are other circumstances too in which the sentencer is virtually required to take notice of what is said in the reports of prison governors or probation officers. Before sentencing anyone under the age of 21, or a 'first offender' of any age, to imprisonment a higher or lower court must '. . . obtain and consider information about the circumstances, and shall take into account any information before the court which is relevant to his character and his physical and mental condition.' Thus if they have a report from a probation officer or prison governor they must take it into account (although they are not obliged to comply with any suggestions in it); and if they do not have one they are practically compelled to remand the offender so that they can 'obtain' it. Similarly, before making a probation order the court must 'have regard to' the circumstances, including the character of the offender,[2] and courts do not often make one without getting a probation officer's report on him. Indeed, if the recommendation of the Streatfeild Committee (q.v.) were adopted the court would be obliged to take notice of a probation officer's report in any case in which, whether asked for or not, it has been submitted before sentence.[3] At present, an obligation of this sort applies only to courts which are considering[4] a borstal sentence; they must 'consider any report made in respect of the accused on behalf of the Secretary

---

[1] In Circulars 188-90 of 1968, which recommend a report before an offender is sent to a detention centre or borstal; before imprisonment of two years or less (suspended or not) is imposed on a male not previously sentenced to imprisonment (suspended or not) or borstal; and before any prison sentence is passed on a female.

[2] CJA 48, s. 3; CJ(S)A 49, s. 2.   [3] 1961.102.

[4] This includes magistrates' courts which are thinking of committing an offender to quarter sessions for a borstal sentence.

of State',[1] which means in effect a report from any prison or remand centre, but not from a probation department.

It is standard practice for juvenile courts to receive social enquiry reports on any children or young persons brought before them either on a criminal charge or under social procedure. The reports are rendered either by the probation department or by the children's department or both, although they need not render one if the case is simply one in which the juvenile is charged with a 'trivial' offence.[2]

Even when they are not obliged to obtain reports, many courts already do so, and in England the Home Office suggested[3] in 1963 that this should be standard practice where a person who is under the age of 31, or has reached that age but has not been convicted since his 17th birthday of an 'imprisonable' offence, or has recently been 'in touch' with the probation service,[4] is committed for trial by assizes or quarter sessions.

This means that the views of probation officers and prison staff can be an important, if not decisive, influence, especially upon the decisions of lay magistrates; and while they are usually advised not to make definite recommendations as to the form or amount of the sentence, in case this appears to usurp the functions of the court, it does not need much ingenuity to make their opinions plain as well as palatable.

Remand. In theory, courts do not begin to consider their sentence before the accused has been found guilty; and at this stage he can be remanded, in custody or on bail, for the necessary investigations.[5] An adult remanded in custody is committed to the local prison.[6] A juvenile remanded in custody is committed to a remand home,[7] unless he is very 'unruly or depraved' in which case he is treated as a young adult. Young adults are committed to remand centres provided by the Prison Division of the Home Office unless there is none available in their area, in which case they are remanded to the local prison.

The practice of remanding has disadvantages. There is often a long interlude between conviction and sentence, during which the offender is under observation, enquiries into his background are proceeding and arrangements are being made for any psychiatric examination that seems to be needed. Moreover, higher courts sit at considerable intervals, so that

---

[1] CJA 61, s. 2. Scottish courts are obliged to obtain such reports, not merely to consider them if they are given (this was the position in England before 1963).

[2] CYPA 33, s. 35: CYP(S)A 37, s. 43.

[3] In Circular 138/1963, which follows the recommendation of the Streatfeild Committee to this extent.

[4] If, for example, he has been on probation or under after-care, it is likely that some probation department has useful information about him.

[5] MCA 52, ss. 14 and 26 (as amended).

[6] In Scotland a person remanded or committed for trial who seems to the court to be mentally disordered can even be committed to a mental hospital (if a suitable one is available) for the interim: see MH(S)A, s. 54.

[7] Except in cases in which the juvenile is under 12, and where the local authority has provided a 'special reception centre' for children of this age-group; in which case he must be sent there and not to a remand home. (Children and Young Persons (Amendment) Act 1952). Not many local authorities have provided such reception centres.

O

even after the reports on the offender are ready he may have to wait for weeks until the next session. When these delays are added to the time spent awaiting trial they can mean that an excessive time elapses before he is finally disposed of. In the case of children, the suspense, and the association with staff and inmates whom they have not time to get to know, are especially undesirable.

Pre-trial Reports. It is therefore obligatory for both the local children's department and the probation department to be notified of any juveniles who are to appear before a juvenile court either on a criminal charge or under social proceedings, so that they can have a social enquiry report ready if the result of the proceedings makes one necessary.[1] There is no such obligation when the accused is past his 17th birthday, but some probation departments and prisons make use of the time during which he is awaiting trial – especially if he is in custody – to arrange for a report on him to be ready for the court. An offender of any age (and his family) can, of course, refuse to submit to the necessary enquiries – for example, on the grounds that they would prejudice his chances of acquittal; but, since only a small minority pleads not guilty, few objections are raised in practice. As a result of the recommendations of the Streatfeild Committee, the Home Office have suggested to courts and probation departments that in the case of those adults on whom social enquiry reports are now prepared as a matter of course[2] this should be done before trial wherever possible, unless the court or the offender sees any objection.

Availability. There is another way in which the freedom of the courts is limited by the executive. Some forms of disposal cannot be ordered unless the court has been told that the facilities in question have actually been provided for their area. An obvious example is attendance centres, which have not been provided and may never be provided in many rural districts, and still do not exist in many large towns. A detention centre order, too, cannot be imposed by a court unless it has been officially notified that there are places available for offenders of the age-group in question from that area; and for several years after the first centres were opened there were courts which had not yet been allowed to deal with offenders in this way. Later, vacancies were 'rationed' between courts, until the supply caught up with the demand. Remand homes often become full in different parts of the country, and thus prevent courts from using them. The shortage of approved school vacancies does not debar courts from sending juveniles to these institutions, but means that, whether the courts know it or not, the juveniles have to spend long weeks in remand homes and classifying centres waiting for places. Finally, as we shall see, the most important ways of dealing with mentally abnormal offenders cannot be used unless a hospital or out-patient clinic is willing to accept the offender as a patient. Roughly speaking, it is only prisons, borstals, the special hospitals (q.v.), probation officers, and children's departments which have to accept offenders however overloaded they are; and of course fines and discharges raise no difficulties of this kind. But the availability of places in institutions for

[1] CYPA, 33, s. 35.
[2] See p. 209.

offenders influences sentencers to an extent that is seldom appreciated, and depends very largely on the efficiency of the executive in providing them.

Appeals. Another important influence is the possibility of an appeal by the offender against the sentence. If a sentence imposed by a magistrates' court seems to him excessively severe, he can appeal to quarter sessions (or to the Queen's Bench Division of the High Court if he can argue that the sentence was actually wrong in law or in excess of the magistrates' jurisdiction). There are certain forms of penal measure against which he cannot appeal: the only important examples are a probation order, a conditional discharge and a penalty fixed by law.[1] A juvenile or his parent can also appeal to quarter sessions against a 'fit person order', an approved school order, a supervision order, or a recognisance, whether any of these is the result of a criminal charge or of 'care, protection or control' proceedings. Quarter sessions may confirm the magistrates' order, remit it back for reconsideration, or vary it themselves; if they take the last course they can even substitute a more severe measure. In 1961, there were appeals against 1,104 sentences, which represented 0·6 per cent of all the cases in which juveniles or adults had been found guilty in summary courts: fully half of the appeals resulted in a variation of the sentence. The prosecutor cannot appeal against a sentence which seems to him too mild.

Similarly an offender – but not the prosecutor – may appeal against the sentence of a higher court to the Criminal Division of the Court of Appeal,[2] which in practice means either the Lord Chief Justice sitting with a Lord Justice and a Queen's Bench judge, or a Lord Justice with two Queen's Bench judges. They may refuse leave to appeal if they see no case to argue; if they agree to hear the appeal they can confirm or reduce the sentence, but no longer have the power to increase it. In 1961 out of 31,283 sentences imposed by higher courts over 7 per cent were the subject of applications for leave to appeal. Only 401 applications – about 1 per cent of all sentences – were granted, and only 175 sentences were finally varied. Nevertheless, the possibility of a successful appeal must operate as a restraint to most judges when they are considering sentence. At the same time the Court of Appeal can also influence sentencers in the opposite direction, as the former Court of Criminal Appeal did when it declared that there was no point in imposing preventive detention for less than seven years, although the statute allowed a minimum of five;[3] moreover, by issuing 'practice directions' dealing not with individual cases but with certain aspects of sentencing the Lord Chief Justice can more or less impose a certain amount of uniformity. Recent practice directions, for example, have dealt with

---

[1] In Scotland even these can be the subject of an appeal.

[2] See the Criminal Appeal Act of 1966. From 1907 to 1966 there was a separate Court of Criminal Appeal, which also consisted of a changing selection of three judges, usually presided over by the Lord Chief Justice. The constitutional change is unlikely to do more than increase the volume of cases which can be heard. In the rest of this book references to the Court of Appeal mean its Criminal Division, while references to the Court of Criminal Appeal mean its predecessor.

[3] In *R. v. Sedgwick*, [1952] 34 Cr. App. Rep. 156.

'antecedents' reports and 'restriction orders' (q.v.). Since the House of Lords in its capacity as a court of appeal is concerned only with points of law it exercises no influence on sentencing policy.

In Scottish criminal cases all appeals are to the High Court of Justiciary. If the sentence was imposed by a court of summary jurisdiction (see p. 15) the High Court may confirm it, vary it or substitute one of their own, provided that they do not increase its severity. If the sentence was imposed by a court of solemn jurisdiction, an appeal can be heard only with its leave or the leave of the High Court; but unlike its English counterpart the High Court can then increase the sentence as well as reduce it. For this purpose three judges are a quorum, although occasionally their decisions have been over-ruled by a full bench of seven.

Consultations between Sentencers. Judges, recorders and magistrates are strongly influenced by the unofficial opinions of their colleagues, and often consult each other before passing sentence. The views of judges, and especially the Lord Chief Justice, carry particular weight. Such consultations help to reduce individual variations in policy, and attempts have been made to exploit this in the interests of uniformity. Many magistrates' benches have drawn up on paper their own rules for sentencing motorists, and some have even published the result.[2] Since 1965 the Lord Chief Justice has held 'sentencing conferences' for judges and recorders, at which selected cases and proposed sentences for them are discussed, in the hope that more uniformity will result.

Guidance by the Executive. The principle that the judiciary should be free from interference by the executive is carried to almost superstitious lengths in the British penal system. Until recently Home Secretaries have virtually confined themselves to three methods of influencing sentences. One has been the limitation of sentencers' freedom of choice by persuading Parliament to pass legislation: examples are the successive provisions restricting the use of imprisonment for young offenders. Another has been to remit questions of sentencing policy to Departmental Committees, to the more permanent Advisory Council on the Treatment of Offenders, or to its successor, the Advisory Council on the Penal System; and to rely on their published reports to influence judges and magistrates: an example is the 1957 report of the Advisory Council which discouraged short sentences of imprisonment. Occasionally judges themselves have asked for and been given information about the value of certain types of sentences, as happened when they decided against sentencing recidivists to less than three years' corrective training.[3] In 1964, however, on the recommendation of the Streatfeild Committee, the Home Office took the step of issuing a handbook for courts on the treatment of offenders.[4] This not only explained the practical consequences of each type of sentence, but presented evidence that in the case of certain types of offender some forms of sentence were

---

[1] See Chapter 13.

[2] See for example the Amersham justices' tariff in *The Magistrate* for June 1960.

[3] A decision which they subsequently revoked in the light of further information from the Prison Department; see the Lord Chief Justice's practice direction of February 1961.   [4] *The Sentence of the Court.*

followed by fewer reconvictions.[1] It will be interesting to see whether the issue of this new type of publication will be followed by a change in the trend of sentences.

OPERATIVE CONSIDERATIONS

In the meantime, the sentencer is chiefly conscious of the probation officer looking over one of his shoulders and the appellate court looking over the other. Moreover, if we wish to assess the weight which he himself attaches to specific considerations, there are further complications. That a given consideration influences some courts on some occasions can be established by the simple process of collecting a few published reports of cases in which judges or magistrates have stated reasons for the form or severity of their sentence. It is usually, however, the exceptional case which is reported, and to discover the considerations which determine the ordinary, everyday sentence is more difficult. The interrogation of the sentencers themselves, even if they are willing to be interrogated, is not likely to be profitable. People are sometimes able to give a fairly accurate account of the thoughts and motives with which they performed some out-of-the-way action, but the more regularly it is performed the less clear is their introspection or their recollection of it. In addition, if – as is the case with sentencers today – they have reason to feel that these thoughts and motives will be subjected to a critical examination, they are likely to edit and censor them if they are subjected to a direct interrogation.

In any case, the assumption that the mental processes leading to the sentencing decision are confined to the mind of the judge or magistrate who pronounces sentence is fallacious. Not only must lay magistrates sit in groups of two or more to deal with all but a few trivial types of offence, with the result that they must agree upon their sentence; but even sentencers who sit alone[2] discuss sentencing policy, if not individual sentences, with their colleagues. Consultations are probably most frequent among the lay members of a bench of magistrates, since such courts run the greatest risk of criticism if there are wide discrepancies between individual sentences.

Studying Sentences. In so complex a situation it is difficult to do more than simply study the sentences which courts pronounce, and the statistical associations between them and such variables as the type of offence and the age, sex, and previous record of the offender, on the assumption that whatever the processes by which judges – or their critics – believe that sentences are decided upon, these associations reveal at least part of the truth. The most thorough study of this kind is probably Professor Edward Green's[3] analysis of the 1,437 sentences pronounced by 18 Philadelphia judges in 1956 and 1957, for 46 kinds of offence. Contrary to popular belief, Green showed that the apparent leniency of sentences imposed on women and

---

[1] The nature and implications of such evidence will be discussed in the next chapter

[2] In England, stipendiary magistrates can and usually do, while recorders of borough quarter sessions and judges of higher courts invariably do so. But in Scotland the only courts which cannot consist of a single person are justice of the peace courts, and the High Court of Justiciary when hearing an appeal.

[3] 1961.

young white males, and the apparent severity of those imposed on negroes, were entirely explained by differences in the type of offence and the previous criminal record. In other words, if in his sample a white adult male, a white woman, a white youth, and a negro male of any age had similar criminal records and were convicted of similar offences, the sentences were usually similar. Evidence of this kind is more convincing than any assertions of impartiality by the judges themselves.

Studies of English Sentences. Unfortunately, there has been no study of any sample of English sentences which has achieved the same degree of thoroughness. R. G. Hood analysed the sentences imposed by a sample of twelve urban magistrates' courts during 1951-4 on adult males convicted of offences of dishonesty or of indecent assault on persons under 16 years' old.[1] Mannheim, Spencer and Lynch analysed the sentences imposed by eight London juvenile courts in 1951 on boys of 14, 15, and 16 found guilty of larceny.[2] The Cambridge studies of sexual offences[3] and robbery,[4] and Gibbens' and Prince's study of London shoplifters[5] contain valuable discussions of the sentences imposed for these special types of offence. The study of robbery is the only one which analyses the sentences of higher courts. What follows is based where possible on these studies, and, where this is not possible, on the Criminal Statistics. In the case of some factors all that can be done is to demonstrate from reported trials that they sometimes operate.

Semi-legal Considerations. The considerations which seem to influence the courts' actual choice of penal measure, or its severity, can be subdivided into three groups. First there are some considerations which the law itself already employs. It provides different maximum sentences for different types of offence, for offenders of different ages, and for offenders with different penal careers. The courts, however, apply these distinctions not only as the law requires but in ways which extend beyond the strict requirements, so that they can be called 'semi-legal considerations'.

Maximum Penalties. The statutes, for example, permit different maximum penalties for different types of offence. These maxima have been fixed at very different periods in the development of the penal system and reflect wide fluctuations in severity. The destruction of registers of births or baptisms has been punishable with life imprisonment since 1861, while the maximum sentence for cruelty to a child was fixed in 1933 at two years. In practice, the maximum sentence is rarely used and bears little relationship to the sentence actually imposed, for courts appear to have their own intuitive limits. As Glanville Williams[6] says:

 . . . the attitude of the courts has always been that there is *in gremio judicis* a moral scale which enables the judge to pronounce what quantum of punishment is justly appropriate to what offence. This is

[1] 1962.
[2] 1957.
[3] L. Radzinowicz (ed.), 1957, III.
[4] F. H. McClintock and E. Gibson, 1961, 73-.
[5] T. C. N. Gibbens and J. Prince, 1962, 55- and 156.
 1963.

the punishment that fits the crime. . . . The just punishment may be
reduced by reference to the circumstances of the particular criminal . . .
but it may not be *increased* by reason of any special circumstances
relating to the offender as opposed to the offence, for such an increase
would be unjust.[1]

This outlook has been described, even by Departmental Committees,[2] as a
'tariff system'.

Consistency. Courts which think in terms of tariffs are bound to consider
that sentences for similar offences should be similar, and are therefore likely
to restrict the operation of the principle of individualisation, retributive or
corrective.[3] The length to which the principle of consistency in sentencing
can be carried is illustrated by the case of *R.* v. *Reeves.*[4] Reeves and another
man were convicted of receiving 20 stolen pitch-fibre pipes. The other man,
who was tried summarily, was fined £25, but Reeves, who had elected to go
for trial by a higher court, was sentenced to nine months' imprisonment.
When he appealed, the Court of Criminal Appeal did not consider that his
sentence was excessive: on the contrary they criticised the fine imposed on
the other man as too lenient. Nevertheless, such was their respect for consistency that they felt obliged to reduce Reeves' sentence by an amount
which had the effect of releasing him immediately.

Not only are lengths of prison sentences or the amounts of fines governed
by intuitively sensed tariffs, but it is clear that certain offences are more
likely than others to be punished with imprisonment. This can be demonstrated very simply by listing the percentages of offenders convicted of
various crimes who are sent to prison by higher courts.[5] In 1960 and 1961
combined, some percentages were:

	percentage
incest	78
manslaughter[6]	75
rape	73
robbery	63
bigamy	56
buggery	54
blackmail	51
attempted murder	50
burglary	46
housebreaking	42
shop-breaking	34
gross indecency between males	11

[1] 1963.

[2] For example, the Streatfeild Committee; see the quotation on p. 223.

[3] See p. 144.

[4] *Times Law Report*, 20th November 1963.

[5] Types of offence which can also be tried summarily have been excluded, since in
such cases only 'serious' examples are sent to higher courts for trial or sentence, a factor
which could bias the imprisonment rate. Female offenders, who tend to receive lighter
sentences, are also excluded. Two years have been combined in order to yield larger
numbers.

[6] Excluding cases of 'diminished responsibility'.

Although we do not know the actual percentages of these offences which were committed by first offenders and by men with previous convictions, and cannot therefore use the imprisonment rates as exact indices of the severity with which courts treat such offences, it is noticeable that the offenders near the top – mostly convicted of personal violence or sexual offences – are of the kind who tend to include only small percentages with previous convictions for the same type of offence. Few men are convicted more than once of incest, manslaughter, or rape, and few embezzlers succeed in re-establishing themselves in posts which give them opportunities to repeat their crimes. On the other hand, the offenders against property, such as housebreakers, include very substantial percentages of men with one or more previous convictions. In other words, if allowance could be made for the previous convictions of the offenders in the list, the comparative frequency with which offences of sex and personal violence incur prison sentences would probably increase and not diminish.

Harm. The table above illustrates the great weight which sentencers attach to the actual harm caused by the offence. It is noticeable that while three-quarters of those convicted of manslaughter in 1960 and 1961 were imprisoned, only half of those convicted of *unsuccessful* attempts at murder were: a difference which is all the more striking if we reflect that man-slaughter includes some cases of unintentional homicide. Furthermore, there is a widespread belief that a property offender may expect a lighter sentence if he can assure the court that he has made complete or even partial restitution, and so reduced the harm caused by his offence. In such cases, the court might presumably argue that it was doing no more than recognise redress as a penal aim; but a court which punishes unsuccessful attempts more lightly can justify this only on the principle of retaliatory retribution. Apart from such cases, it is not easy to generalise about the extent to which the degree of personal injury or the money value of the stolen property influences the sentence. Green did not include this in his data. Hood implies that his magistrates' courts were influenced by the money value of the stolen goods, but does not say how strongly. McClintock and Gibson found that London courts' sentences for robbery were only slightly affected either by the gravity of the injury to the victim or by the value of the haul. Among Gibbens and Prince's shoplifters only a handful of first offenders appear to have been sent to prison because of the high value of the goods stolen. On the whole the evidence suggests that in sentencing courts are influenced by the harmfulness which they attribute to the *class* of offence in question, but that *within* a given class of offence other considerations are more power-ful.

Provocation. Provocation, although it is only in the case of unlawful killing that it can alter the nature of the offence, is often taken into account by courts when considering sentences for other offences; and when doing so they may even interpret the notion more liberally than the law of homicide allows. For example, in the case of *R. v. Thomas*, quoted below, a factor which persuaded the Court of Criminal Appeal to reduce the sentence was the belief that the appellant had lost his self-control because of the events of the previous night, a lapse of time which would have made it difficult, if not impossible, for provocation to be pleaded as a defence had the crime been murder.

The Offender's Penal History Among the considerations which have the strongest influence on the sentence is the offender's 'penal history'; that is, the number of offences of which he is convicted at the current trial, the number of previous occasions on which he has been convicted, the nature of the penal measures which were tried on those occasions, and the length of time since the last conviction during which he appears not to have committed an offence. The factor to which the courts seem to give most weight is the number of previous convictions, a practice which has been encouraged by Parliament; not only do many modern statutes provide higher maximum penalties for subsequent convictions for the same offence, but the First Offenders' Act, 1958, discourages magistrates' courts from imprisoning anyone who has not been previously convicted since his 17th birthday of an offence punishable with imprisonment. In Scots criminal law the sentencing court used to be allowed to take into account only offences which are 'cognate', or akin, to that of which the accused had just been convicted, and while neither Scots nor English courts are now restricted to that extent, they clearly pay more attention to cognate previous convictions. A burglar with a previous conviction for burglary will almost certainly receive a more severe sentence than one whose only previous conviction has been ior bigamy or dangerous driving.

Hood observed that, in those magistrates' courts in his sample which used prison sentences with normal frequency, an adult male convicted of an offence of dishonesty was most unlikely to be imprisoned unless he had more than two previous convictions, or had been convicted of more than one offence at the current trial, or had unsatisfactory 'work habits'. Even in the case of offences for which first offenders have a substantial chance of imprisonment – such as robbery – McClintock and Gibson observed that the chances were markedly greater for men with two or more previous convictions.

Offender's Age. The statutory limitations on the penal measures which can be applied to various age-groups of the immature reduce the court's freedom to an extent which makes it impossible to say how much they are influenced by the age of a minor. Indeed, McClintock and Gibson found that among their London robbers, if first offenders were disregarded, men under 21 were *more* likely to be sentenced to some form of detention, and they suggested that the reason was that special forms of institution – borstals and detention centres – were available for this age-group. In other words, the growth of special forms of sentence for the young, and the statutory restrictions on the penalties applicable to them, have to a great extent discouraged the courts themselves from giving much weight to this factor. At the other end of the scale, there are undoubtedly occasions on which courts take account of the old age of an offender, and refrain from imprisoning him in spite of a long history of petty offences such as larceny. In between the extremes of childhood and old age the extent to which the youth of the offender lightens his sentence is doubtful: in Philadelphia it was believed that it did; but Green showed that this was largely an illusion due to the fact that younger men had fewer previous convictions and had committed less 'grave' offences. When allowances were made for these factors the apparent bias in favour of the younger men virtually disappeared, and what was left was probably attributable to chance. Hood does not discuss the influence of age on his magistrates' courts.

The Reformation of the Offender. The reformation of the offender is recognised by statute as a proper objective of certain penal measures – borstal training and probation.[1] Even when it has been dealing with apparently incorrigible recidivists, who have more than qualified for preventive detention, the Court of Criminal Appeal has several times substituted probation in a last attempt at reform. An example was the case of Bestford[2] who at 38 had 17 previous convictions and had already served a sentence of eight years' preventive detention. For a further offence of breaking and entering he was sentenced to another 10 years' preventive detention, but the Court of Criminal Appeal substituted a three-year probation order on an 'outside chance' that he might still reform (he did not).

Socially Recognised Factors. The next group of factors consists of those which, though not explicitly recognised by penal statutes, are often openly mentioned by sentencers as considerations which influence them, and which can therefore be said to be socially recognised. They seem to include the offender's attitude to his offence, his way of life, the attitude of the victim, the prevalence of the offence in the locality or the country as a whole, and perhaps the effect which the sentence contemplated is likely to have upon his dependants. We shall see, too, in the chapter on women offenders that the offender's sex probably affects the sentence.

The Offender's Attitude to His Offence. There is no doubt that courts take into consideration the offender's attitude to his offence. Sentencers not infrequently say that they are influenced by evidence of remorse or the lack of it. This can be justified as consistent either with the aim of retaliatory retribution – since it is possible to argue that remorse is self-inflicted punishment – or with the aim of reformation, since a contrite man seems less likely to repeat his offence. It creates wide opportunities, however, not only for insincere protestations by the offender or his counsel, but also for impressionistic assessments by advisors of the court, to say nothing of sentencers themselves. This was demonstrated by the case of *R. v. Watson*[3]:

> Mr Gilbert Gray, for the appellant, said that he was now only 19 years of age and had a very good work record. He had married in 1960, the marriage being a forced marriage, and a spastic child was born, for whom he developed a great affection; but the child died when it was 13 months old and shortly after that the appellant went to pieces. His marriage also went to pieces, his wife leaving him and starting proceedings against him on the ground of cruelty.
>
> He had wanted a reconciliation with her, and for that purpose he visited the house where she was living. She was out at the time, but

---

[1] 'Reformation' is expressly mentioned in the statutes dealing with borstal, and is implied in the case of probation, especially by s. 3 (3) of the CJA 48.

[2] 1959, *Criminal Law Review.*

[3] *Times Law Report,* 22nd August 1962.

her sister, aged 15, was in, and it was on her that the offence of rape was committed.

One matter which had weighed very heavily with the Judge in passing sentence was the report of the Prison Commissioners that this young man had been 'supercilious' and had shown no remorse whatever. Counsel's instructions and his own impression were that the appellant was full of remorse and contrition, but he was a particularly inarticulate young person and it would not be fair to hold that against him.

Mr Justice Marshall, giving the judgement of the Court, said that, although nothing which the Court did in this case must be regarded as in any way suggesting that the Court did not regard the offence of rape as extremely serious, this young man was only 19 years of age; he was a traffic clerk with a very good work record; he had not been involved in any previous offence of this particular kind; and the Court knew that the Prison Commissioners' report that he was supercilious and showed no remorse whatever appeared to have had a marked effect on the Judge.

But the appellant's contrition had in fact been conveyed to the Court, which accepted its genuineness. Indeed, the appellant had quite plainly by his conduct on the night of the offence placed beyond all hope any question of reconciliation with the wife, for whom he still appeared to feel some affection. In all the circumstances the Court felt that the sentence of ten years was too severe. The appeal would be allowed and there would be substituted a sentence of six years' imprisonment.

Courts seem especially apt to believe in the offender's remorse if he has tried to undo the harm caused by his offence, for example by repaying stolen money. Attempts at reparation, however, are more convincing evidence of contrition if they are made before detection; and this seems to be rare.

Way of Life. The accused's way of life is usually dealt with very fully in social enquiry reports, which lay particular emphasis on his habits of work. A man who can show that he has held down the same job for a considerable time, and satisfied his employers, is more likely to escape imprisonment, other things being equal, than one with a record of drifting from one job to another. Hood found that his magistrates' courts appeared to be strongly influenced by 'unsatisfactory work habits'. Conversely, the Court of Criminal Appeal has even varied sentences of preventive detention on the ground that since his last term of imprisonment the offender has worked steadily at the same job. Certainly there seems to be an association between irregularity of employment and probability of reconviction, whatever the age and criminal career of the offender.

Attitude of the Victim. A court which is considering its sentence is sometimes influenced by an assurance on the part of the victim that he forgives the offender. This is especially common when the victim is a wife or an employer. For example, in November 1963, a prison sentence of five years imposed on a man who had attacked his wife was halved by the Court of

Criminal Appeal because the wife told the court she had forgiven her husband.

A decision which illustrates the simultaneous operation of this consideration and several other factors that have been discussed is that of the Court of Criminal Appeal in the case of *R. v. Thomas*[1]:

Mr Justice Marshall, giving the judgement of the Court, said that the appellant had been married some four and a half years, when, on the evening of Sunday, May 15, 1962, his wife told him that she might be pregnant. He replied that if she was it was not by him. That had started some argument, which went on throughout the night. The next morning the appellant got up, made some tea, and took a cup up to his wife.

He then went downstairs a second time, armed himself with a hammer, and went upstairs, where he struck his wife several times about the head with the hammer, putting his hands round her throat at the same time, and causing injuries which involved putting 38 stitches in her head. He had then gone out and telephoned the police that he tried to murder his wife and that he had done it because 'she had been mithering and I laid on her with a hammer'.

In assessing the appropriateness of the sentence passed the Court had four points to consider. First, the offence was entirely out of character for this young man, and all who spoke for him spoke of his non-violent personality. Secondly, it was clear that what he did was done at a time when he had lost his self-control because of the events of the previous night. Thirdly, he had an excellent reputation as a workman; and it was also clear that he was extremely contrite for what he had done. Fourthly, the woman whom he had harmed – his own wife – appeared to have forgiven him; and the Court was happy to know that there was a real possibility of a reconciliation.

But the appellant must know that the use of a hammer, the admission of an intent to murder, and the causing of these injuries were matters which the law must meet with a severe sentence. In all the circumstances and for the reasons given, it would be proper in this case to allow the appeal and to substitute for the sentence of ten years one of five years' imprisonment.

Public Sentiment. Occasionally the occurrence of an abnormally large number of offences of an alarming or sensational kind within a short period prompts courts to impose more severe sentences than usual, either as a general deterrent or as an expression of the disapproval of the community. In 1963, for example, a group of young men were convicted for sexual intercourse with a number of 14-year-old girls, and, although courts normally deal lightly with this offence, were sentenced to borstal training or, in one case, eighteen months' imprisonment. Dismissing their appeals against these sentences, which were more severe than is usual for this type of offence, the Lord Chief Justice said:

Bearing in mind the characters of the girls concerned, in an isolated case in which only one girl was involved the Court might find some

[1] *Times Law Report*, 22nd August 1962.

way of not sending the man to prison, but in the present case the Court was faced with a situation which must be causing disquiet in the locality and something in the nature of a deterrent sentence was clearly called for. . . . Treating the sentences . . . as deterrent sentences, there was nothing wrong with them and they might very well have a very salutary effect on the neighbourhood.[1]

A similar policy had been adopted by Scottish courts in dealing with gang warfare in Glasgow soon after the Second World War. At least one Lord Chancellor has commended the principle involved:

Sentences passed by benches in different parts of the country might vary within certain limits. In some parts a particular form of crime might suddenly increase and so warrant sterner measures than in another part of the country where there was little of it. If a sentence was too harsh it could always be corrected on appeal.[2]

Even in cases where this justification is absent courts may look over their shoulders at what they imagine to be the probable public reaction to their sentences. Nor is reasoning of this kind confined to local courts or to lay sentencers. A judge of the Central Criminal Court who was sentencing two 14-year-old boys for a series of 16 offences of breaking and entering and arson in an outer suburb of London, resulting in losses valued at £16,758, is reported[3] to have said 'I think the public would be rightly outraged if I placed these lads on probation'. McClintock and Gibson observed that sentences on their London robbers, which had decreased in severity between 1950 and 1957, had become more severe again by the first half of 1960, although courts in general do not seem to have swung in this direction, as Figure 4 demonstrates. The explanation was almost certainly the publicity given to the rise in the frequency of robberies in the London area.

On the other hand, Hood found that the imprisonment rates for property offences among his 12 magistrates' courts were *not* greater in the areas where such offences were more frequent in proportion to the population. Indeed, if anything, the areas with the highest rates for such offences had the most lenient magistrates; and Hood attributed this to the working-class composition of their benches.[4] However that may be, it seems likely that the severity of sentences is related not to local differences in the frequency of an offence but to sudden and spectacular increases in it.

Tacit Factors. In addition to factors which are recognised as relevant by the law, or openly taken into account by sentencers, it is widely believed that there are others which, though seldom discussed explicitly in court, influence the nature or severity of the sentence. They can be considered

[1] *Times Law Report*, 22nd December 1963.

[2] Lord Dilhorne, addressing the Magistrates' Association, as reported by *The Times* on 20th October 1962.

[3] In *The Times* of 22nd October 1962.

[4] The *Daily Express* of 28th May 1960 reported that the Chairman of a Scottish Justice of the Peace Court in a working-class area, sentencing two schoolboys for thefts, said: 'I hope you realise how mean and despicable are the offences that you have committed – breaking into the homes of working-class folk. Why don't you do a bit of travelling and try breaking into some of the big houses?' He explained afterwards that he had been joking.

under the headings of the plea of the accused, the penal philosophy of the sentencer, the temperament of the sentencer, and long-term changes in sentencing fashions.

The Plea. In at least some parts of the United States the accused is able to secure a lighter sentence by pleading not guilty until his counsel has reached agreement with the prosecutor as to the nature of the charges that will be brought and the severity of the sentence which the prosecution will ask for. When agreement has been reached he pleads guilty.[1] Green's analysis, however, of sentences imposed by Philadelphia courts for serious offences failed to support the theory that merely pleading guilty has a favourable effect on the sentence. In Britain, where the prosecution has no say in sentencing, there is less official scope for bargaining between defence and prosecution, although it does take place. On the other hand, it is some-times alleged that the police will offer to tone down their evidence as to the accused's antecedents if in return he will save them trouble by pleading guilty.[2] To what extent a plea of guilty influences the sentencer himself has not been investigated in this country. The Court of Appeal's Criminal Division seems to regard it as improper to give an offender a heavier sentence than usual because he has pleaded 'Not Guilty', but quite proper to give him a lighter sentence because he has pleaded 'Guilty'..[3]

The Sentencer's Penal Philosophy. The law does not tell a court what is to be its primary aim in deciding between measures. For example, there is no rule that instructs it to think first of the protection of the public. Even when it is sentencing a man convicted for the *n*th time of attempted murder or grievous bodily harm the court has complete freedom of choice between imprisonment, probation, a fine or a discharge. It is true that the statute which allows a court to award an extended sentence in certain cases makes it clear that the object of this sentence is 'the protection of the public', and the object of borstal training is defined as the offender's 'reformation and the prevention of crime'. But these statutes do not tell a court in which sort of case it should decide that one of these must be its objective. Indeed, one of the oddities about the use which courts have made of preventive detention (q.v.) is their tendency to apply it to petty burglars rather than to men with records of serious assault or violent sexual crimes, against whom the public might be thought to need more protection.

The 'ambiguity of aim' which, as we saw in Chapter 8, is a feature of practically all penal measures, makes the reasoning by which a court arrives at its choice of sentence an elusive and difficult subject for study. If a measure could clearly have only one aim, we should be able to assume that this was in the court's mind, but this is hardly ever the case. Where the probation officer makes a report, this sometimes contains a definite opinion that, for example, prison or probation would be the more successful in

[1] See, for example, D. J. Newman's analysis of sentences in a county of Wisconsin (1956).

[2] See, for example, the essay by F. Norman in Rolph, 1962 (*The Police and the Public*).

[3] See *R. v. Harper* [1967] 3 All E.R. 619n (C.A.) and *R. v. de Haan* [1967] 3 All E.R. 618.

reforming a given offender[1]; and if the court takes his advice it is fair to assume that they accept his reasoning also. Where the court acts without, or against, a probation officer's recommendation, it sometimes adds a statement as a justification of its sentence. 'I am going to give you another chance' is often the preface to an absolute or conditional discharge or a probation order. On the other hand 'the public must be protected against criminals of your kind' usually heralds a stiff sentence of imprisonment. It is only in the case of the young that courts are given any general direction: 'Every court in dealing with a child or young person who is brought before it, either as being in need of care or protection or as an offender or otherwise, shall have regard to the welfare of the child or young person . . .'[2], and even here it is noticeable that the statutes do not say that the child's welfare is to be the only consideration or even the overriding one; merely that it is to be among the considerations in the mind of the court.

Consequently there is considerable scope for the operation of personal idiosyncrasies of penal philosophy, and for the influence of individual variations in the strength of the sentencer's distaste for this or that type of offence. Nor have there been any authoritative comments on the penal law in recent years by Home Secretaries or Lord Chief Justices which would help to clear the minds of sentencers. Perhaps the nearest approach to advice was achieved by the Streatfeild Committee, which included a judge, a recorder, a professor of Law, two lay magistrates, a sociologist and a psychiatrist:

> In short, sentencing is becoming a more complex task. In many cases, particularly those appearing at the superior courts, the court can still do little more than punish the offender for what he has done, and in every sentence the offender's culpability has still to be taken into account. But in a considerable, and growing, number of cases the 'tariff system' can no longer be relied on to fit all the considerations in the court's mind. The need to deter or reform the offender, the need to protect society and the need to deter potential offenders may in a particular case be conflicting considerations. . . . These objectives have an importance of their own and have a separate effect on the decision of the court.

As a philosophy of sentencing this represents a compromise rather than a synthesis. Beyond emphasising the extent to which superior courts still think in terms of 'culpability', it gives no positive guidance to sentencers. The Committee did not explain how the number of cases which the tariff system did not fit was growing: it may merely have meant that the number of sentencers who were dissatisfied with retributive thinking was increasing.

The Temperament of the Sentencer. It is widely believed that judges and magistrates vary greatly in the type and severity of sentence which they impose on offenders who do not differ in relevant respects: in other words, that a burglar of given age, marital status, penal history, and record of employment might receive very different sentences from two different judges. Certainly some judges and magistrates have reputations for

---

[1] A practice cautiously endorsed by the Streatfeild Committee (1961.94-).
[2] CYPA 33, s. 44: CYP(S)A 37, s. 49.

severity, others for leniency. But reputations can be misleading. A single sentence may cause a judge to be labelled severe, so that his lenient sentences are ignored as out of character and his heavier ones noted as typical. In any case, the important question from a scientific point of view is not whether one or two judges or magistrates are extreme in their sentencing habits, but whether most of them vary widely.

Hood's study of 12 urban magistrates' courts was an analysis of the sentencing behaviour of groups of magistrates and not of individuals, since lay magistrates do not sit singly when sentencing.[1] This should have had a normative effect which would have restrained individuals who might by themselves have gone to extremes; the amount of variation which Hood did observe was therefore all the more striking. In the early 1950s the average percentage of adult males who were imprisoned by all English magistrates' courts for indictable offences of dishonesty was about 21 per cent, and 60 per cent of such courts imprisoned between 15 per cent and 30 per cent of such cases. But two courts in Hood's sample imprisoned as many as 50 per cent, and two others imprisoned less than 15 per cent. Even when allowance was made for differences in offenders' penal histories, or in the value of property stolen, these two pairs of courts were still well out of line with the majority. The two courts which made extensive use of imprisonment seemed to be further out of line than those which used it very little. Hood's explanation was that these courts were in towns which

> ... have better social conditions and a larger proportion of middle-class people than have the towns with a low imprisonment rate. They are older towns, not heavily industrialised, with a traditional 'conservative atmosphere', and their benches are predominantly composed of members of the middle class, who are anxious to maintain the traditional temper of community life and protect local property through means of deterring criminals by imprisonment.

But he points out that his information about the social composition of the benches is limited, being largely based on a field worker's impressions.

In contrast, Green's 21 Philadelphian courts were all presided over by professional judges. He found that if allowances were made for differences in the proportions in which various types of offence and offender were represented among their cases, there was a surprising degree of uniformity in the *length* of their penitentiary sentences. Rather less impressive was the uniformity of their choices between different penal measures. When the offence was fairly serious or fairly trivial, they showed some uniformity, but a substantial minority of four judges dealt more leniently than the rest with the serious crimes, while six judges dealt more severely than the rest with the minor ones. In cases of intermediate gravity, they fell apart into three quite distinct groups. When it is appreciated that, unlike Hood's magistrates, all these judges sat in the courts of a single city (although five were visiting judges from neighbouring counties) and can be assumed to have known each other personally, the amount of variation is remarkable.

---

[1] Three out of twelve courts, however, had stipendiary magistrates. One of these was responsible for one of the pair of courts which made very little use of imprisonment: he was determined to use it only as a last resort.

Relative Importance of Factors. Which of the factors discussed in this chapter has the greatest influence upon sentences? Only Green's study of Philadelphia Quarter Sessions attempts to provide an answer which is applicable to serious offences in general. Nor did Green's data allow him to analyse all the factors discussed, such as variations in prevalence, or the degree of harm caused by the offence. He was able to analyse the influence of (1) the nature of the offence, (2) the number of offences charged at the same time, (3) the recency of the last prior felony conviction, (4) the prior criminal record of the offender, (5) the sex of the offender, (6) the age of the offender, and (7) the race of the offender. His results – which relate, of course, only to serious offences committed by adolescent or adult offenders in Philadelphia – showed that the influence of sex, age, and race was non-existent or negligible. The order of importance of the other factors was (1) the nature of the offence, (2) the number of offences charged at the same time, (3) the prior criminal record, and (4) the recency of the last prior felony conviction.

British studies have been confined to certain groups of offences – larceny dealt with in magistrates' courts and juvenile courts, shoplifting dealt with by London magistrates, robbery dealt with by higher and lower courts in London, and sexual offences dealt with by higher and lower courts. This has the advantage of largely eliminating the influence of different maximum penalties for different offences, as well as of differences in the extent to which such considerations as the need for protecting the public are in the mind of the court.[1]

On the whole, their results are consistent with Green's finding that, next to the nature and number of the charge or charges themselves, the most important factor is the offender's record of previous offences. In all probability there is no other single factor which approaches it in the strength of its influence on the mind of the court.

TRENDS

Taken as a whole, courts are impressively slow to alter the general pattern of their sentences. The period since the war has seen not only a sharp and much-publicised increase in almost all types of offence, but also several major pieces of penal legislation and a great deal of public discussion of our penal system and its underlying philosophy, all of which might be expected to affect the sentencing policy of the courts. Yet, as Figures 4 and 5[2]

[1] The disadvantage is that the four British studies have taken notice of different factors, or factors measured differently, and have employed statistical techniques of different degrees of thoroughness.

[2] Figures 4 and 5 (based on the annual Criminal Statistics) show the main measures of disposal as percentages of the total number of persons found guilty and dealt with in the year. Figure 4 is confined to offenders aged 21 or over; Figure 5 is confined to offenders dealt with by juvenile courts. Several points must be borne in mind in studying the figures. The imprisonment of offenders under 21 by higher and lower courts was made more difficult by the 1948 Act. A number of measures – preventive detention, corrective training, attendance centre, detention centre, and borstal training orders – which were used for relatively small numbers having regard to the total in the age-group, are not shown.

P

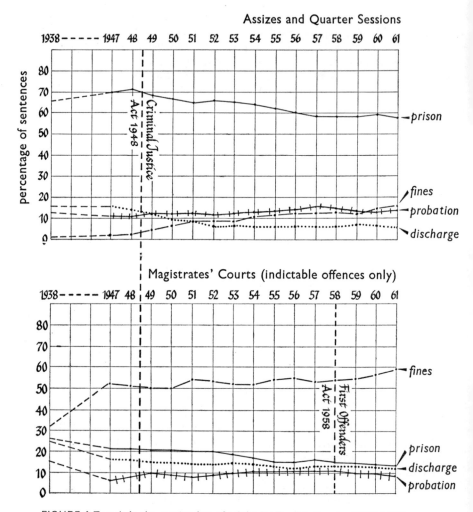

FIGURE 4 *Trends in the sentencing of adults by English Courts, 1947-1961*

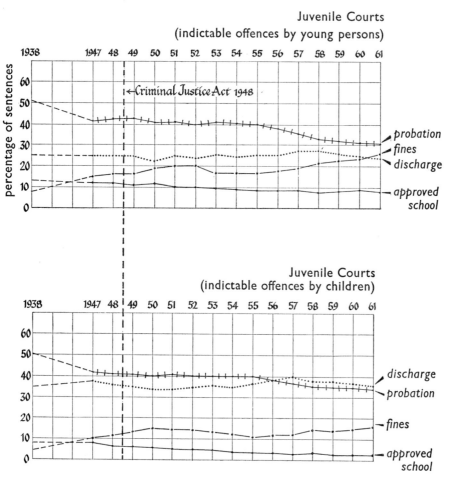

FIGURE 5 *Trends in the sentencing of juveniles by English Courts, 1947-1961*

demonstrate, the pattern of sentences imposed by courts as a whole upon adult and juvenile offenders has not changed markedly during the fifteen years from 1947 to 1961.

Imprisonment. Nevertheless, both higher and lower courts have shown a steady, though very gradual, tendency to make less use of imprisonment.[1] This tendency is rather more marked in the case of higher courts, but the explanation may simply be that since they imprisoned much larger percentages than did lower courts they had more scope for a decrease. McClintock and Gibson observed that in the case of their London robbers, who were dealt with by higher courts, smaller percentages were imprisoned in 1957 than in 1950, a decrease which was largely but not entirely accounted for by reductions in the percentages of juveniles and first offenders who were sentenced to prison or some other form of detention. Thus the percentages of adult male robbers who were imprisoned were:

TABLE 24 Probability of prison for convicted robbers

	1950	1957	1960 (first half)
	%	%	%
first offenders	74	40	(67)
with previous convictions	91	87	(95)

A similar post-war trend towards non-imprisonment was observable in the sentences imposed by London magistrates' courts on Gibbens' and Prince's shoplifters in 1949 and 1959.[2]

Indeed, it is noticeable that the First Offenders Act of 1958, which made it difficult for magistrates to sentence adult first offenders to prison, seems to have done nothing to hasten the downward trend in imprisonment. It is obvious that by the time it was passed such a large majority of magistrates were already following this policy that the statute did little more than ratify their practice.

Length of Imprisonment. Another trend in imprisonment has been the decrease in the popularity of the short sentence of two months or less. For several years after the war the Howard League led a vigorous campaign against prison sentences of less than three months, on the grounds that they were insufficiently long for deterrence or reform, but long enough to enable the first offender to make acquaintance with sophisticated criminals. The campaign led to the production of a report in 1957 by the Advisory Council

[1] There are, almost inevitably, exceptions to this general downward trend. Hood found that among his 12 urban magistrates' courts two, which had made a more or less average use of imprisonment in 1951-4, had increased their use of it by 1960. McClintock and Gibson observed that London courts seemed to be making more use of imprisonment for robbery in the first half of 1960 than in 1957, probably because of the alarm which had been caused by the much-publicised increase in this form of crime in London.

[2] 1962.55-.

on the Treatment of Offenders, discussing the alternatives to short terms of imprisonment, and recommending, for example, the increased use of fines. Table 25 shows how prison sentences in 1937, 1951, and 1961 compared in length. It is noticeable that 67 per cent of magistrates' sentences are now for more than two months, compared with 57 per cent in 1951 and 36 per cent in 1937. We must not jump to the conclusion that magistrates are deliberately lengthening their sentences. It is much more likely that the sort of offender who in 1951 or 1937 would have been sentenced to a short term in prison is now being fined instead, while those who would have received sentences of three months or more are still doing so. Certainly the decline in the use of imprisonment is more than enough to account for the decline in shorter sentences. Similarly, the sentences of higher courts, although no longer than in 1951, are now markedly longer than in 1937, when a larger percentage of offenders was sent to prison.

TABLE 25 Lengths of sentences of imprisonment[1] imposed on adults[2] by English courts in 1937, 1951, and 1961

Length of sentence	1937	1951	1961
Assizes and Quarter Sessions:	%	%	%
up to 6 months	34·4	15·4	16·0
6 months to 1 year	34·4	34·1	34·0
over 1 year	31·2	50·5	50·0
number of sentences (=100%)	4,182	8,351	12,471
Magistrates' Courts (indictable and non-indictable offences):			
up to 14 days	17·6	6·6	4·8
15 days to 1 month	30·9	20·9	16·4
1 to 2 months	15·4	15·4	11·7
2 to 3 months	21·1	29·0	34·6
3 to 6 months	14·8	27·8	32·3
over 6 months[3]	0·2	0·3	0·2
number of sentences (=100%)	19,136	19,064	20,981

[1] Including penal servitude, but excluding borstal, preventive detention and corrective training.

[2] i.e., males and females aged 17 or over. A very few under this age are unavoidably included in the figures for higher courts.

[3] A sentence of over 6 months can be imposed by magistrates only in the circumstances defined in MCA 52, s. 108.

Probation. One of the rather surprising trends is in the use of probation. It might have been expected that the decrease in the use of imprisonment would have been accompanied by a rise in the percentage of probation orders. But this seems to have happened only in the higher courts, and there only to a very slight extent. In magistrates' courts a slightly *smaller* fraction of adults than before the war are dealt with in this way, while in juvenile courts, where probation is most frequently used, the decline has been most marked. This does not necessarily indicate a loss of confidence in probation, since increasing numbers of juvenile courts have recently had detention centres and attendance centres opened in their areas, with all the attractions that novelty confers. It is also possible that probation officers themselves have discouraged the courts from extending probation to a much larger percentage. Although the growth in the number of probation officers has kept pace with the recent increase in the number of indictable offenders, the average case load of probationers per officer rose from 55 in 1954 to a peak of about 65 in 1958 and 1959, and was felt by many officers to be excessive.

Fines. The measure which has undoubtedly increased in popularity is fining, and this seems to be true of all age-groups:

TABLE 26 Probability of a fine

years	percentage of indictable male offenders who were fined[1] in the age-groups			
	8-13	14-16	17-20	21 and over
1938	5	8	15	27
1951	15	20	33	45
1961	17	26	42	48

This upward trend, which seems to be continuing, is too marked to be attributable to any changes in types of offence or percentages of first offenders. It can be observed in the sentences imposed on Gibbens' and Prince's samples of shoplifters in 1949 and 1959. No doubt an important contributory factor has been the increasing number of offenders whose earnings seem to the court sufficient to enable them to pay a fine. During the nineteen-fifties the manual wage-earner's average weekly pay more than doubled, while retail prices increased by little more than a half.

Discharge. It is very noticeable that the measure which shows least change in popularity over the last ten years is discharge. Figures 4 and 5 lump together absolute and conditional discharge because in essence they both imply that the court considers the case to be such that no positive penal measure, whether retributive, prophylactic, or reformative, is necessary. The absence of fluctuations in the percentages of discharges is all the more remarkable when we appreciate that it represents not a constant annual number, but a constant fraction of a steeply rising annual total of appear-

---

[1] In the case of practically all boys aged 8-13, and some aged 14-16, the fine was, of course, imposed on the parents; see p. 184

ances in the criminal courts. Since nobody has so far studied the characteristics of cases which lead to a discharge, any suggestion as to why this might
be so would be mere speculation. Indeed, the most noteworthy feature of
all the trends that have been discussed is that they have taken place not
against a background of a steady level of reported crime, but in a decade in
which reported indictable offences rose from under half a million to well
over three quarters of a million, to the accompaniment of newspaper
leaders, white papers, parliamentary debates, and television documentaries.
It would not have been surprising if judges or magistrates or both had
reacted by discharging a decreasing percentage of offenders; but they have
not done so.

POSSIBLE DEVELOPMENTS

Two sorts of proposal have been put forward in recent years for improving
our present system of sentencing. The less radical of the two is that courts
should be obliged to give reasons for their choice of sentences. They are
already obliged to do so in certain cases: magistrates' courts, as we have
seen, must state their reasons if they decide that imprisonment is the only
appropriate sentence for a first offender or an offender under the age of 21.
But it has been suggested[1] that there would be advantages in a general
obligation of this kind:

1. in that it accords with a principle of 'natural justice', which has come
   to be recognised not only in civil actions but in administrative law.
   As a result of the recommendations of the Franks Committee on
   Administrative Tribunals and Enquiries, Government Departments
   are obliged to give reasons for a decision in any case in which a
   statutory inquiry is or could be held, and a similar obligation is
   placed on many tribunals;

2. in that it would lead to a 'rationalisation' of sentencing, since
   sentencers would have to indicate the considerations which in their
   view justified their decisions, and this would prevent them from being
   influenced by emotional reactions to the offence of the offender;

3. in that this would lead to more consistency in sentencing policy.
   'Certain factors would become recognised as valid reasons for the
   choice of particular sentences, others would be rejected as irrelevant.
   Differences in practice between various courts would become obvious,
   and would be removed as a result of decisions of the Court of
   Criminal Appeal.'[2]

It is noticeable that only the second of these arguments is concerned with
the effectiveness of sentencing in achieving the aims of the penal system.
The other two assume that 'natural justice' and 'consistency' are desirable
for themselves, and many people who would grant this in the case of 'natural
justice' would not do so in the case of 'consistency'. Indeed, it is arguable
that if consistency were achieved this might crystallize sentencing policy
to an extent which would prevent the development of new ideas and
attitudes. Interesting and probably valuable innovations have in the past
been the result of sentencers' originality, as when Clarke Hall, the

[1] For example, by Thomas, 1963.   [2] Thomas, *loc. cit.*

London Magistrate, used probation as a means of requiring certain offenders to undergo psychiatric treatment.[1]

The second argument is more complex. Its claim that 'rationalisation' would prevent sentences from being chosen from emotional motives is exaggerated, since human ingenuity in devising respectable reasons for obeying less respectable impulses is considerable (indeed, this is one of the meanings of 'rationalisation'). The very 'ambiguity of aim' which we have noticed in penal measures would make this only too easy. It must be conceded that the process of justification would reduce the scope for emotional sentencing. The argument seems to imply, however, that sentencers would not only justify their sentences by reference to one of the recognised aims of penal measures (which by itself would be mere lip-service) but would as a result choose sentences which were more likely to achieve these aims. As we shall see in the next chapter there are few recognised aims which sentencers can safely assume that they are achieving, at least unless they have the benefit of considerable technical guidance.

Sentencing Authorities. This leads us to the more radical proposal that the sentencing function should be taken out of the hands of the courts and given to another sort of body. Supporters of this proposal point out that courts are designed to secure a fair trial, and that even where they are presided over by trained judges the training of these judges has been concerned not with the choice or administration of penal measures, but with rules of law which are intended to ensure that a conviction is just and a sentence legal. Moreover, the very position of the magistrate or judge prevents him from observing or talking to the accused except in a formal and artificial setting. For both these reasons, courts are nowadays, as we have seen, encouraged and even sometimes obliged to take the advice of persons with training, experience and the opportunity for assessing the likely effect of different penal measures on the individual offender. Either the sentencer must become the mere mouthpiece of the probation officers, doctors and prison governors who report on the prisoner, or the pronouncing of sentence should be given to a body of experts. To remand the accused for reports, and recall him to court, requiring the attendance of those who have prepared the reports, is to waste the time of judges, recorders, magistrates, clerks, probation officers, doctors, and prison staff.

It would be both ridiculous and impractical to suggest that all of the million or so cases with which higher and lower courts have to deal each year should be referred to a sentencing authority. Ridiculous, because for most traffic offenders and other non-indictable offenders the only questions for decision under our present law are whether the offender should be discharged, fined, have his licence endorsed or be disqualified from driving; and there is little expertise that a sentencing authority could contribute to such decisions. Impractical, because the manpower involved in creating bodies of experts throughout the country would be enormous. From this point of view at least our courts are the most economical sentencing machinery that could be devised.

Once this has been conceded, however, the problem is to define categories

[1] See Chapter 13.

of offenders or offences which might benefit by being remitted to sentencing
boards and which would not be so numerous as to strain our skilled manpower and other resources. Leaving aside juveniles – for whom a rather
different sort of machinery seems likely to develop – examples of possible categories are

1. offenders who have not yet experienced a custodial sentence, but for
   whom the courts consider that one may be needed (from prison
   statistics for 1965 it seems likely that this would include some 15,000
   men and 1,100 women a year);
2. offenders for whom the courts consider that a prison sentence of, say,
   more than two years may be desirable (from 1965 prison statistics
   this seems likely to include some 2,500 men and 50 women a year;
3. recidivists who are eligible for an extended sentence (see Chapter 15:
   the numbers are not easy to estimate, but are unlikely, at 1965 rates,
   to exceed 1,000 men and 50 women a year);
4. persistent and dangerous traffic offenders.

Although these categories overlap to some extent, it would not be illogical to
propose that all of them should be remitted to a sentencing board or boards.
The first category is by far the largest and most miscellaneous, and if it were
included more than one board would be required.

A sentencing board or boards could also perform another sort of function.
An odd feature of our penal system – which is admittedly common to most
civilised systems – is that it makes it very difficult to experiment with new
ideas. The need to protect the offender against inhumane originality has
produced a penal philosophy which frowns on penal measures that are
not expressly permitted by statute; and it is assumed that such statutes
should be general – that is, that what they permit should be permissible for
whole classes of courts or offenders. It is true that there are exceptions. For
example, the idea of an attendance centre for young adults was regarded as
tentative, and only two have so far been provided, in Manchester and
Greenwich. Again individual sentencers have sometimes 'experimented',
by using their powers in an unusual – and sometimes improper – way,
as one or two stipendiary magistrates did in the nineteen-thirties when
they used probation as a means of ensuring psychiatric treatment (an
experiment which was later legalised in section 4 of the Criminal Justice
Act, 1948). In contrast, throughout the long-drawn argument over suspended prison sentences which preceded their introduction in 1967 there
was no attempt to test the arm-chair psychology of either supporters or
opponents by experimenting with the idea; for to do so would have been
illegal. When the idea was introduced, it was made available to all courts for
prison sentences up to two years in length.

A solution to this self-imposed dilemma would be to allow sentencing
boards to experiment with new measures before they are made available
to courts in general. It would be possible to control the sort of measures
which they tried by stipulating that these should have the approval of, say,
the Home Secretary; but it would be desirable to give them rather more
freedom than this. It might be sufficient simply to stipulate the sort of
retributive appropriateness of a three-year sentence for burglary the best
measures with which they could not experiment: obvious examples are

capital and corporal punishment, and long periods of solitary confinement. In practice, the care with which members of the boards would be chosen should ensure that they operate with commonsense and humanity. As a final safeguard, however, the offender should have the same rights of appeal as he has against an ordinary sentence.

THE

EFFICACY

OF SENTENCES

Having discussed the aims of penal measures, the forms which they take in Britain and the use made of them by the courts, I am now approaching the central problem of penology – the assessment of the effectiveness of these measures.

RETRIBUTIVE APPROPRIATENESS

Since some sentencers and many men in the street regard retaliatory retribution as at least one of the main aims of the death penalty, imprisonment, and fines, the question whether these measures achieve this aim must be considered, if not answered. In Chapter 8 I described this form of retribution as the intentional infliction of appropriate suffering upon an offender who is capable of recognising that the suffering is intentionally inflicted because of his offence. As to the suffering caused by such measures there can be no doubt, except in the case of the man who welcomes death, enjoys seclusion or is sufficiently rich or unworldly to be unmoved by a heavy fine. That the intention behind the infliction of suffering is recognised by most offenders is also fairly certain, unless they are too young, mentally ill, or subnormal. The crucial difficulty arises when we ask whether the remaining requirement is fulfilled, namely that the amount of suffering shall be appropriate. If the code according to which it is inflicted prescribes amounts for given offences, then one can simply define 'appropriate' as 'prescribed in the code' and leave it at that, although this does not prevent moralists from questioning whether the prescription of, say, death for forgery is retributively appropriate. A similar question has to be faced even by those who advocate quantitative retribution, as defined in Chapter 8, since they must presumably be able to explain why an upper limit of so many months or years imprisonment is retributively appropriate for, say, burglary. As soon as this question is allowed, the difficulty of assessing retributive appropriateness by any objective standard has to be faced.

Unless the retaliatory retributionist is able to claim divine revelation as a source, it seems necessary for him to find a secular standard, and it is hard to see what form this could take, unless perhaps it were the public opinion of the day. In other words, if one were asked how to test scientifically the

one could do would be to sample public opinion. This would carry with it the corollary that a sentence of imprisonment which was regarded as retributively proper when it was inflicted upon a given offender might, before he had served the whole of this sentence, come to be regarded as excessive or inadequate.

THE ASSESSMENT OF REDRESS

In comparison, the task of deciding the extent to which a measure of redress has achieved its aim seems easy. In civil courts the assessment of the sums to be paid as compensation for injury or damages for loss of property is an everyday task. In criminal cases, although there is often the practical difficulty of identifying the offender, and procedural awkwardnesses which are not relevant here,[1] only one serious problem arises after these have been overcome: this is the fact that many offenders are unable to pay the full sum which would, in the court's view, be adequate. Moreover, some offenders are unwilling to pay, and prefer to go to prison.

There are penal reformers who support measures of compulsory redress on the grounds that whether or not the sum paid is adequate, the payment of it has a remedial effect upon the offender, who is thus made to think about and regret the effects of his offence more vividly. If so, since most offenders who are ordered to compensate their victims have to be given time to pay, we must be prepared to accept a system of repentance by instalments. The theory of regeneration by compensation is so far based not on any factual evidence, but on the belief of some middle-class non-delinquents that if they were working-class delinquents this would assist them to repent. This may be so, but it is equally possible that a man who has to pay a substantial part of his wage-packet to someone whom he injured in a quarrel will in fact have his grudge perpetuated and enhanced: this too, however, is special pleading of an equally speculative kind.

ELIMINATION

One foreseen effect of imprisonment is the temporary elimination of the offender as a danger to society, and since less than 1 in every 200 prisoners manage to escape (usually for only a few days), imprisonment is in this respect extremely effective. There is only one type of prison sentence which is expressly prophylactic, and that is the extended sentence; I shall therefore postpone discussion of this function to Chapter 15, which deals with recidivists. Elimination is also a foreseen effect of capital punishment; but it is more fashionable to judge this measure by other criteria, and in particular its efficacy as a general deterrent.

GENERAL DETERRENCE

The deterrence of the individual offender from repeating his offence will be discussed along with other forms of correction, since it is often not easy

[1] See, for example, the annual reports of the Criminal Injuries Compensation Board (H.M.S.O.)

to apportion the credit for reform between deterrence and other influences. In this section I am concerned with the problem of assessing the deterrent effects of penal measures upon people other than the offender.

Capital Punishment as a Deterrent. The measure whose efficacy as a general deterrent has been most thoroughly discussed is, of course, the death penalty.[1] The most impartial summary of most of the evidence is in the report of the Royal Commission of 1953.[2]

Those who believe that the death penalty operates as a general deterrent have described more than one way in which it may do so. A man who is planning in cold blood to kill someone, whether for gain, revenge or some other motive, must, it is argued, take into account his chances of being detected and the probability of being executed as a result. Even a man who is provoked or startled into an impulse to make an unpremeditated attack is sometimes able to restrain himself, or to confine himself to injuries which are unlikely to be fatal, or to desist before he has caused death; and the fear of capital punishment must sometimes be one of the restraining motives. A man who foresees a situation in which his experience tells him that he may be impelled to attack someone may deliberately make sure that he does not carry a lethal weapon; the example usually given is the burglar who leaves his gun behind.[3]

A fourth way is suggested by the Royal Commission themselves:

.. We think it is reasonable to suppose that the deterrent force of capital punishment operates not only by affecting the conscious thoughts of individuals tempted to commit murder, but also by building up in the community, over a long period of time, a deep feeling of peculiar abhorrence for the crime of murder. 'The fact that men are hung for murder is one great reason why murder is considered so dreadful a crime.' This widely diffused effect on the moral consciousness of society is impossible to assess, but it must be at least as important as any direct part which the death penalty may play as a deterrent in the calculations of potential murderers. It is likely to be specially potent in this country, where the punishment for lesser offences is much more lenient than in many countries, and the death penalty stands out in sharper contrast.[4]

The arguments for and against these beliefs take three forms. There is the argument from introspection, in which the proponent tries to imagine how he would react in certain situations, and reasons that potential murderers react likewise. Since the proponent is usually unfamiliar with the sort of situation in which murder is committed, and is probably the sort of person whose upbringing, education and moral code make him most un-

---

[1] It also happens to be the only measure that can be claimed to be a general but no an individual deterrent.

[2] Gowers, 1953.19- and 328.

[3] Like most legendary figures he may well have existed in some form, although the nearest I can find to a factual account of such a man is on p. 335 of the Royal Commission's Report.

[4] 1953.20. The Royal Commission were quoting Fitzjames Stephen, to whom the theory should probably be attributed.

likely to commit murder whatever the penalty, such reasoning is worth no more than any other kind of armchair psychology.

Secondly, there is anecdotal evidence, based on the doings or sayings of known offenders. Though it tends to be produced in the heat of debate by avowed supporters or opponents of the death penalty, it cannot be entirely dismissed. Good examples will be found in the Royal Commission's Report.[1] Although, like most anecdotal evidence, some of the stories are suspiciously dramatic, they can be summed up as demonstrating that:

1. some men premeditating murder think of the death penalty and do refrain;
2. some men premeditating murder think of the death penalty and do not refrain;
3. some men are actually impelled to commit murder because it incurs the death penalty[2];
4. some men premeditating murder think of the absence of the death penalty and commit murder.

Presumably there have also been cases of:

5. men who have premeditated murder in countries where the penalty is not death but 'life', and have also refrained.

In other words, anecdotal evidence, even at its face value, could not conceivably show that the death penalty *never* operates as a deterrent; it can and does show that the penalty sometimes operates; but could not conceivably show how often, or in what percentage of potential murderers it operates. Since this is of course the important question, we must turn to the statistical evidence.

Statistical Evidence. As the Royal Commission pointed out, 'Capital murder has obviously failed as a deterrent when a murder is committed. We can number its failures. But we cannot number its successes. No one can ever know how many people have refrained from murder because of the fear of being hanged. . . .' This fundamental difficulty can be circumvented in two ways. One is to study the annual murder rates per head of population in countries where the death penalty has been abolished or reintroduced, and where the rates are based on 'murders reported' or 'known to the police' and not merely on 'murders resulting in convictions' or 'persons brought to trial'. Countries which have reintroduced capital punishment probably provide a sounder basis than countries which have only abolished it, since formal abolition is usually preceded by a rather indefinite period during which the death penalty is not inflicted, or only rarely inflicted and it is impossible to know how clearly this is appreciated by the population; whereas reintroduction is preceded by a period in which the penalty is known not to be death,[3] and is accompanied by considerable public discussion.

---

[1] 1953.335-.

[2] Since such men are abnormal and even rarer than other murderers, such stories, though undoubtedly true, are not really evidence for or against the deterrent effect of the death penalty on normal people.

[3] Except where the abolition period has lasted for only a few years, as in the States of Iowa, Colorado, Washington, Tennessee, Arizona, Missouri; such States do not provide reliable evidence.

From this point of view the best evidence is provided by New Zealand, where capital punishment was in abeyance from 1936, abolished by law in 1941, restored at the end of 1950, and abolished again from the end of 1961. New Zealand has the additional advantage of being a country with a small population, which increased from about $1\frac{1}{2}$ million in 1920 to about $2\frac{1}{2}$ million in 1961; every known murder is interesting news in both the islands. It has two disadvantages for our purpose. The annual number of murders is small, which gives an appearance of sudden fluctuations, but this can be overcome to some extent by calculating moving averages over five-year periods. The other disadvantage is that a rather low percentage of murders seem to lead to convictions, which might weaken the deterrent effect of any penalty.

Figure 6 shows the moving 5-year averages[1] from 1924 to 1962 of murders known to the police for every million inhabitants of the main islands of New Zealand, and indicates also the years in which executions took place and the period during which the death penalty was in abeyance or abolished by law. The fluctuations in the murder rate appear to have little or no relationship to the use of the death penalty. There was a sharp rise from 1933 to 1935, before the death penalty fell into disuse and in years when one or two executions were actually carried out. The rate fell equally steeply in the first five years of disuse. It rose again in the first few years after formal abolition, but began to fall again before the restoration of capital punishment. It continued to fall after restoration, but began to rise again four years before the second abolition, and following a year in which all of the four persons convicted of murder were executed. In other words, the fluctuations in the murder rate over the last 39 years seem to be independent of the use of the death penalty.

The other kind of statistical evidence is the comparison of contemporary murder rates in countries or states which do and do not use the death penalty. Since some countries include a wider range of homicides under the heading of murder than do others, comparisons should be drawn only between countries in which the legal definition is roughly the same. From this point of view comparisons between England and a Commonwealth country would be sounder than comparisons between England and a European country, although even the former might be vitiated by other differences – for example, in the degree of urbanisation or in attitudes to homicide. The best comparisons, however, are probably those in the tables and diagrams supplied to the Gowers Commission by Professor Sellin, which show the homicide death rates in groups of American States which he considered similar in social organisation, composition of population, and in economic and social conditions, but of which some used the death penalty and others did not. The comparisons extended over the 29 years 1920-1948. In neither table is it possible to tell from the rates which are the 'abolitionist'

---

[1] The graph is based partly on figures supplied to the Gowers Commission by the New Zealand Department of Justice, partly on figures for the years 1949-60, which have been obtained direct from the same source. In both cases, however, they have been converted into moving 5-year averages per million inhabitants. (The 'moving 5-year average' for any year is the average for the 5 years of which it is the last.)

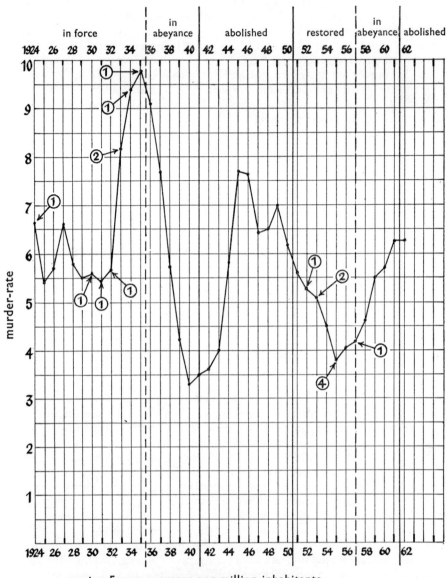

• = moving 5-year averages per million inhabitants
of murders known to the police

① = number of executions carried out in the year

FIGURE 6 *Relationship between the murder-rate and the death penalty in New Zealand, 1924-1962*

states, and both abolitionist and other states have experienced declines in the rates.

If then the death penalty functions as a general deterrent its effect is so small that it is concealed by fluctuations attributable to other so far unidentified factors.[1] This is subject to one important qualification. It is an inference based upon data from countries with low murder rates. It is not only conceivable but also probable that in these countries the murder rate has approached so near to the irreducible minimum that the effect upon it of deterrent measures is negligible; or, expressed conversely, that in countries with higher murder rates a substantial percentage of potential murderers *is* influenced by the prospect of being executed. This is not too paradoxical: countries with a high murder rate may also be countries in which the chances of escaping the penalty for murder are high. Unfortunately there are no satisfactory statistical data about murder rates in such countries.

Other Deterrents.[2] If the difference between risking death and risking indefinite imprisonment is not a decisive one for more than a negligible number of potential murderers, what can be inferred about other crimes and other deterrents? It is reasonable to assume that lesser deterrents do not weigh much with potential murderers, and since – as Chapter 2 pointed out – the distinction between serious physical violence and murder often depends merely on the death or survival of the victim, the same assumption is probably true of a substantial number of people who commit serious physical violence, especially if they do so without demonstrable premeditation.

It would be ridiculous, however, to reason in this way about less impulsive offences, such as frauds, embezzlement, planned robberies and other acquisitive crimes with rational motives. How often are people deterred from these by the possibility of a fine or prison sentence? The only sound test of these penalties as general deterrents would be a drastic and well-publicised increase or decrease in their severity, unaccompanied by any change in the readiness with which such offences were reported: but indisputable examples of this are not easy to find.[3]

A survey of the attitude of young males toward the consequences of

---

[1] The alternative to this inference is the unlikely hypothesis that there is some factor which consistently operates so as to cancel out the deterrent effect of the death penalty; for example, that so many mentally abnormal people are attracted by this form of death – as we know *some* are – that they roughly counterbalance those deterred by it.

[2] The question whether corporal punishment operates as a general deterrent was discussed by the Cadogan Committee (1938.82-). Since corporal punishment is now confined to certain penal institutions, the evidence for its efficacy is not discussed here. The post-war report of the Advisory Council on the Treatment of Offenders (1960) on this subject contains statistical evidence on the effect of corporal punishment as an individual deterrent, but not on its effect as a general deterrent.

[3] An apparent example was the sharp fall in prostitutes' convictions for soliciting when the penalties for this were drastically increased in 1959. At the same time, however, many police forces adopted a practice of cautioning women for soliciting on the first and even the second occasion; and since no central records of women so cautioned were kept, a prostitute could usually escape prosecution by moving to another police district when she knew that she could not expect another caution.

Q

conviction was made by H. D. Willcock in 1963 at the request of the Home Office: it involved interviews with 808 youths whose ages ranged from 15 to 22. Sixteen per cent had been in court, accused of an offence of some kind, serious or trivial: 73 per cent had met someone to whom this had happened: but 73 per cent had never been in a court in any capacity. Asked whether it was the feeling that breaking the law was wrong, or the chances of being found out by the police, which 'put them off' it, half chose the former, a third the latter. The majority thought that their chances of 'getting away with' house-breaking and stealing from shops were less than fifty-fifty; but they were more optimistic about such offences as taking and driving away cars, stealing from coats or breaking into locked shops. When asked to say which of eight possible consequences of being found out by the police would worry them most, next and so on, they tended to rank their family's opinion highest, and the prospect of losing their jobs next. Third was the shame of appearing in court: the actual punishment was fourth. This was less surprising, however, when it emerged that only about one in five expected that someone with a clean record would receive a custodial sentence for an offence such as shop-breaking (and most of them had clean records). The great majority expected either a fine or probation for any of the offences. Interestingly, probation was usually regarded as a slightly more severe penalty than a fine.

Clearly the stigma and other social consequences of conviction were more powerful deterrents than the official penalties as far as this group were concerned. It is true that once a person has been stigmatised as an offender these social consequences must lose their terror for him: but to what extent is their place taken by the official penalties? A system in which the chances of escaping conviction are considerable and the result of conviction un-certain because of the flexibility of courts' sentencing policies is not one in which sentences can have much effect as general deterrents. Their effect might be slightly increased if courts were known to operate a fairly rigid tariff; and this is a genuinely utilitarian argument in favour of sentencing tariffs. These are usually regarded, however, as inconsistent with the aim of correcting the individual, which must now be discussed.

THE CORRECTION OF THE OFFENDER

In assessing the corrective effect of any penal measure, there are three difficulties to be overcome. The first is purely a matter of verbal usage, although none the less important to clear out of the way. Since it is often hard to tell whether an individual offender refrains from repeating his offences because he has lost the temptation to do so, is simply deterred by recollection of the penalty, or, though not deterred but still tempted, resists the temptation from other motives, it is useful to have a word which will include all these states of affairs; and I shall be using 'corrected' in this sense. The offender who feels temptation but resists it for reasons other than deterrence will be called 'reformed', and the offender who is fortunate enough to feel temptation no longer will be called 'regenerated'. Finally, since at least some members of the probation, prison, and approved school services believe that they can make some offenders morally better in ways that are outside the scope of the criminal law, such offenders might be referred to as 'morally improved'.

The second difficulty is to agree upon the sort of things that are to be accepted as signs of correction. If all that is claimed for a penal measure is that it produces deterred, reformed, or regenerate offenders, or a mixture of these, then by definition this will have been achieved if offenders who would have continued to break the law refrain in some or all cases from doing so as a result of the measure, or at least do so less frequently. But if it is claimed that a certain penal measure produces morally improved offenders, or that at least some of its products are morally improved, the criteria by which such a claim can be verified are more difficult to agree upon. Breaches of the law can be counted, at least in theory, but on what sort of scales is virtue weighed? What notation does the Recording Angel use? If, as most people would agree, no objective standard can be offered, then it must be left to the fallible judgements of mortals. But which of us is to say whether an offender is morally improved? Not the offender himself; even if he could be sure, which is doubtful, he is at least as much of a hypocrite as the rest of us, and if he thinks it will make us happier or cut short his punishment he will assure us that he is a better man. Not, I am afraid, the probation officer, or psychiatrist, or prison officer; although they at least know what sort of moral improvement they were trying to achieve, it is a very exceptional man who can be an impartial judge of his own success or failure. Moreover, it is only the exceptional psychiatrist or probation officer who can keep in touch for long with patients or probationers for whom he is no longer responsible. Sometimes it is possible to get a reasonably unbiased report from an offender's wife, or parent or near relative; but even then it is hard to be sure that their standards are those of the psychiatrist or probation officer.

This ideological issue is important because there is a school of thought which rejects mere breaches of the law as adequate criteria of reformation. Nor is this school confined to chaplains and social workers. In a booklet of 1960 on English prisons and borstals the Prison Commissioners had this to say about corrective training:

If, as the figures so far suggest, the system diverts nearly half these young men from their criminal careers, it has already achieved something substantial. . . . But whatever the statistics may prove, the personal judgements of those engaged in the work are that they have been able to achieve remarkable success with many who might well have been written off as hopeless, and that such results could not have been expected from normal sentences of imprisonment.

But perhaps the best exposition of this point of view is to be found in the Morison report on the Probation Services:

. . . But the avoidance of offences is a poor, and even *misleading*, measure of the rehabilitation of the offender and of the degree to which he had learnt to overcome anti-social traits and attitudes, to live happily within the limitations imposed by society, and to meet, or reconcile himself to, material and environmental difficulties that accompanied and, perhaps, occasioned his delinquent behaviour. Conversely, the commission of another offence may mark no more than a temporary relapse in the rehabilitative process. Further, on a wholly material level, it is difficult to regard the offence as showing a total failure with the probationer if, in the period of supervision, he has met difficulties to which he would otherwise have given way or accepted responsibilities which he would otherwise have avoided. No penal treatment can do more than the delinquent's limitations permit and with many offenders periodic breakdowns in behaviour must be expected. . . .[1]

In order to dismiss the evidence of subsequent law-breaking in this way, it is necessary to believe that it is not merely an *inadequate* criterion but also a *misleading* one; and while the Morison Committee actually use the word 'misleading' it is by no means certain that they appreciated the distinction. An analogy will make it clear. Let us suppose that a publisher who distrusts his own judgement of the quality of typescripts submitted to him adopts a policy of simply rejecting those containing a grammatical error in the first ten pages. This would be a very *inadequate* criterion, since the rejected scripts would include many potential best-sellers, and the accepted ones would include many dull books. But if he is right even slightly more often than he would be by tossing a coin, his method can not be called completely useless – merely imperfect; and unless it actually causes him to be wrong more often than he would by tossing a coin, then it is not *misleading*.

In order to be able to say 'whatever the statistics of subsequent law-breaking may appear to prove, we know that they are misleading' one must be prepared to demonstrate, with evidence, that if one divided up the offenders into those who have subsequently broken the law and those who have not, those who had *broken* the law would actually include *more* of the morally improved. In more scientific terms, one would have to show that law-breaking was positively associated with moral improvement in the wider sense. In everyday terms, it is up to the person who rejects statistics of reconvictions to prove that the reconvicted man is likely to be morally better than the man who has 'kept out of trouble'. Until convincing evidence of this is produced, the reasonable assumption is that by using statistics of law-breaking we shall have an imperfect but by no means useless way of identifying most of the men who have been reformed in the most ambitious sense. In the rest of this chapter I shall therefore proceed on the common-sense assumption that such statistics are the only scientific test which we can at present apply to corrective measures.

Incompleteness of Reconvictions. I do not mean to gloss over several defects which have to be kept in mind when reconvictions are used as an index. The most serious defect is, of course, their incompleteness: that is, the percentage of offenders who, though not reconvicted, have committed further offences. Since less than half the thefts known to the police are traced to the thief, the 'incompleteness' of the reconvictions of thieves must be considerable. D. J. West investigated a sample of male recidivist thieves chosen for the very reason that they appeared to have had at least one five-year period in their adult lives without a conviction, but found that at least 40 per cent of his sample had in fact committed offences during that period

[1] 1962.9 (my italics).

without being identified or convicted.[1] This factor of incompleteness is of course much smaller in the case of certain types of offences, such as cases of serious violence, of which over 85 per cent are cleared up.

Elusiveness of Reconvictions. A second, though much less important, defect of reconvictions is the difficulty of being certain that even if an offender is reconvicted his reconviction is traced. Let us call the percentage of convictions which are not traced the 'elusiveness' factor. This is smallest in the case of convictions of adults for indictable offences, since there is a fairly efficient system for collecting a national record of these. Every conviction of a person over 17 for an indictable offence is reported[2] with the offender's name and other identifying information, to the Criminal Record Office at New Scotland Yard, where a search is made for any previous convictions of the same person for indictable offences. If any are found, the latest is associated with them.[3] Thus the C.R.O. index should show any subsequent convictions for serious offences of someone who has already been subjected to any penal measure (including a discharge) for a serious offence. Moreover, the system even records some offences of which a former offender is strongly suspected but has not been convicted. It is possible that the use of aliases may introduce a small element of elusiveness, but the fingerprint system must keep this to a very low level. What the system does not attempt to collate is two categories of offence:

1. *Most non-indictable offences.* If a magistrates' court convicts a person over 17 of an offence for which he *could* have been tried at a higher court, the conviction is reported to the C.R.O. If it is not one for which he could have been so tried, then with a few exceptions it is not reported. The exceptions are important, for they include the non-indictable forms of the indictable offences, and for this reason are sometimes called 'quasi-indictable'. Thus, non-indictable sexual offences, such as indecent exposure and soliciting, are also reported. On the other hand, no motoring offences[4] or offences of drunkenness or any of the hundred and one other transgressions with which magistrates must deal summarily, are reported.[5]

2. *Most offences by juveniles.* Offences committed by juveniles within the Metropolitan Police District are reported to the C.R.O.; but other areas report only the most serious offences by persons under 17, such as murder, attempted murder, or rape. As a result, childhood exploits of a provincial thief are not usually recorded there, although the information can usually be obtained from the probation department and the children's department of the areas in which he is known to have lived.

Finally, the elusiveness of pre-1945 convictions is undoubtedly greater for

[1] 1963.34-.   [2] In theory, at least.

[3] Scottish convictions for a roughly corresponding group of crimes are recorded by a central record office in Glasgow.

[4] Except those resulting in manslaughter or causing death by dangerous driving.

[5] The elusiveness of future reconvictions will be greatly reduced by a new index which the Home Office's Statistical Branch brought into operation in 1963. This will collate the future reconvictions both of adults and juveniles, and will include a wider range of non-indictable offences.

all kinds of offence and offender. Before and during the war reporting to C.R.O. by local police forces was less complete than it has been since. Since children's departments of local authorities did not have an official existence before 1948, few of them have records of children which extend before that date. Probation departments' pre-war records also tend to be scanty. In consequence a middle-aged recidivist's early convictions are very elusive, unless he himself is both communicative and gifted with total recall.

The Success Rate. In spite of these defects, and another which I shall discuss in a moment, claims for the corrective efficacy of penal measures are frequently based on what is called the 'success rate'. When looked at closely, this is found to consist of some sample of offenders who have been subjected to, say, imprisonment, *minus* those who are known to have been reconvicted. It will be obvious from what has been said that the remainder, though classified as 'successes', will contain an unknown number who have in fact committed further offences but because of the incompleteness or the elusiveness of reconvictions have not been classified as reconvicted. It is more honest and precise to base such claims on 'the known reconviction percentage'.

Follow-up Periods. Even the phrase 'known reconviction percentage', however, is not as precise as it could be. Few criminal careers are followed to the grave, so that in fact most figures for reconvictions simply represent those which occurred within some period. The most misleading are those which deal with offenders released at widely different dates but represent reconvictions occurring up to a single date.[1] Since the offenders have been 'at risk' of reconviction for differing periods, such a reconviction percentage must be interpreted with caution, unless the periods are very long indeed.[2] Otherwise, the 'follow-up' period should be roughly equal for each offender. The question how long it should be is also important. No investigation has yet followed enough criminal careers to the bitter end to be able to say that if an offender is going to be reconvicted this will happen within a definite number of years. In Hammond's eleven-year follow-up of Scottish first offenders it was observed that *of those who were reconvicted* during that period, 65 per cent were reconvicted by the end of the third year after the year of release from prison, probation etc.[3] For recidivists the same period would include an even higher percentage of those who would be reconvicted at some date. In this way it is possible to state two rules:

1. the higher the percentage of first offenders in the sample, the longer the follow-up ought to be; conversely, the higher the percentage or degree of recidivism, the shorter it can be;
2. but if for some reason a short period of follow-up has to be accepted, reconviction percentages during the first year 'at risk' will show whether a longer follow-up is likely to yield substantial differences, provided of course that the sample is large enough to render negligible the probability that differences are due to pure chance.[4]

---

[1] See, for example, Andry, 1963.
[2] As they were in Hammond's Glasgow investigation: see below.
[3] Persona communication from W. H. Hammond.
[4] This probability should certainly not exceed 1 per cent.

There is an increasing tendency in British research to insist on a follow-up period of at least two years, and it seems likely that for most purposes three years may become standard. From the point of view of interpretation of results it is obviously necessary to make sure that one is not comparing reconviction percentages based on differing follow-up periods. For precision, therefore, it is desirable to refer to 'known (three)-year[1] reconviction percentages', and for complete precision, to 'known (three)-year reconviction percentages for indictable and quasi-indictable offences (after age 17).' In other words, reports of follow-up of criminal careers must make it clear exactly what they are reporting.

It is also important to know how thorough the follow-up has been. It will be clear from what has been said about the elusiveness of reconvictions that a follow-up of offenders under the age of 17 which relies only on the Criminal Record Office would be most unsatisfactory, just as a follow-up of an adult which did not use C.R.O. would also be incomplete.

Spontaneous Recovery Rate. Let us suppose that we have, as a result of a thorough follow-up, a known three-year reconviction percentage for indictable and quasi-indictable offences in the case of a properly selected sample of offenders. There is one more difficulty to be circumvented. Even if we are reasonably confident that those in the sample who are not reported as reconvicted have in fact 'gone straight', we are not entitled to assume that this is the result of any penal treatment to which they have been subjected unless we can also claim to know how many of them would have gone straight even if not subjected to any penal treatment. Not only do many first offenders who are found guilty but are discharged, absolutely or conditionally, seem to avoid subsequent reconviction,[2] but it is also extremely probable that, even if not detected, a substantial percentage of people commit one or two offences and then spontaneously stop. In other words, we have here very much the same factor to reckon with as psychiatrists have – what is called the 'spontaneous recovery rate'[3] – with the unfortunate difference that whereas psychologists such as Eysenck claim to be able to make at least a rough estimate of the size of this factor in the case of certain groups of mental illnesses, it would be a bold penologist who would make this claim in the case of offenders. As we shall see, however, there is a certain amount of indirect evidence for the existence of a 'spontaneous reform rate' among offenders.

Absolute and Comparative Efficacy. This means that when discussing corrective efficacy we must distinguish between 'absolute' and 'comparative' efficacy. The absolute corrective efficacy of a given measure is the margin by which the percentage of offenders who are corrected by it

---

[1] Or two-year, or whatever th period was. If the date of release is known only by the year, then the best that one can do is to take the end of the first half of the *x*th year after the year of release as being the end of the *x*-year follow-up, unless one has evidence that releases from prison, probation or whatever is being studied are unevenly distributed throughout the calendar year, in which case it may be possible to work out a better assumption.

[2] See Hammond 1960.

[3] See, for example, Eysenck's article on 'The effects of psychotherapy' in Eysenck (ed.), 1960.697-.

exceeds the percentage who would not have repeated their offences even if they had remained undetected. Its comparative efficacy is the margin by which the corrected percentage exceeds that of some other specified measure, for example discharge.

Nobody has yet contrived to assess the absolute efficacy of a penal measure, and the difficulties of doing so are obvious. As for comparative efficacy, even attempts to assess this must avoid at least one fallacy: the comparison of independent studies. Several post-war studies have traced reconvictions, usually for indictable and quasi-indictable offences, following various types of penal measures.[1] But since they were independent studies, with follow-up periods of varying lengths, and using samples of offenders whose ages, types of offence,[2] previous convictions and other penal characteristics were not matched, they provide no basis ɪor estimates of the comparative efficacy of the measures studied. Rather, what emerges from a general survey of this literature is the importance of a few variables:

1. in practically all studies, the fewer the previous convictions the lower the subsequent conviction-rate;
2. the older the offender during the follow-up period the lower the reconviction-rate;
3. women and girls have lower reconviction rates than men or boys of comparable age and penal history;
4. offenders whose crimes are of different types probably have different reconviction rates even after the same kind of penal measure is applied. For example, adult males who have committed heterosexual offences against girls under 16 are apparently less likely to be reconvicted of sexual offences after imprisonment or probation than adult males who have been convicted of homosexual offences against boys or youths under 21, even when those with and those without previous convictions for sexual offences are separately compared.[3] Drunkenness probably has a particularly high reconviction rate.

Figure 7 shows the close association between the probability of reconviction and the age and previous convictions of the offender in the case of males.

From our point of view the most important inference to be drawn from these observations is that any attempt to estimate the comparative efficacy of one sort of penal measure by comparing reconvictions after it with recon-

---

[1] The main independent reconviction studies are
>   for *attendance centres*, McClintock *et al*, 1961;
>   for *approved schools*, P. D. Scott, 1964 and the Home Office's periodical Statistics relating to Approved Schools etc.
>   for *detention centres*, Grünhut, 1959;
>   for *preventive detention*, Hammond and Chayen, 1963;
>   for *probation*, Radzinowicz, 1958 and Folkard *et al* 1966;

The Prison Department's annual Statistical Tables show reconvictions, within stated periods at risk, of corrective trainees, preventive detainees, borstal trainees detention centre inmates and young prisoners discharged on licence.

[2] But Radzinowicz, 1957, pt. 3, gives known reconviction percentages over 3-4 years for various types of sexual offender after imprisonment, fining and probation; and McClintock & Gibson, 1961.86- give reconviction percentages over 5 years for different groups of London robbers.   [3] See Radzinowicz, 1957.202, 227, 255.

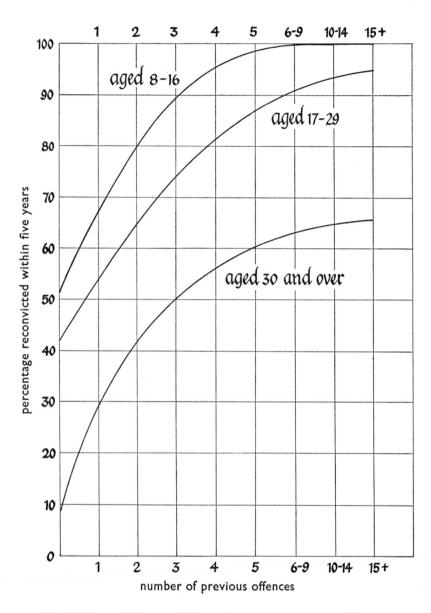

FIGURE 7 *Reconviction according to offender's age and previous convictions*
The graph is taken from the handbook The Sentence of the Court
and is reprinted by permission of Her Majesty's Stationery Office

victions after another sort must be regarded as unreliable unless some way
can be found of eliminating, or at least reducing to negligible proportions,
the effects of at least the following variables – the offender's sex, age, previous
criminal career, and type of offence. Indeed, it would be possible to be even
more rigorous and add other variables, such as differences between the
regimes of different prisons or probation departments, and, if the follow-up
periods do not begin and end with the same calendar year, fluctuations in
the annual conviction rate for the age groups under study. Very few published studies meet those requirements, but there are two which both
illustrate the possibilities of two different statistical methods and at the
same time have yielded interesting results.

Probation Versus the Rest. A striking use of the matching technique for
this purpose was L. T. Wilkins' comparison of the results of probation with
the results of other penal measures.[1] A court of quarter sessions (called
Court 'P') was selected because it used probation in a very high percentage
of its cases (3 times the national average). Ninety-seven males dealt with
by that court in 1952 by means of probation, prison, borstal or fine were
matched one for one with 97 other male offenders, selected from those
dealt with by 194 other courts in such a way that each one corresponded as
closely as possible to his 'mate' in

type of offence;
age of offender;
number of additional convictions at the same appearance;
number of additional offences 'taken into consideration';
number of previous convictions for indictable offences.[2]

Reconvictions for indictable and quasi-indictable offences were traced for
the three years following sentence.[3]

The results can be summarised thus:

1. Court P put 50 out of its 97 cases on probation. But out of the 50
   matched controls in the other courts, only 19 were put on probation;
   instead, 24 were sent to prison or borstal, 6 fined and 1 discharged.
   Nevertheless, the percentages reconvicted were very similar for both
   courts – 40 per cent for Court P, 44 per cent for the other courts.
2. Court P sent 40 of its 97 cases to prison or borstal; out of the 40
   matched controls, most (i.e. 33), were dealt with similarly, though 4
   were put on probation, 2 discharged and 1 fined. Nevertheless,
   exactly 50 per cent of both groups of 40 were reconvicted.
3. The number fined by Court P was very small – 7; none were reconvicted. Of the controls, 3 went to prison or borstal, 2 were discharged,

---

[1] 1958.

[2] On the whole, however, Court P's offenders had worse records, since their previous
convictions totalled 72, with a maximum of 25 for one offender, while the controls had
only 43 between them, and a maximum of 5.

[3] A slight defect was that those sentenced to prison and borstal were 'at risk' for a
shorter time, since they were in custody for some of the three years. But since most of
the prison sentences were for only a few months, the bias in favour of those so dealt
with was slight. Only the borstal boys were likely to have been 'inside' for more than a
few months.

1 was fined, 1 put on probation; 2 were reconvicted, but it is not
stated which.

Some reactions to this result have been emotional rather than rational.
Faith in the superiority of probation to prison and fines was so severely
shaken that it was replaced by an equally exaggerated disillusionment, and
a tendency to regard all three as equally ineffective. In fact what Wilkins did
was to cast doubt on the assertion that if probation were applied wholesale
to males over 17 in place of fines, prison and borstal the reconviction rates
would be markedly less. What he did not do, nor claim to have done, was to
cast any doubt on the absolute efficacy of any of these measures. His results
are equally consistent with the hypothesis that the absolute efficacy of
probation is considerable and with the hypothesis that it is very low, or nil.
But whatever the truth may be, the absolute efficacy of prison and borstal
seems to be roughly the same.

The Use of 'Expectation'. The use of matched samples has disadvantages.
In particular, one-for-one matching entails the discarding of individuals
who cannot be matched with a member of another sample, either because of
unusual characteristics or because of unequal numbers; and if more than
two groups have to be matched the percentage of discards rises. This both
wastes information and disregards the extreme case. A method which
avoids these disadvantages is the calculation of 'expected' reconvictions for a
given penal measure, and the comparison of these with the number of actual
reconvictions of the offenders subjected to that measure.

An imaginary example illustrates the method in its simplest form.
Suppose that of 200 males half are fined, half imprisoned, with the following
results in terms of known reconvictions over the next three years at risk:

> *fined* 100:   reconvicted: 40
> *imprisoned* 100:   reconvicted: 70

A second analysis shows that, irrespective of the penal measure used,
younger men were more often reconvicted:

> *under* 30 120:   reconvicted: 80 $(=\frac{2}{3})$
> *over* 30 80:   reconvicted: 30 $(=\frac{3}{8})$

A third analysis shows that these two age-groups were unevenly distributed
between the fined men and the imprisoned men:

> *fined* 100:   under 30: 80
>   over 30: 20
> *imprisoned* 100:   under 30: 40
>   over 30: 60

Thus, if age were the only variable which had an effect upon reconvictions,
the following reconvictions would be expected:

> *fined:* $\frac{2}{3}$ of the 80 men under 30 = 53 ⎫
> $\frac{3}{8}$ of the 20 men over   30 = 8 ⎬ = 61
> *imprisoned:* $\frac{2}{3}$ of the 40 men under 30 = 26 ⎫
> $\frac{3}{8}$ of the 60 men over   30 = 23 ⎬ = 49

On this basis, the expected reconvictions for the fined men would be 61, compared with an actual number of 40: and for imprisonment the expectation would be 49, compared with an actual 70. It is convenient to express the actual reconvictions as percentages of the expected number, thus:

fined: 66 per cent

imprisoned: 143 per cent } of expectation

The assumption underlying this technique is that the difference between these percentages is a measure of the comparative efficacy of the two different penal measures, so far as offenders of this sort (in this case males) are concerned. The assumption is obviously unrealistic when only one variable – in this case, age – is used to calculate expected reconvictions, and when the comparison is limited to two penal measures. But the same method can in theory be extended to take into account[1] any number of variables, and any number of penal measures; the only limiting condition is that the numbers of individuals in each of the necessary subdivisions should be substantial.

The only studies in which this method has been applied to British penal measures in general have been those carried out by W. H. Hammond and others in the Home Office Research Unit.[2] In these studies the variables used to calculate expected rates have been hard data which appear to be closely associated with the probability of reconviction in all samples of offenders, that is, sex, age, type of offence and previous convictions.

Applying this technique to the known reconvictions within five years of some 27,000 *male* offenders of all ages from 8 upwards, Hammond arrived at Table 27 (*see facing page*).

If this table is taken at its face value, the penal measure which displays the greatest comparative efficacy in terms of reconvictions is fining, since the subsequent reconvictions were markedly and consistently below expectation both for first offenders and for recidivists.

In contrast, the percentages for imprisonment appear to support those who argue that it is not merely ineffective but also detrimental. Here Hammond's separate analysis of Scottish first offenders' subsequent careers is relevant, for it suggested that it is the sentences of less than six months of which this is true, while for longer sentences – that is, in most cases, sentences of six to twelve months – the reconviction rate was better than expected.

The percentages are disappointing for the advocates of probation. They are consistent with Wilkin's finding that in terms of reconvictions the efficacy of probation does not differ much from that of imprisonment. Worse still, it is in the case of first offenders that probation appears least effective. Here the possibility that courts are selecting the more difficult cases for

[1] A logically similar method of using a number of variables to calculate the expected rate is the prediction technique used by Wilkins when comparing the efficacy of 'closed' and 'open' borstals: see p. 113.

[2] See 'The Sentence of the Court', Pt VI (Home Office, 1964) and 'The Use of Short Sentences of Imprisonment by the Courts', Appendix F (Scottish Advisory Council on Treatment of Offenders, 1960).

TABLE 27 Actual reconvictions as percentages of those expected

penal measure	under 17		17-20		21-29		30 and over	
	1st off-enders	others	1st off-enders	others	1st off-enders	others	1st off-enders	others
discharge	89	100	89	98	109	90	133	104
fines	75	83	75	94	63	99	84	65
probation	118	101	122	101	153	115	(150)+	121
approved school	138	102	–	–	–	–	–	–
borstal	–	101	–	95	–	–	–	–
detention centre	–	106	150a	110	–	–	–	–
attendance centre	–	119	–	–	–	–	–	–
imprison-ment	–	–	–	106c	146b	111c	(91)b	104c

+ Percentages in brackets indicate that the numbers were very small.

a The number of juveniles in the sample who were committed to penal institutions of these kinds seems to have been too small to provide a satisfactory percentage; and for similar reasons the first offenders aged 17 to 20 had to be combined for these penal institutions. The report says 'Of the group, the borstal result was the best, being about average in effectiveness'.

b Six sentences of three years or more were excluded.

c The calculation was based on a three-year instead of a five-year follow-up, and sentences of three years or more were excluded.

---

probation must seriously be considered; but there are other possibilities which will be discussed later in this chapter. One minor observation of Hammond's is worth noting because it is so difficult to explain that if it had not occurred in all age-groups it could have been dismissed as the product of chance. This was that although first offenders convicted of 'breaking and entering' had a high reconviction rate in comparison with other first offenders, for those put on probation it was lower than the reconviction rate for other first offenders on probation.

Equally interesting are the percentages for discharges. For young first offenders they are well below expectation, and may reflect (i) the spontaneous reform rate; (ii) the absolute efficacy of the experience of mere detection and conviction; or, in all probability, both. Even in the case of the older offender and the recidivist they are, with one exception, not markedly above expectation.

The exception is the older first offender: unless the high figure of 133 per cent is the product of chance (a possibility that can never be completely eliminated) it may reflect the probability that a first offender in his thirties, forties, or fifties is a person who has committed several undetected offences, and has succumbed at last to the geometric progression of his chances of detection (which is described on p. 13). In this situation he is unlikely to be impressed by a single experience of detection and conviction which does not involve a penalty.

So far I have interpreted the figures by taking them at their face value. What must also be considered, however, is the possibility that they reflect the courts' skill in choosing the right measures rather than the comparative efficacy of those measures. It is not inconceivable that sentencers were, by and large, choosing discharges and fines for offenders who seemed likely to go straight, and probation and imprisonment for those who did not; and that their diagnosis was correct more often than it would have been by chance. Against this are the awkward facts that sentencers, as we saw in the previous chapter, are influenced by age, type of offence and, criminal record; that these are strongly associated with the probability of reconviction; and that Hammond's table takes them into account. In other words, if we believe that the table reflects sentencers' skill rather than comparative efficacy we must be prepared to maintain that sentencers were able to weigh in their minds *not only* Hammond's three factors *but also* a number of subtler ones. Moreover, we must also maintain that sentencers' main aim was to allot offenders to different measures according to their estimated probability of reconviction. It is highly improbable that sentencers are either so skilful in their calculation or so utilitarian in their aims. No doubt Table 27 reflects *some* skill in sentencing; for example, in identifying offenders who will go straight if merely discharged. But it is most unlikely that this is all that it reflects.

Deterred or Reformed? Earlier in this chapter I pointed out that a man who refrains from committing further offences after he has been subjected to some penal measure may do so because he wishes to avoid the same or a more severe penal measure in the future, because he now resists temptation from other motives, or because he no longer feels temptation. Common sense and experience tell us that the last of these is a very rare transformation; we are entitled to assume that in all but the exceptional case the efficacy of a penal measure is attributable either to individual deterrence or to some more subtle process of learning to resist temptation to which I have applied the term 'reform', in an attempt to beg no questions as to its nature. Such evidence as there is suggests very strongly that both processes take place. It is highly unlikely that the after effects of, say, six months spent in an overcrowded local prison can be anything more than a deterrent, just as it is highly unlikely that the influence of probation is mainly deterrent. The apparent efficacy of large fines is a tribute to the deterrent effect either of the fines themselves or in a few cases of imprisonment for non-payment. So much seems obvious. What is more interesting is the question whether a measure which cannot but be a deterrent can also be designed so that it has a reformative influence; for this is the direction in which the Prison Department, under the pressure of penal reformers, are trying to develop the prison system.

The question to be answered seems to be this: on the assumption that both measures which are primarily individual deterrents and measures which are primarily reformative have some degree of absolute corrective efficacy, can the efficacy of the deterrent measure be increased by introducing into it features that are intended to reform? For example, can the reconviction rate after imprisonment be reduced by introducing a reformative regime into the prisons? The study which comes nearest to providing evidence on this question is Benson's[1] comparison of the reconviction-rates of male young prisoners after discharge from Lewes or Stafford prisons with those of youths of the same age range who had instead spent their sentence in borstals. The two groups were subdivided by means of the Mannheim-Wilkins' prediction formula into four categories, each with a different expectation of reconviction. Even so, there was no significant difference between the actual reconvictions, in any of the four categories, of those who had been in borstal and those who had been in prison for roughly the same length of time. This comparison suffered from certain limitations. Although the ages of both young prisoners and borstal youths ranged from 16 to 21 on reception, 80 per cent of the young prisoners as compared with only 30 per cent of the borstal youths, were over 19, and as we have seen the older an offender the lower his reconviction rate is likely to be. Secondly, the borstal regime at this early post-war period had not developed some of its present features, such as group counselling.

Nevertheless there can be no doubt that the borstal regime of those days was intended to differ, and did differ, from the prison regime in ways that were meant to make it more than a pure deterrent. 'The objects of training,' said the Borstal Rules,[2] 'shall be to bring to bear every influence which may establish in the inmates the will to lead a good and useful life on release, and to fit them to do so by the fullest possible development of their character, capacities and sense of personal responsibility.' Staff were specially selected with this end in mind, and there is no doubt that the majority of them were – and are – making a genuine effort to achieve them. Unless, therefore, Sir George Benson's comparison is to be dismissed completely – and its limitations are scarcely serious enough to justify that – they must be interpreted in one of two ways. Either borstal and prison are equally effective individual deterrents for males of this age range, in which case the effort to supplement the deterrent effect by a process of socialisation was unsuccessful; or else borstals deterred a smaller percentage of their inmates than did prisons, but made up for this by socialising some of the others. The latter hypothesis is the more encouraging, but it involves one slightly improbable supposition which must now be discussed.

Mis-classification. At one or two points in these discussions of the evidence for absolute or comparative corrective efficacy I have side-stepped a possibility to which attention was drawn some time ago by a Californian experiment. This possibility is that studies in which known reconviction rates of samples of offenders do not differ significantly after the application of different kinds of penal measure are simply reflecting the defects of our present methods of allocating offenders to these different measures. An experiment in the institutional treatment of adult male delinquents from

[1] 1959.   [2] The Borstal (No. 2) Rules, 1949, r. 4.

the United States Navy and Marines was reported by Grant and Grant in 1959.[1] At Camp Elliott 511 of these delinquents were divided into groups of 20, each of which was confined for 6 to 9 weeks with 3 volunteer non-commissioned officers from the Marines and a psychologist consultant. Communication between delinquents and persons outside these groups was kept to a minimum. Treatment took the form of group discussions on five days a week, and also constant, unrelieved contact with other members of the group (and with supervisors, two out of three being on duty every day). 'Success' was judged by subsequent careers on restoration to duty, although unfortunately the criteria and follow-up period are not described in the published reports. It was found that delinquents classified as of 'high maturity' did better after being in some groups than in others, and so did those of 'low maturity'. But the two groups which seemed to have the best effect on the 'mature' men appeared to have least success with the 'immature men'; two other groups seemed to achieve much the same success with either type, on a level intermediate between the high success rate of the mature men and the low success rate of the immature men under the first two regimes. The difference seemed to lie in the personality types of the supervisors. The interest of the study lay not in what it proved but in what it suggested, namely that a type of treatment which has a high comparative efficacy when applied to individuals of one psychological type may actually have a below average efficacy when applied to another type. In loose terms, which ignore the fact that we cannot estimate absolute efficacy, what does a mature man good may do an immature man harm.

This possibility is obviously very relevant to the interpretation of studies in which penal measures that are obviously different in nature – such as prison and probation – appear to have roughly equal comparative efficacy. An imaginary example will illustrate the possibilities. Let us suppose that in a group of 220 offenders all the 90 first offenders are put on probation, while the 130 with previous convictions are imprisoned; and that a three-year follow-up discloses very similar reconviction rates of 50 per cent and 49 per cent respectively. The hypothesis is that each of the sub-groups is a mixture of men of at least two psychological types (A and B) of which one has a low reconviction rate after probation, but a high rate after imprisonment, and *vice versa*:

TABLE 28 The mis-classification hypothesis illustrated

penal measure	psychological type	number	known 3-year reconvictions	apparent reconviction rate
ex-prisoners	A	60	15 (=25 %)	49 %
	B	70	49 (=70 %)	
ex-probationers	A	40	26 (=65 %)	50 %
	B	50	19 (=38 %)	

[1] Annals of the American Academy of Political and Social Science, March 1959.

Clearly, if all offenders of type A had been allocated to prison, while all those of type B had been put on probation, the reconviction rates of each group might well have been lower. If so, we would have been employing a more *relevant* criterion for classification.

Less obvious is the possibility that what is regarded as a single method of treatment should really be subdivided into two or more categories. For instance, it is possible that men placed on probation are being allocated to a variety of supervisors, in such a way that some are going to supervisors who reduce their chance of reconviction, some to supervisors who increase it, but who would reduce the chance of reconviction of another type of probationer; and that if this were remedied by relevant classification the comparative efficacy of probation would rise above that of prison. Correspondingly, it might be possible to raise the comparative efficacy of prison or borstal in the same way.

Interchangeability of Penal Measures. On the other hand it is premature to assume, as so many discussions of sentencing policy do, that for all or most offenders there is a single correct choice of sentence surrounded by wrong choices; and to insist that sentencing should invariably be preceded by diagnosis for this reason. The fallacy lies not merely in the assumption that our limited and not very sophisticated repertoire of penalties must include one that is effective in each case. Consider what is logically possible in the case of an offender who appears before a sentencer. He may belong to one of a number of groups:

i. those who will go straight whatever the sentence;

ii. Those who will not go straight whatever the sentence;

iii. those who will go straight if given a certain sentence but not any of the others;

iv. those who will go straight if given one of two sentences, but not the others;

v. and so on, until the group is reached for whom there is only one ineffective sentence.

We have no information at present from which we can estimate the relative sizes of these groups, or indeed can be certain that some of them exist at all. We can infer from the existence of recidivists with long penal records that there is a group (ii) from whom none of the sentencer's present choices is effective.[1] Again, it seems probable, from the encouraging results of nominal measures such as discharge, that there is a group (i) of offenders who will go straight whatever measure is applied.[2] It is the existence of the other groups, for which the choice of sentence makes a difference, that is more problematical. The fact that some offenders are reconvicted after being fined, but not after a subsequent prison sentence, suggests that prison

[1] The alternative explanation, that between each successive attempt to correct the recidivist by fines, probation, and imprisonment his personality or circumstances change so that choices which would have been effective at other times happen to be ineffective on that occasion, is too implausible.

[2] No doubt some who go straight after being discharged would not go straight if subjected to some penalty which they considered excessive, such as prison. But to grant this is not to abolish group (i).

R

would have been a better choice on the first occasion. But it is possible that their personality or circumstances changed in the interval;[1] and even if they did not we cannot infer that prison was the *only* correct choice.

What must be emphasised is that there is as yet no empirical evidence which points conclusively, or even persuasively, to the existence of a large number of offenders for whom on any given occasion the sentencer has open to him one and only one effective choice. The common assumption that most offenders fall into this group, and that the right choice can be discovered by a process of diagnosis before sentence, is probably the result of thinking of penal treatment as analogous to medical or psychiatric treatment, or more precisely to an idealised version of it in which diagnosis invariably precedes and points unerringly to the remedy.

In other words, the diagnostic approach to sentencing may well be based on a fallacious model; and even if not is largely impracticable in our present state of knowledge. This is not as defeatist as it sounds, for there is a constructive alternative: 'strategic sentencing'. This assumes that the surest way to find out which choices, if any, will be effective with a given offender are to try them in a rational order.

What is a rational order? Obviously, for example, it is an order which does not try the same choice twice before trying the others (although courts quite often do this with probation). Obviously, too, a choice which does not take long to apply should be tried – other considerations permitting – before one which takes time. In concrete terms, nominal measures or fines should be tried before supervisory or custodial measures. This principle should not, however, be carried to the length of trying a short prison term before a three-year probation order, for there are other considerations. One is the cost in terms of money and scarce manpower, which puts probation before imprisonment. Another is the danger of unwanted side-effects, which is much greater in the case of prison.

The rational order, therefore, in which to try the five main measures offered by our penal system seems to be

> nominal measures;
> financial measures;
> supervisory measures;
> suspended custodial sentences;
> custodial sentences.

This is not to say that each of these measures must be tried before the next can be. In particular, it would clearly be unwise to adopt a wholesale policy of discharging or binding over all offenders on their first appearance; and the choice between, say, discharging and fining must be left to the good sense of the court. Nor would it be irrational to proceed straight to a custodial sentence in those rare cases in which any other measure would involve a substantial risk of real harm (for example, where a man has committed a serious physical assault which he is likely to repeat). Again, if there are indications that the offender is mentally disordered these might justify a special measure of the kind described in Chapter 13. A rational order is

[1] This is not as implausible as the superficially similar hypothesis in note 1 overleaf.

not necessarily one which allows of no exceptions, so long as it is followed in the majority of cases.

The Effectiveness of After-Care. So far we have been considering the efficacy of penal measures proper. But since after-care is being used as an adjunct to institutional measures for an increasing number of categories of offender, the question whether it is effective in reducing subsequent delinquency cannot be ignored. Efficacy of this kind is not the only justification that can be claimed for after-care; it is also a humanitarian measure, designed to minimize the unintentional after-effects of incarceration. There is no doubt, however, that the main assumption underlying the extensive development of it that has been advocated – for example by the Advisory Council on the Treatment of Offenders[1] – is that it reduces the reconviction rate of released prisoners.

Unfortunately, voluntary after-care varies in quality from the inadequate to the non-existent, and all forms of compulsory after-care are accompanied by the threat of recall for misbehaviour during the period of supervision. The deterrent effect of recall seems to be confirmed by Hammond's[2] analysis of the reconvictions of 108 preventive detainees released in 1955. Their periods 'on licence' varied from about a year to over two years, but he found that an unusually high percentage[3] were reconvicted shortly after the licence expired. The consequence is that only an investigation which matched discharged offenders who had received thorough after-care without being recalled during the after-care period, with offenders who had not been subject to after-care but had nevertheless survived a similar period without reconviction, and then studied their subsequent careers for at least 2 years, could be regarded as having eliminated the purely deterrent effect of recall.

In the absence of an investigation on these lines, the next best evidence would be provided by one which compared the effects of two sorts of compulsory after-care, one consisting of little more than supervision and the threat of recall, the other also including positive assistance of various kinds. A study of this kind was carried out by R. G. Hood,[4] who compared the behaviour, during the period of release on licence, of two samples of borstal boys who had been classified as 'homeless', and therefore especially likely to drift into trouble. The samples consisted of 100 boys released in 1953, and another 100 released in 1957 – before and after the establishment of a special unit of the Central After-Care Association to give as much help as possible to this category of borstal boy, and in particular to find them suitable homes or lodgings. After a careful statistical analysis of reconvictions, changes of address and period for which they kept a job, he could find no respect in which the sample subject to special measures had behaved significantly better than those released earlier.[5]

The most probable explanation of his negative finding is either that the

[1] 1958.   [2] 1963.
[3] i.e., having regard to the reconviction curve predicted from the overall reconviction rate.   [4] 1966.
[5] Indeed, there were some differences in the opposite direction, although the numbers in the samples were not large enough to make them significant.

special unit had not raised the standard of after-care appreciably (he found, for example, that one in four of the boys were still going to hostels on release) or that although homeless ex-borstal boys were especially prone to reconviction, the provision of 'homes' for them did not really touch the heart of their problems. (He found, for example, that a factor strongly associated with reconviction was the length of time which they had spent in penal institutions – in particular approved schools – before being sent to borstal, an observation which suggested that their chances of keeping out of trouble had been lowered by 'institutionalization'.) While Hood's investigation cannot be said to have tested more than one aspect of after-care, it demonstrates not only the need for scientific assessment of this kind but also the sort of situation which makes it possible. The introduction of after-care for ex-inmates of detention centres and more recently for substantial numbers of adult prisoners[1] will provide opportunities for further research of this kind.

[1] See Chapter 9.

PART FIVE

SPECIAL CATEGORIES OF OFFENDER

THE DISPOSAL

OF THE

MENTALLY ABNORMAL

If a detected offender is mentally abnormal, there are several possibilities.[1] His abnormality may, of course, remain unrecognised throughout the whole process of arrest, prosecution, conviction, sentencing, and carrying out of the sentence, and he may simply be dealt with on the assumption that he is mentally normal. At the other extreme, it may be obvious from the out- set that he is abnormal, either because of his behaviour or because he is already under care or treatment for his disorder; and in some cases the con- sequence is that he is not dealt with by a criminal court at all: such cases are discussed in the first section of this chapter. More often, he is prosecuted, but his abnormality is formally recognised by the court and leads to a special method of disposal; the procedures by which this can happen are described in the section on prosecuted cases. Sometimes the court merely takes his disorder into account – perhaps as a mitigating factor – when adopting an ordinary method of disposal, such as a fine or conditional discharge; a little is said on this subject in the third section. Finally, his abnormality may either remain unrecognised – or be too mild to be taken into account – until after he has been sentenced, but may then lead to his receiving special treat- ment, or even to a change in his penal status – as when a prisoner is trans- ferred to a mental hospital during his sentence; such cases are discussed in the section on the Mentally Abnormal Prisoner.

Most of what follows is written with adult offenders in mind. It is com- paratively rare for juvenile offenders to be dealt with by the procedures that will be described. The reason is partly that definite mental disorder, with the exception of subnormality, is less frequent among juveniles, and when it does occur is often difficult at first to distinguish from the symptoms of temporary maladjustment which appear at some stage in the development of many adolescents. Another contributory factor may be that since some approved schools and borstals specialise in dealing with maladjusted or subnormal boys, such cases tend to be left to the process of classification

---

[1] The mentally abnormal are even less likely than other offenders to remain un- detected for long (see p. 13). Their chances of detection are increased by the absence or ineffectiveness of their precautions against discovery, or by the repetitive nature of their behaviour. There are exceptions, but they are rare.

which follows the sentence, rather than to be distinguished by one of the formal procedures.[1]

NON-PENAL PROCEDURES

As a result of the recommendations of the Percy Commission, the law controlling the administration of mental hospitals and the admission and discharge of their patients has been greatly simplified by the Mental Health Act, 1959.[2] Under it, the status of a patient varies. He may be an 'informal' in-patient or out-patient, in which case he is free to leave the hospital or break off treatment whenever he wishes. Four out of five persons admitted as in-patients, and all out-patients,[3] are informal.

Compulsory Admissions. About one patient in every six, however, is admitted compulsorily under one or other of three procedures – 'emergency admission',[4] 'admission for observation'[4] and 'admission for treatment'.[4] Under these, an application for the patient's admission must be made to the hospital either by a relative[5] or by a mental welfare officer of a local health authority (as happens when a relative is not available) and must be supported by the written recommendation of a medical practitioner or, in the case of admission for observation, two practitioners. A patient cannot be kept in hospital for more than seventy-two hours under an emergency admission; and unless it has been converted into admission for observation by obtaining the recommendation of the second practitioner before the end of that time, he must be allowed to leave unless he can be persuaded to remain as an informal patient. Admission for observation, however, allows him to be kept compulsorily for twenty-eight days, at the end of which he must either be allowed to leave, persuaded to remain informally, or be the subject of a new application for 'admission for treatment'. This allows him to be kept for a year, and can be extended for further periods.[6] In practice, about two-thirds of patients who are admitted under the emergency procedure or for observation become informal patients, about one in seven is discharged, and about one in fifteen is compulsorily detained for treatment. Between

---

[1] Neither approved schools nor borstals are intended or equipped to serve as psychiatric units, and the staffs of such institutions often feel that some of the inmates with whom they have to deal are so abnormal that they should be sent to more specialised establishments.

[2] And its Scottish equivalent, the Mental Health (Scotland) Act, 1960. They will be referred to in footnotes as MHA 59 and MH(S)A 60.

[3] If we except those required to undergo out-patient treatment as a condition of a probation order; see the section on Prosecuted Cases.

[4] ss. 29, 25 and 26 respectively of the MHA 59. In Scotland there are only two procedures for compulsory admission –'emergency admission' under s.31 of MHA(S)A 60, and 'admission' under s.24. The latter, unlike any of the English procedures, requires subsequent confirmation by the judiciary (in this case a sheriff). An emergency admission allows the patient to be kept for seven days; an ordinary admission for a year, with the possibility of renewal for further periods (see p. 270). The counterpart of the English period of twenty-eight days' 'observation' is the provision for a review of the patient's condition between the twenty-first and twenty-eighth day after admission.

[5] Any relative in the case of an emergency admission; the nearest relative otherwise.

[6] See p. 270.

1 and 2 per cent of admissions are 'for treatment', without any preliminary admission under one of the other procedures.

'*Found in a Public Place*'. About 1 in 200 patients reaches a mental hospital as a result of being found by the police in some public place in a state which seems to them to call for immediate 'care or control'. If the constable thinks it necessary either in the interests of the sufferer or for the protection of others, he can remove him to a mental hospital or some other suitable 'place of safety' which is willing to receive him.[1] He can be kept there for not more than seventy-two hours in order to make it possible for him to be examined by a medical practitioner, and interviewed by a mental welfare officer, and for any arrangements to be made, if they are needed, for his treatment or care. But like other patients admitted in emergencies he may well be kept in a mental hospital compulsorily after that time for observation or treatment.

The Medical Recommendation. The medical practitioners[2] who recommend compulsory admission must be satisfied that the patient is suffering from 'mental disorder'; that it is 'of a nature or degree which warrants his detention in a hospital' (for observation or treatment as the case may be)[3]; and that 'he ought to be so detained in the interests of his own health or safety or for the protection of other persons'. Recommendations for admission for treatment, which may involve prolonged detention, must not merely be based on a diagnosis of mental disorder but must specify one or more of the statutory subdivisions of mental disorder, and both doctors must agree in specifying at least one of these subdivisions.[4]

In the language of the statute, 'mental disorder' is the generic term which includes 'mental illness, arrested or incomplete development of mind, psychopathic disorder, and any other disorder or disability of mind'.[5] Since the law governing the detention of certain types of patient differs, there are four broad administrative subdivisions:

1. *mental illness:* this is not defined, but in practice is used to include psychoses, neuroses, some forms of epilepsy and brain damage, and (by some psychiatrists) alcoholism and other addictions;

[1] MHA 59, ss. 135, 136; MH(S)A 60, ss. 103, 104.

[2] At least one of whom should be on the list of psychiatrically qualified doctors which is kept by the local health authority (in Scotland by the Regional Hospital Board); and at least one should, if possible, have 'previous acquaintance' with the patient.

[3] And in the case of an emergency admission that this is 'of urgent necessity' and that the procedure for admission for observation would involve undesirable delay.

[4] MHA 59, s. 26 (4). For example, if one specified mental illness and subnormality, while the other specified psychopathic disorder, the statute would not be satisfied; but if the other specified subnormality and psychopathic disorder, it would be.

[5] The Scots definition (MH(S)A 1960 s. 6) is simpler: 'mental disorder' means 'mental illness or mental deficiency however caused or manifested'. 'Mental deficiency' includes conditions which in England would be described as 'subnormality' and 'severe subnormality'. The term 'psychopath' is not used; but since similar distinctions are drawn elsewhere in the Scots Act between 'a persistent disorder manifested only by abnormally aggressive or seriously irresponsible conduct' and other forms of mental illness, the concept of psychopathy is as firmly built into it as into the English statute. (See, for example, ss. 23, 40.) There is no express protection for the merely promiscuous or otherwise immoral.

2. *subnormality:* this is defined as a state of arrested or incomplete development of mind which includes subnormality of intelligence and is of a nature or degree which requires or is susceptible to medical treatment or other special care or training, but which does not amount to 'severe subnormality'[1];

3. *severe subnormality:* this is defined in effect as subnormality which is 'of such a nature or degree that the patient is incapable of living an independent life or of guarding himself against serious exploitation . . .'; but it is not essential that it should 'require or be susceptible to medical treatment or other special care or training'[1];

4. *psychopathic disorder:* this is defined as 'a persistent disorder or disability of mind (whether or not including subnormality of intelligence) which results in abnormally aggressive or seriously irresponsible conduct on the part of the patient, and requires or is susceptible to medical treatment'.[1]

A person can be classified as suffering from any combinations of these disorders, except, of course, both subnormality and severe subnormality. These definitions are clearly wide in their terms, and might be used by some people in such a way as to lead to the detention of persons who were guilty of nothing more than sexual promiscuity or immorality, which could be described as 'seriously irresponsible conduct' and so qualify as psychopathy. The same section therefore makes it clear that 'promiscuity or other immoral conduct' alone do not render a person liable to be dealt with as mentally disordered. Moreover, since the Act also stipulates that the nature or degree of the disorder must 'warrant' detention for treatment, and that this must be 'in the interests of the patient's health or safety, or for the protection of other persons', there are forms of mental disorder which seldom justify *compulsory* admission to a mental hospital; examples are most forms of neurosis.

These administrative subdivisions should not be confused with the clinical diagnoses of the psychiatrists, but merely carry certain legal implications. For example, a patient cannot be compulsorily admitted to hospital for *treatment* on the grounds that he is suffering from 'psychopathic disorder' or 'subnormality' if he is 21 years of age or over, and if he is admitted before that age under either of these classifications he cannot be detained after his 25th birthday without a special procedure. These limitations, which do not apply to 'mental illness' or 'severe subnormality', were included because, in the words of the Percy Commission[2]

. . . it is generally agreed that treatment or training is most likely to be effective if it can be given at this stage. Secondly, a society which assumes responsibility for the education of the children of all its citizens, and is prepared to use compulsion if necessary to ensure that children receive education suitable to their abilities and aptitudes, is . . . also justified in using compulsory powers in order to provide special forms of training for young people who, after the normal period of compulsory education, are still intellectually or emotionally immature and who are thought likely to benefit from such special

[1] MHA 59, s. 4.   [2] 1957 125.6.

training. . . . Apart from this we do not consider that there is sufficient justification for special compulsory powers in relation to adult psychopathic patients except where their conduct is anti-social to the extent of constituting an offence against the criminal law. . . .

On the other hand, there is no such limitation on compulsory admission in *emergencies* or for *observation*, which cannot involve more than four weeks' detention, and which the doctors can request without specifying the form of disorder from which the patient is believed to suffer.

Guardianship. Sometimes the disordered person needs no more than a sheltered environment and understanding supervision to enable him to live without being a nuisance to others. This is especially likely in cases of mildly subnormal intelligence, or where a patient has been partially rehabilitated by treatment in hospital. In these circumstances it may be possible to find a relative or other person who is willing to act as 'guardian'. Local health authorities, however, are now required by the National Health Service Acts to make arrangements of this sort for the care or after-care of mentally disordered people in their areas, and, while these arrangements are only in an early stage of development in most parts of the country, all but a few 'guardians' are now the local health authorities themselves. Compulsory guardianship can be arranged in much the same way as compulsory admission to a mental hospital for treatment.[1]

It is important to realise that among the patients who are dealt with in one of these ways there is an unknown but probably by no means negligible percentage of persons who could have been charged with a criminal offence. Rollin found that of the 571 men admitted in 1961 to his mental hospital 98 were offenders; but only two-thirds of these had been admitted as a result of prosecution. Fully a third had been accepted either as informal patients, or as ordinary compulsory patients or as cases found in public places by the police.[2] In such cases the police had exercised their discretion not to prosecute, either because the offence was trivial (as when a schizophrenic vagrant steals food to satisfy his hunger), or because the offender's abnormality had already been formally recognised on an earlier occasion. A good example of this use of police discretion is cited by Radzinowicz[3]:

A woman of 35 was sitting, reading a book, on a seat on the Downs, when a man came up to her, exposed himself and indecently assaulted her. She kicked out at him and he ran away. The woman fetched a police officer, who arrested the man who was still near the spot. It transpired that he was a mental defective resident in a neighbouring mental colony. He was returned to the colony and transferred by the authorities to another institution.

[1] See MHA 59, ss. 33, 34: MH(S)A 60, ss. 25, 29.

[2] 1963. It cannot be assumed that the percentage of unprosecuted cases would be as large in all hospitals, since the 'catchment area' for Dr Rollin's hospital included the Paddington district of London, which has a high concentration of social problems. But the fact that out of 98 offenders 10 were admitted informally, 7 compulsorily and 17 under s. 136 shows that these avenues for the disposal of the mentally abnormal delinquent cannot be dismissed as exceptional.

[3] 1957.43.

In Scotland, if a psychiatric examination of an offender awaiting trial (which is often arranged by the prosecutor) confirms suspicions that he is mentally disordered, the prosecution is sometimes abandoned, and the accused left to be dealt with under the compulsory powers of the Mental Health (Scotland) Act, 1960[1]; this is especially likely if the offence is not regarded as a grave one.

PROSECUTED CASES

If, on the other hand, the offender is prosecuted, there are a number of statutes under which he may be dealt with, according to the nature of his offence, the medical evidence and the tactics of his defence. All but a few cases nowadays are dealt with either under the simplified code introduced by the Mental Health Acts or under the probation sections of the Criminal Justice Acts. But because of the controversy over the penalties for murder, and the defence of insanity (which, however, is hardly ever attempted nowadays), murderers and those who successfully pleaded insanity were expressly exempted from the revised code. The resulting complications will be discussed in this section.

Hospital Orders. From the point of view of the criminal courts, the central provision of the Mental Health Act, 1959, is in s. 60.[2] This allows both higher and lower courts[3] to deal with a mentally abnormal person who has been proved to have committed an offence[4] by means of an order which either commits him to a mental hospital or entrusts him to the guardianship of a local health authority or a person approved by a local health authority. The effect of a 'hospital order' or a 'guardianship order' is that he cannot be discharged from hospital or guardianship, as the case may be, until the responsible medical officer[5] thinks that this should be allowed.

The court's use of this power is limited in a number of ways. It cannot be applied to offences for which the penalty is fixed by law – that is, for all practical purposes, the offence of murder – although it can be applied to cases of infanticide and manslaughter, including murders reduced to manslaughter as a result of a successful defence of diminished responsibility (q.v.). It cannot be applied to offences which are not punishable with imprisonment (q.v.); although the Percy Commission thought that there was no reason why it should not be, it seemed unjustifiable that offences such as keeping a dog or a radio without a licence should be made the occasion for so drastic a procedure.

Restriction Orders. A court of assize or quarter sessions may not only make a hospital order but also, if it thinks it necessary for the protection of

[1] See p. 264, footnote.
[2] Or MH(S)A, s. 55.
[3] In Scotland, however, justices of the peace and burgh courts cannot exercise this power.
[4] Usually, the court must 'convict' him, but if he is diagnosed as mentally ill or severely subnormal, a magistrates' court may act in this way without convicting. In Scotland, neither High Court nor Sheriff Court is *obliged* to convict before making a hospital order, although they may do so.
[5] Or the hospital managers.

the public, make a 'restriction order' either for an indefinite or for a
specified period.[1] The effect of this is that the offender must not be discharged, given leave of absence or transferred to another hospital without
the consent of the Home Secretary. A restriction order cannot be made by a
magistrates' court, which can, however, commit the offender to quarter
sessions with a view to the making of one; if it does so, it must refrain from
making even an ordinary hospital order, since quarter sessions may decide
to deal with the offender in some other way – for example, by imprisonment.

Medical Evidence. The medical evidence which the court must have
before using these powers must conform to some strict requirements. Like
the recommendations which are required for the compulsory treatment of
non-offenders, this evidence must be given by two medical practitioners, of
whom at least one must be on the list of those approved by a local health
authority as having special experience in the diagnosis or treatment of
mental disorders.[2] Both these practitioners must agree that the offender's
mental disorder is of a nature or degree which warrants his detention in a
hospital for treatment (or his reception into guardianship). Whatever their
clinical diagnosis, they must classify his disorder according to the administrative distinctions drawn by the Act – that is, as being mental illness,
psychopathic disorder, subnormality, or severe subnormality; and while
they may of course classify him as suffering from more than one of these
types of disorder, their diagnoses must agree on at least one of them.[3] The
medical evidence may be given in writing or orally, but the court cannot
make a 'restriction order' unless at least one of the practitioners has given
evidence orally. If the medical evidence has not been offered by or on behalf
of the offender himself, his legal representatives must be given a copy of it.
If he has no legal representatives, he[4] must be told the substance of it. The
court must also be assured that arrangements have been made with a
specified hospital for the admission of the offender within twenty-eight days
of the making of the order; or, in the case of a guardianship order, that a
local health authority or approved person is willing to assume this responsibility.

But however clear and consistent the medical evidence, the court is not
automatically obliged by it to dispose of the offender in one of these ways.
It must also take account of 'all the circumstances, including the nature of
the offence and the character and antecedents of the offender, and the other
available methods of dealing with him', and having done so it has to decide
whether this is the 'most suitable method of disposing of the case'. Thus it
might decide simply to fine or imprison him, especially if it came to the conclusion that his disorder was not severe enough to prevent him from being
reformed in this way.

On the other hand, the court is more or less obliged to choose between
penal and psychiatric measures. It cannot combine a hospital or guardianship order with imprisonment, a fine, or even a probation order, although it

[1] MHA 59, s. 65; MH(S)A, 60, s. 60.
[2] This includes most prison medical officers.
[3] See p. 265, footnote.
[4] Or his parents if he is a juvenile.

is allowed to combine it with any other kind of order within its power; examples are absolute or conditional discharge, a recognisance, or a dis- qualification from driving. It would obviously reduce or nullify any benefits of psychiatric treatment or care if the offender had to serve a prison sentence before or after it, while if the treatment could be given in prison it does not require an order of the court to make it possible. The justification for excluding fines and probation is less obvious, and the Percy Commission itself[1] did not consider that they should be excluded. The legislators reasoned that it would be of little use to combine a fine with a hospital order, since the patient was unlikely to have much earning capacity and could hardly be imprisoned for non-payment; while the combination of guardian- ship with a fine or probation though possible would seldom be of practical value, again because the patient would have little or no earning capacity, and the control of the guardian should be an adequate substitute for probation. As we shall see, however, it remains possible for probation to be combined with a requirement of in-patient or out-patient treatment for mental disorder.

Discharge from Hospital. The offender who is subject to a 'hospital order' is in much the same position as other patients who have been compulsorily admitted to a mental hospital in the interests of their own health or safety – as often happens with suicidal patients – or with a view to the protection of other people. Both kinds of patient can be given leave of absence when the responsible medical officer thinks that their progress justifies this; both can be transferred to another hospital – for example, because their worsen- ing conduct calls for a hospital which has more stringent security pre- cautions. Most important of all, both become free to leave the hospital permanently after one year, unless the responsible medical officer reports to the hospital managers that continued detention is necessary in the interests of the patient's own health or safety or for the protection of others.[2] If he does so, the patient is liable to detention for a further year, after which the authority for his detention either lapses or is renewable in the same way.[3] The patient over 16 years of age who feels that he is being unreasonably detained can have his case considered by the local Mental Health Review Tribunal, who can direct the hospital to discharge him.[4]

Moreover, if the patient absents himself from the hospital without leave, or overstays his leave, he can be taken into custody and returned to the hospital only if this can be done within a limited period.[5] The period is normally twenty-eight days, but is extended to six months in the case of

[1] 1957.173.
[2] s. 43: MH(S)A 60, s. 39. Since the statute does not make it clear what 'other persons' are to be protected from, this gives the responsible medical officer wide scope for the exercise of his own views on the treatment of offenders. Thus most psychiatrists would hesitate to release a patient who was likely to repeat an offence of serious physical violence, but many might consider that the risk of a repetition of petty theft or fraud could be accepted.
[3] The first renewal is for another year; subsequent renewals are for two years at a time.
[4] ss. 63, 123, Sch. III. In Scotland, the reviewing authority is the sheriff for the area.
[5] s. 40 (3).

patients aged 21 or more who are classified as psychopathic or subnormal.[1] If at the end of this period he is still at liberty, he cannot be taken into custody again without fresh proceedings.[2] In this respect the offender-patient, unless he is subject to a restriction order, is in exactly the same position as an ordinary compulsory patient.

The position of the offender-patient does differ in certain respects. An ordinary compulsory patient may be discharged if his nearest relatives apply to the hospital for this, since this usually means that they are willing to look after him; but the nearest relatives of an offender-patient can only apply to the local Mental Health Review Tribunal.[3] Again, an ordinary compulsory patient who is not mentally ill or severely subnormal, but is psychopathic or subnormal, can be detained after the age of 25 only if the responsible medical officer reports that he is likely to be a danger to himself or others. Mere irresponsibility or incompetence which does not involve the commission of offences or endanger people is not regarded as justifying the compulsory detention or supervision of an individual for the whole of his adult life. As we have seen, it is only before the age of 21 that a person who has committed no offence can be compulsorily admitted to hospital for treatment or to guardianship solely because he is subnormal or psychopathic. If, on the other hand, he is found by a criminal court to have committed an offence punishable with imprisonment, a psychopathic or subnormal offender of any age can be subjected to a hospital or guardianship order and kept under it in the same way as mentally ill or severely subnormal offenders.[4]

The effect of a restriction order is more drastic. The court may either specify the period for which it is to last, or set no time limit. While the order is in force, the offender cannot be given leave of absence, transferred to another hospital or discharged without the consent of the Home Secretary. If he absents himself without leave, there is no limit (apart from the duration of the restriction order itself) to the period during which he can be retaken.[5] After the first year he can request the Home Secretary to take the advice of

[1] In Scotland, the period is twenty-eight days for all except mental defectives, for whom it is three months, and for persons liable to be detained under an 'emergency recommendation', for whom it is seven days.

[2] If he had been subject to a hospital order of a criminal court, no further proceedings based on the same offence would be possible under criminal law; but both ordinary and offender-patients could be subject to fresh proceedings for their compulsory admission to hospital if their mental condition still justified these. (This would not be so, however, in the case of psychopathic or subnormal ex-patients who had passed their 21st birthday.)

[3] In Scotland, they have no such recourse. The patient himself may apply to the Mental Welfare Commission which advises the Secretary of State.

[4] The only distinction is that a magistrates' court may make a hospital or guardianship order in respect of a mentally ill or severely subnormal offender without recording a conviction (but simply finding that he committed the offence), but cannot do so without convicting if the offender is only psychopathic or subnormal, or both (s. 60 (2)). The reason is historical, connected with the disposal of the insane in summary trials. In Scotland the sheriff has a similar power if he is trying the offender summarily, with the difference that it does not matter what form of mental disorder the offender is suffering from.   [5] MHA 59, s. 65 (3) (d); MH(S)A 60, s. 60 (3).

the Mental Health Review Tribunal on his case; but unlike the discharge of other compulsory patients his discharge can only be advised and not directed by the Tribunal.[1] If he is discharged at any time the Home Secretary can attach conditions to the discharge, much as he does in the case of released 'lifers' and discharged cases under 'Her Majesty's Pleasure'.

The percentage of hospital orders which are accompanied by restriction orders has increased in recent years, and reached 15 per cent in 1965. It has since increased further as a result of the Lord Chief Justice's remarks in the case if *R*. v. *Gardiner*:

it is very advisable that they should be made in all cases where . . .
the protection of the public is required. Thus, in, for example, the case
of crimes of violence, and of the more serious sexual offences, particularly if the prisoner had a record of such offences, or if there is a
history of mental disorder involving violent behaviour, . . . there
must be compelling reasons to explain why a restriction order should
not be made . . .[2]

He also discouraged courts from making restriction orders for limited periods except where 'the doctors are able to assert confidently that recovery will take place within a fixed period'. The determinate restriction order was already declining in popularity (in 1961 44 per cent were of this kind, but by 1965 this percentage had sunk to 14). In Scotland it is rare.

Guardianship Orders. Guardianship orders are much rarer than hospital orders as a means of dealing with offenders. In 1961 only 11 men and 5 women aged 17 or over were dealt with in this way. This method of disposal seems to be designed primarily for the subnormal or mildly psychopathic petty offender who is unlikely to improve markedly under hospital treatment but may well be kept out of trouble if he can live under some sort of supervision, either in a special hostel or in carefully chosen lodgings. Few local health authorities have so far developed arrangements of this kind, and since guardianship orders can be made only if a local health authority or approved guardian is willing to accept the responsibility, this is probably the limiting factor. Discharge from guardianship is subject to very much the same procedure as discharge after a hospital order. A guardianship order cannot be combined with a restriction order.

Types of offences and disorders. The offences which lead to hospital orders, and the predominant disorders of the offender-patients, are broadly classified in Table 29. Personal violence and sexual molestation, which are so prominent in the stereotype of the insane criminal, can be seen to be much less common than stealing and other acquisitive offences, although they are undeniably more frequent than they would be if this were a sample of prisoners. Violence is more likely if the patient is schizophrenic, 'psychopathic' or depressive than if he is subnormal, whereas most of the sexual offences were committed by subnormals. More than two fifths (41%) of the whole sample were schizophrenic; and more than a quarter were subnormal. 'Psychopathy' and similar diagnoses accounted for only one in eight hospital orders, but might well have been more numerous if ordinary

[1] In Scotland his only recourse is to the Mental Welfare Commission.
[2] *R*. v. *Gardiner* [1967] *Criminal Law Review*, 231.

TABLE 29 Types of offences and disorders leading to hospital orders in the year from April, 1963 to March, 1964 (Males only) [a]

Diagnosis/ Offence	Schizophrenics		Subnormals		Person-ality dis-orders	Manic-depres-sives	Others	Total	%
	para-noid	others	sev-ere	others					
Acquisitive	21	113	32	141	54	23	14	398	42·2
Sexual	7	28	20	72	15	7	5	154	16·4
Violence to persons	26	33	3	11	24	17	7	121	12·9
Damage to property	10	26	1	5	5	7	—	54	5·7
Frequenting	4	27	1	—	—	1	2	35	3·7
Arson	3	6	2	14	6	—	1	32	3·4
Assaulting police [b]	7	13	—	1	3	3	2	29	3·1
Vagrancy	2	15	1	1	2	—	1	22	2·3
Taking and driving away vehicles	1	5	1	8	1	2	—	18	1·9
Drunkenness	—	5	—	—	2	1	2	10	1·1
Others	9	23	4	10	5	5	3	59	6·3
No offence [c]	—	5	—	2	1	1	—	9	1·0
Total	90	299	65	265	118	67	37	941	
%	9·6	31·8	6·9	28·2	12·5	7·1	3·9		100·0

[a] Based on the Oxford sample: see Walker & McCabe, 1968.
[b] not included in 'violence to persons' because it is so often the result of intervention by the police rather than a spontaneous attack by the offender.
[c] i.e., juveniles found in need of care, protection or control.

mental hospitals had not been so reluctant to accept such patients. What-ever the diagnosis, most hospital order cases had previous histories of psychiatric treatment, criminal convictions or both.

Juveniles. Mentally abnormal juveniles can be made subject to a hospital or a guardianship order by a juvenile court, either as a result of criminal procedure or as a result of social procedure. But the juvenile court cannot make a restriction order, and if the juvenile is dealt with under social pro-cedure it cannot commit him to quarter sessions for that purpose. English courts make little use of these powers (*see Table 30 overleaf*).

Probation with Psychiatric Treatment. Next in importance – again measured by frequency – is the probation order with a special requirement that the offender shall submit to treatment for his mental condition.[1] Like a hospital or guardianship order, this cannot be applied to persons convicted of murder, or found guilty but insane or insane on arraignment; but unlike that type it can be applied to offences not punishable with imprisonment on summary conviction. The medical evidence, which can be given by a single

[1] CJA 48, s. 4 as amended; CJ(S)A 49, s. 3 as amended.

S

TABLE 30 Juveniles and hospital or guardianship orders in 1961

type of procedure	type of order:					
	hospital		guardianship		hospital and restriction	
	boys	girls	boys	girls	boys	girls
criminal	50	8	3	1	3	1
social	4	15[1]	–	1	–	–

medical practitioner so long as he is approved by a local health authority as having special experience in the diagnosis or treatment of mental disorders, must satisfy the court that the offender's mental condition requires and is susceptible to treatment, but that it does not warrant a hospital order of the kind just described. The court must also be satisfied that arrangements have been made for the sort of treatment envisaged. As in the case of hospital or guardianship orders, however, the court is not then obliged to deal with the offender in this way, but has to take into account the circumstances, including the nature of the offence and the character of the offender. If it does decide to take this course, it cannot compel him to submit to treatment for more than twelve months, although the duration of the probation order itself can be longer, up to the usual maximum of three years. This has the advantage that the offender can be kept under compulsory supervision for a while when he is no longer obliged to undergo treatment. The court can stipulate that he should be a resident or a non-resident patient. It cannot, of course, make a probation order of this or any other kind without his consent (unless he is a child), but if he subsequently refuses to undergo treatment he can be brought before the court and dealt with for a breach of the requirements of the order. This does not necessarily oblige him to undergo such drastic forms of treatment as neurosurgery or electro-convulsion, since he can claim to the court that his refusal to do so was reasonable.[2]

In 1961 English courts made the following use of this power:

TABLE 31 Special probation orders

probation orders with a condition of	juveniles		young adults and adults	
	males	females	males	females
out-patient treatment	80	10	326	48
in-patient treatment	31	2	326	66

It is clear that, unlike the ordinary probation order, this method of dealing with offenders is not often adopted in the case of juveniles.

Grünhut[3] analysed 675 out of the 882 cases dealt with in this way in the year 1953. Offences against property accounted for 43 per cent, sexual

[1] One of these girls was aged 5!   [2] CJA 48, s. 6 (6).   [3] 1963.

offences for 34 per cent, offences of non-sexual violence for 15 per cent, the last two categories being considerably over-represented. Some of the offences were of a kind usually regarded as serious; examples were attempted murder, and housebreaking. Nor were all the probationers first offenders: 14 per cent had more than three previous convictions. Not surprisingly, an offender's chances of being dealt with in this way instead of by ordinary penal measures were greater in the cities with well-developed psychiatric clinics and out-patient departments of hospitals, and this was especially the case in London. In 414 cases for which medical reports could be obtained from the hospitals where the patients were treated, the main diagnoses were classified[1] as follows:

	percentage
'psychopathic personality'	
of 'constitutional' type	37
of 'environmental' type	10
schizophrenia	14
depression	13
illness with physical basis	9
low intelligence	7
anxiety state	4
ill-defined neurotic illness	6
no ascertainable abnormality	1
adolescent neurotic tendencies	0·5

THE SPECIAL DEFENCES

Between them, hospital and guardianship orders, and probation orders with a requirement of treatment, account for about 85 per cent of the offenders who are recognised and dealt with as mentally abnormal The remainder are dealt with in a number of other ways, of which none are numerically important, but some have been the subject of so much legal, medical and Parliamentary discussion for many years that they have attracted far more attention.

The Defence of Insanity. Chief among these is the verdict 'not guilty by reason of insanity'[2]. Unlike the orders just described, made by the judge, magistrate or sheriff after a finding of guilt, this is a matter for the jury. Unlike the Mental Health Acts or the statutes governing probation, a defence of 'insanity' under the Trial of Lunatics Act, 1883, compels the court to decide not only whether the offender 'did the act or made the omission charged', but also whether at the time he was 'insane so as not to be responsible according to law for his actions' – in other words, to face that unlaid ghost, 'responsibility'. In doing so they must hear oral evidence from medical witnesses, often contested or confused by cross-examination. They

---

[1] By two independent psychiatrists.

[2] The form of verdict recognised by statute in 1800. In 1883 it was replaced, at Queen Victoria's request, by the verdict usually known as 'guilty but insane', but without altering the practical effect of the verdict. In 1964, on the recommendation of the Criminal Law Revision Committee, the older form was restored. Scots law preserved the older form throughout this period. For the full story, see Walker, 1968.

are assisted by an explanation from the judge, based upon the explanation given by Her Majesty's judges at the request of the House of Lords in 1843, after the astonishment caused by the acquittal of M'Naghten. The only part of the M'Naghten Rules which is now of importance says that

.. the jury ought to be told in all cases that every man is presumed to be sane, and to possess a sufficient degree of reason to be responsible for his crimes, until the contrary be proved to their satisfaction; and that to establish a defence on the ground of insanity it must be clearly proved that, at the time of committing the act, the accused was labouring under such a defect of reason, from disease of the mind, as not to know the nature and quality of the act he was doing, or, if he did know it, that he did not know he was doing what was wrong. . . .

If he is to succeed in this defence, the accused must produce medical evidence, and the onus is on him to convince the jury 'on a balance of probabilities'.[1] The medical evidence must relate to his state of mind at the time when he committed the crime (although his state of mind at a later stage may, of course, be adduced as evidence of this). The evidence must show not only that he was suffering from some 'defect of reason, from disease of the mind', but also that this was so severe that he did not know the nature and quality of his act, or that it was wrong. This is a very stringent requirement, which M'Naghten himself did not satisfy. For in order to be said 'not to know the nature and quality of his act' the accused must be unaware of, or deluded as to, its physical quality: for example, if he is being tried for murder he must have been unaware that he was killing a human being, or imagined that he was doing something different, such as attacking the devil. Thus Lieutenant Codère, who knew that he had killed a non-commissioned officer, and tried to conceal his crime, was found guilty although he was said to be so insane as to be unable to carry on a connected conversation.[2] Wider and more merciful interpretations have been adopted by some courts in the Commonwealth and the U.S.A.[3]

If, on the other hand, the defence is that the accused did not know that his act was wrong, it is the legal and not any moral wrongness that is in question[4]: a man who knew his act to be morally wrong but deludedly thought it legal would apparently satisfy this test.

Partly because these tests are hard to satisfy, partly because 'insanity' or 'disease of the mind' have been interpreted narrowly, the types of mental disorder which have been the basis of a successful defence of insanity are limited. For example, although the nineteenth-century judges who drafted the rules almost certainly intended 'disease of the mind' to include what was then called 'imbecility', psychiatrists later began to draw a distinction

---

[1] Not 'beyond reasonable doubt' (*R. v. Sodeman*, [1936] 2 All. E.R. at 1138).

[2] And his conviction was upheld on appeal ([1916] 12 Cr. App. Rep. 21).

[3] For example, in the Australian case of Porter ([1933] 55 *Criminal Law Review* 188) Dixon J. suggested to the jury that if a man who intentionally destroys human life has 'so little capacity for understanding the nature of life and the destruction of life that to him it is no more than breaking a twig or destroying an inanimate object' he would not know the physical nature of what he was doing.

R. v. Windle, [1952] 2 Q.B. 833.

between 'insanity' and 'mental deficiency' with the result that offenders of low intelligence have sometimes been held not to be 'insane'.[1] Nor would 'psychopathy' (or its synonyms 'behaviour disorder' or 'personality disorder') be classified by psychiatrists as 'insanity' or 'disease of the mind'. On the other hand, cerebral defects such as epilepsy and arteriosclerosis have been accepted as within the scope of these terms, and psychoses such as schizophrenia have no difficulty in qualifying, although there may be doubt in cases of moderate severity as to whether the accused did not know the nature and quality of his act, or that it was wrong.

The most controversial exclusion, however, is probably what is known to lawyers as 'irresistible impulse'. This term is used ambiguously, for it sometimes seems to mean a compulsive desire to perform some action, which nags at the sufferer until he finally yields to it,[2] but sometimes a sudden overmastering impulse which takes the offender by surprise, as it were, in the way in which provocation may overwhelm the ordinary man. Psychiatrists are readier to recognise the former as a disorder than the latter. However this may be, 'irresistible impulse' was regarded by some judges as within the scope of the M'Naghten Rules until the Court of Criminal Appeal in True's case[3] made it clear that it was not.

These exclusions now matter less than they used to because in trials for murder the defence of diminished responsibility (q.v.) has been available since 1957, and admits a much larger variety of abnormalities. On other charges, the provisions for hospital orders, or probation orders with requirements for psychiatric treatment, offer a wide door to any sort of mental disorder.

The virtues and defects of the M'Naghten Rules have been debated by lawyers, psychiatrists, philosophers, members of Parliament, and examination candidates at frequent intervals for the last hundred years.[4] But the defence of insanity is now obsolescent in England, if not quite obsolete. In 1966 there were only two cases in which it was accepted, and although there may have been others in which it was unsuccessful this is not common. Before the Homicide Act, 1957 it sometimes made the difference between life and death to an adult accused of murder; but even this was rare because of the extent to which murderers who were suffering from mental disorder were reprieved. From 1957 to 1965, the period in which murders were either capital or non-capital, the defence was used less and less often, and hardly ever in capital cases, its place being taken by the new defence of diminished responsibility. Even the restoration of hanging would probably not revive it.

In Scotland, the defence of insanity is found only a few times in a decade. Scottish courts are much readier to accept a plea of 'insanity in bar of trial' (q.v.) than English courts to accept that the accused is 'insane on arraign-

---

[1] See the article by J. A. Hobson, 1955. This is rare, however: Straffen's case is the only example known to me.

[2] See Chapter 5.

[3] [1922] Cr. App. Rep., 164.

[4] See, for example, the Gowers Commission, 1953; Wootton, 1959; Glanville Williams, 1961.

ment' (q.v.). Indeed, in the case of *H.M. Advocate* v. *Kidd*,[1] Lord Strachan's charge to the jury included the forthright explanation that 'The special defence (of insanity) is one which arises very seldom, because in most cases if a person was insane at the time of a crime he continues to be insane until the time of his trial. He is held not to be fit to instruct his defence, and the trial does not proceed.'

The practical consequence of an acquittal by reason of insanity is that the court *must* make an order for the offender's admission to a hospital specified by the Home Secretary – usually, but not always, one of the Special Hospitals (q.v.). There his status is the same as that of a patient detained under a hospital order with an indeterminate restriction on his discharge.[2] This underlines the conflict in the penal system between the principles of distributive retribution and social defence. In the name of retributive justice we regard the accused as not guilty because he could not help doing what he did, but in order to protect society we subject him to an indefinite period of detention.

Automatism. An even rarer defence is what is known as 'automatism'. This is based on the doctrine that in order to be criminal an act must at least be voluntary. Consequently some accused persons have secured an acquittal by arguing in their defence that the acts or omissions with which they were charged were involuntary. Not all these persons were suffering from mental disorder: some had simply committed acts of violence in their sleep.[3] More often, however, the accused is suffering from some defect of cerebral functioning, whether chronic or temporary. Thus a Scots motorist who succumbed to a state of dissociation as a result of carbon monoxide poisoning while driving a car was acquitted of careless driving[4]; and Lord Goddard has implied that a person who had an epileptic fit while at the wheel of a car could not be said to be driving, and so could not be convicted of an offence involving driving.[5] Charlson, who struck his child with a mallet and threw him out of a window, was acquitted on the judge's direction as a result of a defence that he was practically unconscious at the time, a defence supported by medical evidence that he might have been suffering from a cerebral tumour.[6]

Nowadays, however, a defence of 'automatism' which is based on medical evidence of cerebral abnormality is more likely to lead to a verdict of 'not guilty by reason of insanity', and so to compulsory detention in a mental hospital. For example, Kemp,[7] an arteriosclerotic man who attacked his wife, set up a defence, supported by unanimous medical evidence, that because of his condition he did not know what he was doing; the court ruled that his condition was a 'disease of the mind', so that the defence fell within

[1] [1960] *Scots Law Times* 82.
[2] s. 5 of the Criminal Procedure (Insanity) Act, 1964: s. 63 of MH(S)A, 60.
[3] See, for example, *R.* v. *Boshears* (*The Times*, 18th and 19th February 1961); *H.M. Advocate* v. *Fraser*, [1878] 4 Couper 70; *R.* v. *Partridge* (*Daily Telegraph*, 30th February 1952).
[4] *H.M. Advocate* v. *Ritchie* [1925] J.C. 45.
[5] L.C.J. Goddard in *Hill* v. *Baxter*, [1958] 1 Q.B. 277.
[6] [1955] 1 All E.R. 859.
[7] [1957] 1 Q.B. 399.

the M'Naghten rules, and was one of 'insanity'. It is not surprising that the court should have preferred a verdict which made it possible to exercise some subsequent control over the accused to an acquittal which would have placed him outside anyone's power. Here again the principle of social defence seems to be unobtrusively at work.

Diminished Responsibility. There is one other defence which compels the jury to consider the accused's responsibility for his actions at the time of the offence: the plea of 'diminished responsibility'. In Scotland, where the plea originated, it is part of the common law, and is said to have been applied in the past to several sorts of charge.[1] When it was adopted in England, however, this had to be done by statute, which made it applicable only to an indictment for murder, and in practice it is now confined to murder trials in Scotland. The accused can be found guilty not of murder but of manslaughter, 'if he was suffering from such abnormality of mind (whether arising from a condition of arrested or retarded development of mind or any inherent causes or induced by disease or injury) as substantially impaired his mental responsibility for his acts and omissions in doing or being a party to the killing.'[2] In Scotland the interpretation of the common law notion of diminished responsibility is left wholly to the judges.[3] In both countries the effect of a successful defence is to reduce murder to manslaughter (in Scotland called 'culpable homicide'). Since the penalty for this is not fixed by law, the court can impose any sentence from life imprisonment to absolute discharge, or may, if the required medical evidence is forthcoming, make a hospital or guardianship order, with or without a restriction or discharge.

In the first six years that followed the introduction of this defence into the English law of murder, it was successful in three out of every four cases in which it was offered.[4] These successful attempts have included cases in which a defence of insanity would have had no hope of success; examples were 'mercy killers' who put to death sick or defective members of their families after long periods of worry; men and women who killed spouses or lovers while in states of 'reactive depression' caused by unfaithfulness or a broken engagement; men subject to 'mood swings' or 'chronic anxiety states' who killed women in jealous frenzies; a man who suffered from 'violent perverted sexual desire which he found difficult to control'; a mentally subnormal homosexual who carried out a premeditated killing; and other 'psychopathic personalities'.[5] Yet in spite of such cases as these, the defence of diminished responsibility has not significantly increased the percentage of murderers who have been formally recognised by the court as mentally abnormal. In the five years before the Homicide Act, 46 per

---

[1] But is this so? See Walker, 1968. 144.

[2] s. 2, Homicide Act, 1957.

[3] There are already signs that interpretations in the two countries are developing on different lines. In England psychopaths have recently been held to be within the definition (e.g. in R. v. *Byrne*) whereas in Scotland they have so far been excluded (*Carraher* v. *H.M. Advocate* [1946] J.C. 108).

[4] Either at the trial or on appeal: see Wootton, 1963.86.

[5] See the analysis by Wootton, 1960.

cent of indicted murderers were found insane on arraignment (q.v.) or guilty but insane; in the four years after the passing of the Act 47 per cent were found insane on arraignment, guilty but insane *or of diminished responsibility*.[1] As we have already seen, a defence of insanity was seldom attempted between 1957 and 1965 when the charge was capital murder, and these percentages suggest that cases which before the Homicide Act were smuggled through the M'Naghten Rules by the efforts of medical witnesses and juries are now offering the more honest and less risky defence of diminished responsibility.

A successful defence of diminished responsibility does not automatically lead, as a defence of insanity does, to committal to a mental hospital. Since it reduces the crime to manslaughter, it sets the court free to impose any sentence in its repertoire, from imprisonment to an absolute discharge. Moreover, unless the necessary medical evidence is forthcoming – including an assurance that there is a hospital willing to receive the offender in question – it cannot make a hospital order.[2] Out of 139 cases of diminished responsibility which were dealt with in the years 1964-6, only 56 per cent were made the subjects of hospital orders (including 44 per cent with restriction orders added). Another 8 per cent, however, were put on probation, probably in most cases with a requirement of psychiatric treatment. Imprisonment was the measure adopted for 32 per cent. The remainder were disposed of in various ways: one by conditional discharge, one to an approved school and so on.

Finally, there are a few provisions under which the mental abnormality of the offender may determine his disposal in such a way that the court is not allowed to consider the extent to which he or she was responsible for the offence.

'*Insanity on Arraignment*'. Numerically the most important of these is Section 2 of the Criminal Lunatics Act, 1800, under which a jury to whom the accused appears to be so mentally afflicted that he should not be tried[3] may find him 'insane on arraignment'. The issue is usually raised by the defence, and the jury are instructed to ask themselves whether the accused is able to understand the charge, to distinguish between a plea of guilty and not guilty, to challenge jurors, to examine witnesses, to instruct counsel, to follow evidence, and to make a proper defence (on the doubtful assumption that mentally normal offenders are always able to perform these tasks). In practice, only cases of severe mental illness or subnormality of intelligence seem to pass this test: attempts to argue, for example, that amnesia extending over the time of the offence should exempt the accused from trial have not succeeded.[4] Twenty-one men and one woman were disposed of in this way in 1966; they had been indicted for a variety of offences, ranging from capital murder to malicious injuries to property and various types of sexual offence.

In Scotland, the equivalent finding is 'insanity in bar of trial', but it is

[1] See Gibson and Klein, 1961, Table 7, and Walker, 1968.159.

[2] Nor, *mutatis mutandis*, a probation order with a requirement of psychiatric treatment.   [3] Or physically impaired, as a deaf-mute might be.

[4] *R. v. Podola*, [1960] 2 Q.B. 325.

applied rather differently. The Crown arranges for the examination by a psychiatrist of any person who is in custody charged with a serious offence and who is suspected of being mentally abnormal. It has the right to raise, of its own motion, the question of the accused's fitness to plead, though the normal practice is to hand over psychiatric evidence of unfitness to plead to the defence, so that they may raise the plea. In practically every case the judge decides, after hearing the medical evidence, whether the accused is fit to plead, although if he is in doubt he can leave the question to the jury, by allowing the case to go to trial. Although the test is roughly the same – whether the accused is able to give instructions for his defence [1] – in practice, it appears that it is satisfied by a lesser degree of mental abnormality, since it is practically unheard of for an offender to be found fit to plead and yet insane at the time of the crime,[1] as happens in England.

Both in Scotland and in England the practical effect of being found unfit for trial is much the same as that of being found 'not guilty by reason of insanity'. The accused is removed to a mental hospital, to remain there until the Home Secretary is satisfied that he can safely be discharged or it is decided to remit him to stand his trial. Although the latter proceedings is rare,[2] it may take place if it appears that the patient was sane when the offence was committed; if there is good reason to suppose that his insanity was feigned; or if there is doubt whether the offence was committed and it seems desirable to settle the matter. This procedure would not normally be used unless the patient had recovered (or it had become apparent that he was feigning insanity) within a few months of the court's finding that he was unfit to plead.

Infanticide. Finally, a woman who deliberately causes the death of a child under the age of 12 months to which she has given birth, in circumstances which would otherwise make her guilty of murder, must instead be convicted of infanticide if the jury are satisfied that at the time 'the balance of her mind was disturbed by reason of her not having fully recovered from the effect of having given birth to the child or by reason of the effects of lactation consequent upon the birth of the child'.[3] The effect is that she can be dealt with as if she had committed manslaughter; the court has a choice between imprisonment[4] (for life or a specified period), a hospital or guardianship order, probation (with or without a requirement of treatment), a fine, or a discharge (absolute or conditional). It is worth notice that while it is for the jury to decide – after hearing medical evidence – whether the balance of her mind was disturbed in the way defined, they are not required to decide whether it was disturbed to an extent which removed or impaired her responsibility, or indeed, to decide to what extent it was disturbed. The Act is so drafted, however, that if she murders a child other than one to which she gave birth less than twelve months ago – for example, if she

[1] See Lord Strachan's charge to the jury in *H.M. Advocate* v. *Kidd* quoted above (p. 278).

[2] It seems to be rather less rare nowadays than when the then Superintendent of Broadmoor told the Gowers Commission that he (with twenty-five years' experience) could recall only one such case (Minutes of Evidence, 15.352).

[3] The Infanticide Act, 1938.

[4] Or, of course, a young offenders' equivalent: for example, borstal training.

murders an older child, or all her children or someone else's child – such murders remain murders, and a plea of diminished responsibility has to be offered to cover them. In 1961, thirteen women were found guilty of infanticide; twelve of them were put on probation.[1]

The Infanticide Act, 1938, does not apply to Scotland, where women in such circumstances are in theory liable to prosecution on a charge of murder, but in practice are charged only with culpable homicide, or (more often) committed to mental hospitals without prosecution.[2]

MENTAL ABNORMALITY AND ORDINARY SENTENCES

There are cases in which a convicted offender has been found to suffer from some degree of mental abnormality but for one reason or another is not dealt with in one of the special ways described, perhaps because the degree of abnormality seems insufficient to the medical witnesses or to the court, perhaps because the necessary steps have not been taken to produce the evidence in the form required. In such cases the court is free to take his mental condition into account when deciding between, say, prison and probation, or between a fine and a discharge, or when deciding upon the period of imprisonment or the amount of the fine. Thus in May 1961 two women who had pleaded guilty to several shoplifting offences successfully appealed against sentences of nine months' imprisonment on the grounds that they were under great mental strain at the time.[3] But the extent to which courts are influenced in this way has not been studied.

The relative importance of all these different measures can be seen from Table 32. This cannot of course show the number of offenders who are not prosecuted for minor offences because they are already recognised as mentally abnormal, or the number whose disorder is merely accepted by the court as a mitigating factor when an ordinary sentence is passed. What it includes is offenders whose abnormality leads to one of the formal procedures described in this chapter. It is noticeable that the overwhelming majority are dealt with by the post-war procedures, and that a very small minority are found 'guilty but insane', 'of diminished responsibility', 'insane on arraignment', or 'guilty of infanticide'. When it is realised that the 2,054 offenders who appear in the entire table represent only 0·65 per cent of all adults found guilty by the courts,[4] the full insignificance of these traditional procedures will be appreciated.

THE MENTALLY ABNORMAL PRISONER

It sometimes happens that an offender who receives an ordinary prison sentence is later found to be mentally disordered. Sometimes his disorder is one that might have been diagnosed had he received a psychiatric examination earlier. He may be enjoying a remission of his symptoms when he is

---

[1] The Criminal Statistics do not show how many of these were required to undergo treatment, or how the thirteenth case was disposed of.
[2] See the first section of this chapter.
[3] *Daily Telegraph* for 18th May 1961.
[4] Of indictable or non-indictable non-motoring offences.

TABLE 32 Adults and young adult offenders dealt with
as mentally abnormal in 1961 (England and Wales)

method of disposal	men	women
not reported to the police because of abnormality		
reported but not prosecuted[a]	numbers unknown	
found guilty, but sentence mitigated because of abnormality		
transferred from prison to hospital before trial or sentence	16	1
probation with treatment:		
as out-patient	326	48
as in-patient	326	66
guardianship order	11	5
hospital order:		
without conviction	75	22
after conviction, but without restriction order	604	127
with restriction order	134	16
insane on arraignment	41	7
guilty but insane	7	3
diminished responsibility	24[b]	12[b]
infanticide	–	13[b]
automatism	1	–
previously sentenced to imprisonment, but transferred to hospital during sentence	155	27
totals	1,719[b] +	335[b]
	=2,054[b]	

[a] Including those admitted to hospital, guardianship or treatment informally or compulsorily under civil procedures

[b] One of the diminished responsibility cases and 12 of the infanticide cases were put on probation, probably with a requirement of psychiatric treatment; and the totals have been reduced to take account of the unavoidable overlap.

---

arrested and tried; there are cases in which the commission of the offence itself seems to produce a temporary improvement. Other prisoners may develop the first signs of mental illness during their sentence. If the disorder is sufficiently severe, and if two medical practitioners – one of them usually the prison medical officer – report that it 'warrants ... detention in a hospital for medical treatment', the Home Secretary may (but is not obliged to) issue a 'transfer direction' of which the effect is the same as that of a hospital order.[1] Unless the sentence has only a few days to run, he usually also issues

[1] Or release him on licence or under supervision if the sentence is of a kind which permits this.

a warrant with the same effect as that of a restriction order so that if the prisoner recovers before the end of his sentence he can be remitted to prison instead of being discharged. The restriction on discharge has no effect after the sentence expires, and the discharge of the patient then becomes the responsibility of the medical officer, as in the case of the offender-patient who is subject to an ordinary hospital order. A prisoner who objects to being transferred to a mental hospital can presumably appeal to the Mental Health Review Tribunal.[1] In 1961, 155 men and 27 women were transferred out of English prisons in this way, to special and ordinary mental hospitals. Inmates of borstals, detention centres, and approved schools are dealt with in the same way, although restrictions on discharge are not always applied to approved school inmates.

Unsentenced Prisoners. In the same way, a transfer direction, with a restriction on discharge,[2] can be given if it is found that a civil prisoner, or a prisoner who is awaiting trial or sentence by a higher court, or has been remanded in custody by a lower court,[3] is mentally ill or severely subnormal. Since this procedure is intended for prisoners whose need of treatment is so acute that their transfer should not await their disposal by the court, it cannot be applied to prisoners who are merely psychopathic or subnormal (but, of course, such prisoners may be either subjected to a hospital or guardianship order by the court itself or, if sentenced to prison, transferred from it to a hospital). Sixteen men and one woman were dealt with in this way in 1961. In Scotland, such cases can be transferred to a hospital only by an order of the Sheriff, made on the Secretary of State's application and after receiving the usual reports from two medical practitioners.

There are many prisoners whose type or degree of abnormality is not regarded as justifying their transfer out of the prison system. Between 15 and 20 per cent of male prisoners receive some form of psychiatric treatment in the course of their sentence, either in those ordinary prisons which have special units for the purpose (for example, Wormwood Scrubs) or at the borstal (Feltham) or prison (Grendon) which specialise in psychiatry. Transfer to Grendon, like any other transfer between prisons but unlike transfer to a mental hospital, involves no change of legal status, but in practice is not carried out if the prisoner objects. Grendon is a security prison, with a segregated wing for young males. It has, of course, an exceptionally large number of psychiatric and psychological staff, and like the special hospitals (q.v.) is under the authority of a Medical Superintendent, who in this case can refuse to accept any prisoner who seems to him unsuitable. There is, however, a lay Deputy Governor, and the great majority of the staff are prison officers who have volunteered and been selected as suitable for this work.

Insanity and the Prerogative of Mercy. A person's mental condition is occasionally the reason for invoking the royal prerogative of interference

---

[1] In Scotland, to the Sheriff.
[2] The restriction *must* be added unless the prisoner is a civil prisoner or detained under the Aliens Order.
[3] And even certain civil prisoners; the exact definition is in s. 73 of MHA 59.

with the law, which has been mentioned in Chapter 9. When the death penalty was still enforced, the common law of both England and Scotland forbade the execution of an insane person: a special inquiry by psychiatrists was held if the mental condition of a person under sentence of death was suspect, and the result was often the commutation of the death sentence to indefinite detention, either in a special hospital or in prison. Now and again, however, the prerogative is still used in less spectacular ways for the advantage of the mentally disordered. Prison sentences have been remitted because it has been established that for some reason the court failed to take the mental condition of the accused into account; and very occasionally a sentence is shortened to allow a prisoner who has benefited from psychiatric treatment while in custody to be released in the interests of his rehabilitation. More often, the prerogative is used to remit fines imposed on offenders who are found to have entered mental hospitals for what seem likely to be long stays, and who would otherwise be liable to imprisonment for default.

INSTITUTIONS FOR MENTALLY ABNORMAL OFFENDERS

The great majority of mentally abnormal offenders who are committed to institutional treatment or care find themselves in ordinary hospitals provided by the National Health Service for the mentally ill or subnormal; and, unless they are subject to a restriction order, their status and day to day life there are practically indistinguishable from those of ordinary patients.

In particular, the restrictions on their freedom will be determined by the nature of the treatment which they are receiving, and their behaviour during their stay. Some forms of treatment require the patient to remain in bed; others may make it advisable for the patient to spend his day within the ward. A severely depressed patient, who might attempt suicide, or one in a confused state, would be kept under close surveillance. On the other hand, patients who are able to look after themselves, and who show no tendency to do physical harm to themselves or others, will – after a period under observation – be allowed to move in and out of the hospital with a good deal of freedom. They may be allowed to visit shops, cinemas, or the houses of friends. They may even be given leave of absence, which would allow them to spend days or even weeks with friends or relatives. This is sometimes used to test whether they are ready to be discharged.

If the patient is subject not only to a hospital order but also to a restriction order, this does not of itself compel the responsible medical officer to place any special restrictions on his liberty, although he cannot give him leave of absence without the consent of the Home Secretary. But since most patients under restriction orders have committed offences of personal violence, and tend in any case to be seriously disordered when admitted, they are kept under control and observation longer than other patients; and even when they have responded well to treatment the restrictions on their liberty are eased only gradually and with care.

Most hospitals nowadays, however, try to avoid keeping patients under physical restraint if they can do so; sedative or ataractic drugs are gradually replacing the padded cell and the locked ward. The policy of 'the open door' not only improves relations between staff and patients, but also makes life pleasanter for both, and prevents many of the patients (and some of the staff) from becoming 'institutionalised' as they used to become under less free regimes. This means that the relatively few patients who are so intractable or unpredictable that they cannot be kept under such conditions without a risk of serious violence are a disturbing element in the ordinary hospital, and there is an increasing tendency to concentrate them in the 'special hospitals' – that is, in Broadmoor, Rampton, or Moss Side, depending on the diagnosis.[1] These hospitals are for patients who in the opinion of the Secretary of State for Social Security require treatment in specially secure conditions because of dangerous, violent, or criminal propensities. Unlike other mental hospitals of the National Health Service they are administered directly by his Department (and not through local Regional Hospital Boards). They cannot accept informal patients: most of their inmates have committed offences – usually of personal violence or sexual molestation. This is not, of course, an essential qualification for admission; a patient who had been admitted to an ordinary hospital without committing any offence, but whose behaviour there made him unmanageable by ordinary medical techniques could be transferred to a special hospital. Such patients are a very small minority, however; the great part of the population of the special hospitals consists of offender-patients, and at the end of 1966 some 60 per cent of all offender-patients whose discharge was statutorily restricted[2] were in these hospitals.

The After-Care of Patients under Special Restrictions. The patient whose discharge is subject to special restrictions presents the Home Office with a difficult decision. Before they release him they must be satisfied not only that he has recovered but also that there is reasonable ground for regarding the recovery as permanent. A period of observation, therefore, is usually necessary after his recovery, and its duration varies greatly according to the nature of the patient, the type of mental disorder and the nature of the crime. The more serious the crime the more important becomes the protection of the public, and the greater the need to be sure that a relapse is unlikely: the early discharge of a thief is considered more readily than that of a murderer, however similar their medical histories.

As we have seen, hospitals must review the progress of offender-patients (and others who are compulsorily detained) at the end of the first and second years of detention, and thereafter at intervals of two years. But if after any period of observation the responsible medical officer considers that a patient subject to restrictions could safely be released he must then seek the Home Secretary's approval for this step. If the offence was not serious, and the patient's history does not suggest that he might be dangerous to himself or others, he is usually discharged without formal conditions. But in a case in which the patient's offence was murder or some other grave offence against the person, the Home Office, if it agreed to his release, would do so only after satisfactory arrangements had been made for his resettlement. A psychiatric social worker from the hospital visits the house to which he is to go on

[1] In Scotland, the State Hospital at Carstairs serves a similar purpose, having subdivisions for the mentally ill and the subnormal.

[2] Including transferred prisoners, and 'Her Majesty's Pleasure' cases.

release, and finds whether a reliable relative or friend is willing to stand as his guarantor, to submit regular reports on his condition and to undertake to inform the Home Office at once of any sign of mental disturbance.[1] If the patient is of an age to work the Home Office like to be assured that there is a suitable job for him.

When arrangements have been made a warrant is issued directing his discharge and stipulating certain conditions. Typical conditions are:

1. that on leaving the hospital the patient shall go immediately to the home of (his brother) at 3 High Street, . . . ;
2. that he shall reside there under the care and supervision of (his brother) . . . ;
3. that he shall attend a psychiatric out-patient clinic as directed by the Medical Officer of Health for (the appropriate local health authority).

Sometimes the patient is also required to submit to the supervision of the local authority's mental welfare officer or a probation officer. At any time while the restrictions are in force a patient who has been conditionally discharged may be recalled to hospital by the Home Office, for example if there are signs of mental disturbance, if he commits an offence, or if there is any other reason to fear that it would not be in his own or the public interest to leave him at large. If the patient settles down and satisfactory reports are received for a substantial period the guarantor is then relieved of regular reporting on the understanding that he will notify symptoms of relapse. Conditions of residence and supervision may have to be varied as circumstances alter, and may eventually be allowed to lapse. But in the case of patients charged with murder or serious crimes of violence[2] the power of recall is usually retained even when the formal conditions of discharge have ceased to be enforced.

Subsequent Prosecutions. Under whatever procedure a mentally abnormal offender has been dealt with, and even if he is still subject to treatment, supervision, or detention as a result, he does not have any formal protection against prosecution for some other offence, even if it occurred before the offence for which he has been dealt with as mentally abnormal. It is true that, as we have seen, police may refrain from prosecuting someone for a minor offence if he is found to be under psychiatric treatment already; but they are in no way debarred from doing so. For example, a man who, while subject to a hospital order and a restriction order, committed serious motoring offences during a day's absence from the hospital was sentenced to preventive detention.[3] Another, a certified mental defective who had been indicted for the murder of a child but had been found unfit to plead, escaped from Broadmoor and murdered another child. He was tried, unsuccessfully pleaded insanity as a defence, and was sentenced to death; but as a result of psychiatric examination the Home Secretary reprieved him.[4]

---

[1] In the absence of a reliable relative or friend, a mental welfare officer of a local authority or a probation officer is asked to supervise him.

[2] Although, of course, a restriction order in such cases may be for a specified period, in which case the power of control over the ex-patient lapses.

[3] *R. v. Higginbotham*, [1961] 45 Cr. App. Rep. 379.

[4] Straffen, 1952 (see the account in G. W. Keeton, 1961).

DISCUSSION

As this chapter has demonstrated, the ways in which the mental abnormality of an offender may affect his disposal are extremely varied, and not even the Mental Health Acts have combined them into a systematic whole. Moreover, underlying different procedures are different assumptions as to the reason for exempting the mentally disordered from ordinary penal measures.

Some procedures, for example, assume as a justification for this that a certain degree of abnormality removes or reduces the moral blame which can be placed on the offender. The traditional defences that at the time of the offence the offender was insane or suffering from diminished responsibility are of this kind. They are concerned not with the offender's capacity for being tried, nor with his probable response to penal measures, but with the extent to which, in popular language, he 'could help doing what he did'. Historically, these defences arose from the notion that the primary aim of penal measures was retaliatory retribution. Today, the way in which we use them is reconcilable with the more sophisticated forms of the retributive principle which were described in Chapter 8; that is, with retributive appropriateness as a criterion for determining who shall be liable to penal measures, or for setting upper limits to the severity of penal measures, even when the penal measures themselves are merely reformative or prophylactic. It is true that the verdict of 'not guilty by reason of insanity' is two-faced, excusing the offender from retributive punishment but at the same time placing him in prophylactic detention; nevertheless it uses his responsibility for his offence as the criterion. Similarly, a successful defence of diminished responsibility, while it makes it possible for the court to apply measures which are almost wholly reformative – such as probation – does so not because the offender is deemed to be specially likely to respond to such measures, but because he was not fully answerable for his offence, which is therefore reduced to a less culpable one.

Similarly, the special verdict of infanticide is retributive in its implications, since it has regard to the balance of the mother's mind at the time when she killed her child, and not her probable response to penal measures. The effect of this verdict is exactly that of a successful defence of diminished responsibility: the offence is reduced to manslaughter. The only important difference is that the defence of insanity or diminished responsibility requires the jury to decide whether the medical evidence shows that the accused's responsibility was removed or reduced, whereas the defence of infanticide merely requires them to decide whether the balance of the mother's mind was disturbed as a result of childbirth or lactation. If they accept that it was, they do not have to weigh her responsibility.

The justification for exempting from penal measures those who are too insane to defend themselves is also essentially retributive. For whether the penal measures themselves are regarded as retributive or reformative, the procedure assumes that they must not be applied unless we can make fairly sure – by the process of accusatorial trial – that the accused did in fact commit the offence; and this is what has been called earlier 'distributive retribution'. It is true that, like the verdict of guilty but insane, the verdict of insanity on arraignment is two-faced, since it automatically places the accused in prophylactic detention; but this does not mean that its underlying principle is not retributive.

In contrast, the implications of what might be called the 'post-war procedures'[1] – namely, those involving hospital, guardianship, or probation orders – are less directly retributive. The medical evidence must relate to the present mental state of the offender, and presumably to his future prospects of recovery; his state of mind at the time of the offence, though bound to affect the doctors' prognosis, is not otherwise relevant. It appears to have been the intention of this legislation that the court should be swayed partly by the offender's likely response to psychiatric as distinct from ordinary penal measures, partly by the need to protect the public against repetitions of the offence.[2]

Sometimes courts find themselves in a happy position in which they can assure themselves that a psychiatric method of disposal will benefit both offender and public. Thus Mr Justice Marshall, dealing with a mother who had attempted to gas both her children and herself, agreed to make a hospital order because he had 'come to the conclusion, after considering the medical evidence, that the public interest would be best served by her being cured. . . .'[3] On the other hand, there are cases in which the regime most likely to hasten the offender's recovery is one which allows him a certain amount of liberty, so that he may become used to the problems and temptations of the free world; yet this obviously offers the public less protection than imprisonment would. An example of this conflict[4] was the case of Morris, an elderly man who had killed his seriously ill wife while in a depressed state. He was found to have been of diminished responsibility, and doctors suggested a hospital order which would have confined him to a local mental hospital. The judge, however, was so impressed by the evidence of Crown witnesses as to the seriousness of his condition that he did not consider the local hospital secure enough, and sent him to prison instead, leaving it to the Home Secretary to transfer him to hospital if he thought fit; this decision was upheld on appeal.

Moreover, whatever the intentions of those who designed it, the legislation did not completely exclude the retributive approach to ordinary penal measures. Although the court must consider medical evidence which in effect implies that psychiatric treatment or care would be effective, the court is not bound to act accordingly. On the contrary, it must also take into account other considerations: '. . . the circumstances, including the nature of the offence and the character of the offender . . .'.[5] Clearly, the

---

[1] This is a convenient but slightly misleading term, since similar procedures were in operation as early as 1913 (under the Mental Deficiency Act of that year) for what would now be called subnormal patients, and even for some of the types which would now be called psychopathic.

[2] Hence the power to impose restriction orders.

[3] R. v. Russell, [1963] 3 All. E.R., 603.

[4] R. v. Morris, [1961] 45 Cr. App. R. 185. Morris was not in fact transferred to hospital.

[5] s. 3, CJA 48: the wording of s. 60 MHA is almost the same: '. . . all the circumstances, including the nature of the offence and the character and antecedents of the offender . . .'.

T

judge or magistrate is meant to weigh the medical recommendations against these considerations. What the court is not told, however, is what sort of circumstance should dissuade it from accepting the medical advice.

In particular, the court is neither compelled to think in terms of the offender's responsibility for his offence nor debarred from doing so. That this is so seems to be confirmed by the *obiter dictum* of the Lord Chief Justice in the case of Morris[1]:

> Of course there may be cases where, although there is a substantial impairment of responsibility, the prisoner is shown on the particular facts of the case nevertheless to have some responsibility for the act he has done, for which he must[2] be punished, and in such a case, although as the court reads the sentence imposed by the learned judge this was not such a case, it would be proper to give imprisonment. . . .

THE EFFICACY OF PSYCHIATRIC TECHNIQUES

The efficacy of applying psychiatric techniques to offenders is only beginning to be studied in accordance with scientific standards. The difficulties of assessment are even more formidable than in the case of ordinary penal measures. Psychiatric techniques, as we have just seen, are applied as a result of a wide variety of procedures, each of which places the offender on a slightly different formal footing. Some involve compulsion, others do not; some are accompanied by detention, others allow the offender a certain degree of freedom to enter and leave the hospital; others again allow him to be an out-patient. The techniques to which he is subjected vary from pure psychotherapy to electro-convulsion therapy, chemotherapy, and combinations of these. Even if one technique alone is selected – such as psychotherapy – and even if the differences between individual practitioners are ignored,[3] it is difficult to be sure whether any apparent effect is due to the psychotherapy or to the shock of detection and exposure. If the psychotherapy is combined with compulsory detention in prison or hospital, we cannot ignore the possibility that absence of subsequent reconvictions is due wholly or partly to individual deterrence.

Secondly, in most cases the psychiatrist[4] regards his treatment as aimed not merely at the behaviour which has brought the offender into conflict with the law, but at the disorder of which this behaviour seems to him to be only one symptom. The mother who has killed her children in a pathological depression is treated for the depression and not for behaviour which she is unlikely, in the nature of things, to repeat. In such cases it makes little sense to ask whether the psychiatrist has reduced the probability that she will be reconvicted. The only useful question is whether he has removed or alleviated her depression, and whether she is likely to relapse without future

---

[1] 1961, 45 Cr. App. Rep. 185.

[2] Note that he said 'must', not merely 'may'.

[3] In the same way as, until recently at any rate, individual differences between probation officers have been ignored.

[4] The term is used here to include those who apply any recognised technique, whether verbal, surgical, chemical, or electrical.

treatment. The same is true of the violent schizophrenic whose violence ceases while he is under chemotherapy.

It is in such cases, where the offences are clearly symptoms of easily diagnosable disorders for which psychiatry has devised effective cures or palliatives, that it is easiest to be sure of its efficacy. Even the fact that the depressive woman may respond to electro-convulsion therapy, or the schizophrenic to chlorpromazine, only to relapse later, is not evidence against the efficacy of these techniques. It merely shows that in some cases the techniques' efficacy is temporary. From the penological point of view repetitions of the violence are preventable by alleviating the disorder and being on the alert for signs of a relapse.

But such offenders are in a minority. More numerous are cases of the kind which psychiatrists have only recently come to regard as within their province. The best examples are those in which the behaviour that offends society is not so much one symptom as the essence of the disorder, so that they are sometimes called 'behaviour disorders'. Unlike his colleague who has to deal with the depressive or schizophrenic patient, the psychiatrist who attempts to treat this sort of patient can use no other standard than repetitions of the offensive behaviour as a measure of his effectiveness. He cannot say 'Yes, I have cured this man's aggressive form of psychopathy so that unless he relapses he won't commit another assault'; for the only symptom of relapse that is in practice detectable *is* another assault. In this field the effectiveness of psychiatric techniques must be judged by the same criteria as those we apply to ordinary penal methods.

Intermediate between these extremes is, of course, a large group of offenders whose delinquency is their only marked abnormality, but who, when brought to light by the penal system, prove to have mild symptoms of disorders of kinds that are diagnosable in non-offenders. When this happens, and when the disorder is treated with what appears to be a measure of success, the delinquency sometimes ceases, sometimes recurs.

Even this three-fold classification is an over-simplification of what actually occurs. One of the striking features of the case-histories of mentally abnormal offenders is the way in which arrests by the police are interspersed with voluntary or compulsory admissions to mental hospitals. Reconvictions are thus an inadequate measure of the frequency with which these people become entangled in the machinery of the social services, and a better measure is a combination of arrests and admissions to hospital, out-patient treatment or guardianship.[1]

There are other obvious difficulties. Quite apart from individual variations in the techniques of different psychiatrists,[2] some offender-patients are at the same time subjected to compulsory detention, which may be almost as much of an individual deterrent as imprisonment, especially if we compare an open prison with a secure hospital. Even offenders who are

---

[1] For a follow-up which attempts this, see Walker and McCabe, 1968.

[2] These are, of course, most marked in psychotherapeutic techniques, but can be found even in psycho-surgery or the administration of electro-convulsion (for example, the number of treatments and the interval between them varies). But such differences have their parallels in supervisory or institutional measures under the penal system.

receiving out-patient treatment under the terms of a probation order have been subjected to the shock of detection and public exposure. The ideal sample would consist of undetected offenders who have been subjected to out-patient treatment for a specific type of behaviour, such as compulsive shoplifting; but this is a penologist's pipe-dream. Perhaps the nearest practicable approach to this would be a sample of probationer-patients who had already committed repeated offences of a specific kind in spite of ordinary penal measures such as fines and imprisonment, and were now being subjected to out-patient psychotherapy.

No investigation that overcomes these difficulties, to say nothing of others, has been reported. The most interesting study is that of Dr Grün-hut's already mentioned analysis of 414 cases in which offenders aged 17 or over had been placed on probation in 1953 with a requirement of psychiatric treatment.[1] Fully 5 per cent had received no treatment (no doubt because they broke it off[2]); 19 per cent had simply received 'out-patient supervision', 'institutional care', or 'occupational therapy'. In only 288 cases (70 per cent) was a more definite form of treatment administered, and in 261 of these it consisted chiefly of psychotherapy.[2] The careers of 393 of the 414 probationer-patients were followed up not only during the ordinary period of probation that followed the period of treatment but also for a year after the end of probation. The results resembled those of ordinary penal measures. For example, women were less likely to be reconvicted than men; sex offenders less likely than property offenders; heterosexual less likely than homosexual offenders.

In other words, while there was no evidence that psychiatric treatment was being less effective than ordinary penal measures – including ordinary probation – neither was there evidence that it was so effective that it was altering the normal patterns of reconvictions. In particular, although psychiatric treatment (and especially psychotherapy) is usually *more* effective with younger than with older patients, this was not so with these patients, who remained faithful to the tradition that younger offenders have higher reconviction rates. Nor was there evidence that offenders who had failed to respond to ordinary penal measures were responding to psychiatry; as usual, those with previous convictions were more likely to relapse than first offenders.

In other words, Grünhut's results are consistent with the hypothesis that the interchangeability of penal measures, to which I referred in Chapter 12, extends to a substantial number of offenders who respond to psychiatric treatment. Obviously there are cases in which only psychiatric treatment is likely to be effective. Experience has shown that schizophrenics, paranoiacs, epileptics, and depressives do not respond to imprisonment and do respond to specific psychiatric techniques. But the extension of psychiatry to milder and less well defined forms of disorder has undoubtedly resulted in our applying it to some offenders who would also respond to penal measures. The only question is how numerous they are. In such cases – if we can identify them – the choice between ordinary penal measures and psychiatry

---

[1] 1963. The interpretation is mine.
[2] In another 5 per cent the form of treatment was not discoverable.

cannot be made purely on grounds of superior effectiveness. Other considerations will have to be taken into account: for example, whether psychiatrists and mental nurses are scarcer than prison staff, or whether the offender does such harm that security is important. Even irrational arguments might be listened to: for example, that since other things were equal, psychiatric treatment should be preferred as more humane. It should not be assumed, however, that it is always more humane. Some offenders dread the stigma of being classified as mentally abnormal more than the stigma or discomfort of prison. Some psychiatric techniques, such as electro-convulsion, are more alarming, and may on occasion do more lasting damage, than that anathema of penal reformers, corporal punishment.

POSSIBLE DEVELOPMENTS

Apart from technical developments in the diagnosis and treatment of the disorders associated with anti-social behaviour, what developments in the system of disposal seem likely?

The Special Defences. It will probably not be long before the defence of insanity becomes completely obsolete. 'Automatism' is becoming the defence of the motorist rather than the murderer, and increasingly unpopular with the courts. If a mandatory indeterminate sentence, however, is retained for murder there will still be some point in a defence of diminished responsibility because it will set the court free to choose between imprisonment and milder measures, such as probation. But it would be more logical to place all kinds of homicide on the same footing as manslaughter so far as powers of sentencing are concerned, and give the court the same choice between hospital or guardianship orders, probation with or without a requirement of psychiatric treatment, a determinate or indeterminate prison sentence, or any of the other measures at its disposal; and if this were done the need for the concept of diminished responsibility would disappear. (So, for similar reasons, would the need for the special category of infanticide.) As for the insanity defence, its point would be reduced to the fact that it would force a judge (instead of merely allowing him) to substitute detention in a mental hospital for imprisonment, a tactic which might be useful where he was known to be antagonistic to this alternative. It is questionable, however, whether the penal system should be overtly designed so as to enable Her Majesty's judges to be outmanœuvred.

On these premises, the procedures of the Mental Health Acts for dealing with offenders would then be applicable to all offences[1], and so would a probation order with a requirement of psychiatric treatment. Several minor amendments might be made to these parts of the code in the interests of flexibility. Since restriction orders for specified periods are pointless for the reasons already discussed, all restriction orders could be made indeterminate without any disadvantage, even to the offender. More important is

---

[1] All 'imprisonable' offences in the case of hospital and guardianship orders. It is arguable that even this limitation is pointless, since there is no legal obstacle to the compulsory admission under civil procedure of a man who has been convicted of a non-imprisonable offence.

the absence from the Mental Health Acts of any power of compulsory supervision over a discharged offender-patient who is not subject to a restriction order. In contrast, the combination of a three-year probation order with a requirement of psychiatric treatment for one year (the maximum period) gives the probation officer opportunities for after-care and surveillance. As we have seen, too, compulsory supervision is being extended to additional categories of ex-prisoners, and it seems consistent to make it possible where it is needed in the case of offender-patients.

14

WOMEN

OFFENDERS

The previous chapters have deliberately ignored women offenders, partly because they are in the minority, partly because they raise some interesting questions which could not be dismissed with a passing nod.

THE SEX-RATIO

In the first place, why are female offenders in such a minority? In 1961, for every adult woman who was cautioned for or found guilty of an indictable offence, five men were; and for non-indictable offences the ratio was one to seven (see Table 33). The younger the age-group the higher these ratios become. Although as usual it is intellectually tempting to look for a single explanation, there are several factors which probably combine to produce this effect.

Strength and Skill. The most obvious of these is the difference between the sexes in strength and certain sorts of skills. It hardly matters whether this is a physiological or a sociological fact. Whether with a different upbringing girls would have the strength and dexterity of boys or not, in this society they do not. Offences therefore which involve climbing or breaking into buildings are more easily committed by men, and the sex ratio is enormous (almost 1 : 60: see Table 33). Types of personal violence which involve the use of weapons, or which result in injury, are much more frequent among men, although it is noticeable that where minor assaults are concerned, women come nearer to holding their own.

Opportunity. Differences between the ways of life of the sexes must give men greater opportunities for some types of offences, although these differences are probably diminishing. There is an enormous disparity between the 45 women and the 3,556 men who were tried in 1961 for thefts from unattended vehicles. Many of these thefts are committed by men whose jobs involve loading or unloading goods in markets or yards; others are thefts from parked cars by men who can hang about inconspicuously where a loitering woman would attract attention. In contrast, when women have equal or greater opportunities, the pattern changes; women outnumber men among shoplifters, chiefly no doubt because their daily life takes them into shops for a much larger part of their day. Women, too, have more opportunity for cruelty to children and are more often prosecuted for it. They are more likely than men to be consulted about unwanted pregnancies, and so are more often charged with committing or abetting abortion. It is easier to become a brothel keeper if one has been a prostitute, and here again the sex-ratio is reversed.

Conformity. Quite apart from differences in strength, skills, and opportunities, women seem to take a more censorious view of transgressions of codes of conduct. Unlike most generalisations about women this is supported by a little experimental evidence: the best is probably that of Rettig and Pasamanick[1] who found that among students and former students of Ohio State University, who answered a questionnaire on 50 'morally prohibited activities', the judgements of the women were consistently more

TABLE 33 The sex-ratio for selected[2] offences in 1961

type of offence[3]	*number of adults tried*[4]	
	men	*women*
violence		
common assault	8,118 ⎱ 15,281	3,155 ⎱ 3,531
woundings	7,163 ⎰	376 ⎰
cruelty to children	364	424
public order		
simple drunkenness	32,314	2,556
aggravated drunkenness	27,353	1,738
disorderly behaviour	7,820	660
property		
larceny from unattended vehicles	3,556	45
larceny from shops, etc.	3,862	7,637
larceny by a servant (i.e. employee)	6,791	1,004
burglary, housebreaking and shopbreaking	9,923	169
embezzlement	1,297	206
sex		
bigamy	78	16
incest	144	8
brothel keeping	65	106
procuring abortion	19	38
soliciting	–	1,868

[1] 1960.

[2] Most of the offences are selected simply because they are frequent, the rest because they illustrate points of special interest.

[3] Offences tried at higher courts are combined with those in the same group tried at lower courts.

[4] For this purpose, persons tried are preferable to persons found guilty, since it is often alleged that women have a better chance of acquittal. Persons under the age of 21 are excluded, since teenage girls have a greater chance than boys of being cautioned instead of tried.

severe than that of the men,[1] even when the replies were separately analysed under the headings of 'basic', 'religious', and 'economic' morality. Gorer's less scientific survey[2] of readers of a popular English newspaper suggested that women readers were slightly more law-abiding than male readers in their attitudes to 'fiddling' with minor restrictions (such as food-rationing, which must have been particularly irksome to housewives.) This does not necessarily suggest that women are inherently more virtuous than men. They may simply have a stronger tendency to conform to what they believe to be the value-judgements of the society to which they belong. Experiments with groups of students by psychologists such as Crutchfield[3] show that many will change their expressed judgements so as to conform with what they believe to be the judgements of the majority even if these judgements can be recorded anonymously; and that females show more 'conformity' than males. Women with the lowest conformity were those who least readily accepted the conventional feminine role in society.

Motivation. Even if women's moral attitudes, opportunities, strength, and skills did not differ from those of men, another factor would probably result in a lower crime-rate among them. Their motives for breaking the law must in most cases be much less strong. Apart from traffic offences,[4] the most common are those committed for material gain, and in spite of the increasing number of women wage-earners, it is still the man who is expected to provide money for the basic necessities of the family. Even in a vocation where women seem to outnumber men[5] – the procuring of illegal abortions – they seem to make little money out of it, and many claim to do it for the sake of the pregnant woman.[6]

Again, whether by nature or nurture, women are assumed to be less aggressive than men, and this may be part of the explanation of their lower rate of assaults, although part of it may also be that adult women, most of whom are housekeeping, have fewer personal contacts that are likely to result in quarrels.

Reporting of Women Offenders. It is also very likely that a larger percentage of identified women offenders are not reported, particularly where the victim or other person who could identify them is a man. Sometimes the victim refrains out of simple chivalry; sometimes he does not want his association with the woman to be known, as happens when a prostitute steals from her client.

Scope of the Criminal Law. We must also consider, of course, the possibility that the criminal law is biased against men, in the sense that it treats as criminal certain types of male conduct while excluding from its scope the

[1] The exception was the view of 40-year-olds on 'religious morality', where men seemed more severe than women.

[2] 1955.236.   [3] 1962.508-.

[4] In which it is impossible to assess the sex-ratio because we cannot compare the mileage at risk of men and women drivers.

[5] At least if we except medical practitioners, who are seldom prosecuted, partly because their operations lead less often to septicaemia, partly because they are more often covered by a certificate as to the necessity for the operation.

[6] See M. Woodside, 1963.

female counterpart. An obvious illustration is the fact that homosexual behaviour is criminal when it takes place between boys but not between girls. Although it is difficult to find any other case in which the law discriminates as definitely as this,[1] it can be argued that there are whole areas of conduct in which the female analogies of prohibited male forms of behaviour are not criminal. For example, where men retaliate for insult or injury by assault or malicious damage to property, women tend to do so by slander, which very seldom takes a criminal form. Wives nag husbands with impunity, but the husband who hits back commits an offence.

A more controversial instance may be that of prostitution. There can be no question that, officially at least, this is strongly disapproved. Promiscuity is regarded as so unnatural and harmful in women – though not in men – that if the woman is young enough to come within the scope of our juvenile court system it is sufficient to enable her to be dealt with as a measure of social defence. Yet adult prostitution is not itself a criminal offence. It is only certain methods of practising or exploiting it that can be prosecuted. Attempts to use the criminal law to control the dissemination of venereal disease by prostitutes have been so strongly criticised by other women that they have had to be abandoned.

A less well-known type of antisocial sexual conduct which is confined to women is the making of false accusations of rape or indecent assault. Sometimes the woman fears that she is pregnant and is trying to save her reputation; sometimes her motivation is more obscure and irrational. In almost every such case, the best that the accused man can hope for is to cast enough doubt on her evidence to secure an acquittal. The law of perjury is such that she can hardly ever be convicted of it.

Women who co-operate with men in the commission of offences are frequently regarded as unwilling accomplices (often this is the case, but sometimes they are the instigators). This assumption is even reflected by statute: except where the charge is one of treason or murder, a woman is allowed to plead as a defence that she committed the offence in the presence and under the coercion of her husband.[2]

I am not suggesting that these instances of discrimination are indefensible; in several of them it could be argued, for example, that the male variety of the delinquency does greater or more permanent harm, or is more

[1] For example, women are never charged with indecent exposure. This is only partly because the law was clearly aimed at this male aberration (see s. 4 of the Vagrancy Act, 1824), since it would be possible to prosecute a woman under common law or even certain statutes (e.g. s. 28 of the Town Police Clauses Act, 1847). Part of the reason must be that the public exposure of sexually significant parts of the body by women is usually confined to situations such as soliciting or strip-tease performances which are dealt with otherwise by the criminal law. But by far the most important factor must be that women do not seem to have the same pathological urge to do this, with the exception of those who are quite insane. They do it only in situations where there is a rational motive. Better examples of clear-cut discrimination are ss. 3, 7, 8, and 9 of the Sexual Offences Act, 1956; but they deal with behaviour rarely indulged in by women.

[2] It is true that this originated as a legal fiction for the protection of women when they could not plead benefit of clergy, but it is significant that it was perpetuated and not abolished by the Criminal Justice Act of 1925, s. 47.

difficult for the victim to avoid. Nor am I arguing that the criminal code should be so ambitious in its scope as to include the female variety, but simply that if it were as ambitious as this the sex-ratio for offences in general might be slightly less unbalanced.

Age and the Sex-Ratio. The sex-ratio does become less unbalanced, however, as men and women grow older. For example, for those found guilty of or cautioned for indictable offences, the great majority of which were against property, the ratios in 1961 were:

TABLE 34 Age and the sex-ratio

age-group	sex-ratio[1]
14 (peak age)	1 : 7·3
20	1 : 9·8
21-4	1 : 9·4
25-9	1 : 8·5
30-9	1 : 5·5
40-9	1 : 3·2
50-9	1 : 2·3
60 and over	1 : 2·1

It is noticeable that although the 14th year of life, the last year of school for so many delinquents, was the age at which the rates for both sexes were highest, it was not the age at which the ratio was highest, which was the 20th year.

Part of the explanation must be that most of the indictable offences represented in the table are property offences, of which the male variety call for the skill and agility that decline with age; whereas women's property offences – shoplifting, receiving, and minor larcenies – are as easily committed by the middle aged and elderly. Other factors, however, may be at work. Even if property offenders alone are studied, a much higher percentage of women at any given age have had no previous convictions for indictable offences of any kind. In rough fractions, only a half of the adult men but three-quarters of the adult women are first offenders. Either women begin to commit property offences at the same age as men, but are somehow able to avoid detection for much longer, or there is a small but steady trickle of genuine new recruits to crime from each age-group which is proportionately larger among women.

Police and Women Offenders. Even if a woman offender is identified and reported to the police, she is more likely than a male offender to be let off with a caution instead of a prosecution, and the younger she is the more likely she is to be dealt with in this way:

---

[1] To allow for disparities in numbers at risk, the ratios are based on rates per 100,000 in each age-group.

TABLE 35 Offenders cautioned as percentage of those cautioned or
found guilty in 1961

age-group	indictable offences		non-indictable non-motoring offences	
	males	females	males	females
8-13	28	40	36	47
14-16	14	22	25	27
17-20	6	8	7	36[1]
21 and over	3	8	7	24[1]

Part of the reason for the sex difference in the rates of cautioning may be
that the offences committed by the women and girls were more trivial; boys
who are detected in breaking and entering are seldom let off with a caution,
whereas shoplifters often are. We have seen, too, that females are more
likely to be first offenders, and that they are also more likely to be treated as
semi-innocent accomplices, whether this is their true role or not.

Acquittal. Women who are unfortunate enough to be tried seem to have
slightly less chance of being found guilty if tried by juries. For example in
a sample of American jury trials in which one spouse was accused of killing
the other, only 10 out of 17 wives were found guilty, compared with 22 out
of 27 husbands.[2]

THE DISPOSAL OF WOMEN

On paper, our penal system makes few distinctions between the sexes.
Expectant mothers were exempted from the death penalty, and no longer
executed when the child had been delivered. The Infanticide Act (q.v.)
recognises the special form of mental disorder which causes some mothers
to kill their child in the months that follow its birth. Home Secretaries, too,
sometimes reprieved female murderers simply because 'There is a natural
reluctance to carry out the death sentence in the case of a woman'[3]. But
otherwise the sexes are equal in the eyes of the law.

Sentencing. There is nevertheless a widespread belief that women receive
lighter sentences than men. This should be accepted with some reservations.
If one simply compares women sentenced for a given offence with men
sentenced for the same offence, the probability is that a much higher
percentage of the men have previous convictions, which, as we saw in
Chapter 11, have a great influence on sentencers. It is also possible that the
women's offences, though of the same legal category as the men's, appear
less heinous to the court – for example, because the harm done is less.
E. Green's analysis of the sentences of Philadelphia judges showed that
while they appeared at first sight to be chivalrous to women, the apparent
differences disappeared when allowance was made for the higher percentages of previous convictions and aggravating factors among the men.[4]

[1] An interesting minor feature of this table is the high percentage of women over 17
who are merely cautioned for non-indictable offences; many of these are probably cases
of soliciting.

[2] See Kalven and Zeisel, 1966.210ff.   [3] See Gowers Commission, 1953.

[4] 1961,52.

None of the British studies cited in Chapter 11 included women in its sample, and the best data for our purpose have to be extracted from Gibbens and Prince's investigation of shoplifting. This has several advantages: since it was confined to cases dealt with by London magistrates' courts, the nature of the offence cannot have varied widely,[1] and since the courts were confined to London, regional differences in the severity of sentencing were to some extent excluded, although the suburban magistrates seemed to be rather more severe than the central London stipendiaries. Moreover, samples were included of both male and female shoplifters tried in 1959, by which date magistrates could not normally sentence first offenders to prison.[2] Finally, data included the percentages of offenders with previous convictions, so that the following comparison can be made:

	men	women
with previous convictions	49% of 234	20% of 532
sentenced to prison	21% of 234	4% of 532

This strongly suggests that the women were more leniently dealt with, although as we shall see an influential factor may have been the high percentage of them who appeared to be psychologically abnormal.

A similar analysis, based on the English Criminal Statistics, seems to point in the same direction. Let us take an offence to which women are sufficiently prone to provide a substantial number of individuals – for example, 'larceny from shops and stalls'; let us eliminate juveniles, since their disposal is influenced by more factors; let us also take only those cases which are tried in higher courts, thus ensuring that the thefts involved goods to the value of at least £20. To obtain sufficiently large numbers, let us combine the years 1960 and 1961, which give us 161 men and 67 women tried and sentenced by higher courts for this offence. Assume that 50 per cent of the men, and 80 per cent of the women had no previous convictions,[3] and were therefore most unlikely to be sentenced to imprisonment; if so, about 80 men and 13 women were likely to receive prison sentences.[4] In fact the numbers imprisoned were 99 men and 12 women.

Both analyses at least demonstrate that even among those with previous convictions women shoplifters have a slightly higher chance than men of escaping imprisonment.[5] There are two considerations, whether courts are influenced by them or not, which might well be held to justify a sentencer in

[1] Since thefts involving goods to the value of £20 or more would probably have been tried at London Sessions.

[2] See Chapter 9.

[3] This assumption is based on the supplementary Criminal Statistics for 1961, Table V, and tallies with Gibbens and Prince's percentages.

[4] Or the equivalent – i.e. borstal, corrective training, or preventive detention.

[5] We cannot of course exclude the possibility that the average man had *more* previous convictions than the average woman, or that the women's thefts were in some way less 'heinous' by the courts' standards, although by analysing separately cases tried at higher courts and cases tried at London magistrates' courts we have reduced these possibilities considerably.

rejecting imprisonment for a woman offender even in cases where he would regard it as the right measure for her male counterpart. One is the probability that imprisonment is a more severe hardship for women; this will be mentioned later in this chapter. The other is that unless the woman is without dependants imprisoning her will be likely to impose hardship on others; this is especially so if she is caring for small children or elderly people.[1]

Mental Abnormality. Because female offenders are an even smaller minority of their sex than are criminal men, there is an understandable tendency to infer that they are more often psychologically abnormal. Moreover, our conception of the female role is such that a delinquent woman seems more 'unnatural' than a delinquent male; and this presumption is particularly strong when her delinquency takes the form of violence or promiscuity. We know, for example, that among adult women the rates of admission to mental hospitals are higher than among men, and that, among the working population, neurosis is a more frequent cause of absence among women.[2]

Certainly in practice women offenders have a higher chance of being dealt with as mentally abnormal. In 1961, the 347 women who were dealt with by one of the formal procedures described in Chapter 13[3] represented 0·8 per cent of all those in their age-groups found guilty of offences,[4] whereas the 1,720 men represented only 0·5 per cent of male offenders. Although the percentages are minute, the numbers involved are large enough to make the difference very significant. Moreover, the information which we have about offenders who were sufficiently disordered to be dealt with under the Mental Health Act shows that the women have a higher percentage of diagnoses of mental illness, while the men have more diagnoses of subnormality,[5] a pattern which corresponds to that of mental disorder in the population as a whole. Over half of women prisoners, too, receive some form of psychiatry, compared with a fifth of male prisoners.

We cannot, however, exclude the possibility that psychiatrists' diagnoses – which must in the nature of things be impressionistic in most cases – are being influenced by the very presumption which we are trying to test, namely, that there is probably something abnormal about a woman delinquent. This would not necessarily mean that psychiatrists were deceiving themselves, for it might be that by their standards too *few* male offenders were being referred to psychiatrists, or even that a male offender who *is* referred to a psychiatrist is less likely to seem abnormal, either because the psychiatrist is of the same sex or because he has seen so many male offenders.

Moreover, it is now common knowledge among women themselves that mental illness is often accepted by courts as a defence or mitigating circum-

[1] None the less, at least half of the population of women's prisons in 1965 had children young enough to need parental care (see Goodman and Price, 1967.64). We do not know, of course, how many of these mothers had in fact been caring for their children before their sentence.

[2] Unpublished Ministry of Pensions statistics.   [3] See Table 32.

[4] To be precise, of all those aged 17 or over found guilty of indictable and non-indictable non-motoring offences. This seems the soundest basis of comparison.

[5] See Table 29 in Chapter 13.

stance. This is especially true of shoplifting. Gibbens and Prince had to admit that 'the task of assessment [sc. of the shoplifter's mental state] was not made easier by the processes of trial. Some offenders consult their solicitor, who may advise them to see a doctor for the first time, and evidence is produced which develops all that can be said in extenuation. . . .' One of the case histories which they cite seems to demonstrate a certain amount of psychiatric sophistication on the part of the accused, abnormal as she may have been:

A woman of 65 stole some books, a door plate and two door knobs, a china figure, a pill box and a bracelet, totalling £7, from a department store. She had £2 with her but had an account at the store. Her objective seemed practical in some respects and pointless in others. On arrest, she showed no guilt and seemed to accept very calmly that it 'was due to her anxiety'. She was a very genteel and refined lady, with social and material ambitions far beyond her real situation, about which she was very untruthful; however, she was a little more frank after the probation officer surprised her by saying that they had met when she was convicted of shoplifting twenty years before. She was, however, undoubtedly anxious about her husband's illness and her own health. For some years she had had treatment for an irritating skin condition (pruritus) about which she had abnormal fears, and had been referred in this connection to a psychiatrist, who reported to the court. She arrived in the shop with an empty bag which she filled. She insisted that some medical books were the limit of her intention, but she also stole some children's books and was quick to point out that she had no children and did not know any. There seemed some doubt whether her periodic trips from the country were to see the doctor or shoplift or both. It was concluded that she was a chronic neurotic with a 'false pretences' type of neurotic personality distortion, liable to periodic psychosomatic illness and pointless impulses to steal (which were then practised quite deliberately).

This woman probably knew that mentally abnormal shoplifters are said to steal articles for which they have little use. In fact, however, the investigators found that 'the pathological group frequently stole valuable or practically useful articles', and that the nature of the articles was not a good diagnostic clue.

Nevertheless, it is hardly possible to explain away all Gibbens and Prince's diagnoses of abnormality, which accounted for 21 per cent of first offenders[1] and 30 per cent of the recidivists. Moreover, some features of their sample were most unusual: 25 per cent of the women were in their fifties,[2] 30 per cent were from managerial, professional, or clerical families,[3] and a remarkably high percentage were separated or divorced.[4]

[1] Excluding foreign women (mostly visitors and temporary workers).
[2] Compared with about 17 per cent of Englishwomen over 14.
[3] Compared with an expected 20 per cent.
[4] 11 per cent compared with 1 per cent for Greater London in 1951. Only 48 per cent were married, compared with an expected 60 per cent; the rest were single, separated, divorced, or widowed.

Prostitution. Another relatively common form of female conduct often attributed to mental disorder or at least abnormality is prostitution. Promiscuity, especially for gain, is so alien to the usual conception of woman that it creates of itself a presumption that the prostitute is a psychological casualty. As Ann Smith,[1] however, says:

> On few subjects have more contradictory statements been made. Opinions on the tendency of prostitutes towards alcoholism vary widely . . . as do opinions on their tendency to other forms of delinquency. Some writers have suggested that prostitutes are drawn from those individuals precociously developed sexually, or who are over-sexed through inheritance or glandular development. Others consider that the predominant characteristic of the prostitute is her conscious or unconscious tendency towards homosexuality and her frigidity towards the male sex.

Certainly, male psychiatrists[2] find many sorts of psychological abnormality among those prostitutes whom they are able to examine, although it is noticeable that cases of diagnosable mental illness are in a small minority.

In contrast, women who study this problem are more apt to find other explanations. Rosalind Wilkinson's case-histories[3] of 49 London prostitutes contain at least 21 descriptions of women who showed no definite abnormality,[4] and many of the others exhibited merely 'social and psychological isolation' which might well have been a realistic reaction to the way in which society treated them. Ann Smith herself says:

> For the young woman of health and vitality, with little inclination for employment entailing hard work, long hours and a comparatively small salary, the attractions of prostitution are great. Such a woman is unlikely to listen to pleas as to the uncertainty of the future, for no employment which she would find agreeable, or in which she would be likely to be retained for any length of time, would offer greater security financially or emotionally. . . .[5]

The Wolfenden Committee came to a similar conclusion.

TEENAGERS

It is this problem of prostitution which, when we turn to teenage girls, seems to give rise to the greatest concern. Although theft is the commonest teenage offence for both sexes, and reaches a peak among girls at the same age – just before the end of compulsory education – a different pattern develops in later adolescence. Young males turn from schoolboy thefts to casual violence, involving damage to property or each other. A few girls seem to follow this pattern, usually because of their association with a group of youths; but more often they come to the notice of police or social workers

---

[1] 1962.39.

[2] Such as Glover (1960.244-), and Gibbens (1957), who is cited below.

[3] Edited by C. H. Rolph (1955).

[4] Many of them are labelled 'apparently normal' and of others the worst that could be said was that they were untruthful or stole.

[5] 1962.40.

through associations of a sexual kind. They may stay out late at night, associating with older men or haunting cafés used by adult women who are unequivocally committed to prostitution. Girls under 17 are hardly ever charged with soliciting; usually social procedure is invoked to enable a juvenile court to place them under 'care, protection, or control'. It is noticeable that between the ages of 14 and 17 three times as many girls as boys are dealt with by social procedure.[1]

Gibbens, studying 400 girls of this age-group who had been placed in a remand home in the course of social proceedings, found that only a small minority were living by genuine prostitution, or took to it later.[2] 'Prostitution at this age,' he thought, 'is nearly always a transitory phase, unlikely to be permanent but rather likely to recur temporarily in a time of crisis.' Most of this minority were either girls of fairly normal intelligence and stability, or else girls who combined a high intelligence with marked instability. Most of the latter group, unlike the others, had overtly lesbian inclinations, but both kinds appeared to Gibbens to show 'an inability to feel any real affection for men, a fear of being dominated by them and a thinly disguised hostility and contempt for them . . .'.

A girl in this age-group who is found in need of 'care, protection, or control' is, in two out of three cases, handed over to the local children's department by means of a fit person order, and is usually found a place in a home or hostel managed either by the local authority or by some philanthropic organisation. Most of the remainder are sent to approved schools.

INSTITUTIONS

Indeed, one of the striking features of penal institutions for teenage girls is the high percentage who have been sent there not for offences but because they are in 'moral danger'. In the 19 senior approved schools for girls and the 8 intermediate schools 'care, protection and control cases' usually outnumber offenders, and even in the 6 junior schools the percentages are more or less equal. The senior girls' schools, like girls' borstals, must be among the most difficult establishments in the country to manage. Since most of the girls have already freed themselves from parental control – such as it was – they resent attempts to reimpose it, especially if they regard the staff as lacking in experience of 'life'. Moreover, many realise that had they been a year or so older they would have been exempt from this interference with their freedom. They abscond more often than the boys do, and are in many ways more difficult to manage.

In general, although girls under 21 are subject to the same modifications of the law of disposal as teenage boys, in practice the effect is by no means always similar. The law allows them to be committed to attendance or detention centres, but there are no attendance centres for girls and the first detention centre for them, opened in 1962, was closed again in 1969 on the recommendation of the Advisory Council on the Penal System, who considered this form of sentence unsuitable for girls. Similarly, some borstals

[1] In 1961, 1,684 girls and only 491 boys were in the charge of the local authority's children's department. Most of the remainder were sent to senior approved schools.

[2] 1957.

U

for girls are not more than small wings of local prisons, and at times the increasing overcrowding of male offenders has ousted girls from the separate borstals provided for them. Only about 150 girls are committed to borstal training each year, but most of them have histories of theft, 'breaking and entering' and other delinquencies, interspersed with stays in remand homes and approved schools; and they present some of the most difficult psychological and social problems with which the penal system has to deal today. An analysis of a recent sample suggested that they fell into three main groups – the mentally disordered, the members of delinquent gangs and the sexually irresponsible – with a small minority of drug-users of whom at least half had committed offences of violence.[1]

Prison. Paradoxical though it sounds, women's institutions suffer from the small numbers that are sent to them. This is particularly true of prisons. Because women are convicted in smaller numbers, and because fewer of those convicted are imprisoned, there is only about one woman in prison for every 40 men. The smaller a prison is the more uneconomical it is to run, and this has had two unfortunate results as far as women's prisons are concerned. They are fewer and less varied in type than the men's prisons, so that less classification and specialisation is possible. Secondly, since local prisons are necessary both for women awaiting trial or sentence and for short-term prisoners, small sections of what are primarily men's local prisons are set aside for women. In reaction against the sexual exploitation of women prisoners, which in past centuries was one of the worst features of prison regimes, there are now strict rules insisting on the segregation of the sexes, and even prohibiting any male officer from setting foot in the women's part of a prison 'except on duty and in the company of a woman officer'.

Holloway, the large women's prison in London, has to combine the functions of local prison, young prisoners' centre, regional and central prison for long-term prisoners, and girls' borstal. There are now, however, two open prisons for women, and a semi-security one, where the regimes are more informal and relaxed than in larger establishments, and other special units are in preparation.

The typical woman prisoner receives a shorter sentence than a man sentenced to imprisonment. Table 21 in Chapter 9 shows that in 1961 86 per cent of the sentences imposed on women were for six months or less, compared with 67 per cent for men – a difference which must be at least partly due to the more 'heinous' offences and longer records of male prisoners. However this may be, the result from the point of view of prison administration is what Fox called 'a dreary stage army of 'ins-and-outs' to whom these periodic visits to prison are no more than an accepted if unwelcome risk of the trade'.[2]

Alcoholics. Prostitutes, who can be sent to prison for a third or subsequent conviction for soliciting, are of course strongly represented among this stage army; and many of them are girls under 21. But another sizeable group is the 'drunks', who constitute from 13 to 18 per cent of the annual intake –

[1] See Goodman and Price, 1967. 38-9.
[2] 1952. 114.

about twice the percentage among male 'receptions'. Moya Woodside has described a small sample of those admitted to Holloway.[1] They tended to be middle-aged spirit drinkers, with histories of poverty and unskilled employment interrupted by frequent short spells in prison (two of the women had more than 120 previous convictions). Many of them were indeed 'ins-and-outs', returning to the prison within a few days of discharge. Mrs Woodside observes that 'Those coming into Holloway resemble in many respects the vagrant and disordered patients admitted to an observation ward; indeed, it is often a matter of chance into which institution these women are received. . . .'

It is worth noting, however, that the rate of offences of drunkenness has not risen among women as it has among men. During the nineteen-fifties there was a steep rise in the rates for all adult male age-groups, but especially among those nearing the age of 20; in contrast, the rates for women in each age-group remained more or less steady, or even declined slightly.[2] The reason may well be that drink is one of the male wage-earner's favourite ways of spending his pay-packet, and that the young wage-earner has benefited most of all from the post-war increase in wages. Drinking, on the other hand, is not a typical woman's way of spending surplus income; she accepts drinks which are bought for her, but spends her own money on consumer goods which are less quickly consumed, such as clothes. A woman who spends her own money on steady drinking is in some kind of desperation. But, as I pointed out in Chapter 2, offences of drunkenness are a poor index of the extent of alcoholism, and this can be no more than speculation.

Women seem to have more difficulty in adjusting themselves to prison than men do. The reasons may be that they themselves are an even more antisocial selection from the population than male prisoners; or simply that, as is so often said, women in general take less kindly to institutions full of nothing but women. Breaches of discipline, a good index of morale, are more frequent in women's prisons.[3] Many of these are simply gestures of revolt against the staff and incarceration in general. A frequent form, however, is an hysterical outburst, in which the prisoner smashes everything breakable in her cell. These appear in the statistics under the unemotional description of 'damage to property'. Women who react to prison in this way are often referred to a psychiatrist for a special examination, but are not usually found to be suffering from any definite mental illness.

Babies. A special problem is the woman prisoner or borstal girl who is pregnant, or has a newly born baby, when she arrives. In order to save her child the stigma of being born in prison, a pregnant woman is allowed, if she wishes, to be transferred to an outside hospital for the birth of her child, although the hospital wings at Holloway and other women's prisons can cope

[1] 1961.
[2] See Walker, 1963.
[3] Prison Commissioners' Annual Reports, Tables A.1 and A.2. Dietary punishment for disciplinary offences in women's prisons and borstals was abolished in 1967, although the reason for making this distinction between male and female institutions was not explained.

with uncomplicated deliveries, and do so in the occasional case in which the prisoner prefers not to leave the prison.

Unless she is very near the end of her sentence, the mother is brought back to prison or borstal with the child as soon as both are well enough. Like the woman who has a newly born child when she is admitted, she is allowed to keep it with her for a period determined by the prison governor. Mothers who are obviously inexperienced or incompetent are sometimes sent to the domestic training course at Holloway for women who have been imprisoned for neglecting their children.

When the child is approaching the age of 9 months, the problem of his future has to be faced. It seems to be generally assumed that not long after this age the child will begin to be affected by his environment, and that he should not be allowed to remain in prison. If his mother seems likely to care for him properly in the long run, it may be possible for him to be looked after by one of her relatives until the end of her sentence; if not, the local Children's Officer is asked to take the child into the care of the local authority. As we have seen, however, women prisoners and borstal girls are far from typical of the ordinary woman, and in many cases their temperament, previous history, and lack of a home and husband make it most improbable that they will be adequate mothers to their children. If so, it is in the children's interests to provide them with adoptive homes, and, while the mothers' consent to this must be obtained, most of them give it readily.[1] The adoptions are usually arranged by the Children's Officer of the local authority.

PROBATION AND AFTER-CARE

Women, and especially adults, have a much greater chance than men of being placed on probation, even for crimes such as manslaughter, and their probation orders tend to be for shorter periods. In 1961, one woman for every three men was dealt with in this way. Partly to protect women against abuse, partly on the assumption that their behaviour is better understood by other women, a female probationer is not usually placed under the supervision of a man.[2] Although the majority of probation officers are men, the supply of trained women is enough not only to meet this need but also to allow women probation officers to be used in many areas to supervise young boys.

After-Care. The same principle is applied to the compulsory after-care to which women and girls are subject after leaving approved schools, borstals, and in some cases prison. Approved school girls are supervised either by women welfare officers employed by groups of schools, or by women staff from the local probation or children's department. Borstal girls and women prisoners may be supervised by probation officers.

RESPONSE TO PENAL MEASURES

Women seem to respond better than men to penal measures, at least to the extent that fewer of them are subsequently reconvicted. This generalisation

---

[1] A mother who unreasonably refused to consent could be over-ruled by a court under the Adoption Act, 1958, s.5: but this power is sparingly used.

[2] But this is no longer prohibited by statute: see CJA 67, sch. 7.

seems to hold good for probation, fines, and institutional measures, even if we allow for the fact that a higher percentage of women offenders have no previous convictions. It even seems to be true of girls from borstals and senior approved schools, although their behaviour inside these institutions suggests that they find it much harder than young males to adjust themselves to the regime.

This suggests that, if it is the stay in the institution which is producing the corrective effect, it can hardly be because it is socialising the inmates. If this were the explanation, the sex which showed more sign of adjustment to the regime should also show more sign of reformation. A more probable hypothesis is simply that the main effect on both sexes is still one of individual deterrence. This would not explain what appears to be the better response of women to probation; but it is not inconsistent with this tendency, since women may well be more responsive both to deterrence and to sympathetic supervision and case work. We must not however, overlook the possibility discussed in Chapter 12 – that a substantial number of male offenders are deterred by the shock of the initial detection and exposure. If so, since women seem to be more sensitive to the opinions of others, it is quite likely that the percentage of women who are affected in this way is greater still.

15

RECIDIVISTS

The third special group which the penal system distinguishes is the recidivist – the offender who neither mends his ways spontaneously nor learns to avoid detection, and is neither deterred by the experience of conviction nor reformed by any of the measures in the court's repertoire. Since the majority of offenders do cease to become involved with the system for one or other of these reasons, the recidivist constitutes an interesting minority.

THE DEFINITION OF RECIDIVISM

One problem is how to define a recidivist. As we shall see, the British penal system does so largely by reference to the number of his previous convictions, on the assumption that after three or four it becomes clear that he is not responding to ordinary penal measures. Scientifically speaking, there is no magic number of convictions after which one can assume that the offender is markedly less likely to be redeemable. As Figure 7 in Chapter 12 shows, the probability that he will be reconvicted becomes steadily greater with each new conviction. If there were a point at which the curve made a sudden upward leap, it would be rational to use this point both in a legal and in a scientific definition of recidivism; but there is no such point.

The most that can be said is that the sharpest increase in the probability of reconviction occurs at the second conviction. So far as adults are concerned, the majority of 'first offenders' do not become 'second offenders', whereas a much larger fraction of second offenders become third offenders. From the scientific point of view, therefore, a study of recidivism should concentrate on the difference between the first offender who is, and the first offender who is not, convicted for a second time – in other words on 'primary recidivism'.

I know of no investigation which has really attempted to do this. The Prison Department's psychologists have studied the differences between men who return to prison after their first sentence and those who do not. Since most men serving their first prison sentence have previous convictions (for which they have been discharged, fined or put on probation) this was not really an investigation of primary recidivism; but it is the nearest approach to such an investigation that I know of.[1] In this investigation 438 adult males serving their first prison sentence and 242 adult male 'primary recidivists' serving their second sentence were interviewed and tested by prison psychologists in 1958 and 1959. Since it could be assumed on previous experience that not more than a third of the 'first sentence

---

[1] But *juvenile* primary recidivism is the subject of an interesting article by Miss M. P. Callard, 1967.

men' would be reconvicted (as later proved true) the two groups were compared. A $3\frac{1}{2}$-4 year follow-up also made it possible to see what distinguished those in each group who had been reconvicted for indictable offences, from those who had not.

A general finding which confirms the need to study primary recidivism was that, while most of the characteristics which distinguished 'first sentence men' from 'second sentence men' *also* distinguished *first* sentence men who were reconvicted from those who were not (as one would hope) they did *not* distinguish the relapsers from the non-relapsers among *second* sentence men. The chief characteristics which strongly distinguished the relapsers among *first* sentence men were

excessive drinking ;

a poor employment record, chiefly in unskilled manual work ;

close relatives with prison records ;

poor contacts both with their own families and with other relatives and friends ;

earlier first convictions, and experience of Approved Schools ;

previous convictions which included larceny, breaking and entering and violence.

Others will be mentioned later.[1]

As with most minorities, there is a tendency to presume that recidivists are mentally abnormal. Here it is important to distinguish the person who is psychologically abnormal from the person who is psychiatrically pathological. Clearly, if the great majority of offenders do not reappear in court after one experience of penal measures, those who do reappear must be unusually unresponsive to these measures,[2] and to that extent abnormal in personality. And since abnormal personalities seem to be associated to some extent with psychiatric pathology, they will probably include a higher percentage of the pathological than a sample of first offenders.

What are the facts? Straker's primary recidivists had lower mean scores on intelligence tests than his non-recidivists; but other investigators' results showed virtually no difference.[3] Straker's primary recidivists also tended to score higher on a test of neuroticism; but they were no more likely than the non-recidivists to have histories of psychiatric treatment. It is only when 'multiple recidivists', with long records of convictions and imprisonment, are studied that high percentages with unmistakable mental abnormality are reported.

West, who interviewed and obtained psychological test data and case histories of 97 recidivists in Wandsworth prison,[4] came to the conclusion that 12 per cent must be classified as 'non-deviants':

---

[1] See Straker & Blackler, 1966.

[2] Unless we adopt the unlikely hypothesis that offenders simply learn to avoid detection, and that these are merely the unlucky ones who are detected oftener than the average through the slightly random operations of the police. Since the detection rate for property offences is low, especially in cities, this is not impossible, but it is unlikely.   [3] See Marcus, 1955, Anderson, 1958.

[4] An allocation centre for recidivists. 47 were 'preventive detainees' (q.v.); 50 were 'intermittent recidivists', with at least 4 adult convictions, 2 before and 2 after an apparently crime-free gap of at least four years.

These have no formal mental illness, no serious neurosis, and their personality is not such as to prevent them from getting along among their chosen group of friends, or of enjoying satisfactory marital and family relationships. They constitute the so-called 'socialised delinquents' who are well adjusted to a criminal milieu. Such men tend towards the professional type of crime. . . . Although lacking in respect for other people's property, they experience the normal restraints of conscience in their personal life, and are unlikely to commit atrocious or irrationally violent offences against individuals.

On the other hand, he categorised 36 per cent as 'active aggressive deviants'. Although only a minority of this group were physically violent or explosively aggressive, they were all actively 'predatory' and markedly indifferent to the feelings of others – a trait which, as we have seen, is attributed to one type of psychopathic personality (q.v.). They include not only daring thieves and robbers, but also habitual deceivers, confidence tricksters, and pathological liars. By far the largest group which accounted for 52 per cent of the sample, were 'passive inadequate deviants',

. . . ineffective, feckless people, conspicuously lacking in drive, many of them solitary and friendless, but prone to dependency and parasitism. . . . They generally go in for thieving on a petty scale, usually committed alone and on impulse. . . . Their average intelligence was lower than normal, and they included a higher proportion of individuals with psychiatric symptoms. They also included most of those who had been convicted of deviant sex behaviour (homosexuality, molestation of children and exhibitionism). . . .

Childhood. Straker's investigation suggested that primary recidivists are more likely than non-recidivists to have interrupted their education by frequent truancy. They came more often from homes in which the father was an unskilled manual worker and in which their parents were not in harmony with each other. As usual, however, their penal histories were better predictors of recidivism than their recollections of their childhood.

Indeed, West found that a quarter of his sample came from homes that were to outward appearance satisfactory,[1] and that the majority were the only offenders in their families. West was impressed, too, by the incidence of what he called 'the black sheep phenomenon' – the recidivists from thoroughly satisfactory families, all the other members of which seemed to be both respectable and stable. There were nine of these among his fifty preventive detainees, and all but two of them were 'severely deviant' in personality. As he remarked, the minority of recidivists who had criminal relatives seemed to be less deviant. The only definite connection which he observed between the offender's childhood and his offences was in the case of the aggressive recidivists, many of whom seemed to have experienced cruelty or violence in their own early years.

[1] 1963. 90. It must be remembered that a family which was an unhappy one during the recidivist's childhood may well have settled down by the time the offender was investigated as a recidivist, which in most cases must have been at least twenty years later.

So much for the personalities and backgrounds of recidivists. So far as their previous careers are concerned, several investigators have reported at least one interesting feature, which has come to be known as 'the late start'.[1] The mean age at which multiple recidivists were first convicted tends to be at least 18.[2] Various explanations for this apparent delay in coming into operation have been suggested. One is that recidivists tend to avoid their first detection longer than most teenage offenders; but, since they seem to be no cleverer and moreover seem to be liable to frequent subsequent detections, this is implausible. Another suggestion is that their careers began at a date when police records were less thorough than they are now, so that some early convictions are simply lost; but to make a marked difference to the average the loss would have to be enormous. A third suggestion is that in the early days when their careers began penal measures for children were so severe that a smaller percentage of teenage offenders were prosecuted.[3]

In all probability the 'late start' is a myth, originating in fallacious comparisons with the first convictions of samples of young offenders, and overlooking the substantial numbers of first convictions which occur in the twenties, thirties, and forties. Norval Morris, for example, simply assumes that a mean age of 19 is abnormally late. But in 1961, although the *modal*[4] age for a first conviction in England was 14, the mean age was 20, which is *higher* than the means reported for samples of English recidivists. It is unlikely that the mean was much lower when these recidivists were making their first appearances in court, although we have no comparable statistics for so early an era. Straker's primary recidivists tended to have *earlier* first convictions than his first-sentence men. On the whole, until it is reliably demonstrated that recidivists' first convictions are later – or earlier – than those of all first offenders, explanations of either phenomenon seem premature.

Maturation. Another very doubtful hypothesis is what is known as the 'maturation theory'. The Gluecks compared the subsequent criminal careers of two samples of offenders collected about the end of the First World War. One consisted of about 500 young male delinquents referred by Boston juvenile courts, the other of older men from a Massachusetts reformatory. The first group were followed up for fifteen years, the second for ten years. The average age at which the juveniles' delinquencies had begun was $9\frac{1}{2}$, and the average age at which those who reformed committed their last crime was about $18\frac{1}{2}$. The reformatory group had apparently begun later, at an average age of just under 15, and those who reformed did so on

---

[1] e.g. Norval Morris, 1951.

[2] It was 18 for Hammond and Chayen's 'p.d. eligibles' (1963.33) and for Taylor's sample of 100 preventive detainees received at Wandsworth in 1956. For Norval Morris' 272 'confirmed recidivists' it was just over 19 years (1951.339).

[3] See Elkin, 1938.201.

[4] i.e. the age at which the greatest number of first convictions occurred. The great difference between the mode and the mean is due to the fact that there is a sharp rise from zero at age 7 to the peak at 14, and a slow decline thereafter. See the Supplementary Criminal Statistics, Table V.

average about the age of 25½. The Gluecks were struck by the fact that groups with such different ages of first delinquency should take roughly similar periods – 9 and 11 years – to reform; and they concluded that 'The ... scientific implication of our follow-up studies is then the highly important conclusion that not age *per se* but rather the acquisition of a certain degree of maturation, regardless of the age at which this is achieved among different offenders, is significantly related to changes in criminalistic behaviour once embarked upon ...'. The major fallacy in their comparison is that they used the *mean ages* of 'onset' and 'reform'. Suppose that A first steals at the age of 8, while B first steals at 10, and that A's last theft is at 20, while B's is at 16. The Gluecks' method would simply take the average age of onset, in this case 9, and the average age of reform, in this case 18, and infer that the typical criminal career lasted 9 years. In fact, A's career lasted twelve years, and B's six. In other words, to establish the proposition that criminal careers tend to last a certain number of years, one must measure the careers of individual offenders. If the Gluecks had done this, and found that the mean length of their criminals' careers was nine years, and that the deviation from this mean was small, they would have made an interesting observation; but for some reason they did not do this. The other important defect in their method is that they followed up the reformatory sample for only ten years, but the juvenile court sample for fifteen. As a result, they excluded from their calculations the ex-reformatory men who had not reformed by the end of ten years but would have done so by the end of fifteen; these would have increased the mean age of reform of this group by an unknown amount. It should be appreciated, however, that the Gluecks' theory has not been disproved – by this or other arguments[1] – but is merely 'not proven'.

A simpler form of the maturation theory is that there is a 'criminal climacteric' somewhere in middle age, when recidivists tend to abandon crime. We have seen that there is some evidence for this in the case of offenders with abnormal EEGs, whose antisocial acts, like the fits of epileptics, seem to become less frequent in middle age. So far as other recidivists are concerned, however, there is no evidence for such a happy 'change of life'. Sir George Benson, who investigated the careers of some 450 habitual criminals discharged from Dartmoor and Parkhurst in the early nineteen-thirties found no sudden absence of reconvictions at any stage, but simply a slow decline in the number of reconvictions which was almost certainly due to waning powers and deteriorating health.[2]

[1] Lady Wootton has criticised the Gluecks' maturation hypothesis on the grounds that it is 'nothing more than a high-falutin' way of saying what has all along been obvious – that a minority of young criminals become recidivists while the majority do not ...' (1959.164). This is surely a travesty of what is a genuinely meaningful hypothesis, even if it is based on mishandled data. (The Gluecks' other evidence in support of their hypothesis consists of the similarity between the percentages of serious offenders, minor offenders and non-offenders in the two groups at similar intervals during follow-up. The percentages of serious offenders declined at much the same rate, irrespective of age. But this must have been largely due to the elimination of serious offenders by long penitentiary sentences.)
[2] 1952.

Crime-Free Gaps. On the other hand, some recidivists appear to have periods of considerable length during which they refrain from crime. West[1] was able to collect a sample of 59 men in Wandsworth prison in whose criminal careers there occurred at least one period of four[2] years at liberty and free from convictions, which was preceded by at least two convictions in an adult court and followed by at least two convictions. On investigation he found that in at least 24 cases the interlude had not really been so virtuous: the recidivists had simply escaped conviction through skill or luck. But where the gap appeared to have been genuinely free from crime it was usually a period during which a recidivist of the 'passive inadequate' type had found himself in some sort of sheltered environment. Often this took the form of military service, and the recidivist relapsed soon after discharge. Two recidivists' gaps coincided with periods in mental hospitals. The most frequent explanation, however, seemed to be that he had been living with some protective, motherly woman, whether in marriage or some less definite relationship; when this came to an end, he soon got into trouble again.

Specialism. Another myth is that recidivists specialise in some type of offence, and seldom commit other kinds. Hammond's survey of the previous careers of his recidivists[3] showed that irrespective of the offence for which they are serving their current sentence the most frequent offences in their previous careers were larcenies. For example, out of 44 sexual offenders, there were only 5 cases in which it could be said that the commonest offence in their past had been sexual; in 28 cases it was larceny or breaking and entering, and in 3 cases fraud. The same was true of men whose current offence was some sort of personal violence: out of 59 there were only 7 cases in which violence predominated in their careers.[4] The only types who could be said to 'specialise' were the 156 'frauds' or 'confidence men', of whom 88 had careers of fraud (although even so another 66 seemed to have committed more larcenies and burglaries in their past), and the 570 'breakers and enterers'; for 60 per cent of these breaking and entering seemed to be their favourite offence, although for another 35 per cent it was ordinary larceny.

Petty Recidivists. Studies of recidivists as such tend to be confined to offenders whose breaches of the law are classified as serious: in other words, to thieves, burglars, frauds, confidence men, rapists, paederasts, robbers, and other men of violence. It is true that samples of men who receive special sentences for recidivism include some remarkably trivial pilferers; but this is because our penal code treats any kind of larceny as an indictable offence. Types of recidivist who tend to be overlooked are those whose offences are

---

[1] *loc. cit.*, Ch. V.

[2] This length was decided upon because research had shown that among preventive detainees who are reconvicted after discharge, 90 per cent are reconvicted *within* four years; a 'gap' of four years or more therefore suggests that some unusual factor is operating.

[3] In this case, 1291 males who became eligible for preventive detention (q.v.) in 1956.

[4] In each case, however, there were 'mixed offences', some of which may have included offences of sex, violence, or whatever the offender's current offence was.

dealt with summarily, and particularly drunks, prostitutes, and careless drivers. Female drunks and prostitutes have already been discussed in the chapter on delinquent women. The addicted male drinker who becomes obstreperous in his cups is one of the most constant attenders at summary courts. In Scotland during the two years 1960 and 1961 there were 68[1] appearances by men with over 100 previous convictions; at least one man had more than 250. Recidivists of this kind are probably very specialised indeed, although they may commit thefts in order to pay for their drink; a substantial minority of West's sample was given to heavy drinking bouts, but only one or two were seriously addicted alcoholics.[2] Recidivism among careless drivers has hardly been studied in this country; Willet's sample[3] was too small to include satisfactory numbers of individuals with previous motoring convictions.

SPECIAL MEASURES

The problem posed by the offender who, in spite of probation, fine, or imprisonment, repeats his offence is recognised by the penal system in a few rather limited ways. In the case of a small number of offences[4] the statute provides higher maximum fines or terms of imprisonment for repetitions, and since, as we have seen, the only scientific dividing-line is one drawn between the first offender and the primary recidivist, these provisions are by no means illogical. The offences to which they apply, however, do not include many of the most serious. Secondly, a summary court which convicts an adult of an indictable offence can commit him to a higher court for sentence after being given information about his 'character and antecedents'; and this enables the limits on the sentencing powers of summary courts to be avoided if, for example, the offender has a criminal record.[5] Juveniles and young adults with criminal records are usually sent to approved schools and borstals, although some of the boys and girls committed to these institutions are first offenders.

Extended Sentences.[6] For the protection of the public against 'persistent offenders', however, the statute-book provides a special form of sentence, which it calls an 'extended sentence', and which in 1967 replaced the types of sentence known as 'preventive detention' (p.d.) and 'corrective training' (c.t.) The length of the extended sentence is partly governed by the nature of the current offence (that is, the offence for which the offender is being sentenced). If this carries a statutory maximum penalty of two, three or four years, the extended sentence can be of any length up to five years; but if the maximum is five years or more the extended sentence can be of any

[1] Unfortunately, it is not possible to be sure how many separate members of this stage army accounted for these appearances.
[2] *loc. cit.*, 22.   [3] 1964 (see p. 33).
[4] Examples are soliciting, careless driving, assaulting a constable, brothel-keeping, allowing a child to take part in a dangerous public performance; being drunk and incapable in a public place.
[5] The power can, of course, be used even when he has not, if the lower court finds some other reason.
[6] See CJA 67, ss. 37-38: but note that Scotland has retained p.d. and c.t., although the former is seldom used.

length up to ten years. A man serving an extended sentence, however, can *claim* the usual remission, and is *eligible* for release on licence; but unlike the licence of the ordinary parolee his licence will not expire when his remission would have been due, and will continue until the end of his sentence.

At first sight these are odd provisions. What is the point of allowing a court to impose five years for an offence for which it could already impose four years, thus protecting society for an extra two thirds of a year? The answer is not merely that maxima of four or even three years are almost unheard of,[1] for the draftsman no doubt had in mind that future legislation might well provide such maxima for new or existing offences. To make sense of this part of the statute one must appreciate the inherently retributive philosophy of sentencing from which it is an attempt to escape. It is assumed (although no statute says so) that the ordinary maximum penalty for an offence cannot be imposed simply because the person who committed it is a persistent offender, but only because of some particularly heinous element in the circumstances or nature of the offence itself. Otherwise the sentencer is supposed to impose a sentence less than the maximum, according to that unwritten tariff with which every experienced sentencer is assumed to be familiar. Although this is a non-statutory rule, which has not even been described as part of the common law, it seems to need an express statutory provision to liberate courts from the unwritten tariff when they want to impose on a persistent offender a longer period of detention than the tariff would permit for the current offence. Thus a man might commit an offence carrying ten years (or 14 years or 'life') and yet the court might feel that the nature and circumstances of the offence itself did not justify more than, say, seven years, so that it would have to invoke its power to impose an extended sentence in order to impose more than seven years.[2]

Eligibility. Not all recidivists, however, are eligible for the label 'persistent offender' and the extended sentence. First, the offence itself must carry a maximum of at least two years imprisonment, so that many offences, including for example common assault, indecent exposure and most traffic offences, are excluded. Second, a magistrates' court (whose powers of imprisonment are limited to short periods) cannot impose an extended sentence; only a higher court can do so, and it is never *obliged* to, however persistent the offender. It must be 'satisfied, by reason of his previous conduct and of the likelihood of his committing further offences, that it is expedient to protect the public from him for a substantial time'.

Not even higher courts, however, are given complete freedom to decide when his previous conduct and the likelihood of his offending again justify an extended sentence. His penal career must fulfil several complex conditions:

---

[1] Being an armed or disguised smuggler carries 3 years; I can find no other example
[2] This interpretation of the statute, although it was implicitly rejected by the Court of Appeal's Criminal Division, was later upheld by the House of Lords in the same case *R. v. Ottewell*, who had been sentenced to two consecutive prison terms of two years each, both intended by the sentencing judge as extended sentences). See, for example, the Times Law Report for July 29, 1968.

(a) His current offence must have been committed within three years of a previous conviction for an offence carrying at least two years' imprisonment, or within three years of release from a prison sentence for an offence in this category.

(b) He must have been convicted on at least three previous occasions of offences in that category; the occasions must all have occurred since he reached the age of twenty-one; and the convictions must either have taken place on indictment (i.e., in a higher court) or have resulted in his being sentenced to imprisonment by a higher court (either on committal for sentence or on appeal[1]). Convictions of any kind while he was under 21, however serious and numerous, do not count; nor can convictions at the same court appearance be counted separately; and convictions in a magistrates court can be counted only if they led to a prison sentence by a higher court.

(c) Prison[2] sentences totalling at least five years must have been passed on at least two of those occasions.

(d) These previous prison sentences must have included one of three years or more for a single offence, or two for two years or more, each for a single offence. This last condition was the only amendment of substance made to the Bill during its passage through Parliament. It was a Government amendment to meet the criticism that as the Bill stood a man with a series of convictions for petty larcenies could qualify for an extended sentence of ten years. The amendment assumes that if they were all petty none of his previous sentences would be for three years, and not more than one for two years.

These stipulations were an attempt to compel courts to be more selective in their use of extended sentences than they had been in their use of preventive detention. The Act, however, went about this in a half-hearted way. First, it offered no attractive alternative for those with whom courts were meant to deal otherwise. Secondly, for all its complexity it did not tie sentencers' hands much more tightly than they had been tied already. If we take Hammond's sample of 1,384 men imprisoned in 1965 who were then *eligible* for preventive detention, and the 178 who actually received this sentence, the Act, had it then been in operation, would have reduced the former by 40 to 50 per cent, but the latter by only 15 per cent or less.[3]

What is most surprising, however, about the new conditions of eligibility is what they do *not* insist upon: namely, any degree of specialisation in the recidivist's offences. He could satisfy the requirements of the statute as a

---

[1] So that by appealing to Quarter Sessions an offender could risk an extended sentence—a consideration which might well deter him.

[2] Although sentences of preventive detention and corrective training can no longer be imposed, they will continue for a long time to figure in offenders' penal records; and they count of course as 'imprisonment'. A man with a previous sentence of p.d. automatically satisfies condition (c): see s. 37 (4) (c) (i) of CJA 67.

[3] See Hansard (Lords) for 8th June 1967, col. 636. In practice, English courts have so far used extended sentences with great caution, imposing only 27 in 1968 (10 for 5 years or less).

result of four convictions for a wide assortment of offences, of which the following is merely a selection: arson, bigamy, breaking and entering, buggery, carnal knowledge of a girl under the age of 16, causing death by dangerous driving, cruelty to children, disclosure of official secrets, driving when drunk, embezzlement, forgery, living on a prostitute's earnings, malicious damage to certain sorts of property, robbery, sacrilege, theft and any kind of personal violence apart from a common assault. It is true that many of these offences could be grouped together under sensible generic headings, such as irresponsible handling of motor vehicles, harmful sexual conduct, acquisitive dishonesty, and personal violence. Nevertheless there are enough differences between even these broad groupings to justify the criticism that a man could qualify for an extended sentence as a result of an offence of a completely different sort from those in his previous criminal record, in which case his record, although fulfilling the requirements of the statute, would provide no justification for expecting a repetition of his latest offence.

Nor can this criticism be completely met by arguing that no court would be so foolish as to impose an extended sentence in such circumstances; for this is what has been done in at least one such case, *R. v Crehan*.[1] Crehan was a 38-year-old casual labourer, twice divorced, with a history of 14 convictions for various petty dishonesties, who had picked up a girl of fifteen at a fairground. Six months later she was pregnant by him, and he was sentenced to two years' imprisonment for store-breaking and larceny committed during their association. He was brought from prison to be convicted of carnal knowledge of the girl. There was no doubt about his eligibility for preventive detention (the date was 1962), and he would unquestionably have been eligible for an extended sentence had he been dealt with six years later. He was sentenced to seven years' preventive detention, and although the Court of Criminal Appeal gave him leave to appeal because his current offence was the only sexual offence in his record it decided to uphold his sentence. It admitted that when the current offence was wholly out of character with the offender's previous offences 'the court leans against preventive detention'; but it said that his record as a whole was such that the public needed protection from him. This argument would have been sounder had his appeal been against his sentence for store-breaking, which it was indeed correcting in effect if not in law.

What seems to be required is a provision that will restrict extended sentences to cases in which the offender's previous convictions provide good grounds for fearing that he will commit another offence of the same category as his current one. The drafting might be awkward, and might even involve lists of offences of different categories; but it could hardly be impossible.[2]

If such cases as Crehan's are dismissed as too infrequent to legislate against, there is another type of case which was undeniably frequent in the days of preventive detention, and which is not ruled out by the new conditions of eligibility for extended sentences. Men were sentenced to preventive detention as a result of convictions for petty thefts, burglaries or frauds,

---

[1] *R. v. Crehan* [1962] 1 All E.R., 608.
[2] See the fuller discussion in Walker, 1969.

involving a pair of boots or an overcharge of 1s. 10d. for some apples. In
the early nineteen-sixties people began to ask whether the public needed
protection against such petty dishonesties at so high a cost. Sometimes the
questioner was thinking economically, for an investigation by Hammond
and Chayen[1] has produced figures from which it could be calculated that
the cost of the depredations of the average preventive detainee during a
year's liberty was little, if anything, more than the £450 which was the
rough annual cost of keeping him in prison. (It is true that this calculation
did not take into account the manhours spent by police and courts in tracing
and trying the petty thieves, nor on the other hand the cost of maintaining
their families while they were in custody, although few of them can have
maintained their families even while at liberty). Sometimes the questioner
was a humanitarian, and was thinking of the cost in terms of hardship and
unwanted side-effects. The humanitarian point of view is not entirely
countered by pointing out that many institutionalised prisoners seem to
welcome a return to prison (there are well documented instances of preventive detainees who have deliberately incurred another sentence soon after
discharge). For the humanitarian can retort that this is one of the undesirable side-effects that should be avoided if it is at all possible.

To do justice to judges and recorders, it should be pointed out that they
had not been provided with very attractive alternatives for the disposal of
these petty offenders. The case for putting them in a carefully supervised
hostel, from which those that were employable could go out to work and
pay for at least part of their upkeep, was a strong one. Some courts have in
fact dealt with recidivists who were eligible for preventive sentences by
putting them on probation on the understanding that they will live in one of
the 'half-way houses' provided by such bodies as the Norman House Trust.
But these places were few, and the establishment of probation hostels for
adults was delayed for several years largely because the Morison Committee[2]
could see no need for them: it is only recently that official policy has changed.
Again, it was within the power of the Prison Department to put preventive
detainees and other recidivists into prison hostels for most of their sentences; but fear of the public's reaction made them exceedingly cautious in
developing their hostel scheme. Legislators had not, and still have not
provided by statute for a sentence of 'semi-detention' (q.v. in Chapter 9).
Consequently courts – and especially provincial courts – could see nothing
but a choice between another ordinary sentence of imprisonment (which,
for the reason explained earlier in this section, could not usually be more
than a year or two) and preventive detention. Since short sentences were
clearly ineffective with these ex-prisoners, it seemed logical to impose long
ones in the only way that was open.

What led to the abandonment of 'preventive detention' – and its replace-
ment by something very similar – was perhaps the most illogical argument
of all: that it did not reform. It was pointed out that nearly four in five male
preventive detainees were reconvicted after release.[3] Since the conditions
of eligibility for preventive detention were intended to ensure that it was

[1] See W. H. Hammond and E. Chayen, 1963.
[2] 1962.23   [3] See Hammond and Chayen, op. cit.

X

imposed only on offenders who had demonstrated their inability to respond to imprisonment, it was hardly rational to expect reform, although the Prison Commission (as it then was) encouraged such criticisms by claiming that 'Although the preventive detainee is deemed *ex hypothesi* to be incorrigible by any method of penal treatment it is right and necessary that the system should nevertheless be such as will, so far as possible, fit him to lead an honest and industrious life on discharge. . . .'[1] The defenders of preventive detention could have pointed out that a reconviction-rate of nearly four in every five demonstrated how often the courts were right in supposing that the offender would relapse; and that the effectiveness of a preventive sentence could be judged only by asking whether it did in fact prevent while it lasted – in other words, by considering the escape-rate, which was in fact very low.

What the critics of preventive sentences might have asked, and could still ask, is whether it is impossible to identify the one man in five who will not be reconvicted, and so avoid the unnecessary imposition of a long sentence in his case. If we grant the assumption that an absence of further convictions means that he has gone straight, and not merely gone undetected, this is a legitimate question. Hammond, however, tried several prediction formulae to see how practicable this would have been in the case of his sample, with disappointing results. The best formula which he could devise from his data did no more than divide preventive detainees into those with a 64 per cent probability of reconviction within four years and those with an 85 per cent probability. No doubt a slightly better formula could have been devised had Hammond been provided with better psychological and social information about his sample; but this possibility must not be exaggerated. For mathematical reasons, the further the general reconviction-rate of a sample diverges from 50 per cent the less likely is it that a formula which discriminates at a given level of effectiveness will be found: and the reconviction rates of preventive detainees are nearer to 100 per cent. However that may be, so long as it is impossible to pick out a sub-group of these multiple recidivists with a reconviction-probability considerably below two in three, it will be unjustifiable to accuse sentencers of being insufficiently selective in this particular respect.

The fundamental reason, however, for our failure to produce rational legislation on the subject of recidivists seems to be our unwillingness to face three much simpler questions. The first is 'Against what sort of offences do we demand protection at the cost of long custodial sentences?' So far our answers to this question have taken a very oblique form: in effect saying 'a series of any kinds of offence carrying a maximum prison sentence of two years or more'. As we have seen, this includes an assortment ranging from the very harmful to the extremely trivial. A more direct answer could easily be given by scheduling a list of the offences which should qualify for preventive sentences. Such a list would of course be controversial, and there would be periodic demands for its amendment: perhaps this is the reason why legislators have avoided this solution. But it would be a more honest course than one which in effect leaves it to the courts to draw

[1] 1960.45.

their own boundaries, and to face the criticisms of those who disagree with them.

Once a list has been drawn up, however, two more questions must be answered. One is 'How great must be the probability that this man will repeat his offence before we are justified in depriving him of his freedom for a long time?' In practice, whether we realise it or not, we are accepting probabilities of three in four for quite petty offences. Presumably we should be prepared to accept somewhat lower probabilities if the offences involved were more serious. An obvious example is personal violence. Recent research[1] suggests that with each successive conviction for an offence of this kind the probability of a further such conviction rises appreciably, until it passes the 50 per cent mark. In concrete terms, by the third such conviction it is becoming almost as likely as not that the man will commit violence again; and by the fourth it is more likely that he will than that he will not. Is this probability acceptable as a justification for a preventive sentence ?

It is not a satisfactory answer to this awkward question to reply that in any case courts award long sentences for violence on other grounds, such as the need for general deterrence and retributive punishment. McClintock[2] has shown that in fact long sentences for serious violence are uncommon: in 1959 and 1960 some 80 per cent of sentences for felonious woundings were for three years or (in most cases) less, and less than 4 per cent were for more than five years. This brings us, however, to the last, and by no means least awkward, question. How long should a preventive sentence be? A rational, though inhuman, answer would be that if we accept as a justification for a preventive sentence the nature of the offence and a certain probability of a repetition, the preventive sentence should last until the probability is substantially less. In the case of a young man who is given to violence or sexual molestation this might mean a very long sentence indeed; and it would be logical that it should be an indeterminate sentence, since it is impossible to predict even approximately when his tendencies will subside.

The introduction of parole means that preventive sentences are now in theory semi-determinate: it is only their maximum duration that is determined. But can a five-year sentence, which may restrain a man for only a fifth or a tenth of his active life (depending on his age) really be regarded as preventive? How temporary can prevention be before it ceases to deserve the name? We evade this question by hoping – like the Prison Commissioners – that a sentence of this length will act as a corrective; and since this is not impossible but only improbable the irrationality of this hope is less obvious.

Analysed in these blunt terms, the logic of the situation is extremely repellent from a humanitarian point of view. Is the rest of a man's prime to

---

[1] See Walker, Hammond and Steer, 1967.

[2] 1963. 140-2. McClintock was not able to separate these sentences into those imposed on 'first offenders' and those imposed on men with previous convictions for violence, and it is quite possible that the 80 per cent of sentences which did not exceed three years were imposed on 'first offenders'.

be spent in captivity because, if released, he is more likely than not to do serious harm to someone? It is interesting and relevant that we have less hesitation in saying 'Yes' if we are assured that the man is incurably disordered in his mind. Part of the explanation may be that we are then readier to believe in the very high probability that he will do harm again – although in fact it may be no higher than in the case of a mentally normal man. A more important reason, however, is the assumption that he will be treated better in a mental hospital than in a prison. The key to the dilemma posed by the dangerous sexual offender[1] or man of violence is undoubtedly the conditions in which preventive sentences are served. If we knew that these conditions were as tolerable as those of a good mental hospital we should be as ready to accept indefinite detention in them as we are in the case of the mentally disordered.

In fact, the best of our prisons for preventive sentences are preferable – if one is not in need of nursing or psychiatric treatment – to the worst of our mental hospitals. Freedom apart, a preventive sentence could be made more tolerable still if the Prison Department were given both a mandate and the funds. When this has been done, we may be readier to accept long, indeterminate sentences for a very small number of dangerous recidivists.

Meanwhile, we should not overlook the numerically larger problems posed by other sorts of recidivist. These include not only the petty thief and swindler, but also the chronic drunkard and the irresponsible driver. At the moment the full size of these problems is concealed from us because of the absence of a central index of either, and the scientific study of them has hardly begun.

---

[1] I must emphasise that only a minority of sexual offenders appear to do serious harm; but that this harm can be very serious indeed.

PART SIX

★

GENERAL

16

INFLUENCES

ON THE

PENAL SYSTEM

In this final chapter I shall try to put my finger, briefly, on the main sources of the very gradual changes to which the penal system is subject.

OFFICIAL AGENCIES

Several kinds of national and local agencies have as an official function the control of some part of the system. The main local agencies are Probation Committees (q.v. in Chapter 9), Children's Committees of local authorities (q.v. in Chapter 10), police forces and courts. All of these have a certain amount of autonomy, but are closely circumscribed by the law itself, by financial control from local and central government, and by advice, instruction and in some cases inspection from central government. Nevertheless a strong and skilful Chief Constable, Clerk to the Justices, Principal Probation Officer or Children's Officer can have a considerable influence on the local administration of the penal system. In the early nineteen-sixties at least one Children's Officer induced magistrates in her area to abandon to a considerable extent the use of approved schools, and instead make 'fit persons orders' entrusting delinquents to her department.

The Home Office. Of the central agencies, by far the most important is the Home Office. Its influence takes several forms. It is responsible for legislation on criminal law, procedure and the execution of sentences and other orders of the courts. Its Prison Department directly administers the prisons, borstals, detention centres and remand centres. It regulates and advises the local Probation and After-Care Departments, Children's Departments and courts. Its Inspectorates 'inspect' not only local Probation and After-Care and Children's Departments but also approved schools, remand homes, attendance centres and children's homes. 'Inspection' nowadays consists very largely of conveying advice and information not only to these agencies but also to administrators in the Home Office; and the Inspectorates are closely concerned with the selection and training of probation and after-care officers, prison welfare officers, child care officers and the staffs of institutions for juveniles.

The Home Office Research Unit is responsible not only for its own important investigations – most of which have been mentioned in earlier chapters – but also for assisting, with grants and advice, criminological research by other institutions.

The Home Office also provides the secretariats and official 'assessors'[1] for the councils, committees and commissions which give official advice to the Home Secretary, and it has a considerable say in the choice of the chairmen and members (so that it can usually exclude extremists). These advisory bodies are of two kinds – '*ad hoc*' and 'standing'. The former are set up in order to render a report on a subject which is carefully defined in their 'terms of reference', so that they are discouraged[2] from straying beyond it. They receive 'evidence' from interested groups and people, although not usually of a kind which lawyers or scientists would call evidence. They sometimes commission surveys, or visit other countries. Eventually they render reports with specific recommendations for action; but these are not binding on the Government. Standing councils or committees have wider terms of reference, but are often restricted explicitly or implicitly to giving advice on questions within those terms which are referred to them by the Home Office. They may produce reports for publication, such as those of the new Advisory Council on the Penal System.[3] On the other hand, the Advisory Council on Probation and After-Care usually records in unpublished documents its advice on more specific questions put to it by the Home Office, which is thus able to sound opinion, elicit ideas, and obtain official endorsement from people who are regarded as independent, before proceeding to some course of action.

Other ways in which the Home Office influences the system include the prerogative of mercy (see Chapter 9), which for the last hundred years has been used to mitigate the rigidity and severity of the law on sentencing when the consequences would otherwise have alienated public opinion; for example by reprieving young murderers and releasing gravely ill prisoners. Occasionally the Home Office has been in advance of public opinion, as when it advised the reprieve of unpopular but mentally disordered murderers. In time, the principles on which the prerogative is exercised come to be embodied in the law: the reprieve of young murderers is again an example. The abolition of the death penalty for murder has merely removed the necessity for the most spectacular examples of this; but it is invoked in unpublicised ways week in and week out (see Chapter 9).

The personal influence of the Home Secretary[4] himself must not be overlooked. It is never easy to be sure[5] to what extent Home Secretaries

---

[1] In Whitehall, an assessor is a civil servant who is not part of the secretariat of a committee, council etc. but attends its meetings. Assessors are usually as free to take part in the discussion as ordinary members, but are supposed to confine themselves to views and information which their Departments would support.

[2] But not always prevented; a committee or commission can always argue that unless its terms of reference are widened to include this or that it cannot deal adequately with its subject.

[3] And the Advisory Council on the Treatment of Offenders which preceded the Advisory Council on the Penal System.

[4] And to a lesser extent of his Minister of State and Parliamentary Under-Secretaries.

[5] Even official documents, when eventually made accessible to historians, do not always reveal this, since they usually record the outcome of Ministers' discussions with their civil servants rather than the discussions themselves.

have been innovators and to what extent their appointments have coincided with opportunities for which others have been waiting and planning. Some Home Secretaries, however, have had the reputation of being men of action: examples are Herbert Gladstone, Samuel Hoare (later Lord Templewood) and Roy Jenkins, usually because they have been associated with major pieces of legislation. Others have been said, fairly or unfairly, to have been over-cautious at ripe moments. Some, but by no means all, Home Secretaries have been lawyers, sometimes but by no means always an advantage.

Nor can their political positions be completely ignored. Both the Conservative and Labour Party organisations have in recent decades begun to include penal reform in their election programmes, and even to produce reports on specific aspects of it. The Labour Party's proposals have, not surprisingly, been more numerous and radical than their opponents', and it is probably more than coincidence that the major pieces of penal legislation[1] have taken place while they were in power. The influence of backbench M.P.s too, is as strong in penal as in other matters, and made it difficult, for instance, for the post-war Conservative Government to take decisions on capital punishment, the law on male homosexuality and the minimum age of criminal liability.

Backbenchers themselves can also initiate criminal or penal legislation, although here again the attitude of the Home Secretary or his civil servants can make all the difference between success and failure.[2] Examples of successful private members' bills have been the First Offenders' Act, 1958, the Litter Act, 1958, the Murder (Abolition of Death Penalty) Act, 1965,[3] the Sexual Offences Act, 1967, and the Abortion Act, 1967.

Other ministries and their ministers, though their influence is more specialised, must be mentioned. The Treasury and its ministers, with their hands on the purse-strings, can allow, prevent or delay developments such as new buildings (which can make a great difference to institutional regimes) or salary increases (which affect the standard of recruits to the staffs of prisons, probation and after-care departments and other agencies). The Department of Health and Social Security is directly responsible for the Special Hospitals which hold dangerous offenders suffering from mental disorders.[4] Through its influence on Regional Hospital Boards, local health authorities and teaching hospitals it can also affect, though less

[1] The Criminal Justice Acts, 1948 and 1967. Admittedly much of the 1948 Act was based on a pre-war bill, but not all of it. Detention centres and attendance centres were not in the 1938 bill, although not everyone would want to claim credit for the former. The Criminal Justice Act of 1961 and the Children and Young Persons Act of 1963 were not of major importance.

[2] For example, by a formal decision to allow the private member the assistance of Parliamentary draftsmen, or by allowing Government time to be used for a private member's bill which has run out of time.

[3] This would certainly have failed had it not had the blessing of the Government, and it is probably not unfair for the Labour party to claim credit for it.

[4] But the Home Office by law controls the release and after-care of most of the individual inmates, although a few are ordinary patients, or offender-patients not subject to special restrictions on discharge.

directly, the adequacy of psychiatric services for courts and penal institutions. The Department of Education and Science has a similar and even more persuasive role through its influence over local education authorities and their social services, notably child guidance clinics.

The Lord Chancellor – who is always a lawyer – has an indirect but considerable influence through the choice of persons for judicial office. Whether the nominations are officially his – as in some cases – or the Prime Minister's, his personal views are usually decisive. (The most important judicial appointment is that of the Lord Chief Justice, who is personally responsible not only for many of the decisions of the Court of Appeal's Criminal Division, but also for 'practice directions' to courts of first instance, and who is unofficially consulted by the Home Office when any important step which affects the courts is contemplated. Personalities such as that of Lord Goddard have made a considerable impact not only on the attitudes of lesser judges but also on the public image of the judiciary.) The Lord Chancellor's Office is responsible for the selection and training of magistrates, but relies heavily on local advice and resources for this purpose. In their official capacities the Law Officers (that is, the Attorney-General and Solicitor-General)[1] have little influence on penal policy, although their personal views sometimes carry weight with the Home Secretary or the Cabinet. There are a number of offences which cannot be prosecuted except by or with the consent of the Attorney-General – for example, breaches of the Official Secrets Act, 1911 – but they are not numerically important. More influential is the Director of Public Prosecutions, who, unlike the Law Officers, is a civil servant and not a politically appointed Minister. Although the Home Secretary appoints him, and the Attorney-General can give him directions on certain matters (and answers for him in Parliament) care is taken to leave him as independent as possible. He advises not only Government Departments but also clerks to justices, chief constables and other agencies on questions concerning criminal prosecutions, sometimes at their request, sometimes on his own initiative. Some types of offence (such as murder, sedition or obscene libel) are in practice prosecuted only by his Department; others (for example rape and some other sexual offences) must be reported to him in case he considers that they present such procedural difficulty that his Department should prosecute. He thus exercises considerable influence over the extent to which the criminal law is invoked in practice.

OTHER AGENCIES

So much for the most important of the official agencies. Their main concern is to make the existing system work and to meet its obvious needs for

---

[1] In Scotland, the Law Officers are the Lord Advocate and the Solicitor-General for Scotland. The Crown Agent, appointed by the Lord Advocate, corresponds roughly to the Director of Public Prosecutions, but also has under his control a system of local Procurators-Fiscal, who are responsible for prosecuting all but the trivial offences which local authorities prosecute or the very serious ones which the Crown Office prosecutes itself.

mmediate modification. Long-term reforms are more often traceable to agencies which have no official place in the structure of the system.

The Churches. The Churches probably have less influence over public opinion on penal questions in England than in most other Western countries. Archbishops and bishops speak in debates of the House of Lords, and are members of committees and councils which advise the Home Secretary, but do not hold ministerial or judicial appointments. The Established Church has been less interested and active in penal matters than some non-conformists, notably the Quakers. Sometimes, indeed, its leaders have appeared to be in favour of the *status quo*; for example over capital punishment during most of this century. On the other hand, on the subject of male homosexuality both the Church of England and the Roman Catholic hierarchy advised the Wolfenden Committee to take very much the line which its report eventually did. Again, it was not until the Church of England's Moral Welfare Council produced a report in favour of removing attempted suicide from the list of crimes that the Parliamentary campaign for this at last succeeded. Historically it is the pre-reformation Church which is responsible for many of the retributive principles discussed in Chapter 8, as well as for the notion of forgiveness. We have begun to see, however, that both retribution and forgiveness are irrelevant to penal systems.

Professional Organisations. Most of the staffs of prisons, probation and after-care departments, approved schools and so forth belong to organisations created to look after their interests. Salaries and conditions of service however, are only part of the concerns of these organisations, which usually have points of view, drawn from first-hand experience, upon the way in which the system is operating. They are frequently consulted by the Home Office about developments in policy.

Reform Groups. Other organisations exist for the very purpose of influencing the penal system. Best-known and oldest of these is the Howard League for Penal Reform,[1] which in its early days was led by Quakers but is now an entirely secular organisation, with a full-time secretariat, a library and a journal. It has played a prominent part in the campaigns for the abolition of the death penalty and corporal punishment, for limits on imprisonment and the amelioration of conditions in penal establishments. It is now linked to the Howard Centre of Penology, whose objectives include both penological research and the provision of certain forms of training for social workers.

A shorter-lived organisation of a rather different kind and standing was formed in the early nineteen-sixties, with the aim of restoring corporal punishment and the somewhat inappropriate title of 'The Anti-Violence League'.

Mass Media of Communication. Whatever part they play in generating misbehaviour, newspapers, magazines, radio and television are largely responsible for the man in the street's conception of crime and the penal system. Their approach ranges from that of the Sunday newspaper which specialises in sensational crimes, preferably sexual, to the well-informed

[1] For its history, see G. Rose, 1960.

documentaries of the B.B.C. A very few newspapers or magazines have campaigned overtly for specific changes in the penal system, as *The Observer* did for the abolition of the death penalty. In one way or another the more intelligent man in the street is much better informed about the realities of the penal system than he was ten years ago, although it is still difficult to convince him that bad drivers represent a greater threat to him and his family than do men of violence or sexual offenders, or that thieves are not all mentally ill or below average in intelligence.

Academic and Scientific Institutions. Without listing all the university departments and other institutions which are responsible for teaching and research in criminology – a catalogue which would soon become out of date – it is possible to mention some. Undoubtedly the most influential in recent years has been the Cambridge Institute of Criminology, which is responsible not only for most of the criminological teaching of lawyers and graduate students in that University, but also for a large number of factual surveys upon types of offences or their treatment, most of which have been mentioned in this book. Its library of criminological literature has no rival in Britain, and Cambridge has the only Chair of Criminology in Britain. Oxford has a more modest and recently founded Penal Research Unit, and a Readership in Criminology. Edinburgh University has a Department of Criminal Law and Criminology, a Chair of Criminal Law and a Chair of Forensic Psychiatry. The London School of Economics has a Chair and a Readership in this field. The University of North Staffordshire has a Readership and Manchester has a Senior Lectureship in the subject. The London Institute of Psychiatry has a Chair in Forensic Psychiatry and has been responsible for much recent psychiatric and psychological research. Other university departments of law, psychology, psychiatry, sociology or education have individuals or groups of individuals who have interested themselves in teaching or investigating aspects of the subject.

The Institute for the Study and Treatment of Delinquency, which originated from a psychotherapeutic clinic established in 1931, but became formally separate from it in 1948,[1] is responsible for research, public lectures and study-groups, and the well known *British Journal of Criminology*.

Criminology, in one of its protean shapes, is taught to entrants to most of the professions concerned with the penal system, with the exception of lawyers and psychiatrists. It is true that at Cambridge, and more recently Edinburgh and Oxford, undergraduate law students have been offered it as an optional subject. Nevertheless, in general, universities have treated criminology as a graduate's subject, with the result that law students, few of whom take graduate courses, escape contact with the subject. By the time they become sentencers they are mature or middle-aged, and have no time for it, although there are notable and welcome exceptions.

Penal Involvement. Finally, the man in the street himself takes a closer interest in the penal system as it comes nearer to his own doorstep. In

[1] When what is now the Portman Clinic was incorporated in the National Health Service. The two organisations, however, still share the same building.

Chapter 2 I mentioned the startling estimates of the percentage of the male population which is likely to be convicted of theft or some other indictable offence in its lifetime, to which must be added the incalculable percentage likely to be found guilty of traffic offences and other non-indictable misbehaviour. These percentages measure to some extent what might be called the 'penal involvement' of a society. In this country they are probably growing year by year as a result of several developments. The two commonest forms of opportunity for criminal behaviour – private motor-vehicles and other attractive forms of consumer goods – are steadily increasing in number. Adolescents and young adults in search of risk and excitement are finding these harder to come by in legitimate forms, and are resorting to breaches of the law, such as shoplifting, vandalism and marihuana-smoking.[1] Even people who are too serious-minded for speeding, shoplifting, vandalism or drugs, may be involved in clashes with the law as a result of political protest, whether against nuclear disarmament, racial discrimination or the war in Vietnam. Not only are more people getting into trouble with the law, but also those who have been 'in trouble' are finding it easier to communicate their views to large audiences. The increasing interest in crime on the part of mass media means that not only political or motoring offenders but also drug-users, confidence-men, professional thieves and prostitutes can sell their biographies more readily than ever before. The highly personal view of the penal system which they present is understandably more entertaining than the impersonal commonsense of penal agents or administrators, and must strengthen any dislike of law enforcement which is latent in the listener.

It is impossible to measure or forecast scientifically all the effects of this increasing penal involvement. My impression is that there is a growing tendency for the system to discriminate between harmful and harmless offences, and even when an offence is undoubtedly harmful to think in terms of prevention rather than of retributive justice. On the other hand the assumption that criminals are usually suffering from some mental abnormality is giving way to a more realistic, though no less deterministic, point of view, which recognises the inevitability of much criminal behaviour on the part of mentally healthy individuals.[2] In the disposal of the offender the courts are subject to more and more control by law, advice from professionals and criticism from mass media. They are thinking less in terms of justice and more in terms of expediency. The results of their decisions are increasingly liable to be modified by penal agents. In short, the system is becoming more sensitive, realistic and flexible. It is possible that it is also becoming more effective, although this is less certain.

[1] For someone who wants risk and excitement without physical danger, but has outgrown juvenile law-breaking, marihuana is the ideal solution. It is illegal, and therefore risky. Its harmfulness is by no means proved, so that its use is a protest against the unscientific assumptions of the criminal law. It is even said to be enjoyable in itself, unlike many other forms of risk or protest.

[2] For an example, see the discussion of prostitutes' mental condition in Chapter 14, and especially the quotation from Ann Smith on p. 304.

BIBLIOGRAPHY

Since the value of many of the investigations referred to in the course of this book depends largely on the methods by which their samples of delinquents and non-delinquents were selected, the references to major investigations are supplemented by short specifications of the nature of their samples (but not by a summary of their findings, some of which are to be found in the book itself).

The following abbreviations are used:

(ed.)	*indicates that the person named was editor and not author of the entire work*
HMSO	*Her Majesty's Stationery Office, London*
Cd., Cmd., Cmnd.	*indicates the 'command number' by which certain Parliamentary papers are identified*
J	*Journal*

Advisory Council on Treatment of Offenders, reports on:
   Alternatives to Short Terms of Imprisonment, 1957, HMSO
   After-care and Supervision of Discharged Prisoners, 1958, HMSO
   Treatment of Young Offenders, 1959, HMSO
   Corporal Punishment, 1960, (Cmnd. 1213), HMSO
   Non-Residential Treatment of Offenders under 21, 1962, HMSO
   Preventive Detention, 1963, HMSO
   Organisation of After-care, 1963, HMSO
W. Aichorn, *Wayward Youth*, 1936, Putnam, London
American Academy of Political and Social Science, 'Prevention of Juvenile Delinquency', issue of March 1959, *Annals*
J. W. Anderson, 'Recidivism, Intelligence and Social Class', 1958, in *British J. of Delinquency*
R. G. Andry, *Delinquency and Parental Pathology*, 1960, Methuen, London
   The sample consisted of
   (i) 80 London boys aged 12-15 with more than one recorded conviction for theft who were referred for psychological examination to the London County Council's remand home at Stamford House. Rare types of offender such as sex offenders and incendiarists were excluded, and so were boys with IQs below 80 or above 125, boys diagnosed as neurotic or psychotic, boys from broken homes or middle- or upper-class homes;
   (ii) 80 non-delinquent controls selected from two adjacent secondary modern schools in a London working-class area with a high delinquency rate. 'Non-delinquent' was defined as 'never having been brought before a juvenile court nor attended a child guidance clinic because of stealing or neurosis, nor been brought to the notice of the school authorities for persistent truanting'. The controls were group-matched with the delinquents for age, social class and

IQ (i.e., not matched one with one, but so that roughly similar numbers fell within each year-group, social class (Hall-Jones classes, 4, 5, 6, 7,), and IQ group (e.g., 80-90)).

All 160 boys, and the parents of 30 delinquents and 30 non-delinquents, were interviewed. Data analysed covered home atmosphere and relationships in detail, including early delinquent behaviour and parents' reactions to it.

idem, The Short-term Prisoner, 1963, Tavistock, London

Archbold's *Pleading, Evidence and Practice in Criminal Cases*, 1967 edition, Sweet & Maxwell, London

M. Argyle, *A New Approach to the Classification of Delinquents with Implications for Treatment*, 1961, California Board of Corrections Monograph No. 2

Atkin Committee on *Insanity & Crime*, 1923 (Cmd. 2005) HMSO

M. Balint, *Problems of Human Pleasure and Behaviour*, 1957, Hogarth, London

C. Beccaria, *Of Crimes and Punishments*, 1767, anonymous English translation, J. Almon, London

G. Benson, 'A Note on the Habitual Criminal', 1952, in *British J. of Delinquency*

idem, 'Prediction Methods and Young Prisoners,' 1959, in *British J. of Delinquency*

J. Bentham, *Principles of Penal Law*, Works Vol. I, 1837, W. Tait, Edinburgh

C. D. Blackler, 'Primary Recidivism in Adult Men', 1968, in *British J. of Criminology*; and see Straker and Blackler

W. Blackstone, *Commentaries on the Laws of England*, 1809 edition, Strahan, London

F. Boas, *Changes in Bodily Form of Descendants of Immigrants*, 1912, Columbia University Press, New York

A. E. Bottoms, 'Towards a Custodial Training Sentence for Adults', 1965, in *Criminal Law Review*, Oct.-Nov.

J. Bowlby, *Maternal Care and Mental Health*, 1951, World Health Organisation Monographs

C. Burt, *The Young Delinquents*, 1944 edition, University of London Press

Cadogan Committee on *Corporal Punishment*, 1938 (Cmd. 2005) HMSO

C. H. Calhoon, 'A Follow-up of 100 Normal and Sub-normal Delinquent Boys', 1928, in *J. of Juvenile Research*

M. P. Callard, 'Significant Differences Between Recidivists and Non-recidivists', 1967, in *British J. of Criminology*

Cambridge Survey of Sexual Offenders, see L. Radzinowicz

R. Carr-Hill and D. J. Steer, 'The Motoring Offender – Who is He?', 1967, in *Criminal Law Review*, April

A. M. Carr-Saunders, H. Mannheim and E. C. Rhodes, *Young Offenders*, 1942, Cambridge University Press.

The sample consisted of

(ia) the first 989 boys aged 8-16 brought before London juvenile courts after 1st October, 1938;

(ib) as controls, 1,000 London school-boys, each suggested by the headmaster of the school attended by one of the delinquents as being a non-delinquent of the same age;

(iia) the first 964 boys in the same age-range brought before juvenile courts in 6 provincial cities in a slightly later period;

(iib) 970 boys as controls, selected in the same way as (ib).

The data analysed consist of the boys' family background, penal history and school records. The introductory chapter also includes a review of previous English studies of samples of delinquents.

Chief Constables' Association, 'Trial by Jury', 1966, in *New Law Journal* for 9th June

K. O. Christiansen, 'Threshold of Tolerance in various Population Groups', 1968, in *The Mentally Abnormal Offender* (a CIBA Foundation Symposium), Churchill, London

R. A. Cloward and L. E. Ohlin, *Delinquency and Opportunity*, 1961, Glencoe Free Press, Illinois, and Routledge, London

A. K. Cohen, *Delinquent Boys*, 1955, Glencoe Free Press, Illinois

J. G. Connolly and W. Sluckin, *Statistics for Social Sciences*, 1957 edition, Cleaver and Hulme, London

P. Cornil, 'Les Arrêts de Fin de Semaine et la Semi-detention', 1963, in *Revue de Droit Pénal et de Criminologie*

W. M. Court-Brown, 'The Genetic Aspects of Criminal Behaviour', 1966, in *Proceedings of the Royal College of Physicians*, November

D. Cressey, *Other People's Money*, 1953, Glencoe Free Press, Illinois

Criminal Injuries Compensation Board, Annual Reports of, from 1965, HMSO

A. R. N. Cross, 'Indeterminate Prison Sentences,' 1962, in *The Listener*, 15th February

R. S. Crutchfield, in D. Krech, R. S. Crutchfield and E. L. Ballachey, *The Individual in Society*, 1962, McGraw-Hill, New York

Departmental Committees, see under chairmen's names: Atkin, Ellis, Feversham, Cadogan, Gladstone, Ingleby, Kilbrandon, Morison, Morris, Percy, Sellers, Streatfeild, Wolfenden

J. D. Devlin, *Police Charges*, 1961, Police Review Pub. Co., London

P. Devlin, *The Enforcement of Morals* (Maccabaean Lecture), 1959, Oxford University Press

J. W. B. Douglas, J. M. Ross, W. H. Hammond and D. G. Mulligan, 'Delinquency and Social Class,' 1967, in *British J. of Criminology*

W. Elkin, *The English Juvenile Courts*, 1938, Kegan Paul, London

Ellis Committee on *Remand Homes in Scotland*, 1961 (Cmnd. 1588), HMSO

Estimates Committee's Eleventh Report (1966-67) on 'Prisons, Borstals and Detention Centres', 1967, HMSO

H. J. Eysenck, *Handbook of Abnormal Psychology*, 1960, Pitman, London

T. Ferguson, *The Young Delinquent in His Social Setting*, 1952, Oxford University Press

T. Ferguson and G. Cunnison, *In Their Early Twenties*, 1956, Oxford University Press

The sample consisted of 1,349 boys (including unconvicted as well as

Y

convicted) who left Glasgow schools in January 1947 at the earliest permissible date after their 14th birthday (the school-leaving age had not yet been raised to 15). The first book analyses the relationship between their conviction-rates for crimes and offences and data about their home circumstances, school records and subsequent employment up to the age of 18. The second book describes 568 whom it was possible to follow-up until their 22nd birthdays, but who were unfortunately the more easily traceable and therefore probably the less delinquent. Boys who were in special schools for the mentally or physically handicapped are discussed separately, and boys who were in approved schools at that age and date are not included.

Feversham Committee on *Human Artificial Insemination*, 1960 (Cmnd 1105), HMSO

P. J. Fitzgerald, *Criminal Law and Punishment*, 1962, Clarendon, Oxford

S. Folkard *et al.*, 'Probation Research: a preliminary report' (Home Office Studies in the causes of Delinquency and the Treatment of Offenders, No. 7), 1966, HMSO, London

L. Fox, *The English Prison and Borstal System*, 1952, Routledge, London

C. M. Franks, 'Personality Factors and the Rate of Conditioning,' 1957, in *British J. of Psychology*

K. Friedlander, *Psycho-Analytical Approach to Juvenile Delinquency*, 1947, Routledge, London

M. Fry, *Arms of the Law*, 1951, Gollancz, London

T. Fyvel, *The Insecure Offenders*, 1961, Chatto and Windus, London, 1963, Pelican

J. H. Gagnon, 'Female Child Victims of Sex Offences,' 1965, in *Social Problems*, XIII.2

D. Gath, 'The Male Drunk in Court' in *The Drunkenness Offence*, (edd. T. Cook *et al.*) 1969, Pergamon, Oxford.

T. C. N. Gibbens, 'The Porteus Maze Test and Delinquency', 1955, in *British J. of Educational Psychology*

idem, 'Juvenile Prostitution', 1957, in *British J. of Delinquency*

T. C. N. Gibbens and Joyce Prince, *Shoplifting*, 1962, Institute for the Study and Treatment of Delinquents, London

The sample consisted of
(i) All the 532 females aged 17 or over dealt with between July, 1959 and August, 1960 by
(a) a court serving much of the West End shopping area of London;
(b) a London suburban court known to have high rate of shoplifting, 'but where the shopping was essentially local';
(c) a court on the periphery of Greater London, serving an area which is a civic centre in its own right and caters for the shopping needs of a surrounding semi-rural area;
(ii) 100 women 'systematically' chosen from those convicted of shoplifting in the same courts in 1949;

(iii)   200 women shoplifters received into Holloway, on remand or sentence, 'during, as well as some time before, the period of study' (sc. for i);

(iv)   shoplifters of either sex under the age of 17 dealt with by juvenile courts for shoplifting in the areas covered by courts *a*, *b*, and *c*;

(v)   234 adult male shoplifters who appeared in 1959 and 218 who appeared in 1949 before courts *a*, *b* and *c*;

(vi)   98 of the women convicted by courts *a*, *b* and *c* in 1949 of *other* forms of property offence;

(vii) 50 women received into Holloway on remand or sentence for other forms of property offence.

Information from court and police records was studied for all 7 samples. Probation officers interviewed 'as many as possible' of (i) and (iv), and completed a special interview schedule for the purpose of the survey. A woman prison medical officer, Dr Epps, specially interviewed (iii) and (vii). Subsequent convictions over the next 10 years were traced for (ii) and (vi).

T. C. N. Gibbens, D. Pond and D. Stafford-Clark, 'A Follow-up Study of Criminal Psychopaths', 1959, in *of J. Mental Science*

T. C. N. Gibbens, *Psychiatric Studies of Borstal Lads*, 1963, Oxford University Press

E. Gibson, *Time Spent Awaiting Trial*, 1960 (Home Office Research Unit Report No. 2), HMSO

E. Gibson and S. Klein, *Murder*, 1961 (Home Office Research Unit Report No. 4), HMSO; and see McClintock & Gibson.

Gladstone Committee on *Prisons*, 1895 (Cd. 7702), HMSO

D. Glaser & K. Rice, 'Crime, Age and Employment', 1959, in *American Sociological Review*

E. Glover, *The Roots of Crime*, 1960, Imago, London (The third book in the English language to be published under this title by a psychiatrist!)

E. T. Glueck, 'Mental Retardation and Delinquency', 1934, in *J. of Mental Hygiene*, 1935 (Vol. XIX)

S. and E. T. Glueck, *Unraveling Juvenile Delinquency*, 1950, Harper, New York

idem, *Physique and Delinquency*, 1956, Harper, New York

idem, *Predicting Delinquency and Crime*, 1959, Harper, New York

idem, *Family Environment and Delinquency*, 1962, Routledge, London
The sample consisted of

(*a*)   500 delinquents, selected at the rate of 100 a year, beginning in 1939, from boys at Lyman and Shirley correctional schools in Massachusetts as having particularly delinquent records; their ages ranged from 'under $11\frac{1}{2}$' (4%) to 'over $16\frac{1}{2}$' (but under 17?) (11%), with a mean age of $14\frac{1}{2}$;

(*b*)   500 boys with no more than minor misbehaviour in their records which were carefully checked. Each was selected so as to match one of the delinquents in age (within 12 months), intelligence (within 10 points on the Wechsler-Bellevue Scale), ethnic origin and type of neighbourhood in which his home lay (not necessarily the same neighbourhood).

Data analysed cover

(i)   physical health, somatotypes (especially in the 1956 volume);

(ii)   aspects of intelligence, educational achievement, and personality (using the Rorschach test and interviews by a psychiatrist);

(iii) the family's circumstances and relationship to the boy (especially in the 1962 volume);

(iv)   his school record and leisure activities.

W. Goldfarb, 'Infant rearing and problem behavior' 1943, in *American Journal of Orthopsychiatry*

The sample consisted of

(i)   40 children of both sexes who had been in an institution from early infancy to the age of about three, and had then been transferred to foster-homes in which they were placed and supervised by trained case-workers; and

(ii)   40 children who had been in foster homes from early infancy.

The two samples were matched for age and time under care (it is not clear whether they were group-matched or pair-matched). Check-lists of forms of 'problem-behavior' were given to the supervising case-workers, who were not told the purpose of the research.

N. Goodman and J. Price, *Studies of Female Offenders*, 1967, HMSO,

Their samples were

(i)   the 372 girls aged 16-20 sent to English detention centres, borstal or prisons in 1963;

(ii)   the 567 women and girls found guilty of indictable offences in the Metropolitan Police District in March and April, 1967;

(iii) the 530 women serving prison sentences on 1st January 1965 in English prisons.

G. H. Gordon, *The Criminal Law in Scotland*, 1967, Green, Edinburgh

M. Gordon, *Penal Discipline*, 1922, Routledge, London

G. Gorer, *Exploring English Character*, 1955, Cresset, London

C. Goring, *The English Convict*, 1913, HMSO (out of print)

Gowers Commission on *Capital Punishment*, 1953 (Cmnd. 8932), HMSO (with separately published appendices containing written and oral evidence)

J. D. and M. Q. Grant, 'A Group Dynamics Approach to the Treatment of Nonconformists in the Navy', 1959, in *Annals of the American Academy of Political and Social Science*

P. G. Gray and E. A. Parr, *Children in Care and the Recruitment of Foster Parents*, 1959, Social Survey Division of the Central Office of Information: not on sale.

E. Green, *Judicial Attitudes in Sentencing*, 1961, Macmillan, London

The sample consisted of the 1,437 convictions recorded in a volume of the docket of a non-jury prison court of the Philadelphia Court of Quarter Sessions, and tried within a period of 17 months during 1956-7. The sentences studied were awarded by 18 judges, for felonies and misdemeanours of 46 distinct types, ranging from homicide to drunken driving.

M. Grünhut, *Penal Reform*, 1948, Oxford University Press

idem, Juvenile Offenders Before the Courts, 1956, Oxford University Press

idem, 'After-effects of Punitive Detention', 1959, in *British J. of Delinquency*

idem, Probation and Mental Treatment, 1963, Tavistock, London

W. H. Hammond, *Use of Short Sentences of Imprisonment by the Courts*, Appendix F, 1960, HMSO

The sample consisted of the 3,163 men who at the age of 17 or over were convicted for the first time in Scotland in 1947 and whose convictions were recorded in the Glasgow Criminal Records (to which Scottish police forces are supposed to report all convictions).

Data analysed were

(i) type of offence;

(ii) age at the time of conviction;
type of court (Burgh or Justice of the Peace Court, Sheriff Court, High Court);

(iii) type of sentence (e.g., discharge, small, medium or large fine, short, medium or long sentence);

(iv) subsequent reconvictions recorded in the Glasgow Criminal Records at any time in the next 10-11 years.

idem, The Sentence of the Court, Part VI, 1964, HMSO

In addition to the sample described above (Hammond, 1960) the samples consisted of

(a) 4,234 offenders convicted in the Metropolitan Police District during March and April, 1957, and followed up for 5 years;

(b) 400 persons recorded in 1937 in Scotland as convicted of their first offence, and followed up for 21 years;

(c) 400 children born in 1946 who appeared in criminal courts between 1954 and 1963; but excluding those whose cases were 'dismissed';

(d) 4,218 offenders recorded as first convicted in Scotland in 1946, and followed up for 7 years.

Females in the samples were excluded from the calculations.

Data analysed included

(i) type of offence;

(ii) age at time of conviction;

(iii) type of sentence;

(iv) subsequent reconvictions;

(v) (in some cases) the number of offences for which the offender was dealt with at the original conviction.

W. H. Hammond and E. Chayen, *Persistent Criminals*, 1963 (Home Office Research Unit Report), HMSO

The samples consisted of

(a) 1,384 out of the 1,540 male offenders who in 1956 were served with a notice of the prosecution's intention to prove that they were

eligible for preventive detention (178 of these were actually
sentenced to preventive detention);

(b)　108 males released from preventive detention in 1955, whose
subsequent careers were followed up for 3 to 4 years;

(c)　917 males released from preventive detention in the years 1952 to
1959, and followed up for varying periods.

Data analysed included age, type of offence, offences taken into consideration, offences charged at same trial, previous convictions (type
and frequency), results of appeal against sentence, value of property
involved in offences, certain psychological data, certain social data,
prison behaviour, intervals at liberty and length of sentence.

Hansard's Parliamentary Debates, London

H. L. A. Hart, 'Immorality and Treason', 1959, in *The Listener*, 30th July

idem, Punishment and the Elimination of Responsibility, 1962, Athlone Press,
London

idem, Law, Liberty and Morality, 1963, Oxford University Press

C. P. Harvey, 'The Disciplinary Committee and the Courts', 1958, in
British Medical J. for 22nd November

W. Healy and A. Bronner, *New Light on Delinquency and its Treatment*,
1936, Institute of Human Relations, New Haven

D. K. Henderson, *Psychopathic States*, 1939, Norton, New York

A. F. Henry and J. F. Short, *Suicide and Homicide*, 1954, Glencoe Free
Press, Illinois

D. Hill and D. Pond, 'Reflections on One Hundred Capital Cases Submitted to E.E.G.', 1952, in *J. of Mental Science*

J. A. Hobson, 'Psychiatric Evidence in Murder Trials', 1955, in the
Howard.

E. A. Hoebel, *The Law of Primitive Man*, 1955, Oxford University Press

Home Office (for Home Office *Studies in the Causes of Delinquency and the
Treatment of Offenders* see Folkard, Gibson, Goodman, Hammond,
Mannheim and Wilkins)

　Penal Practice in a Changing Society, 1959, Cmnd. 645, HMSO
　Compensation for Victims of Crimes of Violence, 1964, Cmnd. 2303, HMSO
　The Sentence of the Court, 1964, HMSO, with revised editions
　The War Against Crime in England and Wales, 1964, Cmnd. 2296, HMSO
　The Child, the Family and the Young Offender, 1965, Cmnd. 2742, HMSO
　Children in Trouble, 1968, Cmnd. 3601, HMSO
　The Criminal Statistics for England and Wales (annually), HMSO
　Offences of Drunkenness (annual statistics), HMSO
　Offences Relating to Motor Vehicles (annual statistics), HMSO
　*Statistics Relating to Approved Schools, Remand Homes and Attendance
　　Centres in England and Wales* (annually from 1962), HMSO

R. G. Hood, *Sentencing in Magistrates' Courts*, 1962, Stevens, London
The analysis concentrates on sentences imposed on males aged 21 or
over by magistrates' courts in England and Wales in the 4 years 1951-4.
It is principally concerned with local variations in the percentages who
were sentenced to prison.

In the hope of identifying factors associated with these local variations, a closer study was made of two random samples of sentences on males aged 21 or over. Both samples were taken from cases dealt with by 12 courts, selected so as to include courts with high, average and low percentages of prison sentences, and so as to represent urban areas 'both large and small, industrial and residential, old and new'. 'In some of the courts there was a stipendiary magistrate, but most of them had only lay justices'. The main sample consisted of 70 cases of dishonesty from each of these courts, the other of 18 cases of indecent assault on young persons under the age of 16.

Data analysed consisted of the offender's plea (i.e., 'guilty' or 'not guilty'), previous convictions, previous sentences, age, other offences of which he was convicted on the same occasion, occupation, stability in employment, marital status, and the money-value involved in the offence; the area's size, crime-rate, social class composition, and degree of industrialisation; and the investigator's 'impression' of the social class composition of the bench of magistrates.

idem, Homeless Borstal Boys: a study of their after-care and after-conduct, 1966, Bell, London

The sample analysed in the second part of the thesis consisted of 200 borstal boys classified as 'homeless' on reception, and released (on a licence enforceable until the end of what was then a three-year term) either in the year 1953 (100 boys) or in the year 1957 (100 boys). Those released in 1957, but not those released in 1953, had the benefit of 'after-care' from a special unit of the Central After-Care Association set up to assist this special group. 59 of the boys entered the armed forces on release; most of the findings relate to the remaining 141.

A correlation analysis was carried out on 35 variables, covering pre-borstal employment and penal history, borstal records and post-borstal reconvictions, employment, and place of residence.

D. Hume, *Commentaries on the Laws of Scotland,* 1844 edition, Bell and Bradfute, Edinburgh

S. Hurwitz, *Criminology,* 1952, Allen & Unwin, London

Ingleby Committee on *Children and Young Persons,* 1960 (Cmnd. 1191), HMSO

P. Jephcott, M. Carter and W. J. Sprott, *Social Background of Delinquency,* 1954, private circulation, the University of Nottingham

L. Kaij, 'Drinking Habits in Twins', 1957, *Acta Genetica*

H. Kalven and H. Zeisel *The American Jury,* 1966, Little, Brown, Boston

G. W. Keeton, *Guilty but Insane,* 1961, Macdonald, London

Kilbrandon Committee on *Children and Young Persons, Scotland,* 1964 (Cmnd. 2306), HMSO

H. Krantz, *Lebensschicksale krimineller Zwillinge,* 1936, Berlin

J. Lange, *Crime as Destiny,* 1931, Allen & Unwin, London

C. S. Lewis, 'The Humanitarian Theory of Punishment', 1954, in *Twentieth Century*

A. Little, 'Professor Eysenck's Theory of Crime: an Empirical Test on Adolescent Offenders', 1963, in *British J. of Criminology*

A. Little, 'The Prevalence of Recorded Delinquency in England and Wales', 1965, in *American Journal of Sociology*

Liverpool City Police, *The Police and Children*, 1962, published by Liverpool City Police

Longford (Earl of), *The Idea of Punishment*, 1961, Chapman, London

D. T. Lykken, 'A Study of Anxiety in the Sociopathic Personality', in *Studies in Behaviour Pathology* (ed. T. R. Sarbin), 1961, Holt, Rinehart and Winston, New York

F. H. McClintock and E. Gibson, *Robbery in London*, 1961, Macmillan, London

The sample studied consisted of all robberies recorded as made known to the Metropolitan Police in the years 1950, 1957 and 1960 (first six months). Data analysed included the characteristics of cases in which offenders escaped detection, or were successfully prosecuted; the social backgrounds of those convicted, with their historical sentences and subsequent reconvictions.

F. H. McClintock, *et al.*, *Attendance Centres*, 1961, Macmillan, London

The sample studied consisted of 1,449 boys committed to attendance centres in 9 different areas in the period 1950-55. Data analysed included age, previous offences and penal history, social background, nature of current offence, and subsequent reconvictions.

idem, Crimes of Violence, 1963, Macmillan, London

The sample studied consisted of recorded crimes of violence in England and Wales in 1950, 1957 and 1960 (first six months). A more detailed analysis was made of those occurring in the Metropolitan area, including sexual offences in which violence or threats were used (the Metropolitan crimes totalled a little more than 4,000) and data analysed in this part included

the locations, methods and victims, and the injuries to the victims;

the characteristics of crimes not 'cleared up', or not leading to prosecutions or convictions;

the characteristics, histories, sentences and subsequent reconvictions of the convicted offenders.

idem et al., Crime in England and Wales, 1968, Heinemann, London

W. and J. McCord, with I. K. Zola, *Origins of Crime: a new evaluation of the Cambridge-Somerville Youth Study*, 1959, Columbia University Press; and see E. Powers and H. Witmer, *infra*

J. A. Mack, 'Police Juvenile Liaison Schemes', 1963, in *British J. of Criminology*

H. D. McKay: see C. R. Shaw *et al.*

H. Mannheim, J. Spencer and G. Lynch, 'Magisterial Policy in the London Juvenile Courts', two articles in the *British J. of Delinquency* for July, 1957 and October, 1957, London

The sample consisted of 400 boys, selected from the 979 boys aged 14, 15 or 16 who were found guilty of larceny by 8 London juvenile courts in the year ending on 31st March, 1952; the selection was made by taking 50 at random from those dealt with in each court.

Penological, sociological and psychological data about each boy and his family were taken from police and probation officers' reports. Magistrates and boys were not interviewed.

Analysis by factorial and other methods of the courts' decisions between discharge, probation and other forms of treatment (mostly institutional) showed that the 8 courts fell into 5 groups, 3 groups of 2 courts each, and two groups of 1 court each, which were apparently distinguishable by their 'policies'.

H. Mannheim and L. T. Wilkins, *Prediction Methods in Relation to Borstal Training*, 1955, HMSO
The sample consisted of the 720 males committed to English borstals between mid-1946 and mid-1947
Data analysed included their criminal careers and previous sentences; information about family and social background in so far as this was recorded in their files; assessments by governors, housemasters, psychologists (including scores on the Columbia intelligence test); their recorded behaviour in borstal; and their subsequent careers for $3\frac{1}{2}$ years after discharge.
To test the validity of the prediction formula based on this sample a further sample was used, consisting of 338 males committed to English borstals in the second half of 1948.
B. Marcus, 'Intelligence, Criminality and the Expectation of Recidivism', 1955, in *British J. of Delinquency*
J. P. Martin, *Offenders as Employees*, 1962, Macmillan, London
W. Mayer-Gross, E. Slater and M. Roth, *Clinical Psychiatry*, 1960 edition, Cassell, London
J. B. Mays, *Growing up in the City*, 1955, Liverpool University Press
Medical Research Council, *Current Medical Research*, 1967, HMSO
P. Meehl, *Clinical Versus Statistical Prediction*, 1954, University of Minnesota
M. A. Merrill, *Problems of Child Delinquency*, 1947, Harrap, London
Her samples consisted of
(a) 242 boys and 58 girls living in a rural county of California who had been referred to the juvenile court for delinquent behaviour in 1933-5, and representing 95 per cent of all cases so referred during that period. Their ages ranged from 8 to 21, but 90 per cent were between 12 and 18, with a mean of $15\frac{1}{2}$;
(b) equal numbers of boys and girls living in the same neighbourhoods and attending the same schools, with a practically identical age-distribution (the mean was a month older, the standard deviation differing by ·03 months).
R. K. Merton, 'Social Structure and Anomie,' 1938, in *American Sociological Review*
Ministry of Transport, *Road Safety—A Fresh Approach*, 1967 (Cmnd. 3339), HMSO
Ministry of Transport and Scottish Home and Health Department, *Road Accidents* (annual statistics), HMSO
Morison Committee on *The Probation Service*, 1962 (Cmnd. 1650), HMSO
idem, *Approved Probation Hostels*, 1962 (Cmnd. 1800), HMSO

Morris Committee on Jury Service, 1965 (Cmnd. 2627), HMSO

Norval Morris, *The Habitual Criminal*, 1951, Longmans, London
In the course of the book's discussion of the working of the 1908 and 1948 statutes dealing with the sentencing of habitual offenders, two samples are described:
(*a*) the 32 men who were undergoing preventive detention in England and Wales during the week ending on 16th October, 1948;
(*b*) the 270 men received into Wandsworth Prison between 1st July, 1946 and 30th September, 1948, who qualified for Dr Morris' description of 'confirmed recidivist'
Data analysed for each sample covered
(i) penal history, including aliases and types of offences;
(ii) place of birth, early environment, military and occupational history;
(iii) religious persuasion, companions and associates;
(iv) physical and mental condition as it was ascertainable from record sheets (but not usually from psychometric tests);
(v) 'solely out of courtesy to Lombroso', tattooing.

P. Morris, *Prisoners and their Families*, 1965, Allen and Unwin, London
The sample consisted of 837 married male prisoners aged 21 or more, taken from the populations of 17 representative English prisons, and each with at least 3 months of his sentence still to serve. All but 12 consented to be interviewed, and information was obtained from their records and from prison welfare officers; in 70 per cent of cases it was possible to interview their wives as well. The care with which the investigation was planned, executed and described (under considerable difficulties) make it a model from which other investigators can learn.

T. Morris, *The Criminal Area*, 1957, Routledge, London

T. Morris and L. Blom-Cooper, *A Calendar of Murder*, 1964, Michael Joseph, London

Mountbatten Commission, *Report of the Enquiry into Prison Escapes and Security*, 1966 (Cmnd. 3175), HMSO

D. J. Newman, 'Pleading Guilty for Considerations: A Study of Bargain Justice', 1956, in *Journal of Criminal Law, Criminology and Police Science*

Percy Commission on *The Law Relating to Mental Illness and Mental Deficiency*, 1957 (Cmnd. 169), HMSO

Percy Committee of *Inquiry into Allegations of Ill-treatment of Prisoners in Her Majesty's Prison, Durham*, 1963 (Cmnd. 2068), HMSO

S. Porteus, *The Porteus Maze Test*, 1952, Harrap, London

E. Powers and H. Witmer *An Experiment in the Prevention of Delinquency: the Cambridge-Somerville Youth Study*, 1951, Columbia University Press.
The sample was constructed from the names of nearly 2,000 boys, regarded as 'troublesome' or 'not troublesome' by schools, police, probation officers and other social agencies in two areas of Massachusetts. Data on each boy were obtained from home, school and other agencies. Boys who had passed their 12th birthday, or left town or become untraceable were eliminated. A selection committee of three experts (not on the staff of the project) rated each boy's likelihood of

becoming delinquent on an 11-point scale; and likely delinquents were paired with unlikely delinquents. The result was 650 pairs, half of which received no treatment, half were distributed between 10 'counselors', paying attention to the counselors preferences for ethnic groups etc.

All treatment ceased in 1945, having lasted for an average of nearly 5 years for each treated pair; but the actual periods ranged from 2½ to 8 years (some pairs were discarded to lighten counselors' case-loads). The results for treated and untreated pairs were compared up to November, 1948, three years after the end of treatment, and were so disappointing that there have been several later re-analyses, notably by W. and J. McCord (q.v.)

M. Prince, *The Dissociation of a Personality*, 1906, Longmans Green, New York

Prison Commission (from 1963 'the Prison Department of the Home Office'),
Annual Reports, HMSO
Detention Centre Rules, 1952, HMSO
Prisons and Borstals, England and Wales, 1960, HMSO
Prison Rules, 1964, HMSO
Borstal Rules, 1964, HMSO

L. Radzinowicz (ed.), *The Results of Probation*, 1958, Macmillan, London
idem, *Sexual Offences*, 1957, Macmillan, London

The sample consisted of 2,178 cases in which a person was involved or alleged to have been involved in an indictable heterosexual or homo-sexual offence, and 914 cases in which proceedings were taken against a person for a non-indictable heterosexual or homosexual offence, in selected cities and counties of England during the early nineteen-fifties. It represented between 20 and 30 per cent of sexual offences recorded annually by the police at this time.

Data analysed included
(i)   characteristics of cases in which offenders were not detected or, if detected, not prosecuted, or prosecuted but acquitted;
(ii) age and sex of victims;
(iii) characteristics of convicted offenders; their sentences and reconvictions.

An independent part of the book discusses the state of the law.

S. Rettig and B. Pasamanick, 'Differences in the Structure of Moral Values of Students and Alumni', 1960, in *American Sociological Review*, Vol. XXV

The sample consisted of
(a) 489 Ohio State University freshmen and sophomore college students from various faculties, taking the sociology course;
(b) 1,742 former alumni who returned usable replies to questionnaires issued to 2,400, selected at random from those who had graduated in 1932-3, 1942-3, and 1952-3.

The ages thus ranged from just under 20 to just over 50.

Attitudes were tested by a questionnaire dealing with 50 'morally prohibited activities', which respondents could rate on a 10-point scale of 'rightness' or 'wrongness'.

Road Research Laboratory, *Road Accidents* 1962, HMSO

H. R. Rollin, 'Social and Legal Repercussions of the Mental Health Act, 1959', in *British Medical J.* for 23rd March 1963

C. H. Rolph (ed.), *Women of the Streets*, 1955, British Social Biology Council, London

idem, The Police and the Public, 1962, Heinemann, London

A. J. Rosanoff, L. M. Hardy and I. A. Rosanoff, 'Criminality and Delinquency in Twins', 1934 in *J. of Criminal Law and Criminology*

G. Rose, *The Struggle for Penal Reform*, 1960, Stevens, London

idem, Schools for Young Offenders, 1967, Tavistock, London

Royal Commissions, see chairmen's names: Gowers, Percy, Willink

R. Saleilles, *The Individualisation of Punishment*, 1898, tr. R. S. Jastrow, 1911, Heinemann, London

Sarbin, T. (ed.), 1961, *Studies in Behavior Pathology: the experimental approach to the psychology of the abnormal*, Holt, Rinehart and Winston, New York

M. Schmideburg, 'Delinquent Acts as Perversions and Fetiches', 1956, in *British J. of Delinquency*

M. Schofield, *Sociological Aspects of Homosexuality*, 1965, Longmans, Green, London

His samples, each numbering 50 adult males, consisted of prisoners convicted of homosexual offences with adults; prisoners convicted of sexual offences with boys under the age of 16; homosexuals under psychiatric treatment in a hospital or out-patient clinic; homosexuals who have neither received treatment nor been convicted of homosexual offences; non-homosexuals under psychiatric treatment in a hospital or out-patient clinic; non-homosexuals who have neither received psychiatric treatment nor been convicted for homosexual offences.
Data studied included sexual habits, way of life, family background, penal records and scores on a verbal reasoning test.

E. M. Schur, *Narcotic Addiction in Britain and America*, 1962 (USA) 1963, Tavistock, London

P. D. Scott, 'Approved School Success Rates', 1964, in *British J. of Criminology*

His sample consisted of 149 boys released consecutively from one approved school which admitted boys between 13 and 15 years of age, the average on release being 15, and the average length of stay between 18 and 19 months. The follow-up covered three years from the date of release, and included non-indictable as well as indictable offences and subsequent employment record.

idem, 'Gangs and Delinquent Groups in London', 1956, in *British J. of Delinquency*

Scottish Advisory Council on Treatment of Offenders, reports on
Use of Short Sentences of Imprisonment by the Courts, 1960a, HMSO

Custodial Sentences for Young Offenders, 1960b, HMSO

The Extension of Compulsory After-care to Additional Categories Inmates and Prisoners, 1961, HMSO

Custodial Training for Young Offenders, 1962, HMSO

Organisation of After-care in Scotland, 1963, HMSO

Scottish Home and Health Department, *Criminal Statistics (Scotland)*, annually HMSO

idem, Social Work and the Community, 1966 (Cmnd. 3065), HMSO

Sellers Committee (Criminal Law Revision Committee), third report of, on *Criminal Procedure (Insanity)*, 1963 (Cmnd. 2149), HMSO

H. L. Shapiro, *Migration and Environment*, 1939, Oxford University Press

C. R. Shaw, *Delinquency Areas*, 1929, University of Chicago Press

C. R. Shaw and H. D. McKay, *Juvenile Delinquency and Urban Areas*, 1942, University of Chicago Press

C. R. Shaw and H. D. McKay, 'Social Factors in Juvenile Delinquency', 1931, in U.S. National Committee on Law Observance and Enforcement *Reports*, Vol. VI

W. H. Sheldon, *Varieties of Delinquent Youth*, 1949, Harper & Bros., New York

J. Shields, 'Personality Differences and Neurotic Traits in Normal Twin Schoolchildren', 1954, in *Eugenic Review*

idem, Monozygotic twins brought up apart and together, 1962, Oxford University Press

The samples, most members of which were obtained as a result of a radio programme in 1953, consisted of

(a) 29 female and 15 male pairs of monozygotic twins brought up in different households for at least 5 years in childhood, and usually from the first 6 months of life; their ages ranged from 10 to over 50;

(b) 44 pairs of monozygotic twins brought up in the same households; and matched pair for pair with (a) by age and sex;

(c) 11 pairs of dizygotic twins brought up in different households;

(d) 21 pairs of dizygotic twins brought up in the same household.

Monozygosity was tested by blood-grouping, phenylthiocarbamide tasting, colour-blindness tests, finger-printing, and 'anthroposcopy'. Data studied were

(i) intelligence, measured by verbal and non-verbal tests;

(ii) physique;

(iii) personality, measured by self-rating questionnaires.

A. D. Smith, *Women in Prison*, 1962, Stevens, London

B. M. Spinley, *The Deprived and the Privileged*, 1953, Routledge, London

D. Stafford-Clark: see Gibbens *et al.*

K. R. Stallworthy and H. J. Wily, *Mental Abnormality and the Law*, 1963, Peryer, New Zealand

D. H. Stott, 'The Prediction of Delinquency from Non-delinquent Behaviour', 1960, in *British J. of Delinquency* for January

The sample consisted of 415 boys, aged 8 to 15, put on probation in Glasgow for the first time in 1957, and 404 non-delinquent boys from the same schools, matched one for one by date of birth. The Bristol Social Adjustment Guide – an inventory consisting of 161 items indicative of behaviour disturbance and 49 items indicative of stability – was completed for every probationer and control by the boy's class teacher.

A Straker and C. D. Blackler, *Some Correlates of Primary Recidivism*, 1966 (unpublished: no. 17 in Psychologists Monograph series of the Prison Department): abridged version published by Mrs. Blackler (q.v.)

Streatfeild Committee on *The Business of the Criminal Courts*, 1961 (Cmnd. 1289), HMSO

E. H. Sutherland, *Principles of Criminology*, 1955 edition, University of Chicago Press

R. S. Taylor, 'The Habitual Criminal: Observations on some of the characteristics of men sentenced and preventive detention', 1960, in *British J. of Criminology*

C. H. Thigpen and H. M. Cleckley, *The Three Faces of Eve*, 1957, Secker and Warburg, London

D. A. Thomas, 'Sentencing: the Case for Reasoned Decisions', 1963, in *Criminal Law Review*

D. S. Thomas, *Social Aspects of the Business Cycle*, 1925, Routledge, London

G. Trasler, *The Explanation of Delinquency*, 1962, Routledge, London

P. E. Vernon, *Intelligence and Attainment Tests*, 1960, University of London Press

G. B. Vold, *Theoretical Criminology*, 1958, Oxford University Press

C. H. Waddington, *The Ethical Animal*, 1961, Allen & Unwin, London

N. D. Walker, *A Short History of Psychotherapy*, 1957, Routledge, London

idem, *Adolescent Maladjustment*, 1963, Charles Russell Memorial Trust, London

idem, *Crime and Insanity in England*, 1968, Edinburgh University Press

idem, *Sentencing in a Rational Society*, 1969, Allen Lane the Penguin Press, London.

N. D. Walker, W. H. Hammond and D. J. Steer, 'Repeated Violence', 1967, in *Criminal Law Review*

N. D. Walker and S. F. McCabe 'Hospital Orders: an interim appreciation', 1968, in *The Mentally Abnormal Offender* (a C. I. B. A. Foundation Symposium), Churchill, London

J. N. Walton, 'Some Observations on the Value of Electroencephalography in Medico-Legal Practice', 1963, in *Medico-Legal Journal*

D. J. West, *The Habitual Prisoner*, 1963, Macmillan, London
The samples consisted of
(a) 51 'substantially unselected' male preventive detainees who entered the Wandsworth allocation centre in late 1956 or the first half of 1957;
(b) 50 male recidivists in Wandsworth in 1957 whose known criminal careers included an apparently crime-free gap of at least

4 years, preceded by convictions in adult courts on at least two occasions, and succeeded by at least two further convictions.

Data analysed included penal histories, occupational records, family and marital relationships, intelligence and personality ratings, psychiatric diagnoses, nature of offences, and the cost of property involved in the most recent charge.

G. Westwood, *A Minority: a report on the life of the male homosexual in Britain*, 1960, Longmans, London

The sample consisted of

(*a*) 21 men who were asked by doctors and laymen in touch with Mr Westwood to volunteer for interview;

(*b*) 17 men who heard of his research from the press;

(*c*) 89 men introduced by others who had already been interviewed.

The sample thus consisted of 126 men 'who at some period of their lives have admitted to themselves that they are homosexual. All of them agree that at the time of the interview they still have homosexual tendencies'.

Data analysed included occupation, education, family history, past and present sexual behaviour, contact with the criminal law, experiences of remedial treatment.

L. T. Wilkins, 1955: see Mannheim and Wilkins

idem, 'A Small Comparative Study of the Results of Probation,' 1958, in *British J. of Delinquency*, VIII, 1957-8

The sample consisted of

(*a*) 97 males convicted in 1952 by a Court of Quarter Sessions ('Court P') which made use of probation orders in three times the national average percentage of cases;

(*b*) 97 males selected from 194 other courts so as to match those from Court P (as closely as possible) in

   (i) type of offence;

   (ii) age of offender;

   (iii) number of additional convictions at the same time;

   (iv) number of additional offences taken into consideration;

   (v) number of previous convictions for indictable offences (but the P group had 72 between them, with an individual maximum of 25, to the others, 43 and 5.)

Data analysed were the reconvictions over at least 3 subsequent years for each type of sentence (fine, probation, prison or borstal).

idem, *Social Deviance*, 1964, Tavistock Press, London

H. D. Willcock and J. Stokes, *Deterrents to Crime amongst Youths aged 15 to 21* (Government Social Survey Report No. SS 356) (2 vols.), 1968, obtainable from the Librarian of the Government Social Survey. The original sample consisted of some 1300 males aged 15 to 21, and was designed to be representative of males in this age-group in Britain. Nearly 38 per cent., however, were 'lost' for various reasons, chiefly the difficulty of securing agreement to long interviews in private. Evidence suggested that the lost individuals were more delinquent than the 808 who were successfully interviewed: but since the main object

was to study what deterred those likely to be deterred the bias was
probably worth accepting in order to improve the accuracy of the information obtained.

T. C. Willett, *The Criminal on the Road*, 1964, Tavistock Press, London
The sample consisted of adults of both sexes convicted of certain
motoring offences during the three years 1957-9 in a single police
district with over half a million inhabitants, covering one of the Home
Counties of London. The offences were

	cases	
causing death by dangerous driving	5	(100% of cases)
dangerous driving	285	,, ,, ,,
driving under the influence of drink or drugs	104	,, ,, ,,
driving while disqualified	69	,, ,, ,,
failing to insure against third party risks	73	(10% of cases)
failing to report or stop after an accident	117	,, ,, ,,
	653	

In addition, 50 adults not in this sample, but whose convictions for
similar offences were reported in the press during the same period, were
interviewed by the author.
Data analysed included convictions for motoring and non-motoring
offences, occupations, penalties imposed.

G. Williams, 'Language and the Law,' 1945, in *Law Quarterly Review*
idem, *The Sanctity of Life and the Criminal Law*, 1958, Faber, London
idem, *The Criminal Law* (General Part), 1961 edition, Stevens, London
idem, *The Proof of Guilt*, 1963 edition, Stevens, London
idem, 'The Court and Persistent Offenders', 1963, in *Criminal Law Review*
H. V. Willink, Royal Commission on *The Police*, 1962 (Cmnd. 1728),
    HMSO
H. Wily: see Stallworthy and Wily
G. Woddis, 'Depression and Crime', 1957, in *British J. of Delinquency*
Wolfenden Committee on *Homosexual Offences and Prostitution*, 1957
    (Cmnd. 247), HMSO
R. Wollheim, 'Crime, Sin and Mr Justice Devlin', 1959, in *Encounter*
M. Woodside, 'Women Drinkers Admitted to Holloway Prison During
    February, 1960', 1961, in *British J. of Delinquency*
idem, 'Women Abortionists', 1963, in *Howard*.
M. Woodward, 'Low Intelligence and Delinquency', 1963 edition,
    Institute for Modern Study and Treatment of Delinquency, London
B. Wootton, *Social Science and Social Pathology*, 1959, Allen & Unwin,
    London
idem, 'Diminished Responsibility, a Layman's View', 1960, in *Law
    Quarterly Review*
idem, *Crime and the Criminal Law*, 1963, Stevens, London
S. Yablonsky, 'The Delinquent Gang as a Near Group', 1959, in *Social
    Problems*

INDEX

Letters which occur immediately after some of the page references have the following meanings:

e: the page includes an explanation or definition of the term;

f: the page contains a figure illustrating the subject;

t: the page contains a table related to the subject;

n: the reference is relevant to a footnote on that page.

Acts of Parliament will be found under 'statutes'; legal cases under 'cases at law'.

z

z*